Antifeminism in America

A Collection of Readings from the Literature of the Opponents to U.S. Feminism, 1848 to the Present

Series Editors

Angela Howard and Sasha Ranaé Adams Tarrant
University of Houston Clear Lake

A GARLAND SERIES

Contents of the Series

Opposition to the Women's Movement in the United States, 1848–1929

Edited with introductions by

Angela Howard and Sasha Ranaé Adams Tarrant
University of Houston Clear Lake

A MEMBER OF THE TAYLOR & FRANCIS GROUP
New York & London
1997

Library of Congress Cataloging-in-Publication Data

Opposition to the women's movement in the United States, 1848–1929
/ edited with introductions by Angela Howard and Sasha Ranaé
Adams Tarrant.
    p.   cm. — (Antifeminism in America ; 1)
    Includes bibliographical references.
    ISBN 0-8153-2713-7 (alk. paper). — ISBN 0-8153-2712-9 (set :
alk. paper)
    1. Anti-feminism—United States—History. 2. Feminism—United
States—History. I. Howard, Angela. II. Tarrant, Sasha Ranaé
Adams. III. Series.
HQ1426.0934 1997
305.42'0973—dc21   97-38207
                                                CIP

Printed on acid-free, 250-year-life paper
Manufactured in the United States of America

Contents

Series Introduction

Understanding the Opposition to U.S. Feminism

The purpose of this three-volume collection of primary sources is to generate a more complete understanding and appreciation of the social and political context in which the advocates of women's rights have labored and labor from 1848 to the present. The editors have selected original documents from mainstream literature to allow the reader immediate access to this continuing public discourse that accompanies the prospective and the real changes in women's role and status in the United States. Those opposed to the feminist goal of women's equality have addressed to the public, directly through contemporary popular books and magazines, their concerns regarding the particular nineteenth-century issues of the woman's rights movement. These include woman suffrage and dress reform, as well as topics relating to the discerning and enforcing the proper role and status of women. Public discourse over such topics has extended into the twentieth century, as opponents raised arguments against increased opportunities in women's employment and education, denied the propriety and practice of family planning, and admonished against women's involvement in political issues and activities. In these three volumes, the opponents of feminism speak directly to the reader who is free to evaluate the merits of each author's arguments.

    Diversity of opinion and perspective has persisted among those who oppose the assertion of women's rights as reform movement, which challenges the concepts and institutions of patriarchy as well as the gender system that supports and perpetuates a gender-defined, limited, and segregated existence for women. The constellation of conservative definitions of proper womanhood has varied widely in approach, intent, and intensity. Over the past two-hundred years the critics of feminism, of advances in women's rights, and of the increased opportunity in education and employment for women have had to absorb changes in the status of middle-class women. These critics therefore have co-opted and redefined some of the fait accompli changes to maintain that contemporary practices uphold the primary limitation for women in any century, that for women "biology is destiny." All these opponents to sexual equality ultimately assert that an inescapable maternal duty grounds every woman's identity in her relationships to others and especially to men: each woman's usefulness to society through filial, uxorial, maternal, professional, and civic responsibilities define and limit her identity as an individual.

Some opponents merely dismissed or ridiculed advocates for changes in women's status, and eschewed the need to specify particular flaws in the feminist position on any particular issue. Others relied on interpretations of divine ordination, appeals to natural law, and manipulations of public fears of familial and social disintegration. Often opponents sought to discredit the propriety or to challenge the necessity of any change in the gender system proposed by advocates of women's rights. They utilized divisive tactics to separate women by race or ethnic group, religion, or economic class. Frequently, these critics resorted to ad hominum charges of lesbianism, communism, and socialism, or disgruntled spinsterhood against the advocates of women's rights and against the movement itself. Opponents defined the effort to promote the women's movement out of the domestic sphere and into the public arena of political, economic, and social reform as inherently destructive of social order. By focusing on maintaining a limited role for women, adversaries of the women's movement, both women and men, expressed their common fear that has been created by ongoing social, economic, and political changes beyond their control.

Therefore, much of the value in reading these sources is to experience the variety of perspectives that provide the historical and intellectual context for these documents from the distant and near past. The editors offer this varied selection of sources to allow the reader to assess the merit and validity of the arguments presented by these representative opponents of women's rights and equality. Not all opponents of specific feminist reforms would define themselves as antifeminist; most would deny that they are anti-woman, although opposed to expanding women's rights. For the student of women's history, the temptation to look for patterns of opposition will become irresistible. To facilitate an evaluation of the texts in their own historical context, the editors have grouped the documents within three major historical periods. Because the sources of mainstream opponents were more readily available, we elected to focus on the debate among writers who represented the middle class and who exerted a presence in the popular press. Especially for students of American women's history, this collection provides the opportunity to encounter directly the opinions of those who resisted and criticized the goals as well as the tactics of feminism in all its forms.

The documents in volume one, *Opposition to the Women's Movement in the United States, 1848–1929*, cover the initial era of the woman's movement, which began in the antebellum period and produced the *Declaration of Sentiments* of the Seneca Falls Woman's Rights Convention in 1848 as well as the Cult of True Womanhood (1820–1860). The sources in volume one extend through the culmination of the ratification of the Nineteenth Amendment to the U.S. Constitution that enfranchised women. The nineteenth-century critics of the emerging women's movement launched the conservative defense of a delineated woman's sphere and redefined the cult of domesticity with appeals to scripture and history, as well as to contemporary scientific theories that emphasized the physical-gender differences. By the twentieth century, the opponents of women's rights and equality faced formidable challenges to the validity of these translations of scripture, interpretations of historical development, and questionable "scientific" evidence and conclusions.

The sources provided in volume two, *Redefining the New Woman, 1920–1963*, offer reflections of the twentieth-century era from the "Roaring Twenties" through the

World War II period to the rise of the Civil Rights Movement. Both the 1920s and the 1950s were decades characterized by post-war antifeminism and a trend toward intellectually stifling social conformity for women and men; the maintenance of patriarchal values justified this repression. Those opposed to feminism added applications of Freudian psychology to the arguments based on biological and physiological "facts," firmly established before World War I. This psycho-biological approach reaffirmed that "biology is destiny" for women of the twentieth century as well as for the nineteenth. But developments in the postindustrial economy of the mid-twentieth century U.S. fostered changes in the middle class that redounded to increased women's opportunity in employment and education; the consequences of these changes seemed to threaten to lessen women's economic dependence upon men.

In volume three, *Reaction to the Modern Women's Movement, 1963 to the Present*, the readings span an era contemporary to the publication of Betty Friedan's *The Feminine Mystique* (1963), the so-called sexual revolution (in which women were more prisoners of war than combatants), and the rise of the modern women's movement. The impact of the Civil Rights Act of 1964, Title VII especially, no less than the rise of the women's liberation movement (1968–1972) and the development of women's studies within the standard curriculum of higher education created a climate for change that continues to occur throughout the last decade in the twentieth century. The 1980s ushered in the Reagan era with a backlash against the women's movement that capitalized on the insecurities of middle-class women, especially homemakers, that they would be discarded, abandoned, and stranded as single heads of households and the sole support of their children; middle-class men were told to fear the added economic competition of women and men of color. Conservatives reacted to the legacy of the 1970s—the questioning of authority—and bristled at the challenge of the women's liberation movement to patriarchal institutions and values. This generation of defenders of the gender system articulated the threat feminism posed to organized religion, "traditional" family values, the nation's future, and the free-enterprise economy.

This collection of readings developed from a shared experience and exasperation of a professor and her graduate student in a course on U.S. feminism. Dissatisfied with the limited sources available for studying contemporary criticism of the women's movement and feminism in U.S. history, the editors collaborated to find, edit, and present to the reader the kinds of sources that often appear in women's history courses as handouts—assorted items gathered over time and informally assembled. Our division of labor reflected our individual strengths: the professor brought the expertise gained from decades of teaching women's history as well as editorial experience; the graduate student (now well on her way to completing her Ph.D.) contributed impressive state-of-the-art researching skills and determination to locate, screen, and recommend documents most likely to represent the trends and standard arguments of the critics of the women's movement and feminism. From experience, the former knew that good intentions notwithstanding, "no good deed goes unpunished" and therefore anticipated that the best efforts would still garner candid criticism of purpose and selections; the latter maintained a conviction that this "good deed" needed doing regardless of the time and effort demanded. The idealism of youth won out. We drew into our quixotic vision other graduate students who provided crucial research as assistants to the editors:

Pamela F. Wille, Rae Fuller Wilson, and Susanne Grooms. All of us relied on the kindness and expertise of the professional librarians at U.H.C.L., including Susan Steele, and the professional staff of other libraries. The editors therefore accept any compliments on the results of the collaboration as only proportionally ours while we assert our sole claim of accountability for the inevitable errors (which we trust our readers will bring to our attention and that will be corrected in future editions).

Volume Introduction

Representing opposition to the woman's movement[1] before and after the Civil War, popular antebellum women authors and "womanist" activists, such as Sarah Josepha Hale and Catharine Beecher, as well as postwar physician S. Weir Mitchell, progressive era muckraker Ida Tarbell, and others, speak out against aspects of the woman movement. Articles in this volume range from Tarbell's "The Irresponsible Woman and the Friendless Child" (1912) to the earlier work of the less well-known L.P. Brockett's "Woman, Her Rights, Wrongs, Privileges and Responsibilities"(1869). These sources initiate the series of arguments that characterize the basis of opposition to the woman's movement before suffrage was achieved. These authors warn of the dire consequences— to women, children, and nineteenth-century U.S. society—of advocacy and actions for women's rights.

The selections in this volume divide into three eras that extend from 1848–1867, 1867–1890, and 1890–1920. Selections in part one present the issues as defined in response to the initial challenge of the antebellum woman's rights movement. Momentum toward greater political participation for all men characterized the antebellum era and paralleled the growth of grassroots reform movements; among the leaders and supporters of major reform efforts—temperance and abolition, for example—were women assuming a previously forbidden and still censured public role. Sarah Josepha Hale, as editor of the premier antebellum women's magazine, became the high priestess of the Cult of True Womanhood; her writings were distinctly "womanist" for, while she never challenged patriarchy directly, she argued the importance of women's contributions as women, and therefore not in competition with men. This perspective bridged the dissonance between women's role in the rural agrarian gender system and their marginalization in the emerging prewar industrial society.

---

[1] The contemporary terms for the collective effort to promote women's rights and equality reflected the common usage of each era. Throughout the nineteenth century, proponents referred to this social reform movement as "The Woman Movement," utilizing the singular form, or as "The Woman's Movement," with the singular possessive form. In the twentieth century, after the ratification of the Woman Suffrage Amendment in 1920, the modern use of the plural possessive form predominated, and this reform effort was termed "The Women's Movement."

The readings in part two display the adjustments required by opponents to women's rights after the Civil War because of irreversible changes in women's employment and education. The presence of married as well as single women workers in the industrial wage-labor force increased as did the number of sex-segregated and public coeducational institutions, which expanded women's options and participation in the public sphere during the Reconstruction era and the Gilded Age. Improvements of women's legal rights and status proceeded at a glacial pace, as states enacted married women's property reform legislation and the Fourteenth Amendment was interpreted to separate citizenship from political enfranchisement.

The writings offered in part three reflect the response of opponents of feminism to the impact of women's expanded social, political, and economic activities during the Progressive era. The impact of women's volunteer organizations paved the way for the civic activism of the Settlement House Movement and the reform agenda of the General Federation of Women's Clubs that encompassed political participation through petition and lobbying at the local, state, and national levels. The unimpeachable respectability of these middle-class women's efforts required the opponents of women's rights and women's suffrage to expand their definition of women's proper role, but the critics of the women's movement utilized the same rhetoric of sacred motherhood to restrict women to the twentieth-century version of domesticity.

Opposition to the Women's Movement in the United States, 1848–1929

CHAPTER VI.

SOCIAL EVILS—WOMAN THEIR REFORMER.

It has been often repeated, so often that many have grown weary of the repetition, that one of the first principles of our government is equality ; and yet it may be doubted whether some among us would not find it difficult to define what this equality means, or in what it consists. Not, surely, in personal qualities ; for none can be so besotted as to imagine, that by simply being Americans, they may claim equality with all of the same nation in the dignities conferred by high moral or intellectual power. Nor does it consist in an equal participation in all the advantages which wealth and social position confer; for should any one claim this and attempt to enforce his claim, the bolts of a prison or a madhouse would soon teach him that the opinion of the world was adverse to his own.

And yet it is not a vain boast, that we did first, as a people, assert, and have striven to maintain, that all men were born free and equal,—with equal right to enjoy and to improve to the utmost, that heritage derived, under Providence, from their progenitors.

Was thy father a builder of other men's houses—a shoemaker, working at his last—or a blacksmith, wielding the hammer with sturdy arm—and did he, by his honest industry, win for thee, his loved one, a higher, and in the world's judgment, a better fortune? Let him smile as he looks at thy boyish sports, and say to himself—"Thy life shall be of a nobler sort than mine." It shall be thine own fault if this saying prove not prophetic. There is no seminary of learning in the land into which his gold may not buy thee admittance, and there thou shalt stand on such eminence as thy merits shall command. From such seminary thou mayst pass into the profession that best pleases thee; all are open to thee, and that prophetic father may live to see thee a judge on the bench of the Supreme Court, a senator in the halls of Congress, or a President of the United States. No privileged class shall say to thee—"Touch not that honor—set not thy foot upon that eminence; it belongs to us." Thou art free; free to develop thyself as thy will shall prompt, and thy powers permit. This world is God's world, and He hath given thee so much

3

of it as thou, with thy best faculties, canst conquer. Such is the language of our Constitution, to which nothing in our political life gives denial. There the cloth of frieze stands unrepulsed beside the cloth of gold, and may even attain to a higher position; but not thus is it with our social life. There, the intellect may glow with man's noblest powers, the heart throb with his highest aspirations, and the manners may reflect, in their gentleness and refinement, the glory of such powers and such aspirations; yet, if all this be covered by the cloth of frieze, away with it—it may not enter the charmed circle of "*good society,*" or enter only after its own degradation, as Samson, shorn of his locks, was brought before the lords of the Philistines to make sport for them.

And what constitutes this *soi disant* good society ? Wealth, and the senseless fripperies which wealth may purchase. Oh! give us back the old reverence for a noble name. If we must have a privileged class—if we must bear "the contumely which patient merit of the unworthy takes," restore to us the illusion by which we might fancy ourselves doing homage to the kingly spirits of earth in the persons of their degenerate descendants. In such homage there may be something ennobling; but in this worship of Mammon, this bending the spirit to vulgarity and frivolity, because decorated with jewels and brocade, there is every thing debasing.   And to what do we owe the strength of this sentiment of veneration for wealth amongst us ?   Is it not to our having placed before us the social life of Europe as our model ? We cannot command domains associated with ancestral names whose very sound is a spell, stirring the heart like a trumpet-tone, and evoking images of past splendor which throw a halo over ruin and decay ; but wealth will enable us to build houses almost as large as those to which these domains are attached, and a great deal finer.   Base and shaft to our Corinthian column may be wanting ; but we will place the rich capital upon our Doric base, and by covering its decorations with gold-leaf, make it much more showy.

If we would cease to be the world's derision—if we would take the position which God designed us to take among the nations of the earth, we must put from us this low ambition, we must understand our noble work, and elevate our aims to its accomplishment.

Feudalism had its mission—a mission to educate men into reverence and obedience.   The rude, semi-barbarous nations of Europe in the middle ages could not have ap-

6*

preciated the majesty of law, and would neither have reverenced nor obeyed a power so spiritual. These emotions, then, must be excited in their minds by that physical force, and those outward demonstrations of superiority, which strike the senses. The diadem, sparkling with gems, the purple robe, the golden sceptre, all the insignia of royal or of noble rank, all the rigid etiquette which marked the gradations of society, and kept each class hedged in as by an insuperable barrier, which was soon made to appear a divine and indefeasible right—these were all but means towards the accomplishment of this end. That they were wisely-appointed and successful means, we may learn by a glance at the history of the civilized world. Let us take England, the most advanced in Christian civilization of all those nations whose barbarous or semi-barbarous origin required these educational processes. While at every advancing step she has made, some form has been discarded, or has, at least, ceased to awaken the public reverence, has not the inner spirit which that form had represented, the law, been more clearly revealed—winning, in its majestic simplicity, a truer and more enduring homage than had been yielded to its imposing representative? There was a period in her history—the memorable period of the Stuart dynasty—when the forms and the spirit, royalty and the law whose power it had been created to represent and to enforce, were arrayed against each other, and the result proved that forms were fast becoming useless to a nation which had learned well its lesson of reverence to the spirit of law.

Yet, though their work was well nigh done, their use had well nigh passed away, these forms must be reconciled to the spirit of law, not discarded, for they were but branches of that feudalism from which the whole social structure had grown up. They must not be torn away, lest that structure should be shaken to the base; they must be left to the action of time. Slowly, but surely, they will decay and fall away of themselves.

And may it not be that in the neglect of the principles which have thus guided the English people, has arisen the ill-success which has hitherto marked all other European revolutions. The first French revolution, and those lately occurring in some other European nations, released from all the checks and restraints of outward forms those who had been so held down by sheer, physical force, that their dwarfed minds and palsied hearts had room for no emotions but those of selfish terror or mad revenge. No reverence for God or man stayed

their fierce hands as, seizing on these feelings, the demagogue of the hour swayed them hither or thither at his
will.   Their gross senses could not appreciate the force
of the subtle spirit of law, their obedience could be obtained only by the exhibition of material power, and thus
the institutions, on which their whole social life rested,
were torn away root and branch at one time, only to be
built up on the same basis in succeeding years.   But the
English revolution, if the name of revolution may indeed
be given to that contest which ended with a change of
dynasty in England, was begun, continued, and ended in
a spirit of reverence for the law ; and this reverence
made the victorious party wisely careful not to touch
one institution which had become associated with the
law.   " As our revolution was a vindication of ancient
rights, so it was conducted with strict attention to ancient formalities," says Macaulay, in that masterly work
which has left us little to learn in relation to this period
of English history.

And why was it that not till our ancestors had entered
on this great contest, did one of the many attempts
made to plant English colonies on these shores prove
successful ?   Was it that they had now reached the culminating point of their education in the love of liberty

and reverence for law; that beyond this their advance was stayed by the very arrangements which had been necessary to their safe development so far; that to attain to a more perfect external development of their own noble principles, they must be transplanted to a new soil, and begin afresh the race of life, free from those impediments whose demolition, where they have once existed, must ever be attended with danger of anarchy and misrule? Was it that here, on the basis of Christian institutions and equal rights, we might find it easier to construct that fair temple which has for its foundation and its corner-stone, "Love God supremely, and your neighbor, whether he be king or beggar, as yourself?" We believe it was, and we would ask, why have we made so little advance towards this highest attainment in human association? The answer to this question must be found, we think, in the fact already noted, that the principles which we have politically asserted, we have socially denied; striving to establish socially the inequalities against which we have politically rebelled, only substituting for the distinctions of birth those created by wealth.

In the rapid glance which we have taken of the various influences that have combined to form the English

character, we have seen a nation happily " compounded
of every nation's best," trained to reverence of law and
love of liberty.   In America we have seen this same
people taking a position in which that reverence for law
remained the only restraint upon their actions ; in which,
therefore, they were free in the best sense of the word,
free even as God made man, free from all restraint but
that which, at the command of an enlightened conscience, he imposes on himself.   To those who have followed us in this sketch, and who, assenting to the proposition, that each creature in the Providence of God
finds itself in that condition for which it is peculiarly fitted, and may thus discover in its offices the exact correl-
atives of its powers,—these powers being the sum of its
natural capabilities, and of the circumstances under
which these capabilities have been exercised and developed,—also think, with us, that while man has been endowed with qualities which render him the proper con-
troller of the outward machinery of government, the
thews and sinews of society, woman is by nature equally
fitted to preside over its inner spirit, over the homes
from which the social as distinguished from the political
life must be derived ; the conclusion must, it seems to
us, be irresistible, that to American women we must

look to rectify the errors of American society, and that from them we may hope to derive a life freer from factitious distinctions, controlled more by enlightened convictions and less by conventional forms, a life nobler, more spiritual, more in conformity with Christian principles than any the world has yet seen. To such a work are we now endeavoring to awaken the attention of our countrywomen. It is a noble work: a work which, we think, they must themselves acknowledge to be worthy the exercise of all their powers.

Permit us, in illustration of our subject, to place before you a sketch of an American woman of fashion as she is and as she might be—as she *must* be to accomplish the task we would appoint her. Examine with a careful eye "the counterfeit presentment" of these two widely differing characters, and choose the model on which you will form yourselves. And first, by a few strokes of this magic wand—the pen—we will conjure within the charmed circle of your vision, the woman of fashion as she is.

Flirtilla,—for so noted a character must not want a name,—may well be pronounced a favorite of nature and of fortune. To the first she owed a pleasing person and a mind which offered no unapt soil for cultivation; by

favor of the last, she was born the heiress to wealth and
to those advantages which wealth unquestionably con-
fers. Her childhood was carefully sequestered from all
vulgar influences, and she was early taught, that to be a
little lady was her highest possible attainment. At six
years old she astonished the *élite* assembled in her father's halls, and even dazzled the larger assemblages of
Saratoga by her grace in dancing and by the ease with
which she conversed in French, which, as it was the language of her nursery attendants, had been a second
mother-tongue to her. At the fashionable boarding-
school, at which her education was, in common parlance,
completed, she distanced all competitors for the prizes in
modern languages, dancing, and music ; and acquired so
much acquaintance with geography and history as would
secure her from mistaking Prussia for Persia, or imagining that Lord Wellington had conquered Julius Cæsar—
in other words, so much knowledge of them as would
guard her from betraying her ignorance. To these ac-
quirements she added a slight smattering of various natural sciences. All these accomplishments had nearly been
lost to the world, by her forming an attachment for one
of fine qualities, personal and mental, who was entirely
destitute of fortune. From the fatal mistake of yielding

to such an attachment she was preserved by a judicious mother, who placed before her in vivid contrast the commanding position in which she would be placed as the wife of Mr. A—, with his houses and lands, his bank stock and magnificent equipage; and the *médiocre* station she would occupy as Mrs. B—, a station to which one of her aspiring mind could not readily succumb, even though she found herself there in company with one of the most interesting and agreeable of men. Relinquishing with a sigh the gratification of the last sentiment that bound her to nature and to rational life, she magnanimously sacrificed her inclinations to her sense of duty, and became Mrs. A—. From this time her course has been undisturbed by one faltering feeling, one wavering thought. She has visited London and Paris, only that she might assure herself that her house possessed all which was considered essential to a *genteel* establishment in the first, and that her toilette was the most *recherché* that could be obtained in the last. She laughs at the very idea of wearing any thing made in America, and is exceedingly merry over the portraitures of Yankee character and Yankee life occasionally to be met in the pages of foreign tourists, or to be seen personated in foreign theatres. She complains much of the promiscuous char-

7

acter of American society, dances in no set but her own, and, in order to secure her exclusiveness from contact with the common herd, moves about from one point of fashionable life to another, attended by the same satellites, to whom she is the great centre of attraction. Her manners, like her dresses, are imported from Paris. She talks and laughs very loudly at all public places, lectures, concerts, and the like ; and has sometimes, even in the house of God, expressed audibly her assent with or dissent from the preacher, that she may prove herself entirely free from that shockingly American *mauvaise honte,* which she supposes to be all that keeps other women silent. Any gentleman desiring admission to her circle must produce authentic credentials that he has been abroad, must wear his mustaches after the latest Parisian cut, must interlard his bad English with worse French, and must be familiar with the names and histories of the latest ballet-dancers and opera-singers who have created a fever of excitement abroad. To foreigners she is particularly gracious, and nothing throws her into such a fervor of activity as the arrival in the country of an English Lord, a German Baron, or a French or Italian Count. To draw such a character within her circle she thinks no effort too great, no sacrifice of feeling too humiliating.

It may be objected that all our descriptions of the fashionable woman as she is, relates to externals; that of the essential character, the inner life, we have, in truth, said nothing.   But what can we do?   So far as we have yet been able to discover, this class is destitute of any inner life.   Those who compose it live for the world and in the world.   Home is with them only the place in which they receive visits.   We acknowledge that few in our country have yet attained to so perfect a development of fashionable character as we have here described; but to some it is already an attainment; to many—we fear to *most*, young women of what are called the higher classes in our large cities—it is an aim.   Nobler spirits there are, indeed, among us, of every age and every class, and from these we must choose our example of a woman of fashion as she should be.   On her, too, we will bestow a name—a name associated with all gentle and benignant influences—the name of her who in her shaded retreats received of old the ruler of earth's proudest empire, that she might "breathe off with the holy air" of her pure affection, "that dust o' the heart" caught from contact with coarser spirits.   So have we dreamed of Egeria, and Egeria shall be the name of our heroine.   Heroine indeed, for

15

heroic must be her life. With eyes uplifted to a protecting Heaven, she must walk the narrow path of right,
—a precipice on either hand,—never submitting in her
lowliness of soul, to the encroachments of the selfish,
and eager, and clamorous crowd,—never bowing her
own native nobility to the dictation of those whom the
world styles great. "Resisting the proud, but giving
grace unto the humble," if we may without irreverence appropriate to a mortal, words descriptive of
Him whose unapproachable and glorious holiness we are
exhorted to imitate.

In society, Egeria is more desirous to please than to
shine. Her associates are selected mainly for their
personal qualities, and if she is peculiarly attentive and
deferential to any class, it is to those unfortunates whom
poverty, the accidents of birth, or the false arrangements
of society, have divorced from a sphere for which their
refinement of taste and manner and their intellectual cultivation had fitted them. Admission to her society is
sought as a distinction, because it is known that it must
be purchased by something more than a graceful address,
a well-curled mustache, or the reputation of a travelled
man. At her entertainments, you will often meet some
whom you will meet nowhere else; some promising

young artist, yet unknown to fame,—some who, once standing in the sunshine of fortune, were well known to many whose vision is too imperfect for the recognition of features over which adversity has thrown its shadow. The influence of Egeria is felt through the whole circle of her acquaintance ;—she encourages the young to high aims and persevering efforts,—she brightens the fading light of the aged, but above all is she a blessing and a glory within her own home. Her husband cannot look on her—to borrow Longfellow's beautiful thought—without "reading in the serene expression of her face, the Divine beatitude, ' Blessed are the pure in heart.' " Her children revere her as the earthly type of perfect love. They learn even more from her example than her precept, that they are to live not to themselves, but to their fellow-creatures, and to God in them. She has so cultivated their taste for all which is beautiful and noble, that they cannot but desire to conform themselves to such models. She has taught them to love their country and devote themselves to its advancement—not because it excels all others, but because it is that to which God in his providence united them, and whose advancement and true interest they are bound to seek by all just and Christian methods. In a word, she has never for-

7*

gotten that they were immortal and responsible beings, and this thought has reappeared in every impression she has stamped upon their minds.

But it is her conduct towards those in a social position inferior to her own, which individualizes most strongly the character of Egeria. Remembering that there are none who may not, under our free institutions, attain to positions of influence and responsibility, she endeavors, in all her intercourse with them, to awaken their self-respect and desire for improvement, and she is ever ready to aid them in the attainment of that desire, and thus to fit them for the performance of those duties that may devolve on them.

"Are you not afraid that Bridget will leave you, if, by your lessons, you fit her for some higher position?" asked a lady, on finding her teaching embroidery to a servant who had shown much aptitude for it.

"If Bridget can advance her interest by leaving me, she shall have my cheerful consent to go. God forbid that I should stand in the way of good to any fellow-creature—above all, to one whom, by placing her under my temporary protection, he has made it especially my duty to serve," was her reply.

In the general ignorance and vice of the population

daily pouring into our country from foreign lands, Egeria finds new reason for activity, in the moral and intellectual advancement of all who are brought within her sphere of influence.

Egeria has been accused of being ambitious for her children. "I am ambitious for them," she replies; "ambitious that they should occupy stations that may be as a vantage-ground from which to act for the public good."

Notwithstanding this ambition, she has, to the astonishment of many in her own circle, consented that one of her sons should devote himself to mechanics. She was at first pitied for this, as a mortification to which she must certainly have been compelled, by her husband's singular notions, to submit.

"You mistake," said Egeria, to one who delicately expressed this pity to her; "my son's choice of a trade had my hearty concurrence. I was prepared for it by the whole bias of his mind from childhood. He will excel in the career he has chosen, I have no doubt; for he has abilities equal to either of his brothers, and he loves the object to which he has devoted them. As a lawyer or physician he would, probably, have but added one to the number of *médiocre* practitioners who lounge through life with no higher aim than their own maintenance."

"But then," it was objected, "he would not have sacrificed his position in society."

Egeria is human, and the sudden flush of indignation must have crimsoned the mother's brow at this; and somewhat of scorn, we doubt not, was in the smile that curled her lip as she replied, "My son can afford to lose the acquaintance of those who cannot appreciate the true nobility and independence of spirit which have made him choose a position offering, as he believes, the highest means of development for his own peculiar powers, and the greatest probability, therefore, of his becoming useful to others."

Our sketches are finished—imperfect sketches we acknowledge them. It would have been a labor of love to have rendered the last complete—to have followed the steps of Egeria—the Christian gentlewoman—through at least one day of her life; to have shown her embellishing her social circle by her graces of manner and charms of conversation, and to have accompanied her from the saloons which she thus adorned, to more humble abodes. In these abodes she was ever a welcome as well as an honored guest, for she bore thither a respectful consideration for their inmates, which is a rarer and more coveted gift to the poor than any wealth can purchase. Having done this, we would have liked to glance at her in the tranquil evening of a life well spent, and to contrast her then with Flirtilla, old beyond the power of rouge, false teeth, and false hair, to disguise—still running through a round of pleasures that have ceased to charm, regretting the past, dissatisfied with the present, and dreading the future, alternately courting and abusing the world, which has grown weary of her. But to stray into these flowery paths of imagination, would lead us too far away from a graver purpose, to which we return.

CORRESPONDENCE BETWEEN ELISHA BOUDINOT AND GEORGE WASHINGTON.

Copy of a letter from Elisha Boudinot to General Washington. He was Deputy Commissary-General of Prisoners during our Revolutionary struggle. Both (*original* letters) are now in possession of the son of Elisha Boudinot, residing in the city of Burlington, N. J.

NEWARK, N. J., *May*, 1783.

Amidst the general joy which is diffused through the States, on the establishment of our Independence and a restoration of the blessings of peace, will your excellency permit an individual, deeply interested in your happiness, to give vent, if possible, to his feelings on this subject, and most sincerely to congratulate you on the final accomplishment of our most sanguine hopes. The thought that your excellency has survived the contest, adds a pleasure to the enjoyment that no other event could possibly give. It has been my earnest prayer that Heaven would preserve your life to complete the liberation of your country from tyranny, and see her safely secured in peace, independence, and happiness, and to receive the grateful acknowledgments of a whole people. Nothing can afford a great mind more real pleasure than the idea of being the happy instrument of giving birth to *an empire*, the future nursery of every principle that can ennoble man ; an asylum for the persecuted of all nations; and, in fact, rendering happiness to one quarter of the globe. It is a satisfaction that an angel might desire, and which you, sir, are justly entitled to enjoy.

I am confident that the idea of this has supported your excellency in the many distressing scenes you have passed through, to the final accomplishment of our wishes. *You* have finished *your* part. It only remains that your country should equal in gratitude the toils, the dangers, and solicitude you have endured for them. That they will do this collectively, there is no doubt; but something still remains to perfect the reward—to convince you that every individual feels that real affection for and gratitude to you that they ought to the father and deliverer of their country. This only can be done by the representation of private persons, which will, I hope, apologize for this intrusion. My public business calls me to every county of this State, and a very general acquaintance with the people, and I am positive that I should do the greatest injustice to them, did I not assure your excellency that there is scarcely a man or woman among them who do not entertain these sentiments, and who have a monument erected to you in their breasts that can only be effaced with their lives.

Were it possible for your excellency to have a view of the whole country at once, and see the honest farmers around their fires, blessing your name, and teaching their children to lisp your praises, you would forget your toils and labors, and thank Heaven that you were born to bless a grateful land.

When your excellency is retiring from the field, will you indulge the inhabitants of this State to spend a short time, as you are passing through, free from care, where you have spent so much in distress and anxiety of mind, that they may have an opportunity of personally convincing you of their attachment?

I take the liberty of inclosing, and beg your acceptance of, a copy of an ode, written by my father-in-law, Mr. Smith, on the occasion of our rejoicing. Mrs. Boudinot joins with me in entreating that you will be kind enough to make our sincere congratulations acceptable to Mrs. Washington, and to assure her that we participate in the joy that she, above all others, must feel on this occasion; and that you may both long enjoy that cup of happiness which Providence has so completely filled, is the fervent prayer of

Your most humble and obedient servant,
ELISHA BOUDINOT.

Copy of an autographical letter from General Washington to Elisha Boudinot.

NEWBURGH, *May* 10th, 1783.

SIR: Your letter of congratulation contains expressions of too friendly a nature not to affect me with the deepest sensibility; I beg therefore you will accept my acknowledgments for them, and that you will be persuaded I can never be insensible of the interest you are pleased to take in my personal happiness, as well as in the general felicity of our country. While I candidly confess I cannot be indifferent to the favorable sentiments which you mention my fellow-citizens entertain of my exertions in their service, I wish to confess, through you, the particular obligations I feel myself under to Mr. Smith for the pleasure I have received from the perusal of his elegant Ode on the Peace.

The accomplishment of the great object we had in view, in so short a time, and under such propitious circumstances, must, I am confident. fill every bosom with the purest joy.; and, for my own part, I will not strive to conceal the pleasure I already anticipate from my approaching retirement to the placid walks of domestic life.

Having no reward to ask for myself, if I have been so happy as to obtain the approbation of my countrymen I shall be satisfied; but it still rests with them to complete my wishes by adopting such a system of policy as will insure the future reputation, tranquillity, happiness, and glory of this extensive empire, to which, I am well assured, nothing can contribute so much as *an inviolable adherence to the principles of the Union*, and a fixed resolution of building *the National Faith on the basis of Public Justice;* without which, all that has been done and suffered is in vain. To effect which, therefore, the abilities of every true patriot ought to be exerted with the greatest zeal and assiduity.

I am, as yet, uncertain at what time I shall be at liberty to return to Virginia, ánd consequently cannot inform you whether I may be able to gratify my inclination of spending a little time with my friends in Jersey, as I pass through that State. I can only say that the friendship I have for a people, from whom I have often derived such essential aid, will strongly dispose me to it.

Mrs Washington begs Mrs. Boudinot and yourself will accept her best compliments and thanks for your good wishes; and I must request the same favor, being, with sentiments of esteem and regard,

Sir, your most obed't and most h'ble s'v't,
G. WASHINGTON.

ELISHA BOUDINOT, ESQ.

EDITORS' TABLE.

AMERICAN ARTISTS IN ROME.—A recent letter from our correspondent, for several past years a resident in the "Eternal City," informs us that there are now between twenty and thirty American artists studying in Rome. The greatest work of art in progress there, and, of course, the greatest in the world, is that of our countryman Crawford, "The Virginia Washington Monument." Our friend goes on, "This is to be one of the finest monuments ever erected. An equestrian group, Washington surrounded by six distinguished men of Virginia. The statue of 'Patrick Henry'—one of the six—is completed, eleven feet six inches high, dressed in the costume of 1765. This is very much admired. The Roman artists think these the best costume statues ever modelled. Mr. Crawford is now at work on the statue of 'Thomas Jefferson.' These statues are to be cast in bronze in Munich.*

Then follows a eulogium on Crawford's genius, and the honor he is conferring on his country, both doubtless his deserved tributes of admiration. That the sons of America are thus distinguished gives us pleasure as well as pride. Shall we not also rejoice in the successful genius of the daughters of our republic?

AMERICAN ARTISTES AT HOME.—A young lady of Boston, Miss Harriet Hosmer, has lately completed a beautiful medallion, representing the head of Professor J. N. McDowell, of Cincinnati. This medallion, cut from pure white marble, is as large as the natural head, and the features are said to be admirably preserved. What renders this more remarkable is that the resemblance was sketched from memory, only aided by a small, defective plaster cast taken many years ago. The medallion was sent from Boston to Cincinnati; and Professor McDowell, on receiving this beautiful work of art, gave the following history of the young sculptress. We should state that Professor McD. occupies the chair of "Anatomy" in the Medical Department of the State University at Cincinnati, and that Miss Hosmer, a young lady about the age of nineteen, was on a visit to a friend in that city during the fall and winter of 1850-51.

"While the lectures were in progress at the medical school, Professor McDowell says that Miss Hosmer sought an interview with him, and stated that she had resolved to cultivate a taste for sculpture; preparatory to which, she desired to understand thoroughly the science of anatomy. She requested therefore to be instructed by him, and promised indefatigable attention to the study of this difficult branch of learning. Struck with the novelty of such a proposition, from a highly educated young lady, he supposed at first that she was jesting; but, upon being satisfied that she was in earnest, he readily undertook to instruct her. She immediately entered upon the study, and made such extraordinary progress that, in the opinion of Professor McD., when she left for Boston at the beginning of the summer, she had attained a rare proficiency in it. He related further that the now world-renowned Powers and the distinguished Clevenger had both attended his lectures when connected with a medical school at Cincinnati; but that neither of them had then made such progress in anatomy as Miss Hosmer had attained at the time of her departure for Boston. He paid a glowing compliment to the enthusiasm of her genius, her love of art, her brilliant talents, and the maidenly dignity and purity of her character. He predicted for her a brilliant career as an artist, if she should continue to devote her talents to such pursuits."

Whether she does continue to devote herself exclusively to this pursuit of art, so as to win the highest renown, is of less consequence to her sex and to the world than is the example of energy in the pursuit of excellence she has already displayed. She has shown the superiority of the female mind in the study of *anatomy*, thus pointing to woman's true profession in the sciences, viz., the medical. In this science, females will excel whenever they are permitted to enter on the study.

HOW AMERICAN WOMEN SHOULD VOTE.—"I control seven votes; why should I desire to cast one myself?" said a lady who, if women went to the polls, would be acknowledged as a leader. This lady is a devoted, beloved wife, a faithful, tender mother; she has six sons. She *knows* her influence is paramount over the minds she has carefully trained. She *feels* her interests are safe confided to those her affection has made happy. She *trusts* her country will be nobly served by those whom her example has taught to believe in goodness, therefore she is proud to vote by her proxies. This is the way American women should vote, namely, by influencing rightly the votes of men.

HOW THE "MAINE LIQUOR LAW" MAY BE SUSTAINED.—This law, as our readers are, we hope, aware, prohibits the *sale* of all kinds of intoxicating liquors, except for medicinal or scientific purposes. It has been adopted and *sustained* by the people of Maine for the last year or two, and, in that time, has nearly emptied the jails and poor-houses of their miserable inmates, most of whom had been reduced to poverty or incited to crime by INTEMPERANCE. Efforts are now being made to adopt this law in the other New England States, also in New York and Pennsylvania. Will not every woman's heart beat with joy at this prospect of reform, and every woman's voice wish it God speed? And, if women could go to the polls, would not their votes soon decide in favor of this law? Yet that decision could not sustain it, *because the law, in its last resort, must be upheld by physical force!* Herein lies the reason why men should *vote*, and women should not. But have women therefore nothing to do in this struggle between order and disorder, temperance and intemperance, heaven and hell? On women and children fall the deepest sufferings from this hideous vice, which sacrifices home and all that makes domestic life—woman's life—lovely to the vile selfishness and brutalizing appetites of wicked men.

The conflict between the friends of temperance and those powers of evil—the rum-selling landlords and their tippling crew—will be fearfully severe; and woman, in the majesty and power of her moral influence, should aid the right. Every man who comes forward as a leader in the cause of temperance is the champion of our sex. He should be honored as a hero. The smiles and blessings of those he is striving to save from the demon of drunkenness—a more ruthless destroyer than the monsters slain by Perseus or Bellerophon—should cheer and reward the true "Son of Temperance."

293

Some good men lack moral courage. They would face death in the battle-field with less trepidation than they will probably feel when depositing their vote *against the sale of intoxicating liquors!* Though the *sale* of other poisons is strictly guarded, the traffic in the *rum poison* must be free. Though gunpowder cannot be kept or sold but under stringent precautions, every house may be made the receptacle of an agent of destruction more awful than ever issued from the cannon's mouth. Let men who fear that the "Maine Liquor Law" goes too far, remember they are intrusted with a higher duty than any which the mere military commander performs. They are the defenders of society from the powers of evil, which destroy the sources of happiness, darken hope, and deliver over to destitution, disgrace, and death those who cannot defend themselves. Womanhood and childhood rely on the bravery of the *good and noble men* of our country. Every step onward in moral improvement is an added pledge for the security and happiness of the female sex. Every man who hinders, or strives to hinder these reforms, is an enemy to woman, and deserves her scorn, contempt, avoidance. All her influence should be given to the cause of temperance. The men who vote for the "Maine Liquor Law" are her proxies. Let her approval sustain them in their righteous course, and this "LAW" will be enacted and sustained.

To Correspondents.—The following articles are accepted: "The Enthusiast," "Forgotten," "Rome," "The Peasant's Song," "White Violets," "Three Songs for three Belles," "Ballad," "To E. on her Bridal," "Let me die," "Stanzas," and "The Snow-Drop."

The following articles are declined. We give this list to avoid the trouble of constant inquiries about the communications sent us. Some of these are quite good, and may find favor with other publishers. We have no room for: "The Night-Watcher," "My Mary's Dead," "The Dead Hindoo Babe," "Logan Assenting to the Treaty of Peace," "The Lady of Harringshaw," "Song," "Lines," "The Traitor's Doom," "Song," "A Visit to the Hermitage," &c., "To a Red Rose," &c., "To Miss M. A. S.," &c., "To Amanda," "To my Infant Boy," "The North Wind," "My Pets," "Not at Home," "The Butterfly," "Sleeping at Church," "Fancies," "The Knights of the Crusades," and "The Importance of Always Telling the Truth."

OUR TREASURY.

POLITENESS.

BY GEORGE S. HILLARD.

True politeness is a very rare thing, gentle reader, stare though you may.

Of the gentlemen, young and old, whiskered and unwhiskered, that may be seen in Washington Street any sunshiny day, there is not one who does not think himself a polite man, and who would not very much resent any insinuation to the contrary. Their opinion is grounded on reasons something like the following. When they go to a party, they make a low bow to the mistress of the house, and then look round after somebody that is young and pretty to make themselves agreeable to. At a ball, they will do their utmost to entertain their partner, unless the fates have given them to some one who is ugly and awkward, and they will listen to her remarks with their most bland expression. If they are invited to a dinner party, they go in their best coats, praise their entertainer's wine, and tell the lady they hope her children are all well. If they tread on the toes of a well-dressed person, they will beg his pardon. They never spit on a carpet; and, in

walking with a lady, they always give her the inside; and, if the practice be allowable, they offer her their arm. So far, very good; but I must always see a man in certain situations before I decide whether he be polite or no. I should like to see how he would act, if placed at dinner between an ancient maiden lady, and a country clergyman with a small salary and a rusty coat, and with some distinguished person opposite to him. I want to see him, on a hot and dusty day, sitting on the back seat of a stage-coach, when the driver takes in some poor lone woman, with, may be, a child in her arms, and tells the gentlemen that one of them must ride outside and make room for her. I want to be near him when his washerwoman makes some very good excuse to him for not bringing home his clothes at the usual time, or not doing up an article in exactly the style he wished. I want to hear the tone and emphasis with which he gives orders to servants in steamboats and taverns. I mark his conduct, when he is walking with an umbrella on a rainy day, and overtakes an old man, or an invalid, or a decent-looking woman, who are exposed without protection to the violence of the storm. If he be in company with those whom he thinks his inferiors, I listen to hear if his conversation be entirely about himself. If some of the number be very distinguished, and some quite unknown, I observe whether he acts as if he were utterly unconscious of the presence of these last.

There are a great many little offences committed against good manners, which people are hardly aware of at the time. It is not polite, for instance, to tease a person to do what he has once declined; and it is equally impolite to refuse a request or an invitation in order to be urged, and accept afterwards. Comply at once: if your friend be sincere, you will gratify him; if not, you will punish him, as he deserves to be. It is not polite, when asked what part of a dish you will have, to say, "Any part—it is quite indifferent to me;" it is hard enough to carve for one's friends, without choosing for them. It is not polite to entertain our visitors with our own family history, and the events of our own household. It is not polite for married ladies to talk in the presence of gentlemen of the difficulty they have in procuring domestics, and how good-for-nothing they are when procured. It is not polite to put food upon the plate of your guest without asking his leave, nor to press him to eat more than he wants. It is not polite to stare under ladies' bonnets, as if you suspected they had stolen the linings from you. It is—but let me remember it is not polite to be a bore, especially in print.

Let no man imagine that his rank, or station, or talents excuse him from an attention to those rules of good breeding, which cost nothing but a little care, and which make a great deal of difference in the sum total of human happiness. They are as imperative as the rules of morality; and there is no one, however great or high, that does not owe to society a liberal recompense for what he receives from it. There is now and then a man so weak as to affect to be rough, or forgetful, or absent, from a notion that his deficiencies in these little things will be ascribed to the largeness of the objects with which he is habitually conversant, and that his mind will be supposed unable to come down from the airy regions of contemplation to such low matters. But such a one should be put into the same state-room of the great Ship of Fools, with those who twisted their necks to look like Alexander, or spoke thick to resemble Hotspur. A man that can do great things and not little ones, is an imperfect man; and there is no more inconsistency between the two than there is in a great poet's being able to write a promissory note, or a great orator's having the power to talk about the weather.

I will only remark, in conclusion, that good breeding should form a part of every system of education. Not that children should be made to barter their native simplicity for a set of artificial airs and graces, but that they should be early impressed with the deformity of selfishness, and the necessity of thinking of others as well as themselves. Care should be taken that their intercourse with each other be in a spirit of courtesy and mildness. He who has been reared in a brawling and ill-mannered nursery can hardly be expected to ripen into a polite man. The elder members of a family should bear in mind that the influence of their own conduct will encircle the children like an atmosphere. There can be little happiness in that household in which the minutest offices are not dictated by a spirit of thoughtful courtesy and delicate consideration for others. How many marriages are made wretched by a neglect of those little mutual attentions so scrupulously paid in the days of courtship. Let it be borne in mind that the cords of love, which bind hearts so closely together that neither Life, nor Death, nor Time, nor Eternity can sever them, are woven of threads no bigger than a spider's web.

FEMALE ELOQUENCE.

BY ELIZABETH STARLING.

ELOQUENCE may sometimes effect its object by means of splendid images and sublime expressions, but that alone which springs from the heart takes the certain road to success. The flattering results which have on so many occasions attended the exercise of this brilliant talent by the female sex, must be rather attributed to the energetic zeal with which, from their goodness of heart, they have entered into the lists in defence of virtue, than to any studied use of language, as was the custom with the public speakers of their times. The consciousness of being engaged in a virtuous cause has often given rise to the most enthusiastic and splendid eloquence on the part of women, who, weak and helpless by nature, have thus become endued with strength, not only to urge, but to accomplish the most arduous enterprises. There is no doubt that,

> " If the mind with clear conception glow,
>   The willing words in just expressions flow;"

and warmth of feeling in women has amply compensated for any inferiority, if such there were, in their talents, to those of the opposite sex. We ought to set much weight on these superior instances of mental capacity, and endeavor not to degenerate from such worthy examples: such patterns of merit should not be thrown away upon us, for they teach us that, if the too free use of speech is attributed as a failing to our sex, the proper use of that speech may be rendered not only a private, but a public benefit; as there is a time to be silent, so it does sometimes happen that there is a time when it becomes a duty to speak; and eloquence, actuated by sincere and virtuous motives, must ever claim universal respect and admiration.

MEN'S RIGHTS CONVENTION AT ——.

EXTRAORDINARY PROCEEDINGS, EXCITING SCENES, AND CURIOUS SPEECHES.

FROM OUR OWN REPORTER, CHERICOT.

December 20th, 1851.

YESTERDAY, at 10 o'clock in the forenoon, an immense mass meeting of gentlemen from all parts of the country was held at Independence Hall. It was convened upon notices to that effect, which were issued directly after the late extraordinary and treasonable Female Convention at Massachusetts, and which, being distributed among the principal cities in the Union, had resulted in the collection of an enthusiastic crowd of gentlemen of all grades, trades, and politics, one common danger uniting them, in the effort to repel the proposed feminine aggression of their rights.

On taking a survey of the meeting, one thing struck us very forcibly—the uneasy and restless anxiety that characterized the demeanor of most of the men; the slightest noise caused a general sensation; and, in one instance, the shrill cry of a fish-woman threw a gentleman into hysterics, which he explained, on his recovery, to have resulted from his mistaking it for the voice of his wife.

When the excitement had, in some measure, subsided, the meeting was called to order by Mr. Wumenheyter, of New York, who said, the first business being the choice of a president, he moved that Mr. H. P. Husband, of Maryland, be appointed.

Brass Blackstone, of Philadelphia, seconded the motion, which was unanimously adopted.

After the vice presidents and secretaries were duly chosen, and a business committee appointed to draw up resolutions expressive of the sense of the meeting, the president addressed the convention as follows:—

"The object which has called this great assemblage together is one which not only concerns mankind in general, but Americans in particular. This is emphatically a land of liberty—liberty which, achieved by the exertions of our forefathers, has commanded the respect of the tyrannical governments of the Old World, and resisted all unhallowed attempts to subvert it. This liberty, gentlemen, is threatened with destruction by the establishment, within the very bounds of this republic, of a despotism that has no parallel in ancient or modern history. Yes, there is a conspiracy afoot in the very midst of us, which, should it succeed in its aspiring aims, will annihilate us as men, and convert us into mere household appendages to that rebellious sex who, after having for years shown a disposition to encroach on *some* of our rights and privileges, now boldly assert a claim to *all*. Patience, gentlemen, is no longer a virtue; stern determination and resolute action alone can put down this ambitious usurpation and re-establish our authority on its legitimate basis.

"These firebrands on our domestic hearths must

be extinguished, or the sparks, lighting into a flame, will consume us."

Here the sensation produced by Mr. Husband's fiery eloquence was so intense that groans and sobs resounded from all parts of the building, and the gentleman was so overcome by his own flights of fancy that it was some time before he could proceed.

"I have, in the relations of husband, son, and brother, stood aloof. I have borne, with dignity and Spartan fortitude, the assumption, by my female relatives, of those garments which, from time immemorial, have been our rightful badge, trusting that the 'breach' into which they were throwing themselves would prove of such an 'imminent and deadly' nature as to deprive them of any desire to go further. But late events have opened my eyes to the treasonable nature of their designs, and to the danger of the mine on which we have been heedlessly treading ; and, regardless alike of family ties and possible consequences, I have boldly sounded the alarm which has brought us together this day. This terrible danger I discovered by chance, having picked up—in my *own* room, gentlemen—a letter addressed to my wife by a female friend. I will, gentlemen, read a passage from this incendiary production, premising that the preceding paragraphs, after giving an account of the late meeting at Worcester, refer to the female millennium about to commence :—

"'Now then, my dear,
We 'll smoke and cheer and drink our lager beer ;
We 'll have our latch-keys, stay out late at nights ;
And boldly we 'll assert our female rights ;
While conquered men, our erewhile tyrant foes,
Shall stay at home and wear our cast-off clothes,
Nurse babies, scold the servants, get our dinners ;
'Tis all that they are fit for, wretched sinners !'

"Imagine my feelings on finding treason at work in my domestic sanctuary—at detecting the wife of my bosom in a plot against my peace !"

Here Mr. Husband was so overpowered by his emotions that he was compelled to pause for a few moments, ere he recovered his voice. Deep sympathy was manifested by the audience.

"I would now repeat the necessity of prompt action, for which I doubt not the wisdom and intelligence of this assembly will be found sufficient. Our business now is to find a remedy for the evil. Let us therefore, in a bold and uncompromising manner, address ourselves to the duties before us."

While awaiting the action of the business committee, the following letters were read from distinguished gentlemen who had been invited to attend the meeting :—

Mr. Webster stated that the onerous nature of his diplomatic duties prevented his accepting the invitation extended to him. Had it, however, been in his power to do so, he should still have declined it, as the handsome manner in which the ladies had defended him in his native State obliged him to re-main neuter in the conflict between the great contending parties. He would remark, in conclusion, that, devoted as he was to the Union, faithful as he had ever been in maintaining the Constitution, he had no sympathy with anything tending to infringe the conditions of the matrimonial compact, and therefore solemnly recommended that both parties should meet and conclude a treaty of peace.

Mr. Clay regretted his necessary attendance on Congress precluded his presence at this important meeting ; for, faithful to his great principle, he should have endeavored to suggest such a compromise as should reconcile all parties. But he trusted that an amicable spirit would pervade their proceedings, and unity and concord be the result.

Mr. Horace Mann repeated his determination of not siding with either party. He referred again to the book he was writing, which he thought would satisfy both sides.

Mr. Buckeye, of Ohio, wrote to excuse his attendance, as the duties of the pork-killing season required his attention ; and Mrs. Buckeye's absence at a Socialist meeting, in the interior of the State, prevented his leaving home.

Mr. Wumenheyter, chairman of the committee, now rose to say that their report was ready. He then read the following resolutions :—

Resolved, That a crisis has arrived in our domestic relations that admits of no temporizing measures, but requires us openly to insist on those rights so boldly and outrageously assailed by that weaker portion of humanity, whose duty it is to be satisfied with the inferior position assigned them by nature, and to yield in all things to man.

Resolved, That an unblushing claim has not only been made on our clothes, but on all our masculine privileges ; and as this evil has resulted, in the first place, from the impunity with which the women have put their hands in our pockets, and as it will end only in the usurpation of our business, and of our sole right to the ballot-box, it becomes necessary for us to impress upon this rebellious sex our united determination to resist their aggressions.

Resolved, That this effort becomes imperatively necessary when we consider the treacherous nature of women, and remember that, should they succeed in their attempt, we shall meet no mercy at their hands. Universal decapitation of the men, and an Amazonian form of government will undoubtedly be the result.

Resolved, That, while we shall use our lawful and united authority to put down this revolt, we will show clemency to the culprits, and, tempering justice with mercy, render their punishment as light as may be consistent with our own safety.

These resolutions were ordered to be laid on the table for discussion.

Mr. Wumenheyter said he wished particularly for the attention of the audience while he offered a few remarks on these resolutions. "He was," he said, "proud to call himself a New Yorker. His city was the greatest in the world. It had a great canal, a great line of steamships, a great many railroads, a great many banks, and"——

Here a voice from the crowd exclaimed, "And a great many other humbugs!" Mr. W. was, for a moment, disconcerted; but, resuming his remarks, he said—

"I do not regard this rude interruption. I shall still assert the superiority of my State to all others; and, at the same time, acknowledge that, with all our talents and business enterprise, we cannot manage the women. I confess that, in *our* great State, the attempt on our privileges was *first* made ; but I can also assure this convention that we shall be the *first* to defend those privileges. I have been so unhappy as to have had three wives, but, fortunately, have buried them all; and I can assert, from personal experience, that

'Woman, woman, whether lean or fat, is In face an angel, and in soul a cat!'

A spirit of philanthropy urges me to warn you against the female snares which my fatal destiny has inflicted on me, and from which I am therefore desirous to save others, as my several wives were so many different forms of evil, and I suffered intensely in consequence. I hope my misery will deter others from such experiments. If I rescue one wretch from the horrors of matrimony, my purpose will be answered, and my past sufferings forgotten."

Mr. W. urged the adoption of immediate and relentless measures, and trusted that some available remedy might be suggested for the evil that was in their midst.

Cotte Bettie, Esq., from Delaware, said, "I fully agree with the gentleman from New York in his views on this terrible crisis. I am as proud of my State as he can be of his. I am not ashamed to call myself one of the 'Blue Hen's Chickens.' Delawarians are true blue—they always were, and always will be blue. They were the first to rally at freedom's call, and would not now be found wanting. While he thus obeyed his instructions in proffering their aid, he must, at the same time, assure this assembly that it was very advisable for them to keep their proceedings as secret as possible, lest a premature disclosure should put the women on their guard."

C. Colesworth Pinckney, from South Carolina, remarked, "Had any one told him a few months since that he should be meeting in amity with his northern brethren, he should have indignantly denied the possibility of such an act. He did not intend now, however, to allude to the difference of opinion that prevailed between the South and North; the several States of Georgia, Alabama, Florida, and South Carolina, that had appointed him a delegate to this convention, having empowered him to bury all sectional causes of discord in oblivion, and to unite energetically with the representatives of other States in putting down this terrible conspiracy. He had come prepared, then, to assure them of the cordial co-operation of the Southern States in any action that might be taken in the crusade against women. He would only remark that there should be no delay either in their resolves or execution—'if 'twere done, 'twere well 'twere done quickly.' With this end in view, he recommended bringing before the present Session of Congress a fugitive women bill, by which every man might be empowered to reclaim and punish a runaway or rebellious wife."

Mr. Jonathan Whittle, from Massachusetts, "Guessed that there needn't be much talk about the matter. Wimmen's place was tu hum, and it was man's business to keep 'em there. Pretty much all they was fit for was to dry innions, make squash pies, and get a fellow a good dinner on Thanksgivin'. He calkerlated that if each indiwiddiwel present had the spunk he orter have, he could manage his wimmen himself, without anybody to help him. Yankees knew a leetle somethin' besides makin' wooden nutmegs, mushmellion, and cowcumber seeds, and they didn't want anybody to come there and tell 'em how to do : they'd better stay tu hum, and take care of their own affairs."

Here Mr. Whittle was called to order from all parts of the house, and sat down in a state of high indignation, wiping his face with a blue cotton handkerchief.

George Washington Patrick Henry John Randolph Powhatan, Esq., from Virginia, said, "I regret the irritable state of feeling which seems to sway the gentleman from New England. I wonder at his assertion of our Yankee brethren's ability to manage their women, when the fact is notorious that Mr. Whittle's native State was the scene chosen for the outbreak of the rebellion. Belonging, as I do, to one of the first families in Virginia, descended in a direct line from Pocahontas on one side, and Richard Cœur de Lion on the other, collaterally related to the Virgin Queen, and a far-off connection of the present British sovereign, I know nothing of those menial duties which Mr. Whittle thinks properly distinguish the female sphere. I cannot, nor can any one associated with me, be supposed to know anything of such menial avocations. In Virginia, nothing is required of the fair sex but to give orders to their servants, and that sufficiently occupies their time. I feel proud to assert my belief that no lady from that State is mixed up in this sad affair; but, knowing the danger of bad example, I cannot answer for the future, and am therefore ready to give my counsel both as to prevention and cure. I know the female character well enough to assure this meeting that opposition will but add fuel to the flame. In short, my advice is—

'Let them alone and they 'll come home,
And leave their whims behind them.' "

Dr. Singleman, a middle-aged gentleman, from Vermont, thought the gentleman from Virginia mistaken in his opinion that the let-alone system was the best treatment for the epidemic raging among them. " Acute diseases required active remedies. When the pulse of the domestic frame was disordered, every member of the body suffered, and depletion should be freely resorted to, and the constitution restored to a healthy state, or he would not answer for the consequences. His idea—which he advanced with some hesitation, for, being a bachelor, he knew little of the sex—was that every man should try the effect of the three popular systems of medicine on his female relatives, and he would venture to promise the revolt would soon be quelled. A course of bleeding, leeching, and cupping, with blisters to their heads, and sinapisms on their feet, aided by hydropathic douche and plunge baths, and accompanied with homœopathic quantities of nourishment, would tame the greatest shrew that ever lived."

Mr. Easyled, of Tennessee, said, " There is an old proverb about bachelors' wives being well managed—

'As for my wife,
I would you had her spirit in such another:
Were the third of the world yours, with a snaffle
You may pace easy, but not such a wife.'

The measures that the learned physician proposes are easily suggested; but, I would ask, where is the man in this assembly who would have the nerve to try them? There is another old proverb that says, when you sup with a certain personage you should use a long spoon; and, in this case, that precaution is very necessary. It was best to let the ladies have their own way. To quote the immortal bard again—

'Should all despair
That have revolted wives, the tenth of mankind
Would hang themselves.'

He would inform all present, from his own sad experience, that

'He 's a fool who thinks, by force or skill,
To turn the current of a woman's will;
For when she will, she will, you may depend on 't,
And when she won't, she won't, and there 's an end on 't.' "

Mr. Hoosier, from Indiana, " Didn't want to 'front nobody, but he reckoned Mr. Whittle had said about the only sensible things he 'd heerd that day, and them was his sentiments exactly. There was plenty for wimmen to do in the cabin, with mindin' the children and keepin' the pot a bilin', and out of it with takin' care of the cattle and the farm, while the men was hard at work shootin' and fishin'. Corn-dodgers and cracklins was wimmen's business, and just about as much, he reckoned, as they 'd sense for. He, for one, didn't feel afeerd of any of 'em."

General Boanerges Bluster, from Kentucky, said, " He disagreed very much with Mr. Hoosier. He once heerd a Methodist minister tell what Heaven was like, and, after talkin' a great deal about it, he said, ' In short, brethren, it 's a Kentucky of a place !' He reckoned, when he said that, he forgot the wimmen. In their State, where females was three-quarters bacon, and t'other quarter hominy, they was dangerous critters. General, as he was, of the milishy, and holdin' a great many offices under government, he had to mind his wife, who was big enough to lick three of him. Last 'lection he was candidate for Congress ; and, just as he was makin' a stump speech to his constichents, and was tellin' 'em what a great soldier he was, and how he 'd fou't the Ingins under Harrison, and would be sure to stand up for their rights, 'cause he wa'n't afeerd of nothin', his woman walked up to him right cool, and, takin' him off the platform, said to the people, ' This man 's a fool. I know it, 'cause I 'm his wife. He an't fit for nothin' but to mind the house and take care of the children, while I go visitin'. I can't spare him ; and you must 'lect the other candidate.' He expected he felt about as mean as dog-pie, and sneaked off as soon as he could; and everybody hurrahed for Mrs. Bluster, and said she should go to Congress. And, ever since, she 'd done nothin' but snub him, and had gone off to the wimmen's meetin' in spite of him ; and 'twas her that said ' woman was better than man, 'cause he was made out of the raw materi'l, and she was made out of the manerfected ;' and he only hoped she wouldn't find out where he was, or there 'd be an orful time of it."

Mr. Sucker, from Illinois, remarked, " That it wa'n't with his own will he was at this here meetin'; but, bein' 'lected, he had to come ; and, as it was the season for shootin' prairie hens, he wanted to be off agin. He didn't want to make words himself, and hoped that other people would be short and sweet in what they had to say. As to Mrs. Sucker, she hadn't the spirit of a mouse now ; and, if she ever had, which he didn't know, the fever and ager had shuck it all out of her. He reckoned about the best way he could tell 'em of, was to send all the wimmen where they 'd catch it, and, if it didn't end 'em, it would mend 'em."

Captain Salt, of Nantucket, a veteran tar in a blue roundabout and glazed hat, rose, coolly took his quid out of his mouth, and, depositing it in his pocket, made the following short and pithy remarks : " I an't a reg'lar delergate to this here meetin', seein' as I 'm pretty nearly all the time afloat ; but, bein' as I 'm ashore just now, I thought I 'd come and see how things was a purceedin'. I know all about whales, and have a pretty good notion of a vessel, but I don't know nothin' about a woman. Hows'ever, I 've heerd them as did say she was like a ship, 'cause her riggin' cost more than her hull. If so be that 's the case, why she 's easy manoovered. Keep a tight lookout for squalls, and, when you see 'em comin', reef your sails, scud before the storm, and, if she 's bent on goin' down, take to the boats and leave her."

Captain Salt sat down amid shouts of applause, with a very red face after his unwonted exertions, and an earnest request for a glass of grog; but, none being at hand, he contented himself with his quid.

Patrick O'Dougherty, of St. Louis, got up and said, " Jontlemen, this is my first appearance before the public since I left off being an Irishman, and became a native of this country, and I hope yees will excuse all blunders. I needn't tell this enlightened meetin' that, both as an Irishman and 'Merikin, I love the purty cratures of wimmen, and, faith, I 'm sorry they 've got themselves in such a mess. St. Pathrick knows that, with ' my friend and pitcher,' my little Cruiskeen Lawn, and my Molly Astore, I could live all alone in a desert by myself, without any trouble; and sure never a one of me knows why ye can't manage yeer wives. Trate 'em like an Irish pig : drive 'em the way you don't want 'em to go, and they 'll take the right track in spite of you."

Here Mr. O'Dougherty was interrupted by a considerable bustle in the hall. There was a great disturbance, and many gentlemen looked pale and anxious ; but the excitement was allayed by the appearance of an Indian chief in his war paint, who stalked solemnly up to the platform, and spoke as follows :—

" My nation was once a great nation in the lands near the setting sun. It is now a poor, small tribe, that has sold its hunting-grounds to the Great Father, at Washington, for blankets and corn, and have sent me to have a talk with him. Waw-tu-no-bow-te-ma-tu is a brave ; his white brothers call him Big Bulldog, and know that he has many wives. While he smoked the calumet of peace with his Father, in the Grand Lodge at Washington, a little bird sung in his ear that his white brothers had trouble in the wigwam with their squaws, and he has come to help them, for his heart feels heavy for them. Let my white brothers keep their women at work, hoeing corn, pounding hominy, drying venison, and minding papooses, and let them have but little to eat, and they will give them no more trouble. If they do, let my brothers take their scalps. I have said." And, whirling his tomahawk over his head, Waw-tu-no-bow-te-ma-tu gave a shrill war-whoop, and, bounding off the platform, disappeared in the crowd.

Brass Blackstone, from the city of Brotherly Love, remarked, " That he had listened with attention to the proceedings, and had heard with delight the eloquent speeches delivered on this interesting occasion. It was with the modest timidity so characteristic of a Philadelphia lawyer, that he should offer a few remarks on the subject that occupied them; and he hoped it would not be considered presumptuous in him if his views should differ from those hitherto advanced in the assemblage of talent and influence, with whom it was his high privilege this day to be associated. He had deeply sympathized with all the orators it had been his good fortune to hear on this exciting subject : he had, in turn, been thrilled with the surpassing eloquence of Mr. Husband, the resolute determination of Mr. Wumenheyter, the patriotism of Pinckney, the easy indifference of Mr. Whittle, the dignified hauteur of Mr. Powhatan, the professional talent of Dr. Singleman, the commendable meekness of Mr. Easyled, the heroic submission of General Bluster, the laconic sense of Mr. Sucker, the maritime beauty of Captain Salt's similes, the enthusiasm of Mr. O'Dougherty, and the sententious wisdom of Big Bulldog. For himself, he had always been, and should ever continue to be, an ardent admirer of the fair sex. He was proud to say that his mother was a woman—that his native city was distinguished for its devotion to the fairer part of creation. New York might boast of its canals, its railroads, its banks, and its steamships, but Philadelphia gloried in its women. He could lay his hand on his heart, and proudly assert that even this rebellion had not estranged his feelings—

'Woman, with all thy faults, I love thee still !'

He could even say, with the Irish bard—

'Sweet book, unlike the books of art,
   Whose errors are thy fairest part:
In thee, the dear errata column
   Is the best page in all the volume.'

With these feelings, he was present on this occasion to interpose his humble abilities between them and danger. He acknowledged that his clients had not evinced their usual sagacity in risking their quiet, but powerful influence over man, by endeavoring to grasp ' what would not enrich themselves, but make us poor indeed.' *Why* they had done so, was a question more easily asked than answered, and he should therefore not attempt to solve the enigma. It was his business to implore that nothing should be rashly attempted on this delicate occasion which might result in wounding the feelings of his fair clients. He would assure them a little skillful management would be more effectual than open demonstrations of hostility ; and, should the suggestion he was about to offer prove successful, he asked no better reward, as a man and a lawyer, than the friendship of the sex. In his opinion,

'Fee simple and a simple fee,
   And all the fees in tail,
Are nothing when compared to thee,
   Thou best of fees—fe-male.'

Not to detain them longer in suspense, he advised that the gentlemen should fill their houses with looking-glasses, and give the ladies time for *reflection*."

Mr. Blackstone received much applause for his suggestion; and Mr. Bowieknife, of Texas, who succeeded him, said, "I so fully agree with the gentleman from Philadelphia in his love for the sex, and in all the sentiments he has advanced, that I will only add, should the measure he has recommended fail to make peace, I hope all the ladies will come to Texas. We have hearts and arms for all of them.

'If all other States reject 'em,
Ours will freely, *gladly* take 'em.'"

Mr. Placer, from California, remarked, "That he was for no half-way measures. It was his opinion that all the women ought to be seized and sent to California; it was a new country, and the miners wanted wives. When they were once there, he thought they could be managed. Judge Lynch was an active man. Show them that there was only the difference of a letter between altar and halter, and, if they would not marry, why let them hang!"

Mr. H. P. Husband said, "He had listened with astonishment to the proceedings of the day. He really thought that, for all the good that had been done or suggested, gentlemen might as well have staid at home. He had a few words still to offer on the subject, which he hoped they would hear with patience. Among other things, he had prepared a list of all the bad women who had ever existed."

Here Mr. Wumenheyter remarked, "That he must remind the gentleman time was precious; and, as all women who had ever existed were bad, Mr.

Husband had better mention only the worst of them, among whom he must not forget his (Mr. W.'s) three wives."

Mr. Husband was so disconcerted at this interruption, that he forgot what he had to say, and could only remember that his list begun with Eve, and ended with the present generation.

"I see clearly, gentlemen," continued he, "that no one enters so warmly into this subject as myself. Well, be it so. I am ready to fall a martyr in such a cause; and I here solemnly declare that no obstacle shall induce me to swerve from the path that duty marks out for me to follow. I will make every endeavor to extirpate this vile heresy among the women. I will immolate myself on the altar of my country. I will sacrifice my domestic affections on its shrine—Mrs. Husband herself"——

"Here I am, my dear!" said a sharp voice, and a small, thin, vinegar-faced lady entered the room, and walked up to the platform, at the head of a numerous procession of females. "My love," continued she, "it is late; I am afraid you will take cold. Hadn't you better come home?"

"If you think so, my dear, certainly," replied Mr. Husband, turning pale, and trembling so he could scarcely stand, perceiving which, his wife affectionately offered him her arm.

Mr. Easyled meekly obeyed an imperative gesture from Mrs. Easyled, and Mrs. Bluster picked up the general, who had fainted, and carried him out in her arms.

Exeunt omnes, in wild confusion.

AUTHENTIC PARTICULARS OF ALARMING DISTURBANCES CONSEQUENT ON THE LATE MEN'S RIGHTS CONVENTION AT ——.

BY CHERICOT.

WE hasten to lay before our readers a correct account of a terrible excitement among the ladies, caused by the imprudent and impolitic demonstrations of hostility made by the other sex at their late convention in the city of ——. Vague rumors of an alarming character have reached us, from time to time, since that occurrence, for, though a strange and ominous calm prevailed after the sudden and stormy dispersion of the meeting, it was well known to many that the women held continual and secret councils together, from which, events of a startling nature might be expected to result.

We now present to the public the letters and report of our correspondent as they have successively reached us by telegraph, trusting that the disastrous consequences he seems to anticipate may yet be averted by timely and proper concessions on the part of the gentlemen.

June 1st, 1852, 10 o'clock A. M.

DEAR SIR: When I sent to you, in April, a detailed account of the Men's Rights Convention in this place, I privately expressed to you my fears that the gentlemen in question were acting very unadvisedly in thus hastily and openly defying their ruling powers. The nature of the resolutions passed at that meeting, the coercive measures suggested and approved, and the angry feelings displayed in the inflammatory speeches then and there delivered, must, to a reflecting and unbiassed mind, appear sufficient cause for the great excitement now prevailing among the injured ladies. An outbreak is momentarily anticipated, as the town is crowded with the irritated wives and female connections of the offending parties, and agitating and terrible anxieties are aroused when we recall the truth of the poet's beautiful saying, that

"A place not to be mentioned to ears polite knows no fury like a woman scorned."

Through the kindness of a friend in the enemy's camp, I am promised a seat at the meeting, which takes place to-morrow, consisting principally of those ladies who considered themselves personally aggrieved by the proceedings of the Men's Convention, and, though the undertaking is exceedingly perilous, as I can expect no mercy should I be discovered, I cheerfully brave the danger in the

hope of being able to send you a correct report of all that transpires on this interesting occasion.

I am, etc.   CHERICOT.

6 o'clock P. M.

The panic continues to increase, and many of the male inhabitants are precipitately leaving the place, terrible alarm having arisen from the sudden disappearance of all the gentlemen who compromised themselves so seriously at the late Convention. Their wives and relatives have been questioned, but positively refuse to give any information respecting them, and imagination dares not dwell on their probable fate. As most of them were delegates to the Democratic Convention, and it was supposed that our brave and distinguished countryman, General Bluster, had a fair chance of being nominated for the Presidency, you may have a faint idea of the prevailing consternation. How will all this end? *What* will, what *can* become of the Democratic Platform if its strongest props are thus suddenly torn away? I pause for a reply.

June 2d, 1852.

No further discoveries having been made last evening, I deferred writing again until I could transmit you a full and authentic account of this day's proceedings, which have been even more exciting and interesting than I expected.

The ladies met at 10 o'clock this morning in Independence Hall, when the house was called to order, and a nominating committee appointed, which reported the following persons to be officers of the convention :—

President, Mrs. H. P. Husband ; Vice-Presidents, Mrs. G. W. P. H. I. R. Powhatan, Mrs. Cotte Bettie, Mrs. Easyled, Mrs. Sucker; Secretaries, Mrs. Hoosier, Mrs. Buckeye, Mrs. Bluster, and Miss Pattie Prettywhim.

The meeting being organized, the President, Mrs. H. P. Husband, proceeded to read an introductory address :—

"Ladies, the object of this meeting is not only to vindicate and maintain our rights, but also to notice more particularly the insulting and infamous attempts to subvert our liberties made in the very place where we have now met to assert our privileges. I propose to read an account of the disgraceful proceedings to which I allude, and shall then offer such remarks as the subject suggests, trusting your enlightened wisdom will lead you to reflect on our most hazardous position, and that the result of your deliberations will be the proposal of an effectual remedy for our unheard-of wrongs."

(Here Mrs. Husband read an account of the Men's Rights Convention, as reported in our April number, which was received with groans, hisses, and cries of "shame! shame!")

Mrs. Husband continued: "If your feelings generally, ladies, are so affected by this unprovoked assault, what must be the emotions of those among us who are connected by the closest ties with the prime-movers of those seditious measures!

"Thank Heaven! I am a strong-minded woman, and can survive the disgrace; and, had the three unfortunate Mrs. Wumenheyters also been (as I could devoutly wish) strong-minded women, they might have been living to grace this assembly in defiance of their cruel persecutor. He, however, has lived to be punished for his misdeeds, if woman's wit and woman's will can compass it.

"As for Mr. Husband, I can excuse him. You know, ladies, 'no man is a hero to his wife.' He is a harmless sort of person; easily managed, unless he gets into the hands of bad advisers. It shall be my business to see that he does not again offend, and that he makes proper apologies to you all for his misconduct. In reference to the sublime object that now occupies us, I have some remarks to offer, to which I invite your indulgent attention.

"The history of woman, from creation to the present time, has been a sorrowful record of tyrannical oppression. Meek and submissive under the most dreadful wrongs; self-denying and self-sacrificing for the sake of those who do not appreciate her virtues, she has been a spectacle at which 'a world might weep.' Look at the events of past ages! Behold Eve, our first mother, who, because of an act of the most sublime disinterestedness, has been a mark for the scorn and aversion of her posterity; for why did she partake of the forbidden fruit? Ladies, she saw Adam dying for it, without the courage to taste; and, like a true woman, for his sake assumed the responsibility, and meekly bore the blame; while, faithful to the instincts of his sex, he accused her to shield himself. When Lot's curiosity to know what was passing at Sodom was overpowered by his fear of the consequences, did not his faithful wife gratify it, and bear the penalty? But why multiply such cases? The records of woman teem with them, and it is superfluous to recur to them. The time has arrived to define our position, to redress our wrongs, establish our rights, and make our declaration of independence before the world. If all men are created free and equal, we are created their superiors; and as they seem, through our own blamable supineness, to have doubted the fact, it is time to make them know it."

Mrs. Powhatan, a languid-looking, graceful lady, said, in a listless tone: "As my health is very delicate, I must beg the ladies to pardon my remaining seated while I make a few remarks. My nerves are in such a state that I really could not have undertaken to travel so far North, greatly as I sympathize with the important object you have in view, if I had not wished to show my sex and the world at large what a thorough contempt I have for Mr. Powhatan and his assertions. It was with many misgivings that I permitted him to attend the Men's Convention, and I expressly stipulated that he was to say nothing derogatory to me or the ladies of Virginia. As he has thought proper to abuse my condescension by describing us as mere machines, I must assert solemnly that we are at least the motive power which keeps the domestic and political economy in activity. The only truth he told was the facts of our belonging to the very first family in Virginia, our royal descent, and our aristocratic connections. I am proud to add that our cousin, Queen Victoria, sets us an example worthy of imitation in her management of her husband. Let us benefit by it." Here Mrs. Powhatan sank back with a sigh of exhaustion, and resigned herself to the care of her attendants, one of whom supported her head, another rubbed her feet, a third fanned her, and a fourth held a smelling-bottle to her nose.

Mrs. Easyled, of Tennessee, remarked "that she had not come here to vindicate herself from the aspersions cast upon her by her husband, for in truth she was little in the habit of regarding anything he said. In fact, he had shown his docility in acknowledging her legitimate authority, and she thought he deserved some commendation for opposing Dr. Singleman's sanguinary intentions. One plain inference from the men's proceedings was that we had allowed them too much liberty, and are now suffering the effects of that indulgence. Dr. Singleman was a crabbed old bachelor, and, as his remarks proved, very green; but what else could be expected from the State of Vermont? She wished to take this opportunity of acknowledging the gratitude of the ladies to Horace Greeley, of the 'New York Tribune,' for the interest he had shown in their cause, and the obloquy he had endured for his adherence to it. He could afford, she thought, to disregard the invidious reflections on his costume, for all present would agree with her that his old white hat covered more brains than all the black ones at the late convention." (Great applause, and universal cries of assent.)

Several ladies now arose at once to address the meeting, and much disturbance ensued; but quiet was at length restored, and Mrs. Buckeye allowed to speak, which she did as follows:—

"Our attention, I think, ought to be principally directed to the melancholy truth that, while men enjoy all the pleasures of life, we have all the pains except champagne, which they keep entirely for their own use. Whilst we drudge at home, ministering to their whims and caprices in the menial capacities of cooks, housemaids, and nurses, they lounge in their stores and offices, smoking and chewing tobacco, or, worse still, imbibing lager beer and consuming Dutch cheese and pretsels. All offices of omolument are appropriated by them; the privileges of the ballot-box are theirs alone; the bar, the pulpit, and, until lately, the medical profession, are theatres of action where woman has no right to play her part. I ask, is this to be borne? Are we to continue to yield to our tyrants, or, by bold, vigorous, and concerted measures, throw off the yoke, declare our freedom, and compel them to change situations with us? I am aware some of our own sex are so degenerate as to oppose this sublime movement; faint, weak, timid, without the courage to follow our example, they are influenced by the hired and venial press, which is constantly attacking us. They ask how, with our fragile frames and constitutions, we shall endure the labor and hardship of many of the occupations pursued by men? We answer that we have never contemplated such folly, we intend only to superintend those operations, while the men, as heretofore, do all the hard and dirty work. One lady inquires why she should go to the polls, when she controls seven votes by remaining at home? Miserable sophistry! Why shouldn't she go to the polls and give the eighth vote herself."

Mrs. Bluster said: "I reckon everybody knows what trouble I've had with the General, and how I can't take my eyes off him a minute, without his sneakin' away and gettin' me into a scrape. Before the wimmen got up this here notion of our rights, I had kinder sorter made up my mind to keep him at home altogether to nurse the children, and do up chores; but now I'm determined on it, and nothin' sha'n't stop me. Now's the time or never, as Mrs. Buckeye says, for us to have a vote and take our turn in grabbin' the spiles of office. Look what a state of sin and misery things is in. The post-office is delivered to the *males*, the chiefs of all the bureaus is men instead of wimmen; and what's the consekens? We can't draw nothin' out of 'em. They don't even give us the Home Department. My idee is, we should call ourselves independent right away, run up a platform without no compromise, jine together, seize all the men, lay heavy duties on 'em, and keep 'em under Domestic Protection." (Hear, hear, and shouts of approbation resounded from all parts of the house.)

Mrs. Sucker, a pallid lady, shaking so with the ague she could scarcely speak, said: "Sucker told the men I hadn't the spirit of a mouse. Well, maybe I ha'n't; any how, I've got enough to manage him. I'm thankful to say he's got the ager himself, and if he ever gits well he'll find I'm off, and,

If I *am* allus shakin',
I'll never be taken.

46*

I think, like Mrs. Bluster, that we had oughter to have a platform, and stand no nonsense on it."

Mrs. Hoosier remarked "that she felt terrible bad at standin' up to speak afore so many folks, as it was what she wan't by no means used to, but she reckoned it would feel easier after a while, as she meant to talk whenever she got a chance. Wimmen was so trampled upon that they hadn't never got to stand up for their rights; but she was thankful sich things was a comin' to an end, when they could run their lengths without bein' put a stop to. Hoosier had riled her considerable by what he said at that 'ere foolish meetin', and for the sake of her gals as was a shootin' up fast, she was goin' to make a report of her sentiments, and blow away the nonsense he had filled people's ears with. Tharfor, she'd speak out plain, and tell 'em that in futur' he and the boys was to do all the work *in* the cabin and *out* of it; corn dodgers and cracklins was to be *his* business; and she and the gals had nigh calkerlated to try the shootin' and fishin.' She wanted just to say that she, for one, was a goin' to take a stand on that 'ere platform with the rest on 'em, and never git off of it till she stepped into a office."

Mrs. Whittle now came forward, and made the following eloquent oration:—

"Placed as I am in a most unprecedentedly-painful position by the remarkably-singular proceedings of Mr. Whittle; heart sensitive, when I transcendentally reflect upon the tremendously-important consequences the soul-enlightened deliberations of this wonderfully-illumined assemblage of supernaturally-informed females are, morally speaking and intellectually thinking, likely to have upon the cloud-obscured and black-penumbraed future, I must entreat the intense sympathy and mild-cheering indulgence of my hearers to my faint-whispered utterance of the upward aspirations and ascending scintillations of my earth-clogged spirit. Soaring in the blue ether of full-expansive thoughts, bathing the pinions of my mounting-heavenward intelligence in the balm-redolent atmospheres of—of—a—a"— (here Mrs. Whittle, who had got so high up that she didn't exactly see her way clear to the earth again, let herself down in a furious dissolving flood of tears, which carried resistlessly away the deep sympathies of the audience.) "Oh! sisters of my soul," sobbed she, when she had picked up the thread of her ideas, "worldly language fails to express the high-exalted point at which I am upward tending! Let, then, my appropriately-offered apology be that, when earnest discussing the elevating, heart-subduing cause of our down-trodden sex, the ever-running, overflowing emotions of my pent-up bosom must find sorrowful vent in an up-springing fountain of wild-despairing tears. Mr. Whittle's homely designation of what he terms the appropriate sphere of our etherealized sex must be soul-abhorrent to you and anger-inspiring to me. What! shall *we*, the refined intelligences of this earthly planet, be

37

made to be debase our towering aspirations, and be ignominiously forced to extricate from soilful adherence the tear-exciting New-England-beloved vegetable, vulgarly yclept *onion?* Shall our delicate digitals, heaven-destined to nobler purposes than mind-debased man can comprehend, be employed in the contemptible conglomeration of snow-white farina, sparkling-pure water, and the golden-colored product of the cow, to produce crust? Shall our fair arms, instead of being upward-flung in frantic grief at our unheard-of, Heaven-resented wrongs, be moved to and fro in the assiduous combination of discordant materials, squash pie called? Forbid it, maternal earth! forbid it, shuddering skies! forbid it, horror-struck, yawning nature!" (Here the yawns of the audience, in audible sympathy with nature, gave Mrs. Whittle a hint to curb her transports.) "Friends of my heart!" she continued, "partners of my lofty hopes, I will but request your serious-composed attention to a few additional observations, and then I shall cease to weary your angelic, Job-like, Moses-meek patience. I would ask if any among you have perused the wonderful revelations made in now-revolving times from the spiritual-immaterial-intangible world to the benighted dwellers in this orb terrene? Have *you*, beloved partakers of my destined crusade against tyrannous men—have you, I ask, heard the most inconceivable revealings of the life led by our happy sex in the radiant sphere of Venus, that brightest planet in heaven's darkly, deeply, beautifully blue vault? Some pitying spirit, weeping briny tears over the deserted desolation of women here below, tells us that: ' Venus has a truly republican form of government. On this beautiful planet tyranny and oppression are unknown; here the sexes are on an equal footing. Women go to the polls and vote, and can also hold offices under government. The consequence is that they are more strong-minded and intelligent than the females of your mundane sphere.'*

"Now, sister spirits, will you not emulate this starry example? Will you not even excel it, and, instead of low abasing yourselves to the ignoble level of your Nicotian-weed-loving, alcohol-imbibing Neros, soar far above them into the limitless infinitude of transcendental etherealization, alighting on the Mont Blanc summit of exalted wisdom, and stern-compelling them lowly to bow to the severe castigation of their horror-inspiring, past-mind-conceiving criminality?"

With this sublime climax, Mrs. Whittle put a period to her eloquence, and, unable, after such a feast of reason, and such a flow of soul, to descend to meaner things, the meeting adjourned until nine o'clock to-morrow. The friend who procured me access to this Convention assures me that the inte-

* Vide November number of "Buchanan's Journal of Man."

resting orator's florid wealth of language was acquired during a recent visit to England, where she was in constant association with the sublimely-incomprehensible poetess, Lady Emeline Stuart Wortly, and the world-renowned Thomas Carlyle. She also informs me that no one appears to understand Mrs. Whittle since her return home but Mr. Emerson. We hope, therefore, that distinguished personage will do his fair friend the justice to translate her speech for the benefit of your readers.

Up to this hour, nothing has been heard of the missing gentlemen.

Four o'clock in the afternoon.

Shortly after the transmission of my last report, a great crowd collected around the mayor's office, in consequence of a rumor that some startling discoveries had been made, and, on inquiry, I heard that a little boy had left a note at the police station, and then precipitately retreated. The missive in question bore the signature of General Boanerges Bluster, who stated that he had been put in bodily fear by the awful threats of his wife, who had kept him locked up two days on a diet of bread and water. He pathetically appealed to his fellow-citizens for help, emphatically heading his eloquent application with "Democrats, to the rescue!" Such a powerful sensation was created that it was with difficulty the crowd could be prevented rushing *en masse* to the assistance of the imprisoned martyr. A detachment of police was sent to the designated place (one of our principal boarding-houses), and here, after some opposition from the landlady (who is evidently in league with the enemy), the stairs were ascended, and the attic, where the brave hero of Indian Wars was confined, pointed out. But an unexpected obstacle presented itself in the shape of a young Miss of fourteen, who was posted on the landing-place as sentinel, and who obstinately refused admission to the police. Reluctant to use force, the officer resorted to persuasion.

" My little dear," pleaded he, "let us pass."

"Don't fawn upon me," retorted the spirited young lady; "my name's Amandy Malviny Fitzallan Bluster, and mar put me here to keep par *in* and everybody else *out*, and I 'm just a goin' to do it," brandishing a pair of scissors in such alarming juxtaposition to the officer's face that he was fain to retreat some steps from the juvenile jailer. At this crisis, the door slightly opened, and, with heroic disregard of self, the pale face of the brave Bluster appeared, and his trembling voice exclaimed, " Take care on yourselves, folks; she 's a vinimous little reptyle, and would as lieve kill you as look at you. Ta'n't no use tryin' it without the milentary—" (Here Miss Amandy Malviny made such a decided demonstration at the door that it shut suddenly, while the police retreated, in a disorderly manner, down stairs, without any regard to precedence.) The town is in a tumult, and no one seems to know how to act. The sheriff ordered out the military, but they refused to parade, on the ground that it was not right to face the ladies. The mayor has called a meeting of the city councils, and they are now in secret session with closed doors.

9 o'clock in the evening.

The mayor and councils have just published a placard, announcing that they hold it to be their duty to consult the safety of the many in preference to that of the few, and they will, therefore, not interfere, but let the women manage their own business. The public is exhorted to remain tranquil and await the course of events, which an Irish citizen has just assured the crowd means, "if you can't be asy, be as asy as you can."

June 3d, 1852.

The Convention was called to order by the President, and, on motion of Mrs. Buckeye, a committee of five was appointed to draw up a Declaration of Independence.

Mrs. Cotte Bettie then stood up on the platform, and introduced to the notice of the meeting an Indian squaw wrapped in a scarlet blanket, who signified her wish to say a few words.

"Ei-no-moor-den-u, or Little Gray Mare, has come to sing in the ears of her pale-faced sisters that what they do is very good. Waw-tu-no-how-te-mata is great brave, has many scalps in the wigwam, brings Little Gray Mare much venison and buffalo hump, plenty to eat, very good; but Big Bulldog lazy, very; make squaw draw water, pound hominy, hoe corn, sow moccason, and carry papoose. Ei-no-moor-den-u give Waw-tu-no-how-te-mata plenty fire-water, him sleep strong, tie him tight, run away, never go back no more, but stay and help her pale-face sisters tie their braves tight."

The squaw modestly moved aside, and, when the applause with which her speech was received had somewhat subsided, Mrs. Cotte Bettie expressed herself greatly delighted with the untaught eloquence and simple sagacity of their Indian sister, and thought they might all profit by her suggestions. Indeed, it might now be acknowledged that they had anticipated some of her ideas, as the actors in the late gross assault upon their privileges had most of them been secured. She congratulated her audience on the good effects which had already resulted from this bold stroke against their husbands, for it had terrified the rest of their foes into a declaration of non-intervention, which she hailed with delight as an omen of good days coming. She could affirm that the dawn of woman's restoration to her rights was hourly growing brighter in the horizon of Delaware, and she had little doubt that the next Presidential election would take place with female candidates. The happily stringent laws of her native State—its whipping-posts and stocks—offered every facility towards completing the conquest of the men,

and effecting the female millennium. She would only add that, before the members of the Convention separated for their different homes, Mr. Cotte Bettie, with the other prisoners, would be brought before them, when they would publicly apologize for their misdemeanor.

Mrs. Tabitha Higgins said: "I hadn't calkerlated to say a word at this meetin', bein' as I'm a widder, and done with all my own troubles, but I've always made it a pint to look after other people's business, so I came here to see what you was about, and I've really been quite took aback by one thing, which is that none of you ha'n't never spoke a word about the very worst of the men's doins—I mean the way they keep their secrets all to themselves, so that we can't get a inklin' of 'em. It's unknown what I suffered while my husband was alive, cause he wouldn't never tell me nothin', and dear, dear (here Mrs. Higgins wiped her eyes), no one can tell what trouble it's give me since because it's too late to make him. What a blessed thing it would have been for me if you'd got up this notion of our rights sooner; but I suppose it wasn't to be, so I'll just give you a hint to take warning and not to let 'em off by no means till they tell you everything. Fust, I want to know the Mason's secret about buildin' up their lodges, which I think oughter be free to all the women, and hereafter grand mistresses and no masters, which will make sure that what's done under roofs will be told on housetops. Next, it's high time to be even with the Odd Fellows, and give independent orders to the I. O. O. F.s to mind their Ps and Qs, which they must obey to the letter. I'm doubtful scrupulous about the Sons of Temperance; but I guess the Daughters of Temperance will take care of them; so they're safe enough. I hope this meetin' won't take offence at my puttin' in my word, for it makes me feel a deal comfortabler to discharge my duty and report my idees, which I hope'll flash convincin' on your mind, and lighten your proceedin's."

Mrs. Higgins had, indeed, made such a strong impression on the feelings of her audience, that an immediate and unanimous vote of thanks was made to her, by acclamation, for recalling to the recollection of the Convention a duty which had been so unaccountably forgotten and neglected. A committee was instantly appointed to remedy this omission, and to concert measures for accomplishing the wishes of the curious Mrs. Tabitha Higgins.

Mrs. Husband read the following letter from Mrs. Bowieknife, of Texas:—

DEAR FRIENDS: I deeply grieve that distance divides us, and prairies roll between, while running rivers racing to the ocean hinder the accomplishment of my heart's desire, which would be to share your perils in your glorious onslaught on the dastard oppressors of our sex. But I shall fly to you on the wings of fancy, and, in imagination, imbibe the out-pourings of your spirits, which I doubt not will be full of intoxicating eloquence. Accept my dearest sympathies, and the assurance of my ardent attachment to the cause. I regret to say I must warn the Convention to place no confidence in Mr. Bowieknife, who is a gay deceiver, for Texas is by no means so pleasant a place as he represents it to be; besides which, his heart and arms are mine, as his lawful wife, and he had no business to offer them to other people: but I know you will properly reprove his impertinence. Mrs. Placer, of California, who is on a visit to me, desires me to say that, if you can catch her husband, she has not the least objection to your trying a halter on him, as she wants to get out of the noose of matrimony.

Ever yours, BELINDA BOWIEKNIFE.

The next letter that was read was from Mrs. Pinckney, of South Carolina, who expressed herself deeply mortified at Mr. Pinckney's course in the Men's Convention, and the manner in which he had compromised himself and her. If the ladies of Carolina were obliged to secede from union with the gentlemen of that and the other Southern States represented by Mr. Pinckney, it would be entirely his fault, as the extreme measures proposed by him forced them, in self-defence, to nullify his acts. As to the fugitive women's bill, it was easier passed than executed; and, should Congress attempt to enforce it, she wished them, and all other pursuers of their oppressed sex, "short shoes and long corns."

This sentiment was responded to with three cheers by the excited ladies, after which Mrs. Patrick O'Dougherty, of St. Louis, addressed them in a rich and racy brogue.

"I think shame of that craythur Pathrick for makin' sich an omadhawn of himself at the Men's Convintion, talkin' and spachefyin' about his Molly Astore and his Cruiskeen Laun. He 'd better not let me catch him wid aider of 'em. Sure, when he 's got the drink in, the wit 's out; and that 's the rasin the craythur compared the likes of us wid an Irish pig, for he very well knows that pigs have a dale finer time of it than wimmen. So plaise ye, ladies, not to mind his blarney, for sure he 's a decaiver, and Biddy O'Dougherty (that 's meself) wouldn't cry her eyes out if he was under the sod, where it 's wishin' he was I am. Any how I 'll take my lave on him, and stand right forninst him on that platform you 're goin' to rare up, and then we 'll see how he does be gettin' on all alone by himself, with his frind and pitcher."

Miss Patty Prettywhim, a lively adolacious beauty of eighteen, attired in a bewitching Bloomer costume, which displayed to advantage her sylph-like form and small feet, now bounded on the stand, and, in gay tones, addressed the assembly:—

"If the ladies will excuse my inexperience, I will just give them my opinion on the cause which has brought us together, and I hope my youth will not detract from the soundness of my advice, for really I flatter myself I am quite forward for my years. This meeting, I believe, is for the purpose of enforcing our rights and subduing the men, which, so far as I am concerned, is quite useless, for I assure you, ladies, I never had any trouble in making them all do as I like." (Here Miss Patty tapped her boot with her cane, and with a saucy smile continued:) "In fact, their conquest is easy, for, after all, they are harmless creatures, and soon managed when you know the secret. Ladies, I 'll tell it to you in four words—'flatter them, and feed them;' " and, with a merry air, Miss Patty sprang from the platform and ensconced herself in the crowd, where loud cries of "conceited chit," and " vain flirt," proved that her suggestions had not been very graciously received, which, however, did not seem to disconcert her in the least, as she walked carelessly whistling to the door, where Mr. Brass Blackstone took her arm and accompanied her home.

The Committee on the Declaration of Independence now reported the following resolutions, which were unanimously adopted:—

Resolved, That, in the course of human events, it has become necessary for woman to untie the Gordian knot that binds her to the will of man, and to assume the exalted station assigned her by the provisions of Nature and the law of right.

Resolved, That we hold these truths to be self-evident, that woman was created superior to man, and that she is endowed with certain inalienable rights, the most important of which is the right to her own way.

Resolved, That, to secure the liberty of doing as she likes, she is perfectly justified in rebelling against the despotism that would curb her reasonable desires.

Resolved, That woman has hitherto chosen rather to suffer than to assert her natural superiority to her tyrant, man; but it is now her right, her duty, to throw off her trammels and declare herself free.

Resolved, That man has engrossed every privilege, and forbidden her any pleasure; that, while he frequents clubs, theatres, and other places of public amusement, woman must stay at home and work for him.

Resolved, That he considers woman to have no part in her own property nor in his, and that he has acted on the principle that, "what 's yours is mine, and what 's mine is my own," which compels woman, in her own defence, to hold on to all she can get.

Resolved, That he reserves to himself the right of suffrage, thus preventing woman from righting her suffering.

Resolved, That he monopolizes all offices and all the emoluments thereof, yet constantly complains when woman puts her hand in his pockets.

Resolved, That he holds woman's patience to be a virtue that is to be always tried, never found wanting, yet never rewarded.

Resolved, That, as a lover, he exalts woman above the stars, while, as a husband, he conceives her mission to be a descent into the kitchen; that he expects her to sew on his buttons and darn his hose; yet never permits her to wear out his old clothes.

Resolved, That woman will never be properly appreciated until she thinks more of herself, and that this long train of abuses renders female emancipation immediately necessary, to effect which desirable result woman must make herself master of man.

Resolved, That though man may be physically stronger, he is morally weaker than woman, and may, therefore, be easily subdued through this weakness, and frightened into submission by prompt and energetic measures.

Resolved, Therefore, that we hereby publish and declare that we are and ought to be of right free and independent; that we are absolved from all obedience to our tyrant man; that we have full power to vote, hold offices, use our own money, levy war, conclude peace, contract alliances, establish commerce, and to do all other acts and things that we may think proper, to which we pledge ourselves, in spite of our husbands and all the men in the world.

Mrs. Husband made a speech on the foregoing resolutions, and concluded with saying : *This,* ladies, is the glorious assertion of our rights; the stupendous platform on which we take our stand, and, should it ever be overthrown, may we be buried in its ruins ! But that can never happen, for it will become firmer as ages roll away, and our female posterity will bless us for having reared it. I grieve that I must now recall your attention to meaner things, as the offenders against our dignities are in an adjoining room, awaiting your leisure to receive their concessions. I shall now, with your permission, have them brought in.

The President whispered to some of the ladies near her, who left the hall and presently returned with the crestfallen gentlemen, who, as their names were called, successively came forward.

Mr. H. P. Husband, as he prepared to address the ladies, cast a timid glance at the President, who, in rather an audible tone, bade him "not to make a fool of himself," which doubtless caused the extreme nervousness that characterized his demeanor during the following speech :—

"It is my intention, ladies, to say a few words only, for I have not the indelicate wish to make a vain display on this occasion. I know that my fate will meet with sympathy from my fellow-men, and that my efforts in the noble and just cause of their rights will, by them, be duly appreciated.

"With them I leave my memory, my sentiments, and my acts, proudly feeling that they need no vindication from me this day. The liberty of man has been my fatal dream."

"Well, my dear," interposed Mrs. Husband, " it's time to wake up from it, for we can't stay here all day and listen to *you;* so make your apology at once."

The disconcerted gentleman muttered some words which could not be distinguished, and made a hasty retreat. (We would draw the attention of the reader to the fact that Mr. Husband seems to have an intense admiration of the Irish patriot Meagher, as, in the above address, he has adopted both his words and his ideas, and doubtless, if not interrupted, would have given the public the whole of that gentleman's speech when arraigned before the British tribunal. Perhaps, however, it is no plagiarism, but merely a singular coincidence.)

Mr. Wumenheyter, after much resistance, was finally forced to the front of the platform, where he reluctantly confessed that, of all the humbugs peculiar to New York, *he* was the greatest.

Mr. Pinckney seceded from his seditious sentiments, and apologized to the assembly for his aspersions and assaults.

Mr. Whittle promised " to stay to hum in futur, and never be such a right-on-eend fool as to meddle with the women."

Mr. G. W. P. H. I. R. Powhatan was compelled to come forward ; but, as he would not condescend to apologize, he was taken back till his pride should have a fall.

Dr. Singleman promised henceforth to torture his own patients, and not to try the patience of the ladies.

Mr. Easyled said it was a pleasure to submit to his wife and make concessions to the ladies. He begged to offer them his congratulations on the independence they had this day achieved; but here Mrs. Easyled ordered him to mind his own business and get out of the way, which command he promptly obeyed.

Mrs. Hoosier mentioned that she had left Hoosier at home to mind the cabin; but he told *her* to say that he begged all their pardons.

Mrs. Sucker stated that Sucker had the fever and ager, and couldn't come, but she 'd answer for his peaceableness.

Mrs. Husband explained that they couldn't produce Captain Salt, as he was off on a whaling voyage; but, if they could catch him on his return, he would assuredly be tarred and feathered. She would also observe that, if Mr. Placer had not been among the missing, it would have been a pleasure to comply with his wife's request, and hang him.

Mr. Cotte Bettie said that the fact he had asserted on a late occasion, that " Delawarians were true Blue, that they always were and always would be Blue," must now be his justification to the ladies— as he could not have been so rash as to offend them had he not been very blue indeed.

Mr. Bowieknife entreated the ladies to pardon him if he had offended, and deprecated their being prejudiced against him and Texas by the misrepresentations of his wife. He could assure them his love was extended enough to embrace her and all of them.

Mrs. O'Dougherty informed the Convention that "Pathrick, the craythur, was so overcome by the sperit that he could naythur walk nor spake; but *she'd* kape him from evermore spiting them."

General Bluster was carried forward by Mrs. Bluster, who supported him in her arms while he said: "I'm quite riled at myself for givin' Mrs. Bluster and the rest on you all this trouble, and I reckon I won't never do it agin. I'll gin up all politics and offices. I'll let the Democratic platform hold itself up, and the milentary git another gineral. I'll stay at home and never make no more speeches till Mrs. Bluster runs for President, when I'll stump for her through all Kaintuck." The general wanted to say more, but Mrs. Bluster carried him off; the other gentlemen retreated, and the Convention adjourned *sine die.*

Editor's Table.

WOMAN'S RIGHTS—or the movement that goes under that name, may seem to some too trifling in itself, and too much connected with ludicrous associations to be made the subject of serious argument. If nothing else, however, should give it consequence, it would demand our earnest attention from its intimate connection with all the radical and infidel movements of the day. A strange affinity seems to bind them all together. They all present the same attractions for the same class of minds. They are all so grounded on the same essential fallacy of individual right, in distinction from the organic good, or social propriety, that the careful observer could have no great difficulty in predicting the whole course of the man or woman who once sets out on the track of any one of them.

But not to dwell on this remarkable connection—the claim of "woman's rights" presents not only the common radical notion which underlies the whole class, but also a peculiar enormity of its own; in some respects more boldly infidel, or defiant both of nature and revelation, than that which characterizes any kindred measure. It is avowedly opposed to the most time-honored proprieties of social life; it is opposed to nature; it is opposed to revelation. The first charge it might perhaps meet by the plea of reform; the second it would deny; the third, it would confess, not only, but even glory in the confession. Almost every other radical movement claims the Scriptures, in some sense, as its ally, and will stand upon the platform they offer, or seem to offer, until relentless progress causes it to lose its hold. Here, however, the "woman's rights" doctrine is peculiar. We never yet heard a passage of Scripture quoted, either fairly or perversely, in its support. Abolitionists have their pet texts. Fourierism will sometimes employ the dialect of the Bible. But this unblushing female Socialism defies alike apostles and prophets. In this respect no kindred movement is so decidedly infidel, so rancorously and avowedly anti-biblical.

It is equally opposed to nature, and the established order of society founded upon it. We do not intend to go into any physiological argument. There is one broad striking fact in the constitution of the human species which ought to set the question at rest forever. This is the fact of maternity. There is claimed for woman an equal participation in all the outward life of man. Nothing short of this will carry out the "great idea." Any argument, therefore, that halts in coming fully up to it, must affect the whole consistency of the cause it is brought to support. Every such flinching must admit somewhere some physical, and hence, some social or political difference which is fatal to the abstract claim, and shuts us up again to the same distinctions in kind, if not in degree, which have long grown up in society.

Now there is such a physical difference, involving, as a necessary consequence, the most striking differences of social and political position. It is not simply the sexual distinction in itself—but what we have called the fact of maternity. It is the design of God, expressed and carried out in nature, that a moiety of the human race should have a charge—a precious charge, a most honorable charge—but one which must, in the very nature of things, unfit them for the right and regular performance of those duties which the usages of all civilized and all Christian nations have ever assigned to the opposite sex. From this there arise, in the first place, physical impediments, which, during the best part of the female life, are absolutely insurmountable, except at a sacrifice of almost every thing that distinguishes the civilized human from the animal, or beastly, and savage state. As a secondary, yet inevitably resulting consequence, there come domestic and social hindrances which still more completely draw the line between the male and female duties. Any one may carry out this argument. Its greatest force is in its bare presentment. Around the nursing mother God and nature have thrown a hallowed seclusion. Society has framed her laws and usages in obedience to the Divine and physical ordinance. Every attempt to break through them, therefore, must be pronounced as unnatural as it is irreligious and profane.

But it is not in maternity alone that we see the Divine design. The whole *dual* constitution of humanity, with all the affections and duties that grow out of it, reveals the same great intent. This is not simply the perpetuation of the species, but the highest perfection of the earthly human state in the harmony of the domestic and the outer existence. There is an inner and an outer sphere. The first is as honorable as the second; it is even more intimately connected with the essential life, while the latter stands to it more in the position of a means to a higher ultimate good. Woman was meant to be the main influence in the one; man in the other. To this all civilization tends. Its recognition and establishment is ever in proportion to the advance of a pure Christianity. Destroy this dual life, and the merely physical or sexual distinction becomes a source of immeasurable mischief. Preserve the former, and the latter, instead of a hot-bed of sensualism, is converted into a fountain of the purest and most sacred affections of which our earthly nature is capable.

To denote this inner life of which woman is the guardian angel, no term could be better adapted than the one in most common use, and which must be etymologically the same in every cultivated language. It is the *domestic* life—the *res domi* in distinction from the *res foras*. The latter is the out-door life, the life abroad, the *forensic* life, or life of the *forum*, including in that term all political as well as judicial employment. Now we know that to a superficial thinker, the former may present the idea of the narrower sphere; and hence those logomachies about personal rights, and rank, and "equality and subjugation," which such a one would present as the real issues. If, however, there be any question of rank at all, the domestic is certainly the higher sphere; because, as we have said, it is more closely connected with the essential life, or the end for which humanity exists, and to which all that is outward or *forensic*, with all its imagined importance, is but a subordinate means. Men may *act* abroad, but they *live*, if they live at all, at home. The *State* is for the *Family*, the *forum* for the *domus*. The former would have but little value except as it is found in the protection, the refinement, and the elevation of the latter. And so we may say of the reciprocal influence. The best service that woman can confer upon the State, (and thus, through it, obtain the best security for her own personal rights and dignity) is by making the home what it ought to be. In the right education of her children, she exerts a far purer and more effectual political power, than she could ever wield

44

through the freest admission to the ballot-box or the caucus.

But we can only briefly present this aspect of the question, and pass on. The most serious importance of this modern " woman's rights" doctrine is derived from its direct bearing upon the marriage institution. The blindest must see that such a change as is proposed in the relations and life of the sexes, can not leave either marriage or the family in their present state. It must vitally affect, and in time wholly sever, that oneness which has ever been at the foundation of the marriage idea, from the primitive declaration in Genesis to the latest decision of the common law. This idea gone—and it is totally at war with the modern theory of " woman's rights"—marriage is reduced to the nature of a contract simply. Where the wife and the mother are equally engaged with the husband and the father in all the employments of the same *forensic* life, they may be styled joint partners in business, but are no longer " members one of another." And then follows the inevitable consequence. That which has no higher sanction than the will of the contracting parties, must, of course, be at any time revocable by the same authority that first created it. That which makes no change in the personal relations, the personal rights, the personal duties, is not the holy marriage *union*, but the unholy *alliance* of concubinage.

Already have we gone far in this direction, and unless our legislatures retrace their steps, there is danger of the mischief becoming past all remedy. We refer not now so much to direct facilities for divorce, as to another and more plausible mode of proceeding. It is one which imposes even on the most conservative mind by its plea for the defenseless. On the one hand, it presses into its service the rank individualism of the day, and on the other, appeals to that very feeling of chivalrous regard and tender respect for woman which its perverted notion of political equality, or rather political sameness, would ultimately destroy. It is very hard that the earnings of the long-suffering wife should be in the uncontrolled power of the brutal and intemperate husband. It is very hard that her association with him should make her, in any way, the suffering victim of his cruelty and crimes. Such cases do, doubtless, often exist, although jurisprudence in its ordinary and natural channels has done much, and may yet do more, for their relief. There is, however, at the present day, a danger in the opposite quarter, and one that threatens a far sorer evil. There is danger that laws giving the right of separate property, and of course the management of separate property, to the wife, may in time vitally affect that oneness which is so essential in the marriage idea. There is danger here that the reforming knife may cut into the very quick, and actually kill what it pretends to cure. In other words, let this kind of legislation, which is now so great a favorite, only proceed a little farther, until the personal and property interests of husband and wife become as distinct as those of any outward parties, and marriage is at an end. We may call it by what name we please; it is no longer the marriage recognized by the Church; it is no longer the marriage known to that common law of England and America which, with all its alleged barbarisms and feudalisms, was more distinctly built upon the authority of Christianity, and the Christian Scriptures, than any other system of jurisprudence the world ever knew. Let families be brought up with the clear knowledge that *this* belongs to the father, and *that* to the mother—that each party has its separate rights, its separate interests, its separate dealings with the world without—let this become the predominant feeling, we say, and the family itself, with all its sacred associations, will soon be numbered among the " things that have waxed old, and are ready to vanish away."

But the most grievous hardship, as urged by some, is the denial of what they are pleased to style political rights, or, in other words, the right of voting and holding office. This is connected with a wholly false idea of the political relation; and we might meet it, therefore, with a denial of suffrage being a natural right, and prove our denial by showing the inevitable absurdities which must result from the unrestricted proposition. But it is enough in the present case, and for our present purpose, to take issue on the question of fact. Women are the subjects of law, it is said, and should therefore be represented in its enactment. Political action should be co-extensive with political allegiance. Now, without at present formally refuting this egregious fallacy, which is continually contradicted, and must be contradicted, in every government, even the most ultra radical and individualizing that exists on earth, we may say that in this country, and in every other in which there is a representative system based on popular suffrage, married women *do* vote—they *are* represented—they have a part in the political action, and just the part which is most conservative of their true interests, while it is least subversive of those ideas on which the family, and through it the whole social structure, must ultimately rest. The wife does exercise the right of suffrage. Through the husband, as the family representative, she casts a vote, and the only vote which is consistent with the oneness of that elementary political organism we may call the family State.

Some might style this a cavil, and therefore, in answer, we would beg our readers to extend to us the same indulgence they have often done before—in other words, permit a slight abstraction in the argument, as conducive to an eminently practical conclusion. Let us say, then, that every *organic* whole is such in the highest sense, by being composed of organic parts—that is, parts which are themselves severally each an organic unity, or membership, presenting more or less resemblance to the greater whole. Some of these may be entirely artificial; and of such our own General and State Governments present a beautiful illustration. Beside these, there are the lesser corporations of counties, towns, cities, and villages, forming organic parts of organic parts, each having its own diversity of the inner life, and yet each acting as a unit to all without and all above. Many of these municipal unities have given way, and are giving way, to an absorbing centralization, but ever to the injury of the general body politic, as well as the individual welfare. Now these may be called artificial organisms. There is, however, one of nature's construction to which we can not attach too high a value, and that is the family. We might, in a certain sense, regard the individual man himself as such a natural organic existence—a community of interests—sensual, material, spiritual animal, and rational, with outward relations and in ward coherences, all under a sovereign will and a judicial reason, and thus presenting, what has struck the philosophic mind in all ages, a striking resemblance to the political state. But even thus viewed, the individual does not stand next to the larger civil organization. *The family is the natural unit in the State.* In any other sense it is a mere *accident* for secondary interests—an artificial existence, created and dissolved like a railroad company or a bank charter, instead of being an *essential* and indispensable component of the general political life.

If this view be correct, it is the Family, the household, which should be immediately represented in the State, rather than the individual. It is the family that votes, and not the individual. Whoever deposits that vote, deposits it as the agent of the whole domestic community, just as the Member of Assembly represents the town from which he is sent, and the Senator the State by which he is delegated. Since, then, such voting can only be done by one member, the husband and the father is certainly the most proper person for that purpose. In fact, if we are to preserve at all the idea of the domestic and forensic spheres, this is a matter of absolute necessity. He represents this outward life, and is, therefare, the natural embassador of the little organism in its outward relations to other and similar communities.

But the husband may cast a ballot different from that which would be acceptable to the wife. What then? Shall there be separate voting? If so, the family is at an end. The domestic community is sundered, and the organic life expires. No evils arising from separate property would be so terrible, or so completely subversive of the marriage idea, as the separate voting of the husband and wife, the father and the mother, the outward and inner representatives of the family unity.

This, in fact, is the idea of the common law. The household is the true unit in the State. Certain other considerations of property may have modified its action and applications, but have not destroyed the principle itself. We are tempted to dwell upon this idea of household or family suffrage. It would certainly be better than any tests of property merely, since it would have a natural basis, and, in its representative idea, possess that universality which our democratic age demands for suffrage, while it would be in a great measure free from the evils and inconsistencies and inequalities that meet us in every other view.

There are two antagonists whom the modern advocates of "woman's rights" find especially in their way. These are, the common law and the Apostle Paul. A lingering regard for things once deemed sacred presents some check in respect to the latter, but even the Apostle not unfrequently comes in for his share of platform vituperation from the free tongues of the emancipated. Even he, it is more than intimated, did not understand the question. As regards the law, however, there is no such restraint upon their abuse. And yet it is a position that may be most triumphantly maintained, that in real respect for woman and her real rights, no system of jurisprudence ever went beyond the gallant old common law of England. This is especially seen in the laws respecting dower. The surviving husband is entitled to an interest in the real estate of the deceased wife, but only in case of there having been offspring of the marriage, and then only on the ground of guardianship to the wife's legal heir. The widow, on the death of the husband, takes one-third of all the real estate, without any conditions whatever. This embraces not only that of which he dies possessed, but also that of which he may have been seized at any time during the coverture. From the moment of the marriage, no act of the husband without her consent, no alienation, no debt, can ever bar her favored claim. So also she is entitled to one-half of the personal effects, whatever may be the number or nearness of the husband's collateral heirs.

There are other special provisions of a similar kind, fully justifying the remark of Coke, that the widow is the favorite of the English courts, and that in these respects the common law is far beyond the civil.

It is true it styles her, in her married relation, a *feme covert;* and much attempted ridicule, as well as much reproach, has been cast upon the term. But he who reads the true spirit of the common law, must discover in it the same gallant and knightly idea. She is termed a *feme covert*, not as denoting the little value in which the law holds her, but as significant of security and protection. She is a *feme covert*, shielded not only from all legal claims that might assail her in the single state, but also—and which is of far more importance—from the forensic, out-door storm of political turbulence and corruption. Instead of exposing her to such scenes as have been witnessed in our elections, and mass meetings, and political conventions, it regards her as in the sacred inclosure of the inner or domestic life. The term is significant of peace, security, retirement. It is expressive, not of ignominy, not of forgetfulness, but of the most cherished respect, the most sacred honor. The law meant that such *coverture* should be to her a shield from more harm than ever came, or could come, from marital cruelty or neglect. No creditors can assail, no legal strife can interrupt her hallowed domestic duties. Away from mobs, and caucuses, and Syracuse and Baltimore Conventions, she is in a great measure safe from the moral malaria that must ever gather around such assemblies, and to which her own presence—degraded and unfeminine as she must inevitably become by such contact—would only add a deeper and more deadly taint. It is her higher office to keep watch over the ever-burning fire of the domestic altar; and while she faithfully performs this duty, no forensic "pestilence can invade her," no political "plague come nigh her dwelling."

The Apostle, too, if we keep out of sight his claim to an inspired guidance, might seem, in some things, personally harsh and unkind to women. At least, so some might regard his frequent injunction of domestic subordination, and his express prohibition of their taking upon themselves the office of a public preacher, although they were joyfully hailed as co-laborers in other services in the Church. There is here, however, another and higher aspect of the same idea on which we have dwelt before. The Church as well as the State, is composed of families, or may be regarded as having the family for its unit. It is the "*Church in the house*" with its altar, its service, its sacred instruction. Here, as in the other case, the interior religious life is especially intrusted to woman. The outward or embassadorial relations involved in the preaching and episcopal office belong to the other sphere. Any confusion here would destroy, not only that essential idea of harmony involved in the construction of the Christian Ecclesia, but also that sacred similitude through which the Apostle traces the bridal relation of the Church herself to her Spiritual Lord and Head. But what care these platform brawlers for sacred similitudes and spiritual analogies? It is not at all, as they would make it, a question of "equality and subjugation." A true spiritual equality, as we have seen, is best promoted by the Apostle's notion of keeping each sex within its allotted sphere. It is the only way of avoiding that unnatural mixture of habits, of office, of employments, of dress, which would soon bring on a moral degradation, and, through this, as abject a slavery of one to the other as has ever been witnessed in savage life. No fallacy could be greater than that which confounds *subordination* with inequality. The first exists in the co-equal and co-essential tri-unity of the Divine Persons, and there could be, strictly, no oneness without it. So also may we say of the demand for perfect uniformity, or identity of pursuit. No mathematical proposition is more certain than the seeming paradox, that *sameness* here is separation, incoherence, dissolution—*diversity* is union, attraction, strength. The doctrine we condemn is essentially inorganic. Instead of that exquisitely harmonized instrument which comes from the right temperament of the sexual relations, it would make human life, at the best, a tuneless monochord, if not, in the end, a chaos of all harsh and savage dissonance.

"I suffer not a woman to teach," says the Apostle, with a clear reference to public preaching. And yet no man was ever farther from being a misogynist, or woman-contemner, than Paul. His writings, on the contrary, every where manifest the most tender feeling of regard for women, and especially Christian women, "his sisters in the Lord." How large a space do their names occupy in the closing salutations of his fervent epistles! "I commend unto you Phœbe our sister—Receive her in the Lord as becometh saints; for she has been a succorer of many and of myself also." "Greet Mary who bestowed much labor on us." "Salute Tryphena and Tryphosa—salute the beloved Persis—salute Julia and the sister of Nereus." How admirably, too, does this feeling of Christian tenderness and respect manifest itself in his directions to Timothy? "Entreat the elder women as mothers, the younger women as sisters, in all purity." It is felt at once that this style is not in harmony with the coarse spirit which is predominant on the reforming platform. There is about it all a gentle savor of refinement, of delicacy, and Christian tenderness which we instinctively decide would be out of place in any of these hybrid conventions. How kind and manly, too, his regard for the "widows who were widows indeed"—holy and heavenly women—not scolding for "female rights" like some in our day, who, under a Quaker bonnet, can show more fight than many a brigadier-general, but "well reported of" for a very different kind of "good works"—"for having brought up children, for having lodged strangers, for having washed the saints' feet, for having relieved the afflicted, for having continued in prayer and supplications night and day."

Paul was doubtless well aware, that, as far as mere oratorical powers were concerned, some women might be able to preach better than some men. The beloved Phœbe to whom he intrusted his Epistle to the Romans, or those women of "unfeigned faith," the mother Eunice, or the grandmother Lois, who taught Timothy the Holy Scriptures, might have been more intelligent as well as more fluent evangelists than many of the male Corinthians. But had the Apostle, on this account, made them an exceptional violation of his great idea of the Church's constitution, he would have only put forth that same contemptible reasoning to which the public has been lately so abundantly treated from the platform of "woman's rights."

But with Paul there was more than the mere exercise of an ordinary sound intelligence. He possessed a power which enabled him to look down the stream of time, or, at all events, to see the operation of human nature as it would exist in all ages. Hence his graphic pictures which would almost seem to have been drawn from scenes that have been presented to our own eyes. How to the life he limns them?

"Proud, knowing nothing, doting (or diseased) about questions and strifes of words—perverse disputings of corrupt minds, whereof cometh envy, strife, railings, evil surmisings—from such withdraw thyself." Here him again in another strain: "I will, therefore, that women adorn themselves with *shamefacedness*"—did ever any one hear that text read or quoted in a woman's rights convention?—"with sobriety, with good works." "Let them learn in silence; for Adam was first formed, then Eve." Will any man infer from this that Paul had not as much true esteem for woman, and as high a sense of her true value in the family, the church, and the state, as Mr. Channing, or Mr. Burleigh, or Mr. Wendell Phillips—such a one has yet to learn the first rudiments of a question second to none in importance, if we may judge from its intimate connection with some of the worst forms of radicalism that infest our age?

MARRIAGE.

Upon no subject (says an acute modern essayist) is so much good advice given as upon that of matrimony, yet every one knows how seldom such good advice is listened to. It is not in all circumstances that people *can* listen to reason, and it is very certain that people in love seldom *do* listen to reason. It is also a truth, scarcely to be questioned, that, with the circumstances of falling in love, reason has almost nothing at all to do. Taste, perhaps, has something to do with it, and temperament a good deal; but discernment is for the most part at fault upon such occasions, and judgment is not called upon to act. This is a very serious matter, and must be admitted to be so when we come to consider the very important engagements to which mere personal attachments give rise. Doctor Johnson, while stating that he has not discovered that life has anything more to be desired than a prudent and virtuous marriage, observes that there is nothing which so much seduces reason from vigilance as the thought of passing life with an amiable woman; and he warns the gentleman whom he addresses that love and marriage are very different states; and that those who are to suffer often for the sake of one another soon lose that tenderness of look and that benevolence of mind which arose from the participation of unmingled pleasure and successive amusement.

The pleasantest part of a man's life (says Addison) is generally that which passes in courtship, provided his passion be sincere, and the party beloved be kind, with discretion. Love, desire, hope, and all the pleasing emotions of the soul rise in the pursuit.

The hope, then, is more pleasing than the possession of that which has been hoped for; but that which is most curious in our constitution is, that this sort of hope is ready to spring up afresh in spite of known realities which fight against it. When Johnson heard of a man who was going to marry a second time, he said it was the triumph of hope over experience. Seldom has a commonplace matter been resolved into a happier abstraction.

The continual tendency of hope to triumph over experience in such cases is not enough considered by those vehement reformers of the institutions of society who desire to facilitate the process of divorce; and, in short, to enable people to separate when they find they do not live happily together, with as much facility as they could unite, when they believed that union would insure their happiness. If any such facility were admitted, which it could not be without setting aside altogether the religious character of marriage, it would be found that the hope of forming new ties more agreeable than the old would ever be rising up, in spite of experience, and that inconstancy would be promoted without promoting happiness. In this case, as in thousands of others, the philosophy of bearing the ills we have, rather than flying to others that we know not of, is practically the best for us; and the greater liberty of divorce would turn out to be only a greater burthen.

To return to Addison. Seeing that courtship is so pleasant, he wisely advises that it should be of long continuance. This is a point upon which doctors differ. Doctor Addison, however, expressly says, that those marriages generally abound most with love and constancy that are preceded by a long courtship. The passion should strike root, and gather strength before marriage be grafted on it. A long course of hopes and expectations fixes the ideas in our minds, and habituates us to a fondness of the person beloved. Wordsworth supplies a charming illustration of a love of this kind:—

"There was a youth whom I had loved so long,
    That when I loved him not I cannot say;
'Mid the green mountains many a thoughtless song
    We two had sung like gladsome birds in May;
    When we began to tire of childish play,
We seemed still more and more to prize each other,
    We talked of marriage and our marriage day;
And I in truth did love him as a brother,
For never could I hope to meet with such another."

The most serious point of all in wedded union Addison just touches upon, and pursues the point no further; feeling, perhaps, that it was better to suggest it to reflective minds than to dwell upon it in a familiar essay. "There is nothing of so great importance to us," he says, "as the good qualities of one to whom we join ourselves for life; they do not only make our present state agreeable, but often determine our happiness to all eternity."

MARRIED AND SINGLE LIFE.

WE extract the subjoined from a speech delivered by Mr. Alexander Frizell, in reply to the toast of "The Ladies," at the recent banquet of the Quarter Sessions Grand Jury:—

Mr. Frizell, after some introductory remarks, said: I remember reading an anecdote which I cannot forbear mentioning, it so beautifully illustrates the force of female affection. When the Emperor Conrad besieged Hensburg, the women of the city found it was impossible the place could hold out. They, therefore, unanimously petitioned the Emperor to allow them to leave the city with only as much as each could carry with her. The Emperor, believing that the burden of each would necessarily be light, conceded their request. A flag of truce was hoisted, and silence prevailed, when one of the city gates flew open. The women marched out, rank and file—and what do you think they were carrying? Peace be to their ashes, and honor to their memory! Every one of them had *her husband* on her back. (Cheers.) The Emperor was so stricken by their conjugal fidelity that he restored the wives back to their husbands, and the city to all its former privileges.

Now, Mr. Chairman and gentlemen, I ask you, could all the bachelors in the wide world this day produce an action comparable to that? Oh, that I had the reasoning power of Socrates, that I might induce these young men whom I see around me to consult their own happiness by renouncing what is falsely called "single blessedness!" (Great cheering.) Socrates, once, on delivering a lecture to the Athenians on love and matrimony, pressed home his subject so powerfully and convincingly on the hearts of his audience, by showing them the comforts and advantages the married man possessed over the bachelor, that, at the conclusion of his speech, the young men rose up in a body and solemnly declared that they would marry on the first available opportunity. Of course, ladies will not be the first to declare their love. No! they would rather let concealment, "like a worm i' the bud, feed on their damask cheek." They are like the golden nuggets in auriferous regions—they will not come to you unsought. But, do you seek the inestimable treasure of a wife, and you will be rewarded by a bliss, the adequate description of which would alike defy the pen of poet or the pencil of artist. (Great cheering.)

EDITORS' TABLE.

WE have lately received a very interesting letter from a young lady whose home is in the country, and who enjoys the uninterrupted leisure of a country life offers to people in easy circumstances. She has an earnest desire to save the precious hours of youth from running idly to waste; she is anxious to improve her understanding, and make some preparation for the evening of life. So commendable a disposition we are happy to encourage; and, as we hope " Nellie's" wish for advice on this point may concur with that of other young ladies, in replying to her communication, we would address ourselves to our juvenile readers in general.

"What is the use of reading?" said Louis XIV. to the Duke de Montemar, the handsomest and wittiest of his courtiers. " It has the same effect upon the mind, sire, that your dainties have upon my cheeks." The duke was remarkable for a fine complexion.

Sir John Herschel says: " If I were to pray for a taste which should stand me under every variety of circumstance, and be a source of happiness and cheerfulness to me through life, and a shield against its ills, however things should go against me and the world frown upon me, it would be a taste for reading."

This taste for literature, this habit of cultivating the mind should be formed in early life. The mental soil becomes so overgrown with weeds, if these are allowed to take root in the spring, that late in the summer neither flowers nor fruits have room to expand :—

"A youth of folly, an old age of cards."

The young girl whose immortal faculties are all frittered away upon flounces and opera music will grow into a vapid, silly old woman, shunned by the selfish, tolerated by the generous, and incapable of inspiring any higher sentiment than the compassion nearly allied to contempt. A butterfly belle may, at sixteen, attract " the white-gloved beaux ;" but, alas ! for a butterfly of sixty ! Instances of such, and deplorable ones, too, we have seen; there are few more humiliating spectacles. for our sex. Skill in the fine arts is delightful, a source of unfailing pleasure to its possessor and her circle of friends; but it is only in rare instances that nature gives talent for art worth the years of time and the very large amount of money necessary before the woman can attain an excellence that rewards her and her family for their sacrifices. The cultivation of elegant literature is in the power of every one who has leisure; and what young lady has not time on her hands? It is the cheapest, the easiest of accomplishments. Is it the least valuable? Which is the more desirable friend or companion? Which is capable of giving more entertainment at home or abroad, by the fireside or in the largest assembly? the woman who can warble half a dozen *cavatinas* as well as a tenth-rate opera-singer, or she whose well-stored, well-balanced mind is filled with the bright ideas of the best writers of every age; whose ample fund of knowledge is ready on every occasion ; whose wit, not erratic or sarcastic, but properly curbed and tempered with kindness, gives brilliancy to old thoughts; and whose well-cultured judgment is able to produce new ideas? We can dance and sing but a few

172

years at most; we can converse all our lives, unless our intellects have been weakened by years of habitual repression and factitious torpor.

The knowledge acquired at school is generally but a preparation for after gain. Nellie asks us how to proceed. We would recommend, in the first place, *regularity*. The careless can scarcely form any notion of what may be done by an orderly regulation of time. The young lady who desires to improve must determine upon the time for her reading ; this, of course, must be regulated in its length by her circumstances and duties. Not knowing the actual state of Nellie's improvement, it is difficult to mention the books she may require; but supposing her to be like other young ladies who have just left school, we imagine she has studied epitomes, if not histories, and would counsel her now to undertake some work of more extent than schools usually have time for. " Rollin's Ancient History," which gives a very clear, condensed account of the earliest races of mankind, and a good knowledge of Grecian history, may be read with much advantage. When she comes to the affairs of Greece, she had better read " Plutarch" —each " Life" as she meets the hero in " Rollin ;" and while she is upon Athenian affairs, " Bloomfield's Thucydides" will be very interesting and useful. We urge her to read these Greek writers (the translations of whose works are satisfactory), not that they will give her much more of information than she will find in " Rollin," but because she will form a much better idea of what the old Greeks were, and what was their turn of mind, from reading one or two of their own authors, than from all the accounts given at second hand by the moderns, can convey. She must also, while going on with these works, get good translations of the Greek poets, or at least the works of some of them. Pope's Iliad and Odyssey, one or two of the tragedies of Æschylus, of Sophocles, and of Euripides; and standard works of criticism on other subjects that may be within her reach, should be resorted to, as taste demands cultivation as much as any other faculty. By all means let her write a weekly summary of all she has read ; and that this may be done with advantage, she should, as she reads, put marks (movable ones—strips of paper) in the book at all the striking passages, whether of thought, sentiment, or narration. Recurring to these, she will, by a second perusal, have the best part of her author fully impressed on her own mind. When she has thus finished reading " ancient history," she should, in the same manner, take the standard historians of modern nations, beginning with English history, as the most comprehensive, and, from the identity of language, being to us most important. This system, if perseveringly followed, will give her an acquaintance with history, poetry, and criticism. And when she comes down towards the seventeenth century, the interest deepens, because our country then comes out like a new star on the horizon; and the two succeeding centuries, with the seventeenth, are rich in the treasures of intellect. What a store of memoirs, letters, essays, poems, narratives will be found ! Here are pleasures and occupations independent of wealth, of health, of station, of situation, of age, which interfere with no duties, but enable us the better to go through the trials of the world, accommodating ourselves "to that state of life in which it has pleased God to call us.

A CURIOUS LIBRARY.—In 1847 Count Léopold Ferri died at Padna, leaving a library entirely composed of works written by women in various languages, the number of volumes amounting to nearly *thirty-two thousand*. Whether the English and American lady writers were included in his list, we do not know, but we wish some woman of taste and fortune would, in our country, make a similar collection.

LITERATURE IN RUSSIA.—During the past year there have been published in the empire of the czar, ninety-five newspapers, and sixty-six magazines and periodicals, devoted to the proceedings of learned societies. Of these, seventy-six newspapers and forty-eight magazines are in the Russian language; fifteen newspapers and ten magazines in German; two newspapers and six magazines in French; three newspapers in English; one newspaper in Polish; and one in Latin; two newspapers in Georgian; and two in Lettish; also three newspapers in Russian and German, and two in Russian and Polish. In St. Petersburg, twenty-six newspapers and forty-two magazines are published in the languages above mentioned. Thus, the people of Russia are becoming accustomed to the civilization of the press; and the progress is onward.

A GLANCE AT THE WEST:*—
MRS. SARAH J. HALE: I have spent the last hour looking over the pages of the "Lady's Book" for November and December, and am pleased to see that it bears no marks of frost, while it comes richly laden with the fruits of age. "Godey" has some charms, which no other eastern magazines can boast, for western readers. This periodical has been our companion for many years, and its name is a "household word" in almost every home. Long before railroading was a branch of business in the valley of the Ohio; when even a large portion of the "Territory of the Northwest" was an almost unbroken wilderness, the "Lady's Book," like a messenger of good tidings, made its way over the Alleghany mountains, and across the beautiful prairies, to the loveliest hamlets and the most intelligent families of the great States of Ohio and Indiana. Other magazines have sprung into life, devoted by turns to politics, humanity, literature, religion, and science; but "Godey" has varied not, exhibiting in successive chapters, from the beginning until this hour, the elegance, without the fastidiousness, the honesty, without the scrupulosity, and the learning, without the pedantry, of the panorama of American life.

But I did not sit down to write a formal eulogium upon a work which has vindicated its claims to merit by maintaining, through a long series of years, a heavy circulation in the most intelligent and fashionable circles of the country. To say, at this late period, that the "Lady's Book" merits the patronage which it has commanded, would be simply to say whatever everybody admits to be true.

Since your work was commenced, the seat of empire in this country has been removed from New England and the Middle States to the Valley of the Mississippi.

* From George P. Buell, Esq., editor of the "Western Democratic Review." Indianapolis, Nov. 1854.
15*

We have not rivalled you, nor can we hope to rival you, for many years to come, in the walks of literature and science; but we are rapidly building, upon the foundation laid thirty years ago by the pioneers of the west, a superstructure of polite learning and utilitarian philosophy, whose proud proportions will one day attract the united admiration of the Old and the New World.

Literature, *as a science*, has found a home in our midst, and it may be observed that it has a character peculiarly its own. In England, and on the continent of Europe, the dawn of letters was hailed from the mansions of opulence and power. It was considered a condescension on the part of haughty barons to notice with favor the first efforts of the tyro of the press. That feeling of the superiority of "greatness" to the elegant pursuits of knowledge, has been transmitted from generation to generation, and at this day the influence of some distinguished lord appears sufficient to impart immortal renown to even ordinary genius. In the Western World, however, the case is widely different. Learning is linked to no "undying names." It is pursued in the great laboratory of nature. Those are only its patrons who patronize it for its own sake. There is a freshness in its conceptions, and a power in its manifestations, which cannot be separated from originality. The sun of letters which is now rising in this great valley is not a secondary orb, which has shone before, but one which, in its meridian splendor, will eclipse the brightest era of the past. There is every prospect that this vast region will afford a single example of all the powerful incentives to human action operating in the production of isolated men. Greatness has been said not to belong to clime, and occasional instances of the loftiest exhibitions of mind, under apparently the most unfavorable circumstances, seem to justify the conclusion. Still, the general truth is evidenced by the history of all ages of the world, that geographical position has exerted an overwhelming influence in moulding the character of a people. The proximity of Athens, of Carthage, and of Alexandria, to the great "inland sea" of the eastern hemisphere, beyond a reasonable doubt, was the secret of the magnificence, the humanity, and the glory of those beacon lights of antiquity. The stupendous influence which England has so long maintained in the councils of modern nations is perhaps chiefly deducible from that insulated position whose very necessities seem to have tempted her to the Godlike enterprise of using the ocean to subjugate the land. The presence of the beautiful and grand in nature is requisite to the development of the corresponding qualities in man. Our uncounted race form indeed but a type, a purely philosophical reflection of the earth on which we live. The rugged mountain seems to speak in the lofty, fearless, and immutable Alpine mind; the silver streams of Spain observe not a smoother channel than the pensive current of an Andalusian heart; the mighty ocean is not deeper or more grand than the spirit that embraces its sublimity. That mind which shall be wrought upon the scale of nature on this continent will be such as the world has hardly seen.

It is a great organic truth that, from the earliest ages, the march of civilization has been in the direction of the setting sun. As the star of ancient power, and learning, and glory, set upon the regions adjacent to the garden of Eden, it rose upon the mighty West. But a few years have passed since the East paid little regard to the West. Her institutions of learning, her progress, everything not of eastern origin, commanded but little attention, even on the borders of the Atlantic. The editor of "Frazer's Magazine," of London, introducing a beautiful letter, written by the lamented Howard of Indiana, in the year 1833, from the banks of the Wabash, says: "Next comes a voice from Indiana! From the banks of the Father of Rivers, of the glorious Mississippi himself! It is quite clear that we are, as Wordsworth would express it, 'stepping westward.' We give the letter *precisely as we have received it*, and shall take care that Mr. Jackson, our agent at New York, forwards a copy of this number to Rockville!" The editor of the ablest literary journal of the Old World, twenty-one years ago, confounded the noble Wabash and the giant Mississippi; and he not only did this, but condescended to publish, "precisely as it was received," a letter covering two-thirds of a page, from one of the most eloquent orators, one of the most classical scholars, and one of the purest patriots living between the Alleghany and the Rocky Mountains! General Howard was the great champion of common schools in Tennessee; was afterwards District Attorney for Indiana, and finally *Chargé d'Affaires* to the Republic of Texas, having received the appointment, unsolicited on his part, through the influence of John C. Calhoun, under Tyler. General Howard died young. In examining his papers a few months since, for the purpose of writing his life, I found an immense roll of manuscript, which proved to be a literal transcript of the Philosophy of Aristotle, and the principal commentaries upon it, which Mr. Howard, in an attorney's office, had completed in 1833, as an aid in mastering the sublime science of logic. In looking at the identical copy of "Frazer," forwarded through Mr. Jackson, I found it extensively defaced by all sorts of marks calculated to insure its safe delivery to the obscure individual supposed to reside on the confines of civilization.

But the face of things has radically changed. Not many years ago, our own beautiful Ohio did indeed course silently through an almost undisturbed wilderness; now, however, floating upon its waters, are steamers rivalling the most magnificent upon the Hudson; upon its banks are factories differing not in the slightest degree from those of New England; and colleges honored by as high a grade of talent and learning as graces the universities of the East.

The progress of this country, in the last half century, has amazed the world. The additions which have been made to our territory are such as were not anticipated by any. Our progress has been unlike that of other regions and other times. Under the influence of our institutions, the inhabitants of the Eastern World—China and Japan—that so long and so successfully resisted the attempted invasions of European ideas, have become our neighbors. England *attempted* revolution in China by the use of bayonets and cannon; *we* have laid the foundation of a successful and radical revolution in that vast empire, by the annexation of California. No viands which Europe could afford, tended, in the slightest degree, to arouse the cupidity, the curiosity, or the sleeping energies of the Orientals. When, however, the golden fields of the Sacramento were announced, they turned their eyes across the broad blue waters of the Pacific, and contemplated a land which promised them more than the philosophy of Confucius. The day of the political redemption of the East is not distant. The Yankees, and we mean 'the universal Yankee nation,' are on the march for the Pacific; the tide of our civilization will soon roll on an iron road from the shores of the Atlantic to the farther West. We do not now mean by "the West," what was understood by it years ago.

Bacon regarded New England as the West; the inhabitants of Massachusetts call the prairies of Illinois by that name; *we* locate it beyond the Rocky Mountains:—

"It follows the declining sun
   Along the banks of Oregon;
Nor leaves him where he makes his pillow
   On the great Pacific's billow."

In parts of California, "the West" is another name for the Sandwich Islands. We are certainly a progressive and aggressive people. An indestructible feature in the American character is a love of territorial aggrandizement; and we care not how far we shall go toward the east or the west, the north or the south; the banner of the "stars and stripes" is morally wide enough to shelter the world. We believe that this is a great country; that the ground is not yet ours upon which shall be erected its outer walls; and we have almost persuaded ourselves that the sexton who shall blot us from the roll of nations will be deeply interested in the consummation of human affairs.

But, madam, I find I have violated the "unities." Sitting down to request you, in a few lines, to send me a copy of the new work which you have prepared, entitled "The Bible Reading Book," I have wandered into literature and speculations. Begging pardon for the digression, and for occupying so much space in your valuable work, I will trespass a little further by inserting the following beautiful poem, written by MRS. SARAH T. BOLTON of this city, whose fame as a writer is the particular pride of the West, and destined to become the common property of the Union. I think so competent a judge as the editress of the "Lady's Book" will admit that the celebrated saying of Fontaine is beautifully amplified into an illustration of the energy of the Mississippi Valley, under the title of

"PADDLE YOUR OWN CANOE.

"Voyager upon life's sea,
   To yourself be true,
And whate'er your lot may be,
   Paddle your own canoe.
Never, though the winds may rave,
   Falter nor look back;
But, upon the darkest wave,
   Leave a shining track.

"Nobly dare the wildest storm,
   Stem the hardest gale;
Brave of heart, and strong of arm,
   You will never fail.
When the world is cold and dark,
   Keep an aim in view;
And toward the beacon mark
   Paddle your own canoe.

"Every wave that bears you on
   To the silent shore,
From its sunny source has gone,
   To return no more.
Then let not an hour's delay
   Cheat you of your due;
But, while it is called to-day,
   Paddle your own canoe.

"If your birth denied you wealth,
   Lofty state, and power;
Honest fame and hardy health
   Are a better dower.
But if these will not suffice,
   Golden gain pursue;

And to reach the glittering prize,
Paddle your own canoe.

" Would you wrest the wreath of fame
From the hand of fate?
Would you write a deathless name
With the good and great?
Would you bless your fellow-men?
Heart and soul imbue
With the holy task, and then
Paddle your own canoe.

" Would you crush the tyrant wrong,
In the world's free fight?
With a spirit brave and strong,
Battle for the right.
And to break the chains that bind
The many to the few;
To enfranchise slavish mind,
Paddle your own canoe.

" Nothing great is lightly won;
Nothing won is lost;
Every good deed, nobly done,
Will repay the cost.
Leave to heaven, in humble trust,
All you will to do;
But if you succeed, you must
Paddle your own canoe."

EDUCATION OF CHILDREN.—Lord Brougham gives it as his opinion that the child learns more the first eighteen months of its life than at any other period; in fact, settling its mental capacity and future well-being. Dr. Babbington states the period of the first nine years as the seed-time for life. The Roman Catholic priest wants the child for the first seven years of training, when its character is moulded for time and eternity.

If the early training of the child is of such paramount importance, should not those who naturally have the care of infants and young children, *mothers* and *nurses*, be thoroughly instructed themselves before undertaking this great work of educators?

Who will establish a school for children's nurses? It is more needed in our country than institutions for idiots.

LADY PHYSICIANS.*—The corner-stone of a medical college for women is laid at Richmond, Virginia. It will cost $125,000, and will doubtless be well got up and supported. There is no other department of masculine duty which women have a better right to share than the medical. As it is, they do half the physician's work—and the better half. And then, as regards the more delicate and ailing half of the community, their services would be more welcome and efficacious than those of the men; and to this half add all the children. The fact is that, according to the suffrages of common sense, women would have the greater part of the medi-

* From the "Saturday Evening Mail," edited by George R. Graham, and published by C. F. Peters & Co. We commend this weekly paper to families as excellent in its moral and literary influence. Its advocacy of the education of woman, and of her fitness for her duties (among which the medical care of her own sex in feminine complaints, and the thorough knowledge of the diseases of childhood, are included), is earnest, and will, we trust, help onward the good cause

cal work of the world—the women and children; and we believe this will yet be the case. Not that we would confine them entirely to these. We know very well that many of the male people, when sick, would rather have a gentle young lady doctor than a great, grave medico of the other sex. The only drawback in this case would be the increased tendency of all young gentlemen to make complaints of illness on slight occasions, and become *malades imaginaires*, like the man in the comedy.

Let women prepare to take possession of the medical department of human science; they are the fittest for it. At this moment a regiment of them, under Miss Nightingale as colonel—blessings on her soft voice and stout heart!—are setting out from London, in order to tend the sick in the hospitals of Constantinople. They will go there, and they will do more good than the surgeons and doctors.

We do not approve of ladies in the pulpit, or in trousers, or delivering lectures, except curtain lectures, which are womanly things enough, and, in most instances, highly called for. But we hope to see the day when authoritative women will go about with their pills, prescriptions, and so forth, to deal with and diminish the majority of diseases that visit our households.

THE ODIN RELIGION.—Under this head, the " Westminster Review," for October, has a very interesting article gathered from several recent German works. The old Teutonic race were lovers of myth and mystery, and their descendants, who remain where their forefathers worshipped, seem even now half inclined to serve the same shadowy gods. German philosophers live, usually, in cloud-land, and the study of the " Scriptures of Odinism" is for them a congenial pursuit. The article is very interesting; but we notice it here for the sake of the acknowledgment made to the aptitude of the female mind for the reception of the Christian religion. The writer, alluding to the number of the nobler sort who received the new faith, says these were " influenced in many cases—it is astonishing in how many—by the pious examples and the silent persuasions of devout women, to whose tender hearts Christ proved more congenial than Odin."

TO CORRESPONDENTS.—The following articles are accepted: " A Poet's Song in Despondency"—" The Winter Night"—" Gathered to her Babies"—" Skating" —" He doeth all things well"—" Autumn Days"— " Allen's Grave"—" My Heart is thine"—" Invocation" —" The Forest Cemetery"—" Sleep lightly, Love"— and " The Good and Pure of Earth."

The following are declined: " To the Departed"— " Memory's Serenade"—" Youth and Old Age"—" Let come whatever will"—The Lady of the deep blue Eye" —" The Orphan"—" Scraps from a Journal"—" Cleveland Cemetery, with Reflections"—" The Widow." (This effusion did not reach us till the January number was printed. The author had better send the MS. poem to the lady for whom it is designed.)—" To Mary Neal." (Better send the MS. to the poetess.)—" A Midnight Song." (The poem has merit, but the writer can improve.)—" Lines on a Mountain"—" I sing of thee, Love"—" Lines." (Two pieces inclosed in the letter were accepted; see above.)—" My Angel"—" Winter" —" Gold." (Of no value. Better dig than steal other men's thoughts.)—" The wild—wild Ocean"—" Pride" —" A long Journey"—and " The Return Home."

HUMAN NATURE IN CHUNKS.

CHUNK NO 1.—WOMAN'S RIGHTS.

CREDE RATEM VENTIS!

SOME time since, while travelling through the interior of the Empire State, I observed a very showy placard, in large capitals,—" WOMAN'S RIGHT'S CONVENTION *will assemble this evening at the* ODD FELLOWS' HALL. *The Honorable Miss —— and Mrs. —— will address the meeting."* &c. Prompted by that ever-wakeful monitor of the mind, curiosity, I determined to be present, and, if possible, ascertain the "real rights" of the female portion of humanity. Poor women claim that men steal their hearts by the magnetic power of love to make them kitchen slaves,—court them with the witchery of smiles and subdue them with frowns—lead them into the ideal land, canopied with rainbows, to wander back o'er the lonely walks of discontent—flatter them with hope, but give them the tattered garment of sorrow—admire the electric flash of the eye, but sentinel it with tears—call her angel, to give mockery to praise—talk friendship, but wear the signet of hypocrisy.

56

Indeed, Oh! man, thy broken promises to woman's heart, outnumber the jewelry of the sky,—thy broken vows·are in- sults ·to the God that gave thee breath to breathe them. Ho- nor is all scarred with insults. Truth, God's dearest angel, weeps as flattery and falsehood conquer woman's heart, and bury, in sorrow's grave, the queen of her bosom, hope.

The hour having arrived for the meeting of the Conven- tion, I repaired to the hall, which already was overflowing with the anxious maids and matrons, to rear the standard of right. A maiden wearing two score summers on her brow, and attired *a la turquesque*, arose with parliamentary dignity, and called the meeting to order. Said she :—

Mothers and Sisters:

We have convened this day to vindicate our rights. We have rights, as sacred as the eternal Law, but cold hearted man, has fettered them with his stubborn will and cold unyielding heart. The time has come when we should *speak* and *act*. Our *tongues* have too long slumbered in fear. We have been the slaves of man too long, nor have we dared to move, lest we breath the anger of his displeasure. The selfishness of man would forever chain us to the wash-tub and the kitchen. Are not women as progressive as men? Did not God give equality both to man and women? Where is that equali- ty? Men are masters and we are slaves. They look on women as special household furniture in the kitchen of humanity. Down with the lords! Why do they deride assemblages like this? They fear truth and right Man is not truth, but selfishness. Man thinks domestic knowledge is all that a woman should possess. Man thinks too that woman should not waste time in improving the undying part, the mind. What a vain presumptuous piece of humanity is man! They think that the mathematical knowledge of wo- man should extend no farther than the multiplication of little responsibili- ties. Our philosophy, in giving proper motion to the cradle,—our astrono- my, in examining the family group—our geography, the hemisphere of the kitchen—our history, pants and patches—our classics, *mea filia, meus fili- us.* Can we longer, sisters, bear this weight of injustice? Shall we humble mind into slavery? No! We have our rights, we have our *tongues,* and we will speak. We may possess property, but cannot vote to control it. Why are the rights of suffrage torn from us? Because the selfish heart of man says it is immodest, m o-d-est, forsooth. *Duty knows no modesty.* What is not immodest to the eyes of man? If we change our dress for comfort and convenience, we meet—meet, I say—the contemptible gaze of the rabble. Let them look to their own attire, before they whisper immodesty. I have buried long skirts in oblivion. I will wear, in spite of contempt, the Turk ish costume. There is poetry in the " *a la Turque,*"—it is convenient. There

is always poetry in convenience. Sisters! let our rights this day be vindicated, and from this hour, assert those principles that shall govern our actions towards that pretended master, selfish man. I move, sisters, that the
Hon. Mrs. ——— preside over our deliberations.

"I second that motion," exclaimed a dozen voices. "Will
the Hon. Mrs. ——— take the chair?"

The Hon. Mrs. ——— repaired to the seat awarded to her
by the Convention. (Great clapping of hands.) The Hon.
Mrs. ———, the *Chair-woman* of the Convention, in years was
about three score. She wore a plain muslin cap, after the
fashion of the Quakers. She carried her knitting work in
hand, giving evidence of industry. On taking her seat, she
removed her snuff-box from its covert, and fed the olfactories
with a bountiful pinch. After wiping her glasses on one corner of her apron, and adjusting her cape to a proper position,
she arose and said :

Matrons and Maids:

I thank you a *good deal* for giving me this exalted position. It is a proud
day in my history to meet with my sisters to declare our independence. We
have come up here to *do* battle in the cause of right. We have been tor-
mented long enough by the vindictive spirit of man. Although I am a married woman, I hate man prodigiously. I honor all of my sex that are not
under the yoke of matrimony. (Loud applause by the old maids.) There is
nothing in matrimony but squalling babies and washing days. Better by
far be stigmatized as an old maid, than wear the deep furrows of servitude.
The sceptre of woman has been too long the broom. She was created for a
higher and nobler sphere. Man would lie woman out of all her charms to
feed a capacious avarice. They deny us the rights of legislation, but thank
Heaven, they can't deny us negation, when we *will.* There is potency in
"*will*" and "*wont.*" If we set out aright this day, we can establish our
rights and perpetuate them. Let us have a democracy of women—a government of equality—a confederacy of "*wonts!*" Sisters! the chains have
too long fettered our hearts and bowed them into subservience at the will of
man. Let the timid cast off fear—let the strong grow stronger,—and may
our united efforts effect for poor woman, what union did in the proud colo-
nial days, for the fathers. I again thank you for feminine honors. If there
is any business to be presented, now is the opportunity, and I *do* sincerely
trust that we shall have no jars or turmoils so common to male conventions.

(Mrs. Chair-woman:) Miss ——— Ladies.

"I have the pleasure of presenting a resolution for the

consideration of this august Convention, and I do hope, sisters, you will all speak freely upon it."

RESOLVED, That woman wear what she pleases, act as she pleases, do as she pleases, and go where she pleases.

Miss ———, the concoctor of the above resolution, attired in full Bloomer costume, seemed like one forgotten of love and hope. She had unquestionably passed the main street of life, and read in the ominous future no prospects. A volume of determination was written on her saffron cheek. I believe from my surplus quantity of sincerity, that she would have embraced the standard of Hymen, and yielded her heart's devotion to some lord of creation, and daguerreotype the real rights of her sex at the domestic hearth. At least she had a kind of matrimonial squint in her eyes. In presenting her resolution, she spoke as follows :

Mrs. Chairman and Ladies ·

I am an old maid by choice and not through necessity. I am, *so there,* the uncompromising enemy of man. We are called angels, but made slaves. The everlasting prying curiosity of cold-hearted, sordid, phlegmatic man, is continually harping about our dress. Immodest beings, they. I will wear what I please, *so.* I wont sweep the streets with my dress any more. I am a Bloomer disciple. There is elegance and comfort in the dress. Palsied be the tongue that condemns them ! Long skirts are an abomination in the sight of the Lord. They are baptized every time we move, in the mud and filth of the street. Comfort should be our aim, and not to please the whims of the lords, forsooth, of creation. It is a sin to sacrifice comfort for a whim, and man is nothing but a bundle of whims, an organized uncertainty. The Bloomer combines elegance with ease, and comfort with beauty. Physiology claims it as a rich gift to health. But man laughs at the innovation. Let them laugh on. Their smiles are nothing but the reflection of an iceberg, their own hearts. Let us, sisters, dress as we please. We can't please man, any way. Let us be independent and please ourselves. Again, sisters, let us act as we please, regardless of what man may say. Our own independence will conquer man. Resolution of purpose is greatness. Let us do as we please, and not be pinned by necessity to the will of man. Let us go where we please, and show to man the triumph of our determination. Burst, my sisters, the chains that bind you to the cradle and the wash-tub, and set at defiance the incendiary jargon of the " lords." Man is the first to find fault, the first to teach the lessons of coquetry, the first to flatter. *The first flirt was a man* ; and the term fop is only applicable to the genus homo.

5

We will work with that zeal that characterizes our sex till we have our rights at the ballot box, as we now have to the bandbox. We can conquer man, but man cannot conquer the " will and wont" of woman. There is no equality in matrimony—no true love in man. I am proud to wear the title of old maid. It is woman's declaration of independence—the poetry of single blessedness.

Mrs. —— then arose, age having extracted her front teeth, caused her to lisp a little.

Mith Chair-woman:

I arithe to thay a word on that are resolution. I thay that it ith a very important one. Women are thicked about too muth by the breechthes. I think, that it ith time for woman to wear the breechthes too, and I goeths in for the bloomer costhume.When I goeths home, my Thallie Ann shall have breechthes, and I shall have them too. I thay they are the splendidist tings dat I ever thaw. I thay dat thay make a big woman look little. I do thay dat thay will be theeper. I do know dat my Thallie Ann will be the gratifidest dirl in the world. If my husbun stholds about it, I'll put the broom thover his head. My Thallie Ann is a fine gal—she's very fond of muthick. I and husbun fights thumtimes, but I always wips him ; I will do just as I please, so thar—it's thour duty. Now I thay, let us all agree, as that are woman thed, to do as we pleese. God never made us, thisters, to mind the men. Thumbody has thed dat women are the fowers of the world ; thum of us are buds, but when we get on that are dreth, we shall be bloomers. I gothes in all over for the woman's rights. If we don't, thisters, go in for rights, we aint the *right* kind of women. I hope dare is thumbody else dat will tell us somethin.

(*Mrs. Chair-woman.*)   Ladies —— Miss—
             (In a simpering and delightfully sentimental tone.)

I am scarcely out of my " teens," but have had it impressed in my mind, that man is a mockery—a creature of unsatisfied desires. Oh! I can not bring my mind into the matrimonial channel. Oh! the idea of changing names, is full of melancholy to me. As we look abroad through the world and examine the true character of the "rougher sex," we find many are given to intoxication, Oh! how sad the spectacle,—how gloomy the thought. Alas! how many women are deceived by the falsehood of love,—by the deceitful smiles of the deceiver. Oh! tears come unbidden at the thought. Oh! my sisters, my sisters, we must bear our Rights in triumph, else beauty will fade on the parent stem. A drinking husband! Oh heaven! I cannot plight my vows at the altar,—how my heart would bleed to breathe the breath of an intoxicated consort. Oh! how my pride would be humbled to unite my being to one that masticates the obnoxious weed. How I should weep to hear my companion mocking the majesty of Heaven with imprecations. How I should agonize to see my spouse, walking the streets, as a piece of humanity turned into a chimney. Oh, my dear sisters, I go in, soul and body, for the glorious state of single blessedness. Oh! cradles, brooms, mops, patches, and domestic storms, come not to that state. Oh! talk not to me of love, it is but a child of fancy, the battle ground of hearts. Oh! away, away, with that creature man, that would drag angels from paradise and make them slaves. Sisters, mothers, daughters, would it not be the millennium of our hearts, the heaven of our anticipations, were all men created with that same philanthropic regard for our devoted sex as Mr.———, the Alpha and Omega of the American press, whom we anticipated meeting this day,—His heart yearns to escort us to the ballot box and wreathe that safeguard of Liberty with our smiles,—Reformer and philanthropist—the only exalted specimen of man that has a heart to feel and pity our misfortunes.

(*A voice.*)   Where is Mr. ———— ?
(*Speakeress.*) I learned by a telegraphic dispatch that he was to address a meeting of African Spiritualists this afternoon at ——— (cries) (good, good.)
I have a resolution, sisters, and with your permission, will present it—cries of, do—do—do—oh! do.

BE IT RESOLVED, That we in convention assembled, will marry no man that drinks, swears, chews tobacco, smokes, gambles, keeps late hours, or belongs to any secret society, but must be a member of a Church in good and regular standing, efficient in the cause of temperance, mindful; courteous, of gentle deportment, frugal and industrious.

"I move its adoption," cries one.
"I second it," said another.
"Can married women vote, on that a-r-e res-o-lu-tion?" inquired a woman in the corner, with four yards of consequence in her face.
Certainly said the Chair.
"Well gals," said an old spinister dressed in *pea-green*, "I shant vote for 't, *so there.* My old man drinks, smokes, chaws tobacco, swears, and belongs to the free masons. He belongs to Satan's church, and is in plaguey good standing, I should have to break his neck if I voted for that are resolution. You Gals, here, never will git married in this ere world of
5*

ourn if you let that are thing pass, for there aint a man of 'em but what does one or tother of 'em. Better be a little cautious gals, for all on ye' feel just as I did when I was of your age, glad to take the first one that came along. Keep your eyes open, Gals ; I jist as lief as not, wear that are dress that they tell about, for I have told my old man fifty times that if he did'nt quit drinking I'd wear the breeches. That are resolution, Gals, would make a husband perfect. You cant find on arth a perfect man. They all have faults. Take man all in all, Gals, we could'nt git along without him, with ary tolerable degree of comfort."

"I move the adoption of the resolution and call for the vote," said the woman with a flare up bonnet on. " I ask leave to amend the resolution, by adding, that women have the right to go to the polls and vote for their rulers, and that slavery is a sin."—Said another, " Adopted."

" All that are in favor of the passage of the Resolution as amended, will manifest it by saying *I.*"

" *I.* \ *I.   I.   I.*"

" Those opposed will say *no.*"

"No. No. No. No."

"It is a tie, sisters."

" Wall, Gals, I'm glad 'tis a tie," said the woman with a green dress, wiping her specs on her apron, " I see all the married women but me voted for it, and not one solitary one of the unmarried. I'm glad on't Gals, for all on ye would have died old maids, as sure as butter, if it had passed, and I know ye dont want to. My stars, I wish my Sammy was here, and I'd bet a goose he'd git a wife *right off*, without the plaguy fuss of courtin."

EDITORS' TABLE.

"The sword may pierce the bearer—
 Stone walls in time may sever;
'Tis *heart* alone, worth steel and stone,
 That keeps man free forever!"—*Moore.*

A New Year! Yes, a new year—and a happy New Year may it prove to our beloved country—has dawned on the world. Though many prophecies are abroad, which designate this year as not only the time for the great comet to make its visit, but also for awful catastrophes and cruel wars, we, who live under the protecting banner of that true freedom which emanated from the *hearts* of noble Christians, men and women, who feared God, and, therefore, were freed from the fear of wicked tyrannies—we may rejoice and be glad that the *year eighteen hundred and fifty-six* has come with its hopes, its promises, and its opportunities. We might give a true and most pitiful description of the sufferings which now pervade Europe. To wars of the most destructive character are added the scarcity of food and the fears of bloody revolutions. These are, however, well known to our readers through the journals of the day; and we prefer to go beyond the present surface of things, and trace the source from whence such awful evils flow, and we find it in the selfishness, blindness, and wickedness of *heart* which rejects the true freedom that only can come through the Bible way of peace and happiness. Nations must fear God and obey his laws; men and women must make the Gospel precepts their rule of duty; then the New Year would be the harbinger of hope and rejoicing to the whole world.

This *heart service* in the cause of humanity belongs naturally to women. We cannot take the sword to defend the right; we must aid by holier means. There are so many opportunities in our country both of improvement and of employment that we are in danger of forgetting the oppressions of our sex in the Old World. England we have always been in the habit of considering the bulwark of law and of freedom through the law in Europe; the injustice and cruelties which the law in England sanctions respecting women have never been sufficiently considered by us. We have lately had our attention called to this subject; and, partly to illustrate the blessings we American women enjoy under our better system of laws and usages, and partly to awaken public attention to the still existing defects in our own institutions, we show a glimpse of married life in England; and, while we commiserate the sufferings of our sister women on the other side of the Atlantic, we give a warmer grasp of friendship to the hands that are reaching out to us on all sides, and from every section of the Union, as we wish each household where our influence enters a happy New Year! a *heart* happy New Year!

THE NON-EXISTENCE OF WOMAN.

THE Honorable Mrs. Norton has for several years past been as conspicuous among England's women for the domestic wrongs she has endured as for her fine genius and the fortitude with which she has borne her cruel fate. In the August number of the 'North British Review,' we find an elaborate article on this subject. We cannot, by any comments of our own, add to the force of this article; and we prefer to give the sentiments of a man on the question of the *legal wrongs*, as these monstrous iniquities are tenderly termed, to which English women are subjected. The "Reviewer" says:—

"In the course of last year, Mrs. Norton privately circulated among her friends what may be called a thin volume or a bulky pamphlet, entitled 'English Laws for Women in the Nineteenth Century.' It is an illustration rather than a disquisition, a moving example rather than a chapter of formal argumentation, a painful episode of personal history, more weighty and pregnant in its simple details of much wrong and mighty suffering than sheafs of subtle controversy or swelling declamation; and it is one of those 'over-true tales,' the pathos of which goes straight to the heart.

"Into the minuter circumstances of the sad story, it is not necessary to enter; it is enough that we should express our faith in Mrs. Norton's statements, and our sympathy with her sufferings. In the volume which the injured lady circulated last year, she declared that she would not write again except upon this subject; and so far she has kept her word. Within the last few weeks, she has presented to the outside public a 'Letter to the Queen on the Laws of Marriage and Divorce.'

"That the published work deals largely in private matters, we do not complain; the redress of many great public wrongs has been brought about by the exposure of private grievances. But for such reference to individual cases, it would be said, as indeed it often is said : ' All you say may be very true in theory, but the system of which you complain works well. The evils are possible evils; but in fact they do not arise.' To show that they have arisen, and that they do arise, is to show that they may and will again arise; and to demonstrate that they are not possibilities, but actualities, is to enlist the sympathies of many who would turn aside with indifference from the theoretical question, and remain content with things as they are. To talk about the 'bad taste' of obtruding matrimonial quarrels upon the public is simply to talk as a dolt or a *petit maître,* as if such questions as these could be settled by an appeal to taste. It is not to be supposed that Mrs. Norton, a woman with all the generous impulses and fine sensibilities of genius, has any personal gratification in telling the world how her domestic life has been one long scene of conflict and humiliation, how the sweetest of human faces has been clouded with sorrow, and the kindliest of human hearts filled with bitterness by a process too certain in its operation for humanity to resist; as well might you suppose that, when 'Scævola's right hand hissed in the Tuscan fire,' there was personal gratification in the self-torture. For our own parts, knowing well what it must have cost her, we admire the courage and applaud the martyrdom of the English

79

lady who, sustained by her strong conviction of the justice of a great cause, can thus tread down all the delicate instincts of womanhood, ay, even those of much bearing and much forbearing motherhood, while she pleads the common cause of her sister-sufferers, the highest and the lowest alike.

"There will doubtless be among Mrs. Norton's readers many women, prosperous in their love or believing themselves to be thus prosperous, who will say that they deplore her revelations, and repudiate her doctrines. They are in health, or their disease is latent and unsuspected, and they need not the physician; happy are they in their security or their delusion. That Mrs. Norton's case is an exceptional one in degree, we believe, but *only* in degree; even in degree, though exceptional, it is not solitary, and in kind we are afraid it is common. It so happens that in this unhappy instance all the evils of the existing laws, as they affect women, find apt illustration, meeting together and being massed into a strange congeries of multitudinous wrong; but any one of these evils, taken separately, is sufficient to call attention to the existing state of the law, and to clamor loudly for the most earnest consideration that can be given to the great question of human justice which it involves. It is no reason, because there are happy homes in England, and honored and cherished wives, that those who are wronged and outraged should not be protected by the law; and ought not the thank-offering of the prosperous to be boundless sympathy with those poor bankrupts in domestic love whose cause Mrs. Norton is so eloquently pleading?

"As briefly as we can, and as much as possible in Mrs. Norton's own words, we propose to state at the outset what are the individual wrongs grouped together in her unhappy case:"—

MRS. NORTON'S STORY.—"I cannot," she writes in the published pamphlet, "divorce my husband either for adultery, desertion, or cruelty; I *must* remain married *to his name*. I am, as regards my husband, in a worse position than if I had been divorced by him; in that case, Englishmen are so generous that some chivalrous-hearted man might perhaps have married and trusted me in spite of the unjust cloud upon my name. I am not divorced, and I cannot divorce my husband; yet I can establish no legal claim upon him, nor upon any living human being.

"I do not receive," says Mrs. Norton, "and have not received for the last three years, a single farthing from my husband. He retains, and always has retained property that was left in my home, gifts made to me by my own family on my marriage, and to my mother, articles bought from my literary earnings, &c. He receives from my trustees the interest of the portion bequeathed me by my father, who died in the public service. I have also (as Mr. Norton impressed on me by subpœnaing my publishers) the power of earning by literature, which fund, though it be the grant of Heaven, not the legacy of earth, is no more legally mine than my family property. When we first separated, he offered me, as sole provision, a small pension paid by government to each of my father's children, reckoning that pension as *his*.

"In order to raise money on our marriage settlements," says Mrs. Norton, in another place, "my signature was necessary. To obtain my signature, Mr. Norton drew up a contract; he dictated the terms himself, and I signed it. The effect of my signature was that Mr. Norton immediately raised the loan; the effect of

his signature was absolutely *nil*. In 1851, my mother died; she left me (through my brother, to guard it from my husband) a small annuity as an addition to my income. Mr. Norton first endeavored to claim her legacy, and then balanced the first payment under her will by arbitrarily stopping my allowance. I insisted that the allowance was secured by her own signature and other signatures to a formal deed; he defied me to prove it, as by law man and wife were one, and could not contract with each other, and the deed was, therefore, good for nothing.

"I wrote two pamphlets, one on 'The Separation of Mother and Child,' and the other 'A Plain Letter to the Lord Chancellor, by Pierce Stevenson, Esquire.' The 'British and Foreign Quarterly Review' attributed to me a paper I did not write, and never saw: 'On the Grievances of Woman,' and, boldly setting my name in the index as the author, proceeded, in language strange, rapid, and virulent, to abuse the writer, calling her a *she-devil* and a *she-beast*. No less than 142 pages were devoted to the nominal task of opposing the Infant Custody Bill, and in reality of abusing *me*. Not being the author of the paper criticized, I requested my solicitor to prosecute the 'Review' for libel; he informed me that, being a married woman, I could not prosecute of myself, that my husband must prosecute, my husband, who had assailed me with every libel in his power. There could be no prosecution; and I was left to study the grotesque anomaly in law of having my defence made necessary, and made *impossible* by the same person.

*   *   *   *   *   *   *

"My husband, by subpœnaing my publishers to account for my earnings, has taught me that my gift of writing was not meant for the purposes to which I have hitherto applied it; it was not intended that I should 'strive for peace and insure it' through a life of much bitterness and many unjust trials, that I should prove my literary ability by publishing melodies and songs for young girls and women to sing in happier homes than mine, or poetry and prose for them to read in leisure hours, or even please myself by better and more serious attempts to alleviate the rights of the people, or the education and interests of the poor. When Mr. Norton, I say, allowed me to be publicly subpœnaed in court to defend himself by a quibble from a just debt, and subpœnaed my publishers to meet me there, he taught me what my gift of writing was worth; since he would not leave even that source tranquil and free in my destiny, let him have the triumph of being able at once to embitter and to turn its former current. He has made me dream that it was meant for a higher and stronger purpose, that gift which came not from man, but from God; it was meant to enable me to rouse the hearts of others to examine into all the gross injustice of these laws, to ask the 'nation of gallant gentlemen' whose countrywoman I am for once to hear a woman's pleading on the subject, not because I deserve more at their hands than other women. Well I know, on the contrary, how many infinitely better than I, more pious, more patient, and less rash under injury, have watered their couch with tears! My plea to attention is that in pleading for myself I am able to plead for all these others, not that my sufferings or deserts are greater than theirs, but that I combine with the fact of having suffered wrong the power to comment on and explain the cause of that wrong, which few women are able to do. For this, I believe God gave me the power of writing; to this I devote that power. I abjure all other writing till I see those laws altered; I care not what ridicule or abuse may be the result of that declaration. They who cannot bear ridicule and abuse are unfit and unable to advance *any* cause; it is the cause of all the women of England. If I could be justified and happy to-morrow, I would still strive and labor in it; and if I were to die to-morrow, it would still be a satisfaction to me that I had so striven. Meanwhile, my husband has a legal lien (as he has publicly proved) on the copyright of my works; let him claim the copyright of THIS."

Lest our readers should think Mrs. Norton's story impossible, because English laws could not be thus cruelly at war with every sentiment of manliness, as well as justice, we will add the comments and confessions of the " British Reviewer," who doubtless makes out the case as favorable for the laws and the men as truth will permit. He says :—

" In ordinary cases, this non-existence of the wife in respect to the possession of property suggests nothing more than some semi-jocular complaints, some charmingly illogical argumentation, or, at the worst, a little transient soreness on the part of the wife; but there are cases in which it is a source of intolerable aggravation, when the legal non-existence of the wife is as revolting to the reason as to the feelings, when the head and heart alike declare against it. If the wife has the power of earning money, whether by writing books or washing linen, there is no reason, we repeat, why her earnings should not find their way into the common purse, and contribute towards the payment of the rent or the liquidation of the baker's bill; but when there is *no* common purse, when the husband will not support the wife, when she is the victim of his neglect and his cruelty, and he is squandering his earnings perhaps upon drink, perhaps upon some profligate connections, it is surely a case of inconceivable injustice that he should have the power of laying his hands at any time upon the produce of his wife's labor, and declaring that it is legally his. As the English law now stands, a husband may claim from the employer of his discarded wife all the money that she has earned; and the employer is bound to give it to him. Any contract entered into with *her* is mere waste paper; she may earn money for her husband, as his horse or his ox may earn it for him, but not for herself. If she has been permitted to receive her earnings, and has contrived by painful economy and self-denial to save any portion of them, she cannot leave her savings after her death even to her own children; they are absolutely her husband's, and he may take them and give them all to the children of a paramour, or squander them upon the paramour herself. If our creed were the creed of the Mohammedan,

' Which says that woman is but dust,
A soulless toy for tyrants' lust,'

we could not, in this Christian country, and in this nineteenth century, maintain a law in its operation more flagrantly unjust.

" Laws are for the most part made to meet not ordinary, but extraordinary cases. To a vast majority of mankind, it is personally a matter of extreme indifference that the law sends a murderer to the gallows; not one man in a million is murdered in the course of a year. To a vast majority of English wives, it is doubtless a pleasure to cast all that comes to them by inheritance, by gift, or by laborious acquisition into the common

purse. It is their delight to be ' one flesh' with their husband, to have nothing apart from him; but no woman knows, however bright the dawn of her conjugal career, in what storms and convulsions it may close, and the knowledge that under the existing law grievous wrong, for which there is no redress, may be and is committed is sufficient to make every one interested in the application of a legal remedy. It is the boast of Englishmen that women are protected by the law; but every woman's legal protector may violently despoil her of her earnings, and spend them in a drunken revel with the paramour who has taken her place.

" It may be said : ' But redress is open to the woman. She may sue for a divorce ; and, having obtained it, she may profit by her own industry.' Ostensibly, the law promises divorce in such cases, but practically she denies it; divorce is for the rich, not for the poor—for the man, not for the woman. If there were any tribunal to which an injured woman could betake herself and say : ' I come before you with an empty purse, but a full heart. I have no money wherewith to propitiate the divinity of justice, for the law allows me to possess none ; I have only my wrongs to lay at your feet. My husband has deserted me. He is wasting his substance on a strange woman ; but he will not suffer me to eat in peace the bread which I have earned with my own hands. He comes to me in my loneliness, vaunts himself my husband, and takes from me the wages of my industry ; I now ask to be permitted to eat in quietness the bread which I have earned; I ask that, having ceased to be protected by my husband, I may be protected against my husband; I ask to be dissolved of my allegiance to him, to cease to be a part of him, to bear my own name, and to work for myself'—if there were any tribunal, we say, to which an Englishwoman could betake herself, needing only the utterance of such solemn words as these to call forth the prompt response : ' Stand forth and prove it,' then might it be asserted that redress is open to the woman ; but how unlike a tribunal of this kind is the Court of Arches or the House of Lords !*

" We know all that may be said about ' woman's sphere' and ' woman's duties ;' we have the whole formula of expression by rote, and we believe in it as far as it goes. We believe that married women in all conditions of society best contribute to the well-being of the family, and, therefore, to the common purse, by preserving order and harmony at home ; Nature has ordained that this should be their primary duty. Even from the poorest homes we are sorry to see the wife absent, though she be earning money in the factory or in the field ; but the better the education, the higher the faculties of women, the better they will perform these primary duties, and it is not because at some period of their lives they have husbands to tend and children to nurse that we are to take no account of the

* It will be understood that, although our remarks in this place relate more especially to the appeals of a wife against the ill-treatment of a husband, we plead generally in favor of the institution of cheaper and more accessible tribunals for the adjudication of cases of conjugal wrong. As the English law now stands, the dissolution of the matrimonial contract is practicable, but only under certain conditions. The first is that the party seeking it shall be a man ; the second, that he shall be a rich one. It is this reproach which we desire to see removed.

relation they bear to all the rest of the world. There would be more good wives and good mothers if women were better trained to take a part in the active business of life, if they were educated as though they might be neither wives nor mothers, but independent members of society, with work of their own to do seriously, earnestly, and with all their might.

"This theory of the non-existence of women pursues its victims from the school-room to the grave. Trained from the first to be dependent upon men, they pass through different stages of dependence, and at the last find that they cannot bequeath to another man the ring on their finger, which they may have worn from their earliest girlhood, or the Bible in which they first learnt to spell; to attain and preserve a condition of independence, it is necessary that they should abide in a state of singleness, which is more or less a state of reproach. Single women are legally capable of indèpendent action; but they are seldom or never educated for it. It cannot be said that they are educated for the proper discharge of the duties of wife and mother; but they are educated for the non-existence which that condition involves, and it is often the perception of this which drives women into matrimony without any assurance, sometimes scarcely even with a hope of domestic happiness. What are they to do? If they continue in their singleness, having been educated for non-existence, they are incapable of acting for themselves; they are fit, indeed, only to be absorbed.

"And thus it is that this legal fiction of the non-existence of married women sits as a curse upon married and single alike; it taints from first to last the stream of their life, and Heaven only knows what a crop of misery is the rank result. As society is at present constituted, women are educated not to do, but to suffer. In some classes, self-support is a reproach, not only to the self-sustaining worker herself, but to all who belong to her. Society decrees that she shall be non-existent, that she shall depend, perhaps, upon charity grudgingly bestowed, that she shall live in a state of penurious idleness, useless, querulous, unhappy,

' And from red morning to the dewy fall,
Folding her listless hands, pursue no aim at all,'

but outwardly be what the world is pleased to call a lady; in other classes, the curse works more grievously. Our peasant girls are not trained for labor; society does not encourage them to labor. They reach the dangerous age of incipient womanhood ill-educated, unskilled, aimless, useless, fit indeed for nothing, and, if fit, seeing nothing to employ their fitness. They are not trained to make good wives; they are not trained to make good servants; they are not trained for independent employment, and there is little independent employment for them if they were. There is nothing sadder in human life than this; and there is no greater question than that of woman's work. It cannot be entered upon at the end of such an article as this. Please God, we shall, ere long, devote a paper to it; what we have now written is a fitting introduction to the larger theme."

WHAT IS NEEDED IN AMERICA.

THANKS to the spirit of Christian freedom, women in our land are favored above the sex in any other nation. The absurd and degrading customs or usages of the common law, and the partial and, therefore, unjust

statutes of kings, brought by our forefathers from England, are fast passing away, or being rendered nugatory by new enactments, more in accordance with reason and righteousness. The Homestead laws, and the security given that the property of the married woman shall remain in her own possession, are great safeguards of domestic comfort. The efforts made to open new channels of industry and profitable professions for those women who have to support themselves are deserving of much praise; but one great act of public justice yet remains undone. Government, national or State, has never yet provided suitably for the education of women. Girls, as well as boys, have the advantages of the free school system; but no public provision has been made, no college or university endowed where young women may have similar advantages of instruction now open to young men in every State of the Union. True, there are very many private institutions devoted to female education; but these are defective for the want of a higher model than private enterprise has yet given. Of course, the better woman is educated the higher she will be estimated, and the more careful will legislators be to frame laws just and equitable which are to guard her happiness and protect her rights; men will thus improve their own *hearts* and elevate their views. The standard of woman is the moral thermometer of the nation.

Holding these sentiments, our "Book" has never swerved from its straight forward course of aiding women to improve themselves, while it has aimed to arouse public sentiment to help onward this improvement. For this, we keep domestic virtues and home duties before our readers, we give patterns and directions for feminine employments, we show the benefits of female education, and for this we have *twice* brought before Congress our petition for aid; and now we come the *third* time, intending to persevere till some noble champion arises to advocate the cause and win the victory:—

MEMORIAL
To the Honorable Senate and House of Representatives in Congress assembled.

Whereas, there are now more than *two millions* of children in our country destitute of the opportunity of education, demanding *sixty thousand* teachers to supply them at the same ratio as is common in our best educated sections, your memorialists beg to call your attention to these considerations:—

1. That, while the great West, California, and the wide ocean invite young men to wealth and adventure, and while the labors of the school-room offer so little recompense or honor, the sixty thousand teachers needed cannot be obtained from their ranks; and, therefore, the young women of our country must become teachers of the common schools, or these must be given up.

2. That the reports of common school education show that women are the *best* teachers, and that in those States where education is most prosperous the average of female teachers to that of the other sex is as *five* to one.

3. That while, as a general rule, women are not expected to support families, nor to pay from their earnings to support the State, they can afford to teach for a smaller compensation than men; and, therefore, funds bestowed to educate female teachers gratuitously will in the end prove a measure of *economy*, and at the same

time will tend to render education more universal and more elevated by securing the best class of teachers at a moderate expense.

4. That those most willing to teach are chiefly found in the industrial class, which as yet has received few favors from National or State Legislatures.

5. That providing such gratuitous advantages for women to act as educators will secure a vast number of well-educated teachers, not by instituting a class of *celibates*, but by employing the unoccupied energies of thousands of young women from their school-days to the period of marriage, while, at the same time, they will thus be qualifying themselves for the most arduous duties of their future domestic relations.

In view of these considerations, your memorialists petition that THREE OR FOUR MILLIONS OF ACRES OF THE PUBLIC NATIONAL DOMAINS be set apart to endow at least one *Normal School* in every State for the gratuitous education of female teachers.

These institutions could be modelled and managed in each State to suit the wishes of its inhabitants; and young ladies of every section would be trained as instructors for children in their own vicinity; this would be found of immense advantage in the States where schools have hitherto been neglected.

While such vast portions of the national domains are devoted to national aggrandizements or physical advantages, we humbly petition that a moderate share may be conferred to benefit the daughters of our Republic, and thus at the same time to provide educators for two millions of its most neglected children.

MOUNT VERNON.—The ladies of the Mount Vernon Central Committee of the Union are deeply gratified in being able to "report" to the readers of the "Lady's Book" the interest which is being created in behalf of their "patriotic objects," and the very encouraging prospects which now cheer the "Mount Vernon Association of the Union." Not only have individuals in every portion of our country, from New England to Louisiana, promised to commence exertions, and form "associations" for the collection of "money" to aid in raising the requisite sum to purchase and improve that spot *so sacred to all;* but the second city of the United States, Philadelphia, has come forth in a manner which promises the *most important results.* No other city has so many "revolutionary associations," or is so intimately connected with the military and civil career of the "*Father* of our Country !" It seemed appropriate then that her patriots, with the spirit of '76 still animating their hearts, should announce their intention of uniting with the Mount Vernon Association, and assisting in such a beautiful "tribute" to his "memory" *in the Hall, and on the same spot* which he has immortalized! On the 19th of October, therefore, a number of ladies and gentlemen assembled in the Hall of the Declaration of Independence, and, after a fervent prayer by Rev. Paul Goddard, and an eloquent oration by Mr. Brewster, formed the State Committee for Pennsylvania and an "association" for the city, and, with the portraits of General and Mrs. Washington before them, and of the noble "Signers" around—sent from them "woman's" earnest appeal that Philadelphia would do *her* duty in this work of patriotic gratitude."

In order to place the subject more fully before their community, a "meeting" was held on the 25th of October in Sansom Street Hall (generously given for their use), where Mr. J. C. Montgomery presided; and the Hon. J.

R. Chandler and Judge Penrose eloquently advocated their cause to a gratified audience. The hall was exquisitely decorated with "flags," shrubbery, and flowers. Back of the speaker, an eagle held two flags, which was gracefully festooned over "portraits" of General and Mrs. Washington, while the "flag" of his generous "ally," France, waved to his right; over the "speaker" was an arch of green moss, with *Mount Vernon* in *white rosebuds,* while its sides were pillars of evergreens and flowers! A fine band entranced the listeners with our inspiring "national airs," winding up with the "Marsellaise" in compliment to a French society in New York, which had appealed to the French in the "United States" to raise a "donation" for Washington's home and grave! Truly, the ladies of Philadelphia have set an "example," which, we trust, will not be lost upon their sisters everywhere, but especially of Boston, New York, Baltimore, Cincinnati, St. Louis, and New Orleans!

We are happy to find that the chivalric sons of Virginia are evincing a patriotism equal to that of her daughters! On the 19th of October, the Henrico Light Dragoons celebrated the anniversary of the battle of Yorktown by a "tournament, held for the benefit of the Mount Vernon Association." An elegant oration, music, beauty, the military, with gay knights, and their gallant contest, made it a fairy-like scene, resulting, however, in something more than passing enjoyment; for *seven hundred dollars* were presented by the dragoons as their offering to the *tomb* of Washington!

In consequence of a regulation having been adopted by the Central Committee that all "donations" of $50 and upwards, should be publicly acknowledged, the ladies of the Mount Vernon Association take this occasion to return their grateful thanks for the following patriotic contributions:—

Mrs. M. H. Drayton, Philadelphia,		$100
Miss Ann Leamy,	"	50
Mrs. E. H. L. Stout,	"	50
Mrs. H. L. Hodge,	"	50
Mr. Pierce Butler,	"	50

OUR LIST.—The Editors of the "Lady's Book" acknowledge the receipt of the following subscriptions to the Mount Vernon fund :—

Mrs. Julia A. Cade, Anthony's Shoals, Elbert Co., Geo.					$1
Miss Sallie Cade,	"	"	"	"	1
Miss Mary E. Cade,	"	"	"	"	1
Miss Victoria D. Cade,	"	"	"	"	1
Mrs. Mary A. Starke	"	"	"	"	1
Miss Antoinette Turman,	"	"	"	"	1
J. C. Y. Watkins,	"	"	"	"	1
A Friend, Dubuque, Iowa,					1
" " "					1

To CORRESPONDENTS.—The following articles are accepted: "Forget"—"Enigmas"—"Low-Voiced Ella"—"To A. C."—"Heart-Blighting"—"June"—"To Emma"—"Ancestry"—and "A Child's Opinion."

The following are declined: "The Past and the Future" —"The Memory of the Past"—"Hope"—"My Village Home"—"The Beggar Woman"—"A Fact"—"Letter to the Editors"—"The Eastern Bird"—"Autobiography" (a very sweet poem for a little girl to write, but more suited to a juvenile work than to the "Lady's Book")—"A False Alarm"—"Scenes and Sentiments" —"A Good Joke"—"Temperance"—"Tobacco"—and "The Land I Love."

COLLEGE TEMPLE, NEWNAN, GEORGIA.

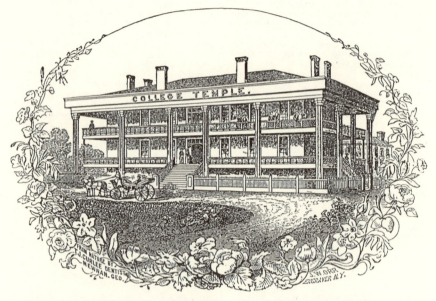

THE spirit of the age exhibits a manifest tendency, among other laudable phases, towards preparing, for the education of woman, institutions. of learning of a grade more nearly allied to our best male colleges. These schools are springing up in every part of the Union. In the South they are becoming numerous, especially in Georgia, which State is far in advance of her sisters in this respect—the number of her chartered female colleges being about twenty-five, and most of them well attended.

Some of these are under the patronage of the different denominations of Christians. Others have been built and furnished by donations from various sources, and one is under the tutelage of the Grand Lodge of Freemasons; but "College Temple," located at Newnan, Georgia, is the result of the individual enterprise and benevolence of M. P. KELLOGG, M. A., President and sole

proprietor, who built and furnished it at his own expense.

No pecuniary considerations, no ambitious motives, no partisan strifes, no sectarian influences prompted the founder in establishing this institution of learning; but it was to elevate woman, to prepare her for the able discharge of her numerous and arduous duties in the domestic circle and society, to qualify her for wielding the pen in defence of right, morals, and the Christian religion, that he undertook the laborious and expensive project of building and supporting a first class female college.

A beautiful building on the left, which. does not appear in the engraving, contains rooms for Music, Preparatory Department, and Philosophical and Chemical Laboratory, well supplied with the best of instruments.

To secure the most rigid mental discipline in

each' pupil no specified time is assigned for a
young lady to complete her education at College
Temple, but she is allowed to advance as rapidly
as her mental and physical abilities will permit;
and the degree, "*Magistra in Artibus*," is conferred upon her, accompanied with a diploma in
Latin, whenever she shall have thoroughly
mastered the extensive course of study adopted
by this institution, and manifests a ripeness of
scholarship sufficient to entitle her to such distinction.

It is not the number of her pupils, but the
ability of her graduates, that forms the just pride
of the friends of College Temple.

To aid the Senior Class in forming a correct
style in composition, they publish semi-annually
"The Fly-Leaf," composed by themselves and
previous graduates of the Temple. This quarto
of sixteen pages has received much praise from
its friends, and the press in many places. This
applause speaks more for the educational facili-
es of College Temple than a multitude of
nominal graduates.

The college has been in successful operation
three years. It now numbers one hundred
pupils in attendance, and six graduates. The
founder is determined to make this a. model
school for *educating* young ladies. The motto
of her seal is "FEMINA, DIVINUM DONUM,"
and as such woman is here sought to be trained
in a physical, mental, and spiritual harmony
worthy of her origin.

EDITORS' TABLE.

" SHE shall be called woman because she was taken out of man."—*Bible.*

In our October number of last year we alluded to the habit of many writers who use the term *female* as a substitute or synonym for *woman ;* and we endeavored to show the impropriety of this mode of expression. We were gratified to find our suggestions well received, many of the popular journals fully indorsing our views. Still, there may be some (*one* individual at least) who take the Bible record, " God created man male and female," to mean that the *latter* is the proper cognomen. If such caviller would read the second chapter of Genesis, he would find the true name of the feminine human being is given in our motto.

The Bible is remarkably clear on this point, as we might expect the Word of God would be—carefully distinguishing the human from the animal female. The name of WOMAN being, by divine inspiration, given, she is always thus designated throughout the sacred books, excepting when the distinction of sex in contrast with man is in question. In the whole Bible the term *female,* applied to woman, is only used in eleven places, and each time in contradistinction to man as male. We will particularize the passages.

1. *Male* and *female* created he them.—*Genesis* i. 27.
2. This is the law for her that hath borne a *male* or a *female.*—*Lev.* xxvii. 4.
3. If it be a *female,* thy estimation, &c.—*Lev.* xxvii. 5.
4. For the *female* ten shekels.—*Lev.* xxvii. 5.
5. For a *female* a month old, &c.—*Lev.* xxvii. 6.
6. Both *male* and *female* shall ye shut out.—*Num.* v. 3.
7. The similitude of any figure, the likeness of *male* or *female.*—*Deut.* iv. 16.
8. There shall not be a *male* or *female,* &c.—*Deut.* vii. 14.
9. God made them *male* and *female.*—*Matt.* xix. 4.
10. God made them *male* and *female.*—*Mark* x. vi.
11. In Christ there is neither *male* nor *female,* &c.—*Gal.* iii. 28.

The reader will see at once that these instances are to designate the sex; not to express the name which, in the Hebrew, was always significant of character. If we use the feminine we must also use the masculine term of sex as a name, because in every instance the inspired writers do this, never putting *man* in contradistinction to *female,* which, if it had been done, would have inferred the inferiority of the latter, as bearing the animal designation. To make this matter more clear, let the term *female* instead of *woman* be substituted in the following passages of Scripture :—

1. I will put enmity between thee and the *female.*—*Gen.* iii. 15.
2. *Man* that is born of a *female,* &c.—*Job* xiv. 1.
3. Who can find a virtuous *female,* &c.—*Proverbs* xxxi. 16.
4. Oh, *female !* great is thy faith, &c.—*Matt.* xv. 28.
5. And he (Jesus) turned to the *female,* and said unto Simon, Seest thou this *female,* &c.—*Luke* vii. 44.
6. Of the chief *females* not a few.—*Acts* xvii. 4.
7. Help those *females,* &c.—*Phil.* iv. 3.
8. God sent forth his son, made of a woman.—*Gal.* iv. 4.

Who would dare substitute the term referring only to the animal in the sex, where the hallowed humanity of our divine Redeemer is disclosed? Thus we have proved that the word of God is true to the feminine nature, giving its testimony to the honored name of *woman,* which is repeated, in the singular or plural, over *two hundred* times in the Holy Book. If any man doubts these statements, let him search the Bible. We assure him that the perfect appropriateness of its language will be a profitable study.

While divine precedent thus establishes *woman* as the true name of the human feminine, let us see what the highest authorities among men have sanctioned. The poets are the best expounders of language, because they must use the most appropriate words in their truest, which is their noblest signification, in order to exalt, beautify, and perfect their themes of song. Let us take a few examples, changing the style in regard to *woman* to the vulgar mode of *female.*

1. I grant I am a *female ;* but, withal, a *female* that Lord Brutus took to wife.

I grant I am a *female ;* but, withal a *female* well reputed—Cato's daughter.
Shakspeare's Julius Cæsar.

2. For none of *female* born shall harm Macbeth.
Hamlet.

3. To whom thus Adam fervently replied : " Oh, *female !* best are all things as the will of God ordains them."
Milton's Paradise Lost.

4. Oh, *female !* in our hours of ease,
Uncertain, coy, and hard to please ;
When pain and sickness wring the brow,
A ministering angel thou.   *Scott's Marmion.*

5. *Female !* blest partner of our joys and woes.
Sand's Yamoyden.

6. Ah, *female !* in this world of ours
What gift can be compared to thee?
George P. Morris.

7.   Earlier than I know,
Immersed in rich foreshadowings of the world,
I loved the *female.*   *Tennyson's Princess.*

The absurdity of these substitutes is at once apparent, and the beauty as well as truthfulness of the word *woman* in place of *female* must be acknowledged. But there is yet another and clearer demonstration. If we are to be influenced by the letter of that particular verse of Scripture—" God made them male and female"—for the term to define the one sex, we are equally bound to apply this rule to the other. Let us see how this would influence our classics.

He was a *male,* take him for all in all,
We shall not look upon his like again.
Hamlet.

Oh ! but *male,* proud *male,*
Dressed in a little brief authority, &c.
Measure for Measure.

An honest *male*'s the noblest work of God.   *Pope.*

The lamps shone o'er fair *females* and brave *males.*
Byron.

Male is but half without *female.*   *Festus.*

Oh, *male!* while in thy early years
How prodigal of time!   *Burns.*

Then, if we come to the plain prose of common life, we should see accounts of the *males* who had robbed the mail being arrested; of a drunken *male* taken up for insulting a *female;* of an honest *male* returning some valuable article he had found; of a noble *male* who had given largely for the relief of the poor, distressed *males* thrown out of employment, &c. Should this phraseology be adopted by journalists, and the term *male* for man be used as *female* now is for woman, the ridiculous impropriety of the language would be seen at once. It would be a good subject for satire. We have looked chiefly at the serious results of the misnomer. One is that it degrades the woman, and thus deprives her of the sympathy and respect of men. Names are significant, and while woman or lady indicates that the being is a *female,* the latter term does not certainly include woman, and rarely, if ever, excites the idea of a lady. We naturally think of females as women of the lower if not lowest order. Is not this one of the chief reasons why our brave American men seem to have become careless of the championship of women, and leave them to go down in the foundered ship, or to perish in the burning boat? In commenting on that dreadful catastrophe, the destruction of the Camden ferry-boat, the editor of one of our leading papers, describing the awful scene, which he did with great power, boldly condemned the selfishness of the "strong men who only sought their own safety, and left the helpless *females* to their fate." *Females,* indeed! They might have been sheep.

Why not shout the rallying cry of Saint Paul— "Help those women!"—and you would awaken the best feelings of man's nature, the sympathies of his heart, the honor of his manhood, the sensibilities of his Christian faith. History has many noble examples of the romantic chivalry, the self-sacrificing generosity of strong, brave men who have laid down their lives, not in the heat of battle, but calmly awaited death on the sinking wreck to insure the safety of women; but never for animals.

Editors are not, however, the only writers in fault. Our swarming works of fiction are nearly all infected by this low taste of using *female* for woman or lady. The word occurs so often in some of these books that it alone would give vulgarity to the style. Many, perhaps most of these works, are written by women whose lack of self-respect in this is the more remarkable, except we consider that the authors are not aware of the effect of their style. If they would study the best writers more, and exercise their own pens less, our literature would be much benefited. Prescott's histories are models of language, and the term *female* for *woman* is never used by him; nor by our best poets.

There is still another source of this popular corruption of words which we are considering, more important and more to be lamented than any we have mentioned. We allude to the almost universal habit of the clergy of our country to speak of woman only as a *female.* Thus, the terms "*female* hearers," "*female* converts," "*females* of the Church," "*female* Bible societies," "*female* associations," &c. &c., are constantly enunciated from the pulpit; while rarely is the beautiful Bible name of woman pronounced by a preacher of the Gospel, except it happens to occur in his text. Might not a Brahmin, if he could hear from our preachers this oft-repeated word "female,' applying equally to all of that sex which brings young, from the elephant to the em-

met, draw the conclusion that Christian ministers held the Eastern doctrine of woman's inferiority, even that she had no soul! Has an animal a soul? Is it not strange that the order of men, whose province it is to refine, purify, and exalt language as well as morals, should adopt the lowest term of designation for the largest portion of their friends and followers? Christ did not speak thus. The apostles did not so teach. The terms they used were WOMAN and LADY. These are the Scriptural mode of defining man's companion, not for earth only, but for an immortality of glory. Would it not be as easy to say, "women of the church," "women of the congregation," "women who are converts," "ladies' Bible societies," "ladies' associations," &c., as to use the present vulgar style? We would humbly present this question to the clergy of the United States. They might, by their influence and example, soon correct the present improper, inelegant, and unscriptural modes of expression.[*] Nor is this a matter of small importance. Language is a powerful instrument for good or evil. Words are things of mighty influence. The manner of speech indicates the habit of mind. If we seek to improve our taste, we must be careful that our expressions are appropriate and refined. A vulgar word will often destroy the good effect of a moral lecture; while "words fitly spoken are like apples of gold in pictures of silver."

---

[*] The custom has become prevalent of styling "colleges for women" "female colleges," "female institutions," &c. This is quite vulgar, if not improper. A school cannot be *female,* though it may be for that sex. Why not give the true name—"school for young women," "college for young ladies," &c.?

SOUTHERN LITERARY MESSENGER.

A MAGAZINE DEVOTED TO LITERATURE, SCIENCE AND ART.

RICHMOND, MAY, 1859.

INTELLECTUAL CULTURE OF WOMAN.*

The Delight of Knowledge—Desire for Knowledge Universal—Different Knowledge Desired, according to Mental Cultivation and Natural Aptitude—The Metaphysician—The Lover of Natural Science—Retailer of Scandal—Office of Education in awakening Proper Curiosity—Superiority in this Respect of Educated Women—Results of this Superiority—What Conduct it Should Produce—Haughtiness to Inferiors—Gratitude and Obedience to Parents—Ordinary Household Duties—Another Office of Education—Empiricism and Quackery—Political, Social and Religious Quacks—Noted Examples—The South Sea Bubble—Joe Smith—Relics—Strolling Pedlars—Foreign Dignitaries—Humbug—The Triumph of Right—Empiricism and Science Contrasted—Advantages of Thorough Instruction: to One's Self, to the Family, to Society, and to the State—Authors Recommended—Monod's Mission of Woman—Conduct at Home, in the Circle of Families, in Society—Society Described—Slavery—Duty of Educated Women to master the Subject, and to Educate a Proper Sentiment Concerning It—One of Her Duties to the State—The Highest Knowledge—Conclusion.

Augustin Thierry, a man distinguished for intellectual power and indefatigable research, who lost his sight in making the investigations the results of which he has recorded in his history of the Norman Conquest, at the close of his long and brilliant career, writes thus of his employment:

"If, as I delight in thinking, the interest of science is counted in the number of great national interests, I have given my country all that the soldier, mutilated on the field of battle, gives her. Whatever may be the fate of my labours, this example, I hope, will not be lost. I would wish it to serve to combat the species of moral weakness which is the disease of our present generation; to bring back into the straight road of life some of those enervated souls that complain of wanting faith, that know not what to do, and seek everywhere, without finding it, an object of worship and admiration. Why say, with so much bitterness, that in the world, constituted as it is, there is no air for all lungs, no employment for all minds? Is not calm and serious study there? and is not that a refuge, a hope, a field within the reach of all of us? With it evil days are passed over without their weight being felt; every one can make his own destiny; every one employ his life nobly. This is what I have done, and would do again if I had to recom-

---

* An Address delivered before the Hollins Female Institute, at the Commencement, on the 6th April, 1859. By ALEXANDER H. SANDS, of Richmond, Va. Published by request of the Faculty and Board of Trustees of the Institute.

VOL. XXVIII—21

mence my career; I would choose that which has brought me where I am. Blind, and suffering without hope and almost without intermission, I may give this testimony, which from me will not appear suspicious; there is something in the world better than sensual enjoyments, better than fortune, better than health itself; it is devotion to science."

I might multiply examples of similar character, in illustration of the hold that the desire for knowledge obtains over the mind which has once experienced its delightful and soul-stirring effects. This desire is universal. It is common alike to the swarthy African and the red men of America; to the cold, calculating and conservative Englishman, to the mercurial Frenchman and the keen-sighted, sharp-witted Yankee; to the refined and educated and polished scholar, and to the clumsy and uncultivated clown. In a term of life now nearing middle age, I have never known a man who had not a thirst for knowledge—to a greater or less degree. It may have been thirst for wrong knowledge; for knowledge not of the right sort and of the right things. It may have been confined within narrow limits and called forth by unworthy or trivial objects. Every where, at all times, among all peoples you will find this principle at work. For knowledge man digs into the *strata* of the earth to find there the record written by the Almighty's hand of the earth's history; for knowledge, he scales the summit of the skies and marks with wonder and delight the movements of the spheres; for knowledge, stretching forth with expectant look, he gazes into the opening vistas of *the future*, and with equal zeal grasps at and commits to imperishable record the transactions and doings and dealings of the present and the past. At one time, he traverses wide and perilous seas to hold converse with the rude and unlettered peasantry of some distant country, that he may record their modes of social being—what they think and what they do; at another, with almost infinite danger, he perils his life to fathom the mysteries of State secrets and to unfold State intrigue. At one time, he tells us

of the accomplishments of mind, at another he witnesses and records the varying changes of matter. At one time, with immense labour and toil, he masters the mysteries of an unknown and barbarous tongue; at another, he is clothing in living forms of beauty and eloquence the emotions of the passing hour, that they may be caught by sympathetic hearts and "echoed down the corridors of Time."

Now we find him engaged in minute and laborious effort, spending his weeks and months and years in the solitude of his study in the solution of some difficult problem, and crying out at its successful close, almost with a mad joy, "I HAVE FOUND IT! I HAVE FOUND IT!" And then, with toilsome footstep we follow him amid the varied realms of Nature's boundless limits as he gathers from her caverns, from her hills and valleys and streams, from her ocean-depths and her mountain summits, fact after fact to enrich his treasury, and discovery after discovery awakening the pleasurable emotion of knowing!

While the desire is thus universal, it is, by no means, equally diffused or called forth alike by the objects of interest around and within us. One thirsts for knowledge with an irrepressible longing. He desires truth for its own sake, and would willingly forego enjoyments of no common type to realize and reap the golden fruition. It matters not to him whether the great world without shall repeat his name with honour, or allow it to sleep in obscurity forever. Another pursues it, for the gain it brings, for the crown it bestows, for the reward it proffers. A third, stimulated by a languid desire to know, would willingly resign the ripe enjoyment of knowing, if he could thus secure exemption from the toil of accumulating, or the trouble of safely keeping it when already acquired.

The desire will be ample or contracted; will be various and useful, or narrow and mean, according to the measure of the mind's original capacity and its aptitude for acquiring, and its opportunities for enlargement.

Take a familiar illustration, drawn from our physical constitution.

We have been so formed by our Creator that every exertion of power brings its enjoyment. We cannot stretch out an arm, if it be in a healthful condition, without experiencing a pleasurable emotion. The senses are so many channels of gratification and delight. For sight, for hearing, for feeling, for the senses of smell and taste, there are appropriate objects and excitants, communicating in the contact at times inexpressible pleasure. We all remember the beautifully apt remark of Paley, in evidence of the Divine beneficence. "If He had wished our misery, He might have made sure of His purpose by forming our senses to be so many pains and sores to us, as they are now instruments of gratification and enjoyment; or by placing us amid objects so ill suited to our perceptions as to have continually offended us, instead of ministering to our refreshment and delight. He might have made, for example, everything we tasted, *bitter;* every thing we saw, *loathsome;* every thing we touched, *a sting;* every smell, *a stench;* and every sound, *a discord.*"

Now, if we take from any part of our physical frame any of its original functions, either in whole or in part, we shall, to that extent, rob ourselves of the enjoyment we should thence derive. If an arm be maimed, or an eye bleared, or an ear deaf, so far as we could have experienced pleasurable emotions from these, so far will we be deprived by the defect of the sum total of enjoyment. This will be the more apparent, if we shall select some power of the body which has not its counterpart. Take from us *the sense of hearing altogether,* and we shall lose all the emotional excitement occasioned by the harmony of sound. The ravishing notes of Mozart and Handel, the liquid music of the summer's waterfall, the majestic roar of the Niagara, even the crash of the terrible voice of the lightning will fail to excite on the one hand *delight,* and on the other that sense of positive enjoyment derived from the highest sublimity of terror. In some sort, the mind which has not compassed

a particular department of thought, which has not "realized" the entireness of a complete area of sentiment, is deprived of one of its faculties, and has excluded itself from sources of delight open to the mind of him who has conversed familiarly with such topics and fully mastered them. Here is one, who ignores altogether the department of metaphysical research. He has learned to echo the stale and absurd reproaches of the superficial and arrogant empiric, who denies that the world of mind needs to be explored, and who ridicules all attempts on the part of mental philosophers to fathom its depths. To such a one the sublime speculations of Kant and Cousin, the nervous, strong and practical good sense of Reid, and the severely logical acumen of Sir William Hamilton, afford neither entertainment nor delight. He prefers to follow some explorer into the realm of physical being, to number the penfeathers of the antennæ of an insect, or to analyze the parts of the most insignificant animalcule. Another stalks through life utterly unconscious of the world of matter around him. He delights in knowing what in himself is worth knowing. He finds there enough, he says, of nobler type to engage his thought, and until he has explored the depths of his own consciousness, he is unwilling to take the time to learn the comparatively unimportant matters of physical nature. A third has no higher employment for the principle of curiosity which nature has implanted in him, than the amusement of the passing moment: and the incidents of daily life, its little scandal, its trivial conversation, the news of the hour, afford him sufficient mental food, and gratify to the full his intellectual appetite. The whole realms of fancy and imagination—of the highest art and of the loftiest aspirings, are to him an utter blank; and for all practical purposes, he is living as if not endued with the capacity to understand, appreciate and enjoy them. Alter now if you will the modes of life of the three. Convert the lover of natural science into the severe student of the laws of the mind. Transform the daily retailer of the latest news in the market-place, or behind the counter, or on the farm, into an intelligent and wise observer of the wonderful operations of Nature, and you at once introduce them into a new world of emotion and delight. So to speak, they have become by the transformation changed into new beings; they have had added to them the possession of other faculties, whose existence they had not suspected or imagined before. The man feels—he knows—new things; and the possession of this new knowledge creates new and fresh sympathies; and he realizes the enjoyment of putting forth hitherto undiscovered or unused powers!

Now it is one of the offices of education to kindle and keep alive the entire intellectual man—to open to him the widest fields of intellectual research and emotional sympathy—and in proportion as we have secured the true advantages of such acquaintance, in proportion as the area of science or art we have explored is enlarged; in proportion to our natural or cultivated capacity to understand aright the objects of thought or of feeling with which we are brought into contact, in *that* proportion are our opportunities for intellectual exercise increased, and in *that* proportion is the enjoyment of pursuing such objects enhanced. We shall find then that the truest and best education is that which capacitates us for the amplest enjoyment and secures for us the ripest attainments, is that which awakens into active life all the faculties and powers of our minds, and suggests for them all appropriate exercise and employment. To be, in other words, a mere lawyer or a mere doctor, a mere professor of languages and nothing else, suggests to us the idea of but half-manhood-ness, and the mind instinctively revolts from it. To be a mere seamstress or landlady, a mere teacher of music or a mere writer of poems or of novels, suggests the same idea of incompleteness, and the mind instinctively recoils. We must have for complete happiness something more than these would indicate the possession of.

If properly instructed, I remark, the educated lady has had a proper and in-

telligent curiosity awakened—she desires to know proper things, and to know them thoroughly.

In this she has an inestimable advantage over her less favoured sisters, whose views are contracted within narrower limits, and who have not cultivated or enlightened sympathies with much that brings out and develops, in highest and noblest form, the capacities of the mind and heart.

But this superiority does not beget haughtiness of demeanor or a neglect of so-called inferiors : least of all does it inspire contempt for any living being? The school-girl who imagines that an acquaintance with the classics or facility in music or in painting exempts her from the obligation to respect her acquaintance, and allows her to ignore and neglect altogether the companionship of her neighbours, has much indeed to learn not only of the *humility*, but of the enjoyment of true learning? Depend upon it, my young friends, it is no mark of superior attainments, in any department of study or school of science, to despise any of the beings God has made.

I need not, I am sure, add to this, that gratitude and obedience to your parents will characterize the truly educated lady. If fortune has not favoured them—if they be rough-handed and toilworn—if they cannot enter into discussions of topics most interesting to the scholar and the woman of ripe attainments, the educated lady will gently, carefully hide the defect, and remedy, as she may, their want of information by imparting to them what she knows in an unpretending and unassuming way.

Into what infinity of contempt does the daughter sink, who, by the *toil of an honest* and rough-handed father, has secured the advantages of ripe training and requites the service with contumely or neglect. Ask the universal opinion entertained of such an one—whether by young or old, rich or poor, male or female, and the kindling glance of indignation in every eye, and the prompt response from every lip, condemn almost beyond reprieve, the crime of ingratitude and folly.

No! no! Young ladies who have been trained at school, who have been well educated, know that it is their first and main duty to love those who, by honest labour and with many prayers, have aided them in their efforts to acquire knowledge. This sentiment should not expend itself as mere sentiment. It must live in the life—it must speak alike in the tongue and by the act. " The old folks at home" are to have the earnest and undivided sympathies of the child of their love; and even though the tuition be harsh, and at times their conduct be rude and uncouth, a heart that has learned the lesson of love aright and a head well instructed, will be led into proper deference and respect.

Again: Least of all should this instruction be imagined to exempt one from the ordinary routine of household duty. It begets a contempt for learning when it contents itself with moping over books and dreaming of sentiment, when the objects and occasions of duty are all around us neglected and unimproved. We shall find, (I doubt not,) ample employment for the largest wisdom and for the utmost stretch of capacity even in managing the ordinary occasions of difficulty as they arise.

But I must return from this digression. *Another office of education is to deliver one from empiricism.* By empiricism I mean quackery of every kind. There is an empiricism in science, in morals, in religion, in politics as in medicine. There are " universal nostrum " men, who go about in search of victims to their impostures; who forego no effort to make disciples of the unwary; and who would be willing, in order to compass their favourite object, to sacrifice not only the fortunes, but the lives of individuals, and to peril the happiness and welfare of entire communities. In looking over the wrecks of fortune and of honour scattered as monitors along the reefs of time, we shall find not a few who have been stranded on this rock; not a few who started in their career with high hopes and unfaltering purpose, who fell victim to some mad delusion, the vagary of some vile and vicious impostor or

madman. Human history is crowded with examples—in the moral and mental—in the political and commercial worlds! And we shall do well to hear and to heed its voice pleading for suffering humanity. In politics the wild extravagancies of the first and second, and third French Revolutions are recent and convincing instances ; in commerce, the Southsea bubble and its almost innumerable copies on a diminished scale, which while not equalling it in the extent and enormity of the conception, have vied with it in the mischief and injury they have effected ; and time would fail me to tell the numberless examples of empirics in morals and religion whose Babel voices have assaulted the heavens from the day on which heavenly harpers hymned the praises of the Infant Redeemer until the present. Look to the collection of sects and divisions of opinion ; to the leaders and followers of leaders who have been named in the religious world, gathered into some modern Encyclopedia of Religious Knowledge; and you will confess that surely here, on the highest and most momentous interests, there has been the amplest display of folly, and that the magnitude of the topic has but served to allure into its domain empiricism and quackery.

In an entertaining article contributed to one of Chambers' Papers for the People, I find the following:

" Superstition has in nothing more plainly manifested at once its foundation in ignorance and its mighty hold upon the popular mind than in the extraordinary variety of *relics* which have claimed and received the homage and adoration of mankind. It is but a few weeks since at Stonyhurst College, in Lancashire, we were shown a piece of the real wood of the Cross; and the following are some mentioned in Brady's 'Clavis,' which either have received, or are receiving the wondering adorations of folly :

" *A finger* of St. Andrew.

A finger of St. John the Baptist.

The thumb of St. Thomas.

The hem of our Lord's garment which cured the dsieased woman.

The seamless coat.

77

A tear which our Lord shed over Lazarus. It was preserved by an angel, who gave it in a vial to Mary Magdalene.

Two handkerchiefs, on which are impressions of our Saviour's face ; the one sent by our Lord himself as a present to Agbarus, Prince of Edessa ; the other given at the time of his crucifixion to a holy woman named Veronica.

The rod of Moses with which he performed his miracles.

A lock of hair of Mary Magdalene's.

A hem of Joseph's garment.

A feather of the Angel Gabriel.

A finger of a cherub.

The waterpots used at the marriage in Galilee.

The slippers of the antediluvian Enoch.

The face of a seraph, with only part of the nose.

The snout of a seraph, thought to have belonged to the preceding.

The coal that broiled St. Lawrence.

The square buckler, lined with red velvet, and the short sword of St. Michael.

A vial of the sweat of St. Michael, when he contended with Satan.

Some of the rays of the star that appeared to the Magi."

Do we laugh at these follies ? In our own day, we have witnessed the rise of a sect, led on by an impudent ignoramus, who declared to us another gospel, and who bid defiance to the government of law and the decency of morals, and yet professed to be an inspired prophet of the Almighty ; and not a few have followed him in his wild and wanton crusade against law and order, and have abandoned home, and country, and kindred, to take up their abode in the haunts of depravity and vice, and to be the willing serfs, and worse than serfs, of the deluded followers of this false prophet.

That Joe Smith has numbered among his adherents some who ought to have known better—some who were trained in the schools and had the advantage of thoroughly furnishing the mind with useful knowledge, I will not deny ; but the mass of his followers were found among those who could scarcely distinguish the right from the wrong, and of those who have followed his fortunes,

above the capacity of idiocy, many were induced to do so by motives very far removed from sheer fanaticism.

I must apologize for taking up so much time in the discussion of these glaring examples of empiricism. It is not here, alone, that the woman of true education is superior to those who have not had her training. In the ordinary routine of daily life, a thousand temptations or occasions occur to mislead the unwary. In the choice of companions, in giving and heeding advice, in yielding to solicitations, in refusing proffered friendships, in rejecting useless or hurtful remedies, opportunities almost innumerable occur for the educated lady to vindicate her good sense and the advantage of ripe training. Let me say it. It is a burning shame that a lady of education should yield to any of the latter day superstitions—it is a burning shame that she should give countenance, even under the stress of repeated importunity to strolling imposters and quacks, to fortune tellers and the like. Every act of the kind lessens the respect entertained for them by intelligent and competent men, and should lessen their own. I know it is sometimes very difficult to throw off and disencumber one's self of the superstition of youth, but the mind well regulated will strive against every such occasion of superstition, and will never yield itself willingly to its sway. Examples are frequent in which a strolling pedlar, peddling some innocent or noxious nostrum, has amassed a princely fortune in the course of a few years : And instances crowd upon the memory in illustration of the fact that honest and intelligent merit at home is overlooked, while with eager gaze and almost Oriental Idolatry, we seek the favour of some arrogant pretender, who has at once the impudence and the shrewdness to affect a profound (or a foreign) air, and pass for a distinguished savant. This evil has grown to such an extent, that at our watering places of common resort, French Counts and foreign dignitaries are the only individuals in the masses that gather at them who can be quite sure of meeting with a cordial and gracious reception. The latter day philosophers tell us with a knowing look—"Great is the power of Humbug! Men will not live without it." And the idea is gaining currency, that the man or woman who utterly ignores and rejects it, forfeits a considerable share of opportunity to make his or her mark in the world! It is a low and specious philosophy, nevertheless. It betrays the corrupt condition of public sentiment which produced it—a sentiment we trust which will soon sink into decay. Bad as man is, there is some good in him after all; and the great heart of humanity will only respond to the truly noble and pure. Petty villainy, and sharp and shrewd empiricism may for a season hold their sway; but the barriers to a right public opinion will, after a while, be swept down, and it will resume its appropriate course, and right will reign. Now it is the province of the educated man or woman to stem the tide of error—to change the current, and to direct public opinion into proper channels. So far from following popular error, it is his office to renounce and expose it, and lift up the standard of truth and purity. Instead of embracing every newly fledged system, because it is new, he ought to question its authority and doubt its verity on that account; with the *modesty* of true science, he will pronounce no harsh, or impulsive, or vehement denunciation against the promulgator of any new system, but with its *honesty* too, he will question closely and examine accurately, and test with rigid scrutiny its claims to credence and support.'

Empiricism is intolerant—science is tolerant. Empiricism is impulsive and bows to one idol, the idol of its peculiar devotion, whose priestly office it fulfils. Science knows no idol but *truth*, and accepts its teachings, though the lesson may never have been learned before. Empiricism teaches one to know every thing, and is content. Science boasts only of its present possessions, and craves to be instructed. Empiricism would disorganize and disarrange the world to enforce obedience to its maddest behests: true science sits at the feet of Nature as a scholar, and asks to know yet more of her revealings.

Time would fail me to enlarge farther upon these thoughts. Thus far we have learned the true offices of education—

—In educating and training a proper and intelligent curiosity; creating a desire to know proper things and to know them thoroughly—and

—In delivering us from the power of empiricism and quackery; in other words, in bestowing upon us an accurate judgment.

I might mention, in detail, others—but you will find them embraced under one or the other of these divisions.

Having briefly detailed your advantages, I approach the second topic of discussion—your responsibilities; and these I shall consider under a four-fold aspect; to yourself, to the family of which you are a member, to the society in which you live, and to the State.

To yourself!

I have already hinted at some of these duties. If it be worth your while to spend at school or some collegiate institution the best years of childhood in amassing information and in quickening into active exercise your mental faculties, it surely would be a matter of surprise and mortification if you should leave at the school door all the desire for knowledge you have acquired—it would surely be marvellous if you should put off all your possessions as no longer fit to be used, so soon as you began to reap other pleasures; so soon as you entered upon "the wide, wide world." You will find, I doubt not, the companions of your school hours, the writers you have studied, your wisest monitors and sincerest friends, your most certain guides and helpers in the hour of need. And then you go out from your school, as I have said, with enlarged and ever active sympathies. The triumphs of science and the trophies of literature, will be to you an ever fresh and delightful source of enjoyment. Nature's volume is being constantly unrolled to the student, and every year contributes its quota of hitherto undiscovered truth; and in literature how ample are the stores of information and pleasurable excitement. The really *"good"* books already written, the product of the giant minds of our race, are waiting to be conned over and learned. You have just been introduced to their society, and have barely learned their names. A brief course of lectures may perhaps have afforded you a passing glance at their various merit and ample instruction. Perhaps you have followed with delight your professor in the departments of English literature, and are already acquainted with the master-work of Milton, the plaintive notes of Blair, the elegy of Gray, the rich and varied eloquence of Cowper, (one of England's best poets, and her most inimitable letter writer,) the stirring and passionate appeals of Burke, the ripe learning and sonorous periods of Johnson, and the sweet, tender and natural descriptions of Goldsmith and Irving. But these men have had their history—a history sometimes crowded with incident of more thrilling interest than the works they produced, and each of these has excited, or will excite, your eager curiosity. And there, too, are the ample pages of the history of nations, and of intellectual philosophy, and of physical research, some of which have already been adorned and illustrated by woman's genius—a Mrs. Somerville in the old world, and a Mrs. Willard in the new.

In some sense, these responsibilities are peculiar to yourself; but the capacities you enjoy may afford occasion of entertainment and instruction to your family. Let not, I beseech you, the list of favourite authors embrace any production, however sparkling with genius, if it be not pure and chaste—if it have aught to corrupt or contaminate the heart—if it be the work of a low and cringing or merely carnal philosophy, or boast the liberty of the libertine, or the irreverence of the profane.

As on this point I must of necessity assume the office of a Mentor, if you ask me should you "altogether ignore the reading of works of fiction," I should answer unhesitatingly, no. Many of the writings of Edgeworth and Cooper, not to mention all of those of the prince of novelists, Scott, and the sketches of

Irving are worthy of all praise, and may be read with profit; and there are some, a few of the writings of the more recent novelists, Dickens and Thackeray, and the later works of Bulwer, which you would do well to read. Do not—oh, do not let this form the staple of your reading. Of religious writers, I should select among the old divines the writings of Taylor and Barrow, Chillingworth and Butler, and among the moderns, the discourses of Robert Hall and Thomas Chalmers. I will point you also to a young man of extraordinary genius, and (it is said) of sterling piety, who has recently arisen in England. His sermons, though hot-pressed and fresh from the mint, are weighty and powerful, and grapple with the mind of the young especially with startling power. You have already anticipated me. I refer to the distinguished and evangelical Spurgeon. Again: another writer of sermons, and I shall close a catalogue of divinity, perhaps already too amply extended in an address of this kind.

Adolphe Monod is a recent French divine, who, we are told, was as distinguished for "simple and truly Christian manners," as for a fascinating eloquence and great and almost unrivalled talents. His "Mission of Woman" is a gem of priceless value, and I commend it to you as a wise counsellor, assistant and friend.

If you shall converse with such companions as these, your minds will be improved, and your hearts enlarged, and you will more faithfully discharge some of the offices you owe to yourself.

And to your family!

The meekness of true learning will exhibit itself in arrogating nothing of superiority over your seniors in age, or superiors in position. You will find it even a pleasant thing to yield to authority, sometimes when its exercise is in your opinion inexpedient; because from large considerations of right, you will feel that the right to rule should be placed in one hand—the head of the family—your father, or mother, or husband, as the case may be. To your younger sisters you will be kind and considerate, having regard to their welfare and not to your mere caprice, in chiding a fault or correcting a blunder. For your brothers you will ever have a kind word of encouragement, when right, but not a word of reproof when wrong. If you should unfortunately be afflicted with an intemperate brother or husband, you will find his habit not cured by a harsh or bitter tone, but rather by persuasion and the tenderness of affection, which a sister or a wife only can feel and appropriately express. You will not, you dare not, under such circumstances, and I would hope under any, offer to your brother the inebriating cup. Remember the curse it has inflicted on our earth—remember the families it has ruined—the fortunes and characters it has wrecked—the splendid intellects it has destroyed for all of good, and nerved to all of ill—the hardships, and sufferings, and agonies of body and mind it has entailed on your sex and on ours—and shun as you would shun the sting of an adder or the deadly bite of a serpent, the occasion of leading your brother into temptation and wrong-doing.

And to the circle of families around you. No wise counsellor would say, "select them all for companions!" Many of them have not similar tastes; they have not common sympathies with you—their enjoyments and your own might, and probably would, widely differ. You could not, if you would, choose them for companionship. But they have their claims upon you, and to these you will promptly respond, in acts of beneficence and benevolence; in courtesy and politeness; in refusing to believe ill of them until compelled to do so by inevitable necessity, and even then in refusing to retail the evil or the scandal you may have heard. And many other things which would as a woman of sense readily occur to you.

You owe also a duty to "Society," strictly so called. "Not the society that boasts itself of splendid array and brilliant equipage; that flounces in silks and flirts in brocade. But the society of the truly noble, gentle and pure; in which thought and heart are the masters, and

form, and so-called Fashion shrink into their native diminutiveness of proportion. The society in which to do a good action lends a sweeter flavour to the life, and to utter a pure thought gives a charm to the conversation. The society of men and women, rather than of puppets and shams; of the gentle and the good, not of the vain and vicious. *This* society has its claims upon woman, and they are not slight. The society, which this is not, needs the reforming touch of woman's genius, before it can lawfully lay claim to its boasted title. Did woman always aspire to occupy the position for which nature designed her, society, ordinarily so called, would be quite a different thing from what it is. Woman would then be as little seen, and perhaps excite as little, or even less attention than now, but she would more surely secure the approbation of her own conscience, and receive more of true homage—would excite more respect and win less admiration. 'The social life of the country is the reflected image of woman's character and culture.' Men may rule 'the court, the camp, the grove;' they may dictate the statutes for the regimen of the State; their mere physical power may nerve its arm, and as counsellors they may give voice and aim to the wisdom of the nation; but after all, the social problems which are the subject and the origin of laws, the manners and customs of the people which originate and produce these laws, are the product, directly or indirectly, of the women. It is no slight duty, then, to which woman is called, in the discharge of her offices to society. She finds it a thing of form, she should give it substance. She finds it a hypocritical sham and a pretence; she should tear aside the veil from hypocrisy and make it real. She finds it cold, without true sympathy, and selfish; she should make it heave with the emotions of earnestness, beat responsively to the calls of sorrow, and cause it to prefer another to itself. She finds it boasting of wealth, gloating in the splendour of its retinue and the pomp of its luxurious entertainments; she should make it rather rejoice in truthfulness and virtue, and adorn itself with quietness and humility." *

In this necessarily hurried glance at the responsibilities of educated women, I must overlook much that it would be well to dwell upon in detail. I pass to notice the claims of the State upon educated womanhood. I call especial attention to but *one*—a matter of vital moment, and one which our women are (shall I not say) culpably neglecting.

It is well known that we have an institution in the Southern States of this confederacy, around which some of the dearest interests of the State are gathered. Thrust upon us at first without our consent, it has grown into our social system and has become a part of the fibre of the body politic. To rend asunder the ties which now bind it to us, would be rudely to sever relations which are of the tenderest character, and would redound to the lasting injury of both parties to the relation—would inflict a curse both upon the slave and his master. This species of property is now estimated as worth, at the least, $1,600,000,000. Its products furnish staples of commerce for the world. One article alone, the product of this relation and almost wholly dependent upon its existence for continued production, furnishes a commerce to our country amounting to more than $150,000,000 per annum. To emancipate our slaves instantly or in any brief space of time would thus reduce as to poverty if not to beggary: and as a nation we should be put back more than a half century in the scale of enlightened improvement.

Granting that emancipation were feasible, and that Northern beneficence would step forward and generously supply the means to transport and settle our slaves abroad, the actual diminution of labour, and the cutting off of this single article of commerce from the South, would entail upon us and upon the country at large an amount of evil not readily to be estimated.

I do not mention these facts as bearing upon the moral question of slavery, but simply to show the magnitude of the interests at stake in the proper solution of this difficult problem. In debating the question of emancipation it is surely not out of place to consider what *we have to lose,*—if for no other reason, at least for this, that if in other regards, there be a balancing of the scales in the argument, the consideration of cost alone should determine our proper course of action. This question of slavery is a question, I admit, on which even good men are divided into opinions.

There are those who maintain the utter immorality of the institution; and, on the other hand, there are those who with equal zeal and ability, support its expediency and affirm that it is morally right; and there are those who go further still, who assert that the institution is a blessing to the inferior party to the relation. Time would fail me here to enter fully into a discussion of the topic. I have no hesitancy, however, in declaring the conviction of my own mind, formed after some attention to the subject, and a somewhat elaborate examination of it in its various phases, that the Southern position is impregnable when viewed in its political and social aspects; and that it can be successfully maintained by the argument from the Scriptures. I have no hesitancy, moreover, in saying that I do not believe any man can approach the question, not having the prejudices of education against it, without saying that the institution has the clear sanction of the Omnipotent and Omniscient Being, who has ordered the relation for the wisest and best purposes and ends. This being true, it is not to be wondered at, that improper and illegal interference with the healthful operation of this institution should have bred dissension and strife in our national councils, and should have arrayed the one section of the country against the other. If it were merely a transient question— if it contained within itself the seeds of its own dissolution, it might not be worth

---

* From an article contributed by the writer to the Messenger, 1857.

while to vex with the question those who ought only to seek for the quietude and seclusion of a private station. If it were such a question, I should be the last to commend it to your study and attention, when so many questions of less difficult solution and of riper enjoyment in the solving are inviting your inquiry. But it is not a transient question. It is intertwined with the dearest and best interests of your homes and firesides. You shall need to know its full import and significance; and whether you will or not, by the rending of domestic ties, by the clash of popular opinion and clamour; it may be, in civil and fraternal strife; you may be called on to take a part, and no slight part in its settlement. I do not propose that you shall prepare yourselves for the national councils, or for seats in the legislature of your native State to settle it. I do not propose to arm you with arguments that you may mount the rostrum and dole out political instruction to your husbands or brothers or sons. I am not prepared to import into Virginia this new-fangled system of Woman's Rights, any more than any of the other thousand and one empiricisms and isms which have been poured upon us by the North. But I do ask you to look well to the surroundings of this question—to read and understand the argument urged in behalf of slavery, and to correct a false sentiment, which I fear is already too prevalent among females, that the institution is wrong. It is not wrong. It is right. The Bible sanctions it. True philosophy sanctions it. The wisest and truest statesmanship has found in it the conservative power of the South—and our educated women ought to know it that they may imbue their children with it and educate in the truest and best method a popular sentiment in conformity to right reason and to the word of the Living God.

This is one of the duties (and but one) which an educated woman at the South owes to the State,—that she may contribute to its good order by promoting the growth of a proper popular sentiment on this subject and lend sympathy and encouragement to her home in its strife with Northern fanaticism and folly.

But a truce to farther discussion of this kind. I began by telling you of the delights of knowledge. It is the chief aim of our existence *to know.* My language is not unguarded. I mean what I say. Take, however, into your mental view, in ascertaining the delights of knowledge, the interests and endowments of two worlds; and you will acknowledge it true. For perfect happiness, unquestionably, nothing save infinity will suffice. No merely temporal exaltation, however high; no transitory sensation of pleasure, however thrilling; no present attainments of the mind, however grand and magnificent, will meet and fully gratify the immortal thirstings of an immortal spirit. You need an object of contemplation and study, infinite—infinite in resources, infinite in duration, infinite in capacity—you need a life long enough to measure infinity. To meet these wants is to meet, and fully meet, the measure of your capacity and satiate this thirst. Add to this high knowledge, what indeed is inseparable from its full attainment, other attributes of emotion and delight experienced by a change of relation to the only Being in the universe we can properly adore—a change which involves the transformation of his attitude towards us, from Judge to Parent, from Condemner and Accuser to Protector and Justifier—add the gratitude and adoration consequent upon the forgiveness of sin and salvation from ruin—a ruin infinite, immeasurable, utter and irretrievable—to a condition of security and bliss, security infinite and bliss which language may not aptly express; add the ripe enjoyments of *home,* and the companionship of beings like circumstanced with yourself, rescued from a similar ruin and saved to a similar security—and you have fulfilled all the conditions of happiness without alloy. To KNOW THUS is indeed to swell the heart with gratitude, to kindle affection into its liveliest exercise, and to give sweep to our highest and noblest powers. When the human mind converses with and studies an Infinite God, in the state of pure spirits, in the courts of heaven, in the expanse of the universe of worlds, and during the duration of eternity, it needs no farther, no other or higher excitant to action; it needs no other and no farther stimulant to perfect enjoyment and perfect bliss.

II. EDUCATION OF THE FEMALE SEX.

Who can find a virtuous woman? for her price is far above rubies.

The heart of her husband doth safely trust in her, so that he shall have no need of spoil.

She will do him good and not evil all the days of her life.

She seeketh wool and flax, and worketh willingly with her hands.

She is like the merchants' ships; she bringeth her food from afar.

She riseth also while it is yet night, and giveth meat to her household, and a portion to her maidens.

She considereth a field and buyeth it; with the fruit of her hands she planteth a vineyard.

She layeth her hands to the spindle, and her hands hold the distaff.

She stretcheth out her hands to the poor; yea, she reacheth forth her hands to the needy.

She is not afraid of the snow for her household; for all her household are clothed with double garments.

She maketh herself coverings of tapestry; her clothing *is* silk and purple.

Her husband is known in the gates, when he sitteth among the elders of the land.

Strength and honor *are* her clothing; and she shall rejoice in time to come.

She openeth her mouth with wisdom; and in her tongue *is* the law of kindness.

She looketh well to the ways of her household, and eateth not the bread of idleness.

Her children arise up and call her blessed; her husband *also*, and he praiseth her.

Favor *is* deceitful, and beauty *is* vain: *but* a woman *that* feareth the Lord, she shall be praised.

Give her of the fruit of her hands; and let her own works praise her in the gates.

A gracious woman retaineth honor.

A virtuous woman *is* a crown to her husband; but she that maketh ashamed *is* as rottenness in his bones.

A prudent wife *is* from the Lord.   Bible, *Proverbs.*

Wives, submit yourselves unto your husbands, as unto the Lord.

For the husband is the head of the wife, even as Christ is the head of the church.

Therefore as the church is subject unto Christ, so *let* the wives *be* to their own husbands in everything.

Let your women keep silence in the churches.

That they may teach the young women to be sober, to love their husbands, to love their children, *to be* discreet, chaste, keepers at home, good, obedient to their own husbands, that the word of God may not be blasphemed.   Bible; *Eph.*, v; 22–24. 1 *Cor.*, xiv; 34. *Titus*, ii; 4, 5.

The authority and dominion remain with the husband, for the wife, according to God's commandment, must be subject and obedient. The husband must govern the house and exercise authority, go to war, defend his property, plow, sow, build, plant, &c.

The wife, on the other hand, must sit at home and be busy in the house. Thus Venus was represented standing on a snail-shell, showing that as the snail carries his house with him, so should the wife always be at home and be busied about the occupations of the house.

Among the first virtues of a wife is, that the heart of her husband shall trust in her; that is that he shall love her truly and wholly, shall anticipate no evil from her, but shall feel certain that she loves him in return, and that she will be careful of his comfort.

A pious wife should be honored and loved; first, because she is God's gift and bestowal; and secondly, because God has given to women great and excellent virtues, which far outweigh some small defects and faults, especially when they hold fast to modesty, truth and faith.

Women, when they learn the gospel, are much stronger and more fervent in faith. Mary Magdalene was more bold than Peter.

"It is not good for man to be alone. I will make him a help meet for him." These are the words of God; and can not be understood without faith.

Weak woman has nothing more precious and noble than her honor.

And thus she should be so minded as not to over-estimate ornament.

Otherwise, when once absorbed in seeking it, she will never cease from the pursuit. Such is the female character.

Therefore a Christian wife should contemn it.

A woman should be adorned, as St. Peter saith (I, iii; 3, 4), with the hidden adornment of a meek and quiet spirit.

A wife is sufficiently adorned when she is adorned for her husband.

Christ will not have you adorn yourself to please others, and to have men call you a handsome strumpet.

But to this you should look; that you have a hid treasure and a rich adornment in your heart; and that you live an unspotted and honorable and modest life.

It is a good indication that there is nothing very attractive in the mind, when too much attention is paid to ornament. (*Esther*, ii; 15.)

Gold and jewels are before man, splendid; but before God, an ill savor.

Why do foolish young women try to attract young fellows?

Do you not know that a young fellow will be afraid to choose you, if he thinks you will cost him so much in maintenance and clothing?

If you would gain the love of a young fellow, take this good advice: Be modest and speak little, and adorn yourself not much, and do not look straight at him with bold eyes.

The greatest adornment of a woman or a maiden is, a modest shamefacedness; for men's hearts are more attracted by that than by all adornments of attire.

And if this ornament departs, love also departs. LUTHER.

See, in the tender child, two lovely blossoms united; youth and maiden, but thus far the bud conceals them both. But softly its bonds are dissolved, and their fresh young natures develop, and from her lovely modesty parts his fiery strength. Suffer the boy to play; give his furious impulses freedom; only when sated, his strength will return to her grace again. Forth from the bud, the blossoms are both beginning to struggle; each is lovely, yet neither is all that the heart desires. The maiden's graceful limbs are inspired with glowing feeling; but pride, like a girdle strong, represses closely their glow. Shy, like the trembling roe-deer, that flees from the forest bugle, she flees from man as a foe; even hates him—until she loves. But the youth looks, defiant and boldly, from under his shadowing eye-brows; and, hardened to strife and battle, stiffens his sinews amain. Far in the throng of spears, along the dust-covered race-course, enticing glory calls him, and boiling courage drives. SCHILLER.

Let your daily occupations, dear girls, like those of your brothers, be industriously pursued, and apply yourselves diligently to what is commanded you ; thus you will escape many useless thoughts and many follies.

Read diligently the Psalter, Jesus the son of Sirach, and Paul Gerhard's Hymns.

Read not foolish books, but flee from them as a poison which may destroy your soul.

For a young girl's hand these two things are proper, a prayer-book and a spindle.

Be much more cautious of doubtful or false friends, than even of open enemies.

A young woman should apply herself earnestly to domestic affairs ; for a wife who can not keep house is the ruin and destruction of her husband.

But if God permits, practice, besides writing, arithmetic and housekeeping, also music and singing.

If you have yet time, devote it to prayer.

Sacred singing especially, is a truly angelic and heavenly employment, and a foretaste of the beautiful and lovely music of the angels of God ; especially where not overloaded with ornament, and where it proceeds from heartfelt devotion, and not from pride and conceit.

Always show modesty, and act in an unobtrusive manner.

Where there is no discipline, there is no honor ; but vile passions, bad thoughts and bad deeds.

A young woman ought not to use many words ; for she ought not to be crammed with mere knowledge.

May God preserve us from an over-wise learned woman !

Prayer, writing, arithmetic, singing and housekeeping, are knowledge enough for a young woman.

Also a young woman should neither curse nor swear, should never speak unless spoken to, and should always answer as briefly as possible.

Also, she should live a quiet, orderly and blameless life, not running into every corner after news and new fashions, as Ringwald says,

" Avoid her who takes pleasure in gadding, in standing at the window or the door, talks with everybody, and works or spins lazily ; who is addicted to roguish tricks, is proud and irritable, and determined always to be above everybody ; who is obstinate, and will not be controlled."

It is almost a born trait of women, to be able to search out, discuss and find fault with almost everything. A hateful vice ! How many maidens have come to great misfortune, and been prevented from all prosperity, by their own mouths !

Therefore a young woman should guard herself from pride and vanity.

For pride is not merely a foolish vice because it costs much, but is above others to be condemned, because it turns us aside from God ; and every right-minded man should therefore diligently avoid it.

A proud person is an enemy of God, who is all mildness, benevolence and goodness ;—is a jest and an abhorrence to all his neighbors, and his own destruction.

Young women should strive after humility, orderliness and purity.

Modesty distinguishes a pure mother of a family ; humility, an intelligent one ; order and neatness, a reliable one.   MOSCHEROSCH.

First, let there be nothing froward in your voice ; and let your soft glance, full of goodness, not go idly forth from under your modest brow ; and be neither too loud, nor too slow, in speech ; for such persons are not welcome here.   *Danaus to his daughters, in Æschylus.*

The husband, in hard-working life, must work and labor, and plant and contrive, and plot and scheme, and strive and venture, to secure success. Thus will he obtain ceaseless riches, and his warehouses will be filled with precious goods; his lands will increase, and his house will increase. And in it is presiding the modest housewife, the mother of his children, wisely ruling his domestic circle, teaching her girls and restraining her boys, and incessantly directing their industrious hands, and with judicious, orderly management increasing her husband's gains, and filling the fragrant chests with treasures, and spinning the humming thread on the spindle, and laying up in the polished box the bright wool and snowy linen, and keeping all his household goods bright and shining, and never resting.

SCHILLER. (Poem.)

Woman both needs, and may easily fail of securing the proper development of her immortal part, for the thankless labors and detailed occupations of her sex render her especially liable to neglect in this particular, and to be bound down and chained to earth, by the restricted limits of her sphere of action.

It is therefore time that not only amongst the lower classes, but among the middle and higher ranks, woman should raise herself out of the intellectual poverty, ignorance and restraint, the empty struggles after externals and the worthless tinsel of a shallow universal knowledge of social affairs, to which the egoism of men has hitherto usually condemned her.

To desire to place woman in a condition exactly similar to man's, is ridiculous; and to undertake this by means of the vain parade of school knowledge, is nonsense.

But she should stand as high as man, in her own department. So much is her right. And it is upon the attainment of this object that her hopes depend for a better mental development in the future. SOLDAN.

For girls, no cold speculative instruction, but a training of the susceptibilities; and one as nearly as possible adapted to the relations of the female sex.

Women can very well spare any other instruction. KANT.

All male characters show more independent activity; all female ones, more passive susceptibility.

But their difference is rather in tendency, than in natural endowment; and thus it is the difference of intellectual tendency which chiefly distinguishes the male from the female character.

The former begins by performing some action, and afterwards receives a reactive impression, through the receptive faculties. The latter pursues the opposite method, first receiving the impression, and then reproducing it by means of the active faculties. W. VON HUMBOLDT.

Man endeavors after freedom; woman after propriety. GOETHE.

The morality of women is a propriety, not a principle.

Boys may be improved by the bad example of a drunken Helot; but women only by a good example.

None but boys can pass through the Augean stable of this world's life with only a little of its odor upon them.

But girls are tender, white Paris-apple-blossoms, hothouse flowers; from which dirt must be removed not with the hand, but with a delicate brush.

They should be trained up like the ancient priestesses, only in holy orders; and should never hear anything coarse, immoral or violent—not to mention seeing it.

Magdalena Pazzi said in her death-bed, that she did not know what an offence against chastity was. Education should at least try to proceed according to that pattern.

Maidens, like pearls and peacocks, are valued most when they are whitest.

A corrupt young man may lay aside a good book, walk up and down his room with hot tears, and cry out "I will change my life"—and hold to it.

But I have heard of but few women who have thus changed themselves.

In the world's opinion, men's faults are specks, leaving little or no scar; but women's are pock-marks, deeply traced in the memory after recovery —in the public memory at least.   JEAN PAUL RICHTER.

In education, the peculiar qualities of each sex need an appropriate treatment.

The nature of girls, predominantly susceptible, dependent therefore upon immediate feeling, sensitive, introverted, adapted to a narrow sphere, troubled at small things, should not be trained to noisy cheerfulness, to predominant mental activity, to clear and comprehensive generalizing, to universal tendencies in science, to a strictly logical process of thought, to rough openness of manner, to the more vivid, general, and outward phases of activity, such as are proper for boys; unless it is desired to carry them quite out of their sphere and to destroy in the germ the charm of lovely womanhood.

And on the other hand it should not be required of the predominantly active and outwardly tending minds of boys, to be as easily affected, as diligently applied to little things, as delicate in externals, as girls, whose proper sphere of action is that of propriety;—unless the pupil is to be made a pedant, and his faculties, which are intended to be exerted outwardly, are to be crippled.   BENDA.

As the natural character of the sexes is different, physically and mentally, and as their departments of destined exertion are different, so must their education, while similar in general, yet be essentially different in subordinate details.

The home of the man is to be the world; the world of woman, her home.

However fearful would be the punishment of bringing up a man for woman's sphere of duty, as heavy a curse would rest upon the endeavor to bring up a woman for the occupations of a man.

The boy is endowed with clear understanding, predominant reason and firm will, corporally fitted to strive with fate, to exert a powerful activity outwardly: the girl, with lively and tender feelings, a vivid imagination, a weaker will; she is corporally unfit to act upon the outer world, to operate on a large scale, to generalize. Thus do the two sexes differ; from this point must their respective educations proceed; towards a corresponding purpose must their discipline be directed, in order to the protection and development of the nobler germs of character, and to the improvement or extirpation of bad ones.

In plainer terms: Boys should be trained to be men, citizens, husbands, fathers; girls, to be true and tender women, wives and mothers.

Anything short of this, or beyond it, is wrong.

In the education of boys, maxims of boldness should be applied; in that of women, those of prudence.   SCHLEIERMACHER.

The future sphere for man is outside, in the world; in pushing and striving amongst men; there is his school.

The future theatre of feminine greatness is the family; and that is the school for girls.

90

To be a loving wife, a cheerful life companion, a diligent housewife, the guardian of her children, such is woman's vocation.

To-day, as much as in gray antiquity, these are still the requisites of the wife of a farmer or of a prince; except that each should also possess the easily acquired knowledge which is needed.

Easily acquired—for the daughters of the great have been seen living in a low estate and earning a living by the labor of their hands; and the daughters of low-born men have nobly filled royal thrones.

Woman is, in her nature and in her perfection, a noble counterpart of man.

He is formed to labor and act in the struggle of the outer world; she, to govern the quiet world of domestic life, beneath the roof of her home. He is fearless, defiant, bold in danger, that he may combat opposition, or bear it down by sheer strength; she governs by grace and mildness. He, investigating and estimating everything, skillful in all manner of handiwork and arrangement, becomes almost able to create; she, the priestess of natural duties and destinies, exhibits her most valuable qualities in controlling these.

As the outward world is contrasted with the inward, art with nature, strength with gracefulness, so is man in this world contrasted with woman.

Beyond this world the destiny of both is the same; religion is the everlasting crown of life to both.

These principles enable us to recognize the principal points of woman's vocation, and the clearly marked boundaries of the course of her education. ZSCHOKKE.

Mighty art thou, O woman, by the quiet charm of thy presence.
But what thou canst not do in quiet, by violence ne'er can be done.
Power I look for from man; and laws are made to restrain him.
But woman governs by sweetness; should govern by sweetness alone.
'Tis true that many have ruled by might of will and of action;
But the loftiest crown of all was never attained by these.
The true queen ruleth alone by woman's womanly beauty—
Ruleth wherever seen; because she is seen, she ruleth. SCHILLER.

The utterly false assumption that a girl needs to know but little, has already borne bitter fruit in the education of the female children of our people.

We consider all over-education—and of course that of the female sex— a misfortune. But it is not a less one, to have youths and maidens go forth into the world and enter upon their duties in life without such knowledge and skill as is indispensable; without having acquired such an extent and profundity of moral, intellectual and æsthetic training, as to feel themselves fully prepared for the vocation that awaits them.

Unfortunately, however, the education of girls is quite insufficient, especially in comparison with that of boys.

This ought no longer to be the case; in part for the sake of the female sex themselves, and in part for the sake of the human race collectively.

For to what other hands will the coming generation confide the bringing up and education of their children, than to those of their mothers?

But where shall these find the power, capacity and skill, required for instructing others, if they do not themselves possess it? (*Luke*, vi; 39.)

It is not entertaining too sanguine hopes, to expect that a more appropriate and thorough, comprehensive and systematical education of females, having a wiser and more practical reference to their future situation and duties, would produce improvements among our common people, which could scarcely be reached by any other means.

91

For as is the root, so is the tree; and as is the tree, so is the fruit. The answer of Madame Campan to Napoleon's question, what deficiency was preventing the prosperity of the education of youth, notwithstanding all the institutions for the purpose? namely, that "There was a deficiency of mothers," is a very significant one, and suggests many reflections.

MENCKE.

The purer the gold of a vessel, the more easily is it bent. The highest grace of feminine excellence is more easily corruptible than the masculine.

Nature herself has provided a born protection and guard for these delicate souls; namely, modesty in speaking and hearing.

This protection should be observed; and should be used as an indication of nature of the proper method in education.

Mother, father, husband, children even, are the best company for young women. Their acquaintance with other young women of about the same age consists of an exchange of their weaknesses rather than their good qualities.

Some dissuasives are such as to serve at once for a persuasion and a bait.

If parents set a good example, they will not find themselves under the necessity of adding any further reinforcement to the natural power of modesty, that wing-cover of the wings of Psyche.

Instruction despoils the child, first, of his innocent unconsciousness of modesty, and afterwards of the quiet influence of it.

The children of Quakers are of mild dispositions, without any punishment; for they see their parents always as calm amongst uncongenial surroundings as snow-white stars looking forth among stormy clouds.

Girls, instead of silly ornamental occupations, should occupy themselves in the various employments of the household; whose constant change and incessant demands on the attention will prevent all dreaming and reverie. In their earlier youth they should learn cooking, and then gardening; afterwards, the administration of the household, and account-keeping.

A wife is like the minister of a small state; she is at the head of all the home departments at once. The husband has charge of foreign affairs.

Girls should learn whatever develops and trains the application of the bodily senses and the use of the eyes; such as botany, that inexhaustible, peaceful, ever fruitful science, which knits us to nature by soft flowery chains; and astronomy, not merely mathematical, but religious; which widens our world, and expands our souls along with it.

I would also advise mathematics, especially the simplest principles of pure and applied mathematics, and a corresponding portion of geometry.

Geography; not a mere register of localities, which would be of little value for the mental culture of women, and of little practical use; but with reference to what it contains of solid and real history, both of man and of the earth.

History; that variety of it which only leads from one antiquity to another, as studied by girls, can not contain too small a number of dates and names, nor can it be rich enough in great men and great actions, the knowledge of which elevates the soul above mere histories of cities and suburbs.

Music, vocal and instrumental, belongs to the female soul; it is the Orphean sound which will lead her safely past thousands of siren songs; and whose youthful echo will accompany her far within the autumn of married life.

Drawing, on the contrary, at least if cultivated beyond a sufficient knowledge of its rudiments to train the eye and the taste, deprives children and family employments of too much time; so that time spent in it is usually lost.

One foreign language is necessary as a means of intelligent companion and study with our own ; but one is enough.

Inspire the heart; and then it will long not for light, but for the ethereal atmosphere of heaven. JEAN PAUL RICHTER.

A husband should be earnest and industrious, and should support his wife and children honestly and respectably. He should not be a spendthrift, nor waste in drinking what his wife saves at home. Also he should be of good conduct; neither a wolf nor a lion, so that his wife may not be fearful and afraid of him And lastly he should be upright; so that his word may be a Yes, and Amen.

A wife should be domestic, industrious, and should economically manage all that her husband so laboriously and honorably earns; not given over to sloth, laziness, and gluttony, which would bring both husband and children together to beggary. And she must be obedient; not growling, murmuring, grumbling, snarling, complaining, &c. ; and good natured too.

With one judicious pleasant word, a wife can bring over her husband, and gain his consent.

But a contrary and obstinate wife is a great burden to her husband.

And who would not rather live among the wolves, than with a bitter-tempered wife ?

What is more destructive to the lovely peace which should prevail at home, than the bad temper and obstinacy of a disobedient and ill-conducted wife ?

For disobedience is followed by contempt for the husband ; and that by violent anger.

It is far better to obey and live in peace, than to strike and bite and quarrel.

It is and must be the prerogative of the head—the husband—to govern ; and the members must do the will of the head.

Lastly, a wife should be serious ; not running after follies, but finding her enjoyment in managing her household. MOSCHEROSCH.

Girls, of all ranks and of whatever circumstances, should obtain practical skill in housekeeping ; for during subsequent married life, even should they be in the easiest circumstances, they should always have a general oversight of their household, and be able to judge correctly of its affairs. They must know what can fairly be required of their servants ; for too much is as often demanded of them as too little.

Early practice will enable a wife to conduct even a difficult household, and at the same time to do this with such ease and despatch as to have strength and leisure for intellectual employments.

A woman of good judgment, even without previous experience, can learn to keep house, by means of a firm resolution and diligent application; but her mind will be much absorbed in the work, and she will never be free from a certain anxiety, arising from the unaccustomed nature of the employment.

A Christian and well educated wife, whose quiet, intelligent and patient activity makes little display in words, and still less in constant, restless haste and scolding impatience, whose virtues and abilities will make her house so comfortable to her husband that he desires to stay in no other place, who educates her children judiciously to a Christian piety, without suffering any of the faculties which are the gift of the Lord only to be neglected or perverted into a false and narrow pietism,—such a wife should be the ideal of female education ; in such an ideal is intimately united a mastery of domestic duties, and a high grade of mental training. VON RAUMER.

Nothing is so much neglected as the education of girls.

Have not women duties which are the basis of their whole lives? Is it not they who destroy or build up families? They exert a most powerful influence upon the good or bad morals of almost all the world.

An intelligent, industrious and deeply religious wife is the soul of a whole great household; she controls it both in its temporal and eternal welfare.

Ignorance is often a cause'which occasions girls to be at a loss for employment, and to busy themselves in ways not innocent.

If women reach a certain age without being accustomed to serious employments, they can neither acquire a taste for them, nor learn to value them properly.   FENELON.

Attractiveness is more valuable than beauty.

Beauty is an earthly quality, and fades in a few years; but attractiveness is a charm of the soul, and adorns even old age.

There are many beautiful forms and regular features. But what pleases the senses does not always attract the mind.

It is often the case that beautiful women are destitute of that charm whose sweetness, unfeigned regard for others, and undefinable dignity, enchants the hearts of all.

Beauty quickly gives pleasure, but does not continue always to do so. Attractiveness renders even serious defects loveable, and establishes, though slowly, an enduring dominion.

It is too commonly the case that women, in their desire to please, and to rule by pleasing, exchange their native agreeableness, even during the period of education, for external politeness, gracefulness of attitude and motion, and elegance of manners. But this is only painting a faded cheek; a counterfeiting what is not really possessed.

As beauty is the charm of the senses, so is attractiveness of the mind; a charm which beams through the corporeal envelope of the body, and ennobles it.

As the strength, mental power and tone of thought in a man, are indicated without his knowing it, in his features, his words, the tone of his voice, his step, his motions, so are the innocence, mildness, and nobility of the feminine character indicated in woman's exterior, without any artifice or design.

It is not a fashionable taste that gives attractiveness; but attractiveness, which often shows itself in trifling matters, which gives the laws of good taste.

The nobler the internal character, the nobler will the external be.

Therefore a higher degree of attractiveness accompanies outward purity and simplicity, than the richest adornment; for the former exemplify the virtues of the possessor, the latter her vanity.   ZSCHOKKE.

While a man who devotes himself to any elevated calling, should always have well studied the fates of the most important nations of the world, it would be inappropriate to require the same of women.

History, as studied by girls, should be directed to the cultivation of their sensibilities, their feelings, their sense of the great and noble; not the mere cramming of the memory.

The extent of what is to be committed to memory should be as limited as possible.

A chronological error is much less injurious to a young girl, than the least appearance to a pretension to historical learning.

It is self-evident that it will be of great service to a young girl, to be made acquainted with the lives and characters of the best feminine models.
                                                          VON RAUMER.

The instruction of girls in history deserves special consideration; it has been too much neglected. There should be more adaptation to their peculiar wants; and actual and ideal representations should be afforded, of the condition of women in different ages. RUEUS.

" The best fruit of history," says Goethe, " is the enthusiasm which it creates." Accordingly, the historical studies of young women should be of an elevating character; and the actual facts communicated should be explained by their respective ideals.

In a history for girls, the chief object should be, to give a biographical and ethnographical representation of the human mind, in single characters, scenes and parties; but not by means of those interminable genealogies of rulers whose names and existences are often much more uncertain than many of the facts in mythology.

Wars, campaigns and battles, can least of all have any interest for them; it will be sufficient to acquaint them by a few representations, with the results of human efforts.

More time should therefore be occupied in following the progress of civilization, manners, customs, arts and religion; and most of all, in the consideration of eminent female characters.

Great wickedness, and outbreaks of brutal vileness can not be entirely passed over; but it will not be a blamable caution, in treating of such things, to make use of much regard to the feelings of the young, and especially to the tender sensibilities of the female sex.

In a history for girls, the chief object should be to bring out the relation between the narrative and actual life; especially with that of women.

Our young women should study history, in order to learn to recognize the earnest purposes of life, and the hand of God as seen in the fates of individual men and whole nations; to avoid becoming similar to those creatures who are carried away with the frivolous sillinesses which French manners and governesses have imparted into our father-land; that in studying Greek history they may follow back to its natural condition that society which a period of affectedness has modelled into stiff and unnatural fashions; to acquaint themselves with the sensible and plain-spoken Socrates; to learn how to understand Jesus and his divine instructions; to secure themselves from falling under the dominion of either sneerers or mystics, and of thus becoming either skeptical or superstitious.

Our daughters should study history, that they may be domestic, true and honorable, after the model of the ancient German wives; that they may appreciate the important duty confided to them by Providence, of training men, from infancy upwards.

For whenever we see a great man, we may see behind him a noble mother, who carefully and lovingly watched over the seeds of his future greatness.

Our women should be acquainted with history, that they may learn how in times of barbarism and degeneration, arts and sciences, virtue and faith, have found a place of safety with them and them only; and also how bad women have caused the destruction of whole nations.

History should also be a protection against silly tattling and vulgar amusements, and all the miserable superficiality and emptiness which characterizes so many women; and also against the excessive sensibility and fancifulness which have carried away many nobly endowed women from themselves and their duty, and plunged them into irreconcilable quarrels. OESER.

As soon as a mother becomes aware that her daughters are no longer contented to be playing all the time, that they have occasional seasons of idleness and *ennui*, she must set about supplying all manner of little occupations to prevent it.

Knitting and sewing should be taught to all girls, of whatever rank, as soon as their aptitude for handiwork is developed.

As soon as they are skilled in these occupations, they are thus fitted to learn artistic and ornamental work; lessons in which may be allowed them as a reward for industry in doing the sewing of the family.

It is desirable that girls should become sufficiently acquainted with ornamental work to be able to do all that is necessary for the tasteful adornment of a room or a dress.   Von Raumer.

The very idea of a public institution for female education is at variance with the best education for women.

The sphere of action of the future man is out in the world; and there should be his school.

But the scene for the exercise of the womanly virtues is a domestic one; the family; and this should be the girl's school.

The life of a family is entirely different from that in an educational institution.

In the former is to be found God's wisely ordained association of young and old persons of both sexes; varieties of thought and feeling, and the duties and the rights of those of different ages. Girls have an opportunity of learning what are right and wrong ways in housekeeping, and in fulfilling the duties of social life; they learn to obey the old, to take charge of the young, to be companions of those of their own age, and to direct those under their authority. Therefore the home life amongst brothers and sisters and parents, small and great together, is the proper school for girls.

In public institutions there are no parents, to conciliate the confidence of the childish heart; there are only teachers, from whom the inmost heart is cautiously concealed, for fear of misunderstanding; while outward propriety is carefully watched over, and at last comes to be the principal thing. The hundred instructive little daily occurrences of domestic life are wanting; and the peculiarities of character which make the deepest impression on the heart. Instead of these there is a cold uniformity in listening and in doing, and with the best teachers and companions, none are seen but strangers. And thus, during the most critical years of the young woman's life, her character takes an impress which is in future life to be seldom necessary, but often injurious.

She returns to domestic life, with a scientific half-education, skillful in concealing her thoughts from others, accomplished in external decorum, with an increased desire and capacity for shining before the world in little things.

Well for her if she finds there again the ancient happiness, naturalness and innocence of her childhood.

Her parents' home and those of her relatives must anew become her school.

But often it is too late, and she is ruined forever for the labors, the sameness, and the little enjoyments of domestic life.

She becomes a wife, but without becoming the cheerful companion for life of her husband; the head of a family, without being able to govern her house with consistent diligence and with equal care and wisdom both in great things and in small; a mother, without taking pleasure in maternal duties.

We have many instructions for the education of girls. But pious parents will instruct them best, in their own family.

What constituted a perfect woman thousands of years ago, constitutes her still. (See Proverbs, xxxi; 11 to 31.)   Zschokke.

DESIGN FOR RESIDENCE.

HOW TO REDEEM WOMAN'S PROFESSION FROM DISHONOR.

IN this Magazine for November, 1864, it was shown that woman's *distinctive profession* includes three departments—the training of the mind in childhood, the nursing of infants and of the sick, and all the handicrafts and management of the family state. With perhaps the exception of the school training of children, it was claimed that the profession of woman is *socially disgraced*, so that no woman of culture and refinement, in the wealthy classes, would resort to cooking, chamber-work, or nursing infants and the sick for a livelihood, scarcely any more than their brothers would resort to burglary or piracy.

It was shown also that women are not *trained* for their profession as men are for theirs; that there is no provision made for ít in public or private schools; and that every school, as well as other social influence, tends at once to disgrace woman's profession and to destroy her health.

Woman, as well as man, was made to *work;* and her Maker has adapted her body to its appropriate labor. The tending of children and doing house-work exercise those very muscles which are most important to womanhood; while neglecting to exercise the arms and trunk causes dangerous debility in most delicate organs.

Our early mothers worked and trained their daughters to work, and thus became healthy, energetic, and cheerful. But in these days, young girls, in the wealthy classes, do not use the muscles of their body and arms in domestic labor or in any other way. Instead of this, study and reading stimulate the brain and nerves to debility by excess, while the muscles grow weak for want of exercise. Thus the whole constitution is weakened.

In consequence of this there is a universal lamentation over the decay of the female constitution and the ruined health of both women and girls. At the same time vast numbers are without honorable compensating employment, so that in the wealthy circles unmarried women suffer from aimless vacuity, and in the poorer classes from unrequited toil and consequent degradation and vice.

It is believed that the remedy for all these evils is not in leading women into the professions and business of men, by which many philanthropists are now aiming to remedy their sufferings, but to train woman properly for her own proper business, and then to secure to her the honor and profit which men gain in their professions.

A young man finds endowed institutions all over the land, offering a home and a good salary for life for teaching only one or two branches to only one class for one or two hours a day. Is there any reason why his highly-educated sister should not have similar opportunities if she does not marry or is a widow?

The public and private high schools have filled the country with women of high culture. The unequal distribution of the sexes and a dreadful war must enforce a single life on many thousands. Many are widows with families; many others would gladly rear the orphan children of relatives and friends or of our slaughtered heroes. Why, should not such have as good advantages to do so as if they were men?

Each department of woman's profession is a science and art as much as law, medicine, or divinity. They are equal also in importance. Why should they not be equally honored by a liberal course of training and competent emolument?

When men seek to elevate their own profession they endow professorships so as to secure men of the highest culture to study and teach it as a science and art.

At one time the farmer's profession was without skill, honor, or liberal reward. To raise it to an honored art and science, *endowments* have been given to sustain men of culture and learning to lecture, practice, and teach; and now this business is taking rank as an honorable and remunerative profession.

Let woman's profession be thus honored and its disgrace would speedily be ended. Let endowed institutions be provided to sustain women of high culture to study, practice, and teach all the branches included in woman's profession *properly*. Let each of our large cities and towns have at least one institution so endowed, and then there would be created *a liberal profession* for highly-cultivated women suited to their nature, and meeting the wants of those who are unmarried or widowed; such a profession as their brothers and fathers now enjoy as college professors in educating men.

Woman's business being thus honored and taught in the higher institutions the lower schools would follow, and thus women of the poorer classes also would be properly trained for their proper business. And when thus trained they would find abundant and compensating employment; for the universal complaint of all who try to find employment for poor women is, that they are not trained to do any kind of woman's work properly, and that this is the fatal difficulty.*

There is as much need for *training* women for the distinctive duties of the family as there is of training boys for their different trades. A housekeeper or a cook, who has been taught to economize in using and preserving family stores and fuel, can supply a table at half the expense incurred by an untrained, inexperienced hand.

A properly trained nurse for young children would relieve a mother of half her care as to the health and training of her children; while an ignorant, unfaithful one rather adds to her responsibilities.

A well-educated, gentle, and faithful nurse for the sick is a treasure in any community as rare as it is valuable.

A woman of education and refinement who can cut and fit dresses, make bonnets, make and mend all household stuffs economically, and at the same time help in cooking, and in keeping chambers and parlors in tasteful order, is a treasure that wealth rarely can command at any price.

Women of good sense and culture, if highly qualified for such domestic duties, could soon command prices equal to artists in music, dancing, and drawing, and an equal social position.

To secure all this, there needs only systematic plans and efforts such as American women are fully competent to organize and carry into successful operation. Institutions should be established where women will be trained to be scientific, healthful, and economical cooks; to be intelligent, loving, and careful nurses of young children; to be skillful seamstresses and mantua-makers, and yet prepared so to aid in the *active* family work as not to injure their health by exclusive sedentary employments.

So, too, there should be institutions to educate women not only as physicians for their own sex, but to be skillful and tender nurses of the sick. And when all these important offices of women are filled, and our school-rooms well supplied, there will be few women remaining to urge into the professions of men.

This project will, of course, be met with the inquiry, How can this kind of training be carried on in schools? Is it not the part that belongs to mothers in the family, and not to the school?

To this it is replied that mothers have not been trained themselves, and so can not teach *properly*. Moreover, with poor servants, feeble health, and multiplied cares, they can not do it. If a house is built for servants, and servants employed, it is as much as a woman can do to superintend all the complicated duties of wife, mother, and housekeeper, without attempting to teach what she herself never was properly taught to do. Moreover, when there are servants enough to do the work, the daughters of a family can not be made to take their places. How can the parents turn off the servants and put the daughters in their places? Every mother who superintends a family of children and servants in the present style of living in the more wealthy classes, will say it is impossible for her to train her daughters *properly* in all branches of woman's business.

But whatever *ought* to be *can* be done, and American women, if they undertake, can discover the best way.

Queen Victoria set up schools for young women to be trained not only to read and write, but to perform all the work of woman in a thorough and proper manner. Her nobility followed her example, and with success.

American women can do the same, and in a way adapted to our democratic system, as the Queen's is adapted to the aristocratic. In an aristocracy it is assumed that one class is to work for the benefit and enjoyment of an upper class. In a democracy it is assumed that every class is to work for their own welfare and enjoyment. In an aristocracy *work* is dishonored, in a democracy it is honored. In an aristocracy it is assumed as a distinctive mark of rank not to work, but to live to be waited on and worked for by a subordinate class. In a democracy it is assumed that both rich and poor

---

* A lady at the head of one of the largest mantua-making establishments in New York, employing over one hundred and fifty women and girls, informed the writer that her greatest difficulty is in finding women taught to work properly; and that, in her finishing-room, of twenty-five of her best hands not more than *four* could be trusted to complete and send off a dress without her standing by to oversee.

are *to work*, and that to live a life of idle pleasure is disgraceful.

When, therefore, the attempt is made to introduce industrial training into our schools, we are simply aiming to carry out practically the true democratic principle.

But there is a still higher aim. It will be found that the democratic principle is no other 'han the grand law of Christianity, which requires *work and self-sacrifice for the public good*, to which all private interests are to be subordinate.

Children are to be trained to live not for themselves but for others; not to be waited on and taken care of, but to wait on and take care of others; to *work* for the good of others as the first thing, and amusement and self-enjoyment as necessary but subordinate to the highest public good. The family is the first commonwealth where this training is to be carried on, and only as a preparation for a more enlarged sphere of action.

Jesus Christ came to set the example of self-sacrificing labor for the good of our race; and family training and school training are democratic and Christian only when the great principle of *living for others more than for self* is fully recognized and carried out.

It is clear that great changes are to be made in all the customs and habits of our nation, especially among the wealthy, before the true democratic and Christian principle will triumph over the aristocratic and unchristian.

One of these changes will be in the style of *house building*.

When houses are built *on Christian principles* women of wealth and culture will *work themselves, and train their children to work,* instead of having ignorant foreigners to ruin their food in a filthy kitchen, and ruin their children in the nursery.

When houses are built to honor woman's profession, and to secure the beauty, order, and comfort of a perfected house, the kitchen, as it usually exists, will be banished. Instead of the dark and comfortless room for family work, there will be one provided with sunlight and pure air, and well supplied with utensils and comforts in tasteful and convenient forms. So woman's dress will be not only neat and convenient but tasteful, as much so in the working-room as in the parlor.

Woman's work will be honorable and tasteful and agreeable when *cultivated* women undertake to make it so.

And when women of refinement and culture build houses on the Christian and democratic plan, work themselves, and train their children to work, they will never suffer for want of domestic helpers. Instead of coarse and vulgar servants, who live in the cellar and sleep in the garret, they will have refined and sympathizing friends to train their children, nurse their sick, and share in all their comforts, joys, and sorrows.

American women have abundant power to remedy all the wrongs and miseries of their sex.

by simply *educating them properly for their proper business.*

Many wealthy ladies would as readily endow institutions for their own sex as for men, were they aware of what might thus be accomplished. Few know what woman has done to aid men in elevating their professions. To gain authentic information on this point, the writer wrote to the Treasurers of only six colleges and professional schools, and gained these facts:

Miss Plummer, to Cambridge University, to endow one professorship, gave	$25,000
Mary Townsend, for the same	25,000
Sarah Jackson, ditto	10,000
Other ladies, in sums over $1000, to the same, over	30,000
To Andover Professional School of Theology ladies have given over	65,000
And of this $30,000 by one lady.	
In Illinois, Mrs. Garretson has given to one Professional School	300,000
In Albany, Mrs. Dudley has given for a Scientific Institution for men	105,000
To Beloit College, Wisconsin, property has been given by one lady valued at	30,000

Thus half a million has been given by women to these six Colleges and Professional Schools, and all in the present century. The reports of similar institutions for men all over the nation would show similar liberal benefactions of women to endow institutions for the other sex, while for their own no such records appear. Where is there a single endowment from a woman to secure a salary to a woman teaching her own proper profession?

But a time will come when women will give as liberally to elevate the true profession of women as *the ministers of home*, as they have to elevate the professions of men.

The remainder of this article will give drawings and descriptions to illustrate one house constructed on democratic and Christian principles. It is designed for persons in easy circumstances, who begin housekeeping with the true Christian idea of training a young family *to work* as well as to practice all the other social and domestic virtues.

Every family, as the general rule, includes the parents as the educators, and the children to be trained to Christian life. To these are added aged parents or infirm and homeless relatives. These are preserved in life after their active usefulness ceases, and often when they would gladly depart, for the special benefit of the young, as the only mode in which, in early life, they can be trained to self-sacrificing benevolence, to reverence for the aged, and to tender sympathy for the sick and unfortunate. Instead of regarding such members of a family as a burden and annoyance, the wise and Christian parents will welcome them as suffering helpers aiding to develop the highest Christian virtues in their children.

This house is planned for a family of ten or twelve, which may be regarded as the average number in healthy families.

The *site* is a dry spot with a cellar well drained, in an open space, where the health-

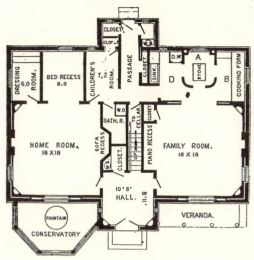

PLAN OF FIRST FLOOR.

the like. Small windows open on one side to the conservatory, and on the other to the veranda. A close staircase, and under it a large closet for overgarments.

When the house has bathrooms and water-closets in the second story there is no need of back stairs. But if they are desired, a narrow flight can descend from the broad stair to the back entry by giving up the recess and the closet of the Family Room.

The East Room, called the Family Room, is for the family eating and sitting room. A working room should always have the pleasant *morning* sun. It is 18 feet square, and opens with sliding-doors to the *cooking-stove* A, *cooking closet* B, with the cooking-form. In the drawing of the cooking-closet, given below, is an illustration of the *close packing of conveniences.*

In front of the window is the cooking-form. The door, F, admits a barrel of flour, and a lid on the top, G, is to raise when using flour. In the barrel a scoop and sieve. On the left of this is the moulding-board C, where bread is made, and other articles for baking prepared on a board which may be turned on one side for cooking, and the other side for other uses. Next to the flour closet are large drawers, the under ones running on rollers, in which are stored the Indian and Graham flour, the rye, tapioca, rice, etc., and two kinds of sugar used in cooking. On front and at the side are shelves, on which are stored every utensil and every article used in cooking.

Still farther to the left hand of the flour closet is the form, x, for preparing meats and vegetables, on the top a board turned on one side to

giving sun falls on every part, and the house so placed that the rooms in common use shall have the sun all day.

A *form* nearest a square best secures sunlight, perfect ventilation, and economical arrangement. Every projection increases expense and diminishes the chances of sunlight, proper warming, and ventilation.

The *close packing of conveniences*, so as to save time and steps, and contrivances to avoid the multiplication of rooms to be furnished, cleaned, and kept in order, is indispensable to economy of time, labor, and expense. In many large kitchens, with various closets, half the time of a cook is employed in walking to collect her utensils and materials, which all might be placed together.

The plan given above is rather a hint to be farther wrought out than a completed effort.

The house is fifty by thirty on the outside (excluding the projections of the back and front entrance). It faces south, giving to the two large rooms the sun all day.

The entrance hall is finished with oiled chestnut and black walnut mouldings, being handsomer, cheaper, and easier to keep in order than painted wood. All the inner doors of the hall finished with Gothic arches to correspond with the outside door. Niches for busts and flowers, each side of the front-door, with small closets under the niches for over-shoes and

COOKING FORM.

cut meat and vegetables, and the other side for other uses. On shelves in front are stored all the utensils and articles used in cooking meats and vegetables, and in preparing them for the table. In this cooking closet, by an economic arrangement, is stored all the family stores and supplies, and all the utensils for cooking and taking care of food. The shelves should reach to the ceiling, and the highest have small closets to hold articles not often wanted.

In the dish closet, D, is the sink, near both to the stove and the eating-room. Over it, and each side, are stored all the dishes. Thus two or three steps bring the dishes to the table, and from it to the sink and shelves. The sink to be of marble, with plated cocks to furnish hot and cold water. Nice small mops for washing dishes hung over the sink, and a convenient contrivance for drying towels over the stove.

The *stove* is placed between the dish and cooking closet, inclosed by partitions to the wall, with rising or sliding doors. A sliding closet, D W, to raise wood and coal from the cellar. Thus the stove can be entirely open in cold weather, and in the warm season closed tight with a contrivance to carry off the hot air and the smells of cooking into a ventilating flue.* In warm weather the stove is used for baking by moving the sliding-door, to be immediately closed after using the oven. These sliding partitions or doors, hung like windows, are made of wood, and lined with tin next the stove.

By this arrangement when the folding-doors of the Family Room are open there is a large and airy room for work-hours, and every article and utensil close at hand. When work is over and the folding-doors closed the room is a cheerful sitting-room for the family. It is furnished with a cheerful green carpet, and the appended work-closets are covered with a light green oil-cloth to match the carpet. On one side is a closet, for china, glass, and silver, with a small sink for washing them. In two corners are niches for busts and flowers, with small closets under them for working conveniences. A fire-place and mantle ornaments tempt the family gathering around the social hearth. The room opens to the piazza by sliding-doors. Glass roof and partitions in winter can turn this into a green-house, warmed by a register. On one side is a recess for a piano. This and the adjacent room to have *deadened* walls, so that the mother, if weary or ill, can find perfect quiet in the Home Room below or the Library above. The wearisome practicing of children on a piano will be thus escaped.

The stationary dining-table has appendages and conveniences *under* it, as do the *ottomans with lids*, which serve to store newspapers and

other matters. By such arrangements many steps are saved and order promoted. The covers of the sofa, ottomans, and table, and the wall-paper should match in color and design with the carpet, as also the window-shades. Such arrangements as these save the labor and expense of separate kitchen and dining-room, and also the expense of wasteful domestics. In such a house parents could train their children to be their happy associates in both work and play.

The West Room is specially for parents and children, and is named the *Home Room*. On the north is a bed recess concealed by folding-doors or curtains. On one side is the parents' dressing-room, with drawers on one side to the ceiling, and a clothes-press. The other side is the children's room, with drawers and clothes-press, close to the bath and water-closet and back outside door, so that children can run out and in without using other parts of the house. On one side of the back-door is a closet for garden tools and shoes, and on the other side a wash-bowl and towel, with a towel closet at hand, near both to this and to the bath-room.

The Home Room opens to a south conservatory and small fountain. Here parents can train their children to love and rear flowers, *not for themselves* alone, but for those who are less favored. Every child can not only give flowers to friends, but save seeds to give to some poor children, and *teach them how* to adorn their own homes with such blossoms of love and beauty. A sofa recess is in this room, and two niches in the opposite corners with work-closets under, while the centre-table and ottomans are provided with hidden places for storing conveniences. The bed recess and dressing-rooms are so provided with drawers and closets, *reaching to the wall*, that every article needed by parents and children may be stored close at hand. Windows in each division, and openings over partitions, secure ventilation.

At night, the parents and two little ones have a large and airy bedroom. In the day, these doors being closed, the same room is a nursery or a parlor at pleasure.

The carpet, wall-paper, covers of furniture, and window-shades, all are in harmony—blue and buff, or white and green, or gray and pink, as the taste may lead.

The drawing on the top of page 715 gives the second-floor, with its dormer-windows and balconies, the roof being so contrived that a current of air passes between the walls of the chambers and the roof, preventing excessive heat in summer. There are five good sized bedrooms, each with a closet. The largest can be finished with an arched ceiling, and furnished as a drawing-room and library, where parents and guests can retire from the work and children below. A method of *deadening* the walls also is provided, so that the noise of one room will not pass to the others.

A ventilating flue may be made, with a current of warm air from the stove in summer, and

* In these drawings there are no arrangements to secure perfect *ventilation*, besides the open fire-places in every room, except the two small chambers. The securing perfectly pure air in all rooms in a house, at all seasons, is the most difficult problem of the family state. A separate article will be devoted to this object hereafter, in which drawings to illustrate this method of escaping the heat and smells of cooking will appear.

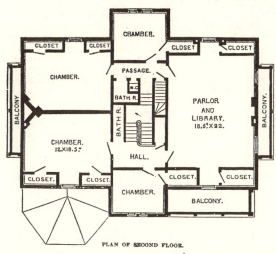

PLAN OF SECOND FLOOR.

close to the stove, filled once a day, and easily raised (like a dumb-waiter), supplies fuel with little labor. A room is parted off for vegetables that should be shut out from the light and warmth of the furnace, a safe being close to the cellar stairs, and a form raised close by these stairs to hold articles to be kept in a cellar, which save steps and waste.

All the inner wood-work to be combinations of chestnut, walnut, white wood, black walnut, or pine—oiled or varnished.

The engraving which heads this article gives a perspective view of the house and grounds, with trees, etc. The trees are in a thick clump, to make a dense shade *near* the house, but not so as to shut out the sun from all parts of the roof.

the furnace and stove in winter, and connected with every room, securing perfect ventilation, *without care and in spite of false notions*, in all seasons, and by day and night. Fire-places in every room but two give these sources of comfort and health.

There is only one stair-case, with a broad stair and two landings; to which, by giving up a closet below, may be added a narrow stair from the broad stair to the back-door, under the narrow stairway to the garret. There are two bath-rooms and a water-closet, with easy access from the chambers. In the country water can be gathered on the roof, or raised by a forcing-pump to a reservoir in the garret, for the use of the water-closet.

The annexed drawing gives the cellar, with its white plastered walls and hard water-cement floor. The south front portion is fitted up with tubs for a *laundry and drying - room*, having windows admitting sun and air. Should it be wanted for a kitchen, the cellar should be extended under the veranda, arches being used to support the wall of the room above. The windows of thick glass placed in the floor of the veranda would admit sunlight, and if made to rise would also admit air. The outside door to this room also could be made of glass to admit light.

The north part receives the wood and coal, and a sliding closet, D W,

A house on this plan will accommodate a family of ten, and afford also a guest-chamber, and it offers all the conveniences and comforts and most of the elegances of houses that cost four times the amount and require three or four servants.

If a new-married pair commence housekeeping in it, the young wife, aided by a girl of ten or twelve, could easily perform all the labor except the washing and ironing, which could be done by hired labor in the basement. The first months of housekeeping could be spent in perfecting herself and her assistant, whom she could train to do all kinds of family work, and

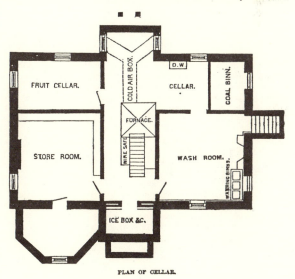

PLAN OF CELLAR.

also to be her intelligent and sympathizing helper when children come.

While it should be the aim to render woman's profession so honorable that persons of the highest position and culture will seek it, as men seek their most honored professions, there must still be the class of *servants*, to carry out a style of living and expenditure both lawful and useful, where large fortunes abound. For this class the aim should be to secure their thorough preparation and to increase their advantages. Should both aims be achieved, then a woman who prefers a style of living demanding servants, will be so trained herself as not to be dependent on hirelings at the sacrifice of self-respect. On the other hand, a woman who chooses another style of living, so as to work herself and train her children to work, can do so without fear of losing any social advantages. Or, in case more helpers are needed, she can secure highly cultivated and refined *friends* to share all her family enjoyments, instead of depending on a class inferior in cultivation and less qualified to form the habits and tastes of her children.

But it is not the married alone who are privileged to become ministers in the *home church* of Jesus Christ. A woman without children, and with means of her own, could provide such a house as this, and take one child and a well-qualified governess to aid in training it. Then, after success inspires confidence, a second child might be adopted till the extent of her means and benevolence is reached.

There are multitudes of benevolent women, whose cultivated energies are now spent in a round of selfish indulgence, who would wake up to a new life if they thus met woman's highest calling as Heaven-appointed ministers of Christ, to train his neglected little ones for that kingdom of self-denying labor and love of which he is the model and head.

Thousands and thousands of orphans are now deprived of a father's home and support. Thousands of women, widowed in the dearest hopes of this life, are seeking for consolation in the only true avenues.

A great emergency in our nation has occurred, in which thousands of women are forever cut off from any homes of their own by marriage. Of these many are women of wealth and influence among Protestants, who in hospitals and battle-fields have been learning the highest lessons of self-sacrificing benevolence. Such will not return home to be idle, but will press toward those avenues that offer the most aid and sympathy; and if it is not provided by Protestants they will seek it in the Catholic fold.

Catholic convents provide their inmates with a comfortable home and opportunities of benevolence toward neglected children, the sick, and the poor. But they are burdened with a round of observances and rules involving the sacrifice of reason and conscience, and of personal independence. For complete submission to the Superior is the first duty. Moreover, this is not the family state designed by God,

with its simple and natural duties, where two, united in love, or sometimes the widowed one alone, has an independent home and a small flock all under her own control, with none but God and her own conscience to rule.

There have been various attempts made to form *communities* on various modifications of the Fourierite plan, which brings individuals of all ages, tastes, and habits into one family, with no parents or superior or bishop to control. Such are, and ever must be, failures.

So the boarding-school system, which takes children from parental love and close watch of the family state, giving them to strangers amidst new and multiplied temptations, this is, and ever must be, a failure.

The true Protestant system, yet to be developed and tried by women of wealth and benevolence, is the one here suggested; based not on the conventual, nor on the Fourierite, nor on the boarding-school systems, but on the Heaven-devised plan of the family state.

One aim of this article is to attract the notice of conscientious persons commencing the family state with means sufficient for a much more expensive establishment.

Many such really believe themselves the followers of Christ who have seldom practiced that economy which denies self to increase the advantages of the poor, especially in deciding on the *style of living* they adopt. Most wealthy persons provide houses, equipage, servants, and expenditures that demand most of their income, while the waste in their kitchens alone would, by careful economy, such as we see in France, feed another whole family.

When houses are built on Christian and democratic principles, and young girls in every condition of life are trained to a wise economy, thousands of young men, who can not afford to marry young ladies trained in the common boarding-school fashion, will find the chief impediment removed; and thus healthful and happy homes will multiply with our increasing wealth and culture.

CHAPTER XVI.

THE suffrage laws of the United States seem to have been based on no well-defined principle, but to have been the outgrowth of circumstances, without any clear comprehension of the character of the liberties they were granting. In some instances important franchises have been conferred on classes not qualified to use them judiciously, merely to appease a popular and unreasoning clamor. The suffrage, originally, in the older States, the privilege of freeholders only, was subsequently granted to those who performed military duty, and, in some States, to those who were members of a volunteer fire department, if of suitable age. It was next conferred on those who had served as volunteers in the war of 1812, the Mexican war, and later, the recent civil war, where they were not, on other grounds, voters. In a fit of democratic generosity, the freehold qualification was swept away in most of the States, and all white male citizens, natives of the country, or naturalized under United States laws, which required five years' residence and three years' declaration of intention, except convicts, lunatics, and idiots, were permitted to vote under certain restrictions of residence. A provision was made by the Constitution in regard to the Southern States, by which a Congressional district should be deemed to have the requisite population, when the white and free colored population were added to three-fifths " of all other persons " (the constitutional euphemism for *slaves*), to make up the necessary number to entitle the territory to a representative. Thus, in one sense, the Southern vote was increased by three-fifths of its slave population, although these cast no vote, and literally, none was cast for them. The late civil war abolished this method of increasing the congressional representation of the South, by abolishing slavery. A considerable number of former voters at the South were at first disfranchised in consequence of their participation in the insurrection, but by successive amnesties they were nearly all restored to their civil rights, and by the action of the constitutional conventions of the reconstructed States, most of them were permitted to vote and hold office again. The emancipated slaves had in many instances contributed all in their power to the success of the national government; nearly 300,000 of them had borne arms, and others in various ways had given aid and comfort to the national soldiers. It was proposed to grant them the suffrage as a compensation for their patriotic sacrifices; and so earnest and loud was the popular clamor to grant this privilege to all the adult men of color in the South, that an amendment to the Constitution was passed by Congress and ratified by the States, and provision made to this effect in all the new constitutions of the reconstructed States. The measure, though prompted by the best of motives, was injudicious; there was some reason for according the privilege to those colored men who had been in the Union service, either as soldiers, teamsters, or servants, though even they were scarcely qualified by their intelligence for the exercise of so important a right; but to extend the same privilege to all the plantation negroes, before they had acquired any knowledge in regard to the government, or were able to understand the Constitution, was exceedingly unwise. They were, of course, very liable to be influenced, in regard to their vote, by designing men, one of the worst evils of a free suffrage. It might be said, indeed, in partial justification of this measure, that they were generally very nearly as intelligent as the poor whites of the South, who already possessed the right of suffrage, but two wrongs do not make one right, and the remedy should rather have been the establishment of an educational test, and the refusal of the privilege to all, black or white, who did not come up to it.

But the popular heart was still unsatisfied, and now the cry was for the abolition of all distinctions of race or color, as a ground of withholding

268 SUFFRAGE IN THE UNITED STATES.

the privilege of suffrage throughout the Union. The amendment to the Constitution prescribing this will undoubtedly be ratified. So far as the negroes in the Northern States are concerned, the measure is not seriously objectionable, while such facilities exist for conferring the privilege upon ignorant and often degraded foreigners,—as the negroes are generally the better citizens of the two; but, with the near prospect of a vast influx of Chinese, mainly of the lowest class, who can, in five years at the most, become citizens and voters, we must think this further extension of the franchise should have been better guarded.

The advocates of universal suffrage in the United States have now only women and minors left upon whom they can confer the right; and there are those who argue that, having swallowed and digested every inch of the camel, we should not so carefully strain out the gnat.

To this reasoning we can not agree; if we have done wrong in the past, if we have conferred privileges on those who were unworthy of them, or who, if not unworthy, were not entitled to them, it does not follow that we should continue to err in the same or any other direction. If there is but little left to contend for, that little, if right, should be as valiantly defended as if it were more, since it is *all* that we can retain.

We are prepared, then, to consider the reasons why, in this country, suffrage should not be granted to women, as women; a different question, be it observed, from that which agitates the public mind in England, the question there being, whether the suffrage should be granted to some women, not as women, but as holders of property.

These reasons may be divided for convenience sake into four classes : those concerning the political, social, intellectual, and moral relations.

Beginning with the political aspect of the question, we may remark, in the first place, that woman has no need of the suffrage, since she is already represented in the legislative bodies, whether State or municipal, as well as by the officers of the State and nation. The family basis of representation, which, however unwisely it may be extended, is the true basis, makes the husband and father the true representative of his entire household, and the intelligent American voter generally feels that the responsibility appertaining to this representative character rests upon him. The members of our municipal, State, and national legislatures forgetful, as they too often are, of other interests confided to them, or of duties required of them by their constituents, are seldom, we might almost say, never, unmindful of the wants and requirements of the women whom they represent quite as truly as they do the men of their respective districts. Whatever may have been the case in the past, it is certain that, at the present day, women makes no reasonable request of our legislators which

11   Q

passes unheeded; on the contrary, the danger is rather that of excess in their liberality in gratifying the wishes of woman than of denying her what are her just rights. In all directions in which it is in the power of a legislature to improve the condition of woman, she has but to ask to receive. This general sentiment of tenderness and regard for the sex on the part of men, both in high and in low station, is invaluable to women. It is their greatest protection and safeguard, and it would be the greatest of misfortunes to them were it to be, by any means, blunted and lowered in its tone.

But there is another power which women exert, independent of this general deference which they command, the power of personal influence, not only over voters, but over their elected representatives. An earnest, determined woman, possessing those graces of person or intellect, which fit her to influence and control men, can carry almost any measure on which she has set her heart, over every obstacle, in either the State or national legislature. Take the case of Miss Vinnie Ream, who is engaged in making a statue, for the Capitol, of President Lincoln. Miss Ream may prove a sculptor of remarkable ability, and her statue may be, when completed, the eighth wonder of the world, as a work of art; on this point we have no right to express an opinion, since it is not yet completed; but whether it be so or not, one thing is certain, that it was not the consideration of her extraordinary abilities as an artist which led to her obtaining this commission, for she had done nothing worthy of note, and of the few busts or figures in plaster which she had executed, the members of Congress, either senators or representatives, had generally no knowledge, and many of them were incompetent to judge, if they had seen them. No! it was her daring, young girl as she was, in proposing to undertake such a work; her determined personal canvass of the members of Congress for their votes, and the magnetic influence of her powers of fascination over grave and venerable senators, and intelligent representatives, which enabled her to procure an order for a statue, more liberal in its terms and more remarkable for its perfect confidence in the, as yet untried, ability of the artist, than any commission of the sort in modern times. Instances of this power of woman's personal influence in political matters are innumerable. Who has not heard of the beneficent efforts of Mrs. Husband, during the war, in procuring from President Lincoln the commutation of sentence, and often the pardon of, soldiers condemned to die under the barbarous military laws? Who does not know of the success of the infamous Mrs. Cobb as a pardon-broker during the late administration?

In the second place, the exercise of the suffrage by woman would be an attempt to make suffrage individual instead of representative, and so against the natural order of things. The other extensions of the voting privilege, to which we have referred, however injudicious they may have been, did not materially interfere with its representative character, as based on the family as the *unit* of society ; but this would inaugurate an entirely different principle; the right of the individual, as such, to participate in the government, a claim incompatible with the organization of society, and subversive of its best interests. In all large communities and States, the principle of representation must obtain in the government. The executive represents and is responsible to, not merely the party which elected him, but the whole people of the State or community. The member of Congress, or of the State legislature, represents all the people of his district, and it is his duty to further their interests so far as is compatible with justice; and every voter who casts his ballot, represents, on an average, five people who do not and can not vote. Abrogate this principle of representation, and let each voter represent only himself or herself, and you loosen the bond which holds society together ; the male voter will say at once : " I have no need to consider anybody's interest but my own ; my wife, my sister, my daughter, may desire to see a certain man elected, or a certain measure voted for, which will prove beneficial to their interests ; but they must vote for it themselves; I shall consult my own interests solely." The representative elected by the votes of those who exercise the suffrage solely for the gratification of their own whims, will cease to regard his representative character as essential; he has no longer to look upon the families of his district as his constituents, or to feel a responsibility to them. They are merely an aggregation of individuals who cast their votes for him, because he was nominated, and not because they expected to hold him accountable for his acts, and he must make the most of his opportunity, for he may not have another. Hence will come rings, corruption, public plunder, and subserviency to great corporations, to an extent far beyond that which has already awakened the indignation of the public.

In the third place, by woman suffrage women will gain nothing, while they will lose much. From what we have already said, it will be seen that they will lose all the advantages which they now possess from the representative character of the suffrage, all that chivalric regard for their interests, which now prompts our legislators to grant all their reasonable and some of their unreasonable requests, as a matter of course; all that their personal influence is now able to effect, and all that is gained now from family, in the place of individual interest in the ballot.

Women would be, in almost all communities, a

minority at the polls; there would be so many who could not, and so many who would not, vote, that it would be remarkable if their vote ever exceeded that of men. It would hardly be possible that, in any case, even in matters concerning their own interests, they would all vote alike. They would be likely to be divided, as their husbands, brothers, and fathers were between the two parties, perhaps unequally, but never to such an extent as to enable them to rule or control either party. Generally, they would have to vote for men, often for men whom they greatly disliked, for legislators, or State, or national officers. They might, and doubtless often would, contribute to place in power some unprincipled demagogue, but very rarely would they be able to rally votes enough to succeed in electing an upright and honest man; they might, at times, be allowed, as a special favor, to elect one or two of their own sex to the legislature, or to some petty office; but such an election would prove any thing but a favor to the unfortunate candidate; in a hopeless minority, so far as any action in relation to her sex was concerned, all her prestige as a woman gone, without influence or position, yet expected to do for her sex what chivalry had previously prompted men to do, it would be strange if the poor representative of women's suffrage did not very early resign her seat, in an uncontrollable fit of home-sickness.

Naturally enough, the measures which concerned women would be referred to them in a legislature in which there were a few (there never would be many) female members; but their power to effect their passage would be infinitely less than if they were not members of the legislative body. In such a body, and as a member of it, the most eloquent of women would find her oratory out of place, and her pleas would fall cold and dead. All legislation in the interests of women would be paralyzed, and their progress in the attainment of their legal rights arrested, and postponed for a full half-century.

In the fourth place, there is no possible plea in justification of woman's intrusion into the realm of political action. The admission of some of the classes which have latterly received the privilege of the suffrage might be justified as an act of self-defense; the foreigner, after a certain period of residence and naturalization, might plead in favor of his admission to the suffrage, that he had property to protect, that the attitude of the native-born citizens toward him was one of hostility, and that he must have the ballot for his own protection. In like manner, the men of color might ask for the suffrage to protect them from the encroachments and oppressions of the whites, and the disfranchised citizens of the South might seek it to save them from apprehended aggressions on the part of the blacks.

But the relations of men and women can never be, to any extent, such as under ordinary circumstances to array them in hostility to each other, or make one fear the aggressions of the other.

Mother, wife, sister, or daughter; one or other, and perhaps more than one, of these relations every woman holds to the men around her ; and, if he would, man can not make any laws or take any measures seriously detrimental to their interests They are bone of his bones, and flesh of his flesh and if he is made their representative and trusted to act for their interests, he will, from the sheer selfishness of relationship, do his best for them. But separate the two sexes; let man understand that woman is determined to stand for herself, and neither desires nor needs his assistance, and how soon would an antagonism be engendered, which many waters could not quench. All such interference with the laws of nature, and the relations in which the All-wise Creator has placed his creatures to each other, can only be productive of evil and misery.

In the fifth place, the exercise of the privilege of suffrage would not be, and, in the nature of the case, could not be a remedy for any one of the wrongs or evils from which women now suffer.

We have all heard of the pope's bull against the comet, and we remember how the comet kept on its way undisturbed by the fulminations of his holiness. The comet moved in obedience to

116

natural laws, over which the pope's missives could have no control. Precisely similar is the case of the principal wrongs of which women complain, and which are, undoubtedly, real wrongs : low wages—we might say, starvation wages—too many hours work in the day, want of employment, over-crowding in many branches of business, and, perhaps, also, more stringent enactments against brothels, seduction, &c.

In a former chapter we have shown that the evils complained of in regard to employments were not, in any respect, subjects for legislation; that the laws of supply and demand must regulate the prices of labor as of every thing else, and that they must be remedied, if remedied at all, by an increase of intelligence which should lift up a considerable number to a higher plane, where the demand was greater than the supply; by trades-unions, which would enable women to control the price of their labor; by the suppression of the practice of underbidding, both by the poorest class of partially skilled working-women in the cities, and by women in the country, who, having homes and food furnished, undertake this kind of work to supply themselves with a little pocket-money; and by co-operation, which should enable them to obtain food and rents cheaper, and, perhaps, to become their own employers. It is obvious that the suffrage is not required for any of these purposes. As to the legal enactments sought, is it not plain

11*

to every thoughtful mind, that the probability is a thousand-fold stronger of obtaining the desired legislation speedily, by appealing to existing or soon-to-be-assembled legislatures, and asking for the enactment of such statutes as are needful, on the ground of good order, good morals, and the moral and social rights of women, than by attempting, what would prove a perfect failure, the election of a sufficient number of women to any legislature, to pass, by their votes, the desired enactments?

The arguments which we have adduced will, we believe, be sufficient to show the inexpediency of women's suffrage as a political measure.

ART. IV.—1. *History of the Female Sex.* BÖTTIGER.
2. *History of Women.* 2 vols., 4to. ALEXANDER. 1779.
3. *Les Femmes.* 3 vols. SÉGUR. 1802.

It is seldom agreeable to argue with the ladies; to refute them is ungallant, and to pass censure on them is odious. Sometimes, however, they have to be argued with, refuted, and even censured, for their own good. We cannot but regard the present as one of these occasions; for we hold that the "woman's rights" movement is no honor to our civilization, but rather discreditable. If its tendency were to improve the condition of the sex, none would give it more hearty support than ourselves; it is precisely because it has the opposite tendency that we oppose it.

If we are wrong in this, a question or two may produce a train of thought that will aid in explaining the fact. We,

119

therefore, ask, what is woman most esteemed, loved and honored for? Is it for her boldness? for her courage? for her independence of man, or for her readiness to compete with him publicly, late and early? In other words, is woman most endeared to man in proportion as she is like himself? Do men prefer women who are masculine to those who are feminine, or womanly, in their habits and manners?

It may be replied that there are a class of men who do. Those who want their wives and daughters to work and earn for them, value them, not in proportion as they are modest, timid and gentle, but in proportion as they are strong and willing to use their strength for the common benefit. But among this class there need be no clamor for woman's rights; the women have an undisputed right to do everything that is coarse and unwomanly. It is not necessary to go back to the savage state for illustrations of this; a tour among the poorer classes of the peasantry in any country of Europe would furnish abundance. The tourist would readily discover that women may work in the field from sunrise till sunset; that they may go out before their husbands in the morning and remain out after them in the evening; that those who have no husbands may work in the field as long as they are able, side by side with men, and get as much pay as men, when they perform as much labor. But are the women proud of all this? Do they boast of their equality with the men, or have they cause to boast? Do they excite the envy of the wives and daughters of their landlords or employers because the latter are such tyrants that they prefer doing the rougher work themselves. This, perhaps, will serve to explain why it is that the theory of "woman's rights" has so few votaries even in the most romantic countries of Europe.

But the peasant women are not merely allowed the right of doing every sort of work; they are also allowed the right of advising their husbands. Nor is this anything new or exceptional; it is no "modern improvement." Among all the principal races of mankind, "woman's rights" were fully conceded by the most barbarous. It may seem incredible to many that it was the most barbarous who were most liberal in this respect; but such, nevertheless, is the fact. The ancient Germans * and ancient Gauls † alike engaged in no important enterprise without consulting their wives.‡ There is no part of Guizot's excellent History of Civilization more interesting than that in which he shows, from the testimony of numerous historians, that woman's rights were well understood among our rude ancestors, both Teutonic and Gallic, more than two thousand years ago.§ True, the historian does not call the privileges enjoyed by the ladies of those distant ages "woman's rights." Cæsar and Tacitus, as well as Guizot, were evidently of opinion that the women of those times would have been much better off had their "rights" been somewhat more limited than they were; and there is good reason to believe that the women themselves, accustomed as they were to compete with men, even in the field of battle, would willingly have surrendered several of their "rights"‖ in exchange for just such tyrannical treatment as their fair posterity are so solemnly and vehemently protesting against at the present day.

But this is not the only evidence of the short-sightedness of our woman's rights advocates. They would have the world believe that they are in advance of the age, but we can assure them that only the credulous and silly part of the world believe any such thing. It is idle to deny that the intelligent and thoughtful regard them, at best, very much in the

---

* The ancient Germans regarded woman as something holy and inspired, and consulted her accordingly as an oracle that seldom, if ever, was mistaken in regard to the future. We quote the words of Tacitus: "Inesse quinetiam *sanctum aliquid et providum* putant."—*De Moribus Germanorum*, c. 8.

† See Cæsar *De Bello Gal.* l. vi., c. xix., *et seq.*

‡ When Hannibal complained that the Gauls had done wrong to his countrymen, they replied that if the Carthaginians felt themselves aggrieved they must present their case to the Gallic women:

"Les Gaulois consultaient les femmes dans les affaires importantes; ils convinrent avec Annibal que *si les Carthaginois avaient à se plaindre des Gaulois, ils porteraient leurs plaintes devant les femmes gauloises, qui en seraient juges.*"—*Mém. de l'Académ. des Inscript.*, t. xxiv., p. 374; Mémoire de l'abbe Fénel.

It is well known that even the North American Indians regularly and carefully consulted their wives.

"Les Hurons, en particulier, *consultent soigneusement les femmes.*"—Charlevoix, *Hist. du Canada*, pp. 267, 269, 287.

§ *Hist. de la Civ. en France*, vol. i., pp. 215–225.

‖ The most degraded tribe of the Siberian women enjoyed woman's rights to

light of the innocent frogs who were so clamorous in their demands for a king from Jupiter. We have shown that nowhere are the sexes more on an equality than among the rudest classes, and that it has always been so. If, instead of "equality," we use the term "liberty," there will be no change in the circumstances, since no women can be said to enjoy more liberty than those whose "inalienable right" it is to roam the forest. But this is equally true of man. If any mortal may be said to be entirely free it is the savage in his hunting grounds, armed with his bow and arrow; nor can he cease to be a savage without surrendering a portion of that freedom!

When man attains to civilization he submits to a certain restraint on his liberty, in order that he may be protected by the state. Woman surrenders a portion of her liberty to man precisely on the same principle ; as a return for the protection and support which she receives from him she renders him obedience, and does what she can to contribute to his happiness. At least, she is expected to do those things. Seeing that her husband does not wish her to do men's work, or to place herself in a position in which her virtue would be in danger, she thinks it her duty to abstain, if only to please him. This is what she is supposed to do in a well-ordered community; and most cheerfully do we admit that in general the supposition is a correct one. Nor do we think there are any women more obedient, more gentle, or more faithful, than those of our own country; none are less disposed to oppose, set at defiance, or otherwise annoy their husbands. Although there are more advocates of woman's rights among the ladies of the United States than among those of any other country, it is true, at the same time, that there are fewer Xantippes or disagreeable wives; and we believe that if the matter were duly investigated, it would be ascertained that three-fourths of the latter class, if not a still

---

the fullest extent, when their inhospitable country was first explored by civilized men. They fought in battle habitually with their husbands; but the historian tells us that they were not the less maltreated on this account:

"Les femmes tunguses, en Sibérie, vont aussi à la guerre avec leurs maris; elles n'en sont pas moins maltraitées."—Meiners, *Hist. du Sexe Feminin, en allemand*, t. i., pp. 18–19.

larger proportion, are to be found among the advocates of woman's rights. Assuming this to be the fact, the question would arise, whether it would not be better, upon the whole, that our American Xantippes had pursued the course of their ancient prototype than that they do pursue. It seems that even the wife of Socrates attended pretty carefully to her domestic duties. It does not appear from the account of either Plato or Xenophon that she neglected her children, or required the philosopher to do the nursing or the dish washing. If she sometimes gave him a bath when he did not wish it, and was not particular whether it was clean or otherwise, we have the best evidence that she was attached to him nevertheless. Her deep grief at his condemnation showed that, no matter what she said or did to her husband, she was still a true woman at heart, and an affectionate wife.

Be this as it may, it is very generally believed among the most sensible and most intelligent classes of mankind, that women who are fond of hearing themselves speak in public, anxious to see their names in the newspapers, as reformers, and ever ready to inveigh against man as a tyrant, rarely, if ever, make good wives. Indeed it would seem that a large portion of our young men have adopted this theory; we prefer to arrive at this conclusion, rather than to say that there are so many old maids and neglected young widows among the women's rights sisterhood, only because they have fewer personal attractions than the sex in general, and fewer womanly qualities. It is probably nearer the truth to attribute the state of things alluded to, partly to one cause and partly to another: for several honest young men, who do not seem at all wanting in courage, have assured us that they would rather remain single for ever, than marry a peripatetic female reformer, but especially a reformer of the woman's rights type.

It is true that there are many young men, and old men, too, who regard the matter in a different light; but they form but a very small minority. This is fortunate, because it is this class — sometimes called the Miss Nancy class — that urge the women to forget that they are such. If there are more woman's rights women in the United States than in any other country equally enlightened, it is chiefly, if not solely, because we have more of this species of men in proportion to our population. The excess is the result of causes which might be easily pointed out ; but it will be sufficient for our present purpose to remark, in general terms, that our climate and mode of life have a great deal to do with that phenomenon.

We are very unwilling to give any needless pain to either the men or the women engaged in the woman's rights movement, much as we dislike it ; but, happily, it so happens that the feelings of neither are very sensitive; if the blush of modesty or delicacy ever mantles the cheek of either, after they have devoted a certain time to the cause, we think it is very seldom ; and if anything like a blush does appear, we think its genuineness may be doubted.

Here we are reminded of certain facts which science has fully demonstrated. It is sometimes remarked, in jest, that this or that individual, in female garments, is but half a female ; and, for a similar reason, it is remarked that this or that individual, in male garments, is but half a male—that he is half, or more than half, a female! In general the observation merely creates a smile ; although it is a smile of assent to the justice of the satire, in a metaphorical sense, not one out of five hundred having the least idea that the fact may be literally true.

Now, if women are like men, or men like women, why should we blame either if it is the result of malformation, or of a *lusus naturæ ?* It would be much more rational, as well as more charitable, to commiserate their condition. If there are any who think that we merely jest in attempting to account for some of the woman's rights phenomena in this way, they can easily ascertain for themselves that the assertion we make on the subject is substantially correct.

From the most remote antiquity up to the middle of the eighteenth century, no doubt was entertained as to the reality of hermaphroditism ; it was universally admitted, at least among scientific men, that in many instances both sexes were combined, in different proportions, in one individual. Not only had all naturalists and physicians, who had written treatises on man, spoken of it as an incontestible fact, but the most eminent artists represented it both in painting and sculpture. But in the earlier part of last century, all opinions which seemed in conflict with the general course of nature, were regarded as superstitious or fabulous; and, accordingly, hermaphroditism was denied or declared doubtful. But modern science has demonstrated, that, as in numerous similar instances, the ancients were right, after all. Several works have been written on the subject within the present century; but we need only mention that of Geoffrey Saint-Hilaire.* None who examine this remarkable and learned work will entertain any doubt on the subject. Those who may not be able to procure the treatise itself, as it is scarce in this country, may find an analysis of the part of it bearing on our present subject, in the supplement to the *Encyclopédie Moderne*, vol. v., article "Hermaphrodisme."

Saint-Hilaire fully describes the different kinds of hermaphroditism, designating them respectively, as "masculine," "feminine," "neuter," and "mixed;" and illustrating them with plates. Nor does the philosopher overlook the moral and intellectual characteristics of each variety. Even the peculiarities of the voice and gestures are clearly indicated. He shows that if many ancient authors spoke of women *who became men*, as instances of the marvellous, they did not do so either through ignorance, or a disposition to impose on the credulity of their readers.

Among the ancients the phenomenon under consideration was regarded as foreboding some terrible calamity in the family to which the individual exhibiting it belonged; and it may be doubted whether the moderns should not regard it in the same light, though for different reasons. Be this as it may, the great anatomists of our day regard it as a "*simple anomalie, arrête de développement*," &c. Sometimes the complications are such that it is impossible to determine whether the individual, in this condition, be male, or female. † For the proofs of this we

---

* *Historie générale et particulière des anomalies de l'organisation chez l'homme et chez les animaux*, 2 vol, in 8vo, 1856; t. ii. *des Hermaphrodismes*.

† L'hermaphrodism *neutre* comprend les cas dans lesquels les parties sexuelles ont une caractère tellement ambigu qu'il est *impossible* de *distinguer* si elles sont mâles ou femalies, en sorte qu'il parait évident que l'individu qui les possèae n'appartient à aucun sexe.— *Complt de l'Ency. Mod.*, tome v., p. 411.

must refer to the treatises alluded to — especially to that of M. St.-Hilaire — for we wish to abstain carefully from every remark and allusion that might have a prurient tendency, and confine ourselves exclusively to such of the scientific facts as are necessary to afford at least a reasonable clue as to what the real difficulty is, in certain cases, altogether independently of styles of garments.

In the mixed species other phenomena present themselves — phenomena which also extend to the voice, gestures, habits, &c. Again, to all external appearance, one may seem to be a man, or a woman, except so far as the habits or the conduct may excite suspicion, as intimated; and yet the experienced and skilful anatomist may be able to demonstrate that the fact is but partially true at best. * These facts are now so fully recognized, that they have been embodied in the medical jurisprudence of all the enlightened nations of Europe, so that it is by no means a rare occurrence for the physician to be called into court to tell, on his oath, if he can, what is the sex of a particular individual !†

Now, let the reader reflect for a moment, and try to remember what are the general characteristics of both the ladies and gentlemen who are the most active and zealous advocates of "woman's rights." It is not sufficient to examine those who go about from town to town to attend meetings, get up resolutions, and deliver speeches, although we humbly think that such examinations, occasionally made, under proper auspices, by medical men of acknowledged skill, virtue, and discretion, would prove the best remedy for those revolutionary hysterics yet applied. It is, however, also necessary to see who are the chief

---

* "L'hermaphrodisme *mixte*, au contraire, mériter*éelement ce nom*. Un individu sera mixte s'il présente réunis des organes mâles et des organes femelles, non pas réunis chacun au complete, mais partieillement, quelques organes mâles remplaçant quelques organes femalles, et réciproquement."

† L'hermaphrodisme donne lieu à des *questions de médecine légale fort délicates* et que nous ne ponvons *qu'indiquer*; c'est aux médecins appelés par les tribunaux à *rechercher*, autant que *cela est possible*, sur un individu vivant les caractérés propres à déterminer le sexe.   Toutefois nous devons dire, pour la décharge des médecins appelés à résoudre ces questions, qu'il y a des *difficultés considérables* et quelquefois *insurmontables* à *préciser* le *sexe ;* car rien à l'extérieur ne peut faire *deviner* l'état des organes intérieurs. Ainsi, lorsqu' à un appareil génital féminin complet s'ajoutent à l'intérieur quelques organes mâles, le médecin ne saurait reconnatre l'existence de ces derniers ; la difficulté est encore plus grande quand l'individu est *neutre.— Complément de l'Encyc. Mod.* t, v., p. 411.

aiders and abettors of the movement among the members of the press, the clergy, the medical faculty, the bar. We think that if the investigation be impartially made, and extended in this manner, it will be found, in nine cases out of ten, that those who are in favor of woman's rights, are, or have been, equally in favor of various other visionary projects. Those who consult the work of Sainte-Hilaire will see that the sex of an individual may be even doubtful; and yet he or she may possess a certain kind of talent, especially a talent for speech-making, and making a general noise in the world; nature being disposed to make amends in this way for her carelessness in arranging, or rather disarranging, certain details. Some may think that because they have a family they are entitled to exemption from examinations of this kind; but although such a plea would seem a very plausible one, science has proved, in a hundred instances, as the reader may ascertain, that it is by no means conclusive!

If, upon the other hand, we inquire who are opposed to "woman's rights," we shall have to place in that category the greatest women, as well as the greatest men of all ages and countries. The great philosopher, the great poet, the great soldier, the great scientific discoverer, the great jurist, the great divine—those who love woman best and esteem her most—are all equally opposed to woman's rights. In short, those who would be the first to die, if necessary, in defence of woman, would be the last to concede those rights, precisely because they are too precious of her to expose her to what would inevitably degrade her, even though no rude or lascivious hand should ever be laid upon her in her competition with men.

It is needless to enter into particulars on this point; the most short sighted can see for themselves, that, in accordance with the scientific facts just glanced at, it is the women who are most like men, and the men who are most like women, that in ninety-nine cases out of a hundred are advocates of woman's rights. Hence it is that when some of our journalists compare a woman ambitious to vote, to hold political office, and to reform her male neighbors by her public speeches — to a *crowing hen*, he does not merely perpetrate a joke, or indulge in well merited satire; for if the crowing hen were placed in the hands of any competent comparative anatomist, it would be found that if the poor feathered biped imitated some of the performances of the male of its species, it was not without substantial reason.

But, assuming that anatomy has nothing to do with the matter—an assumption which is certainly not justified by the facts—it requires but very little research and reflection to ascertain that the woman's rights doctrines confer no credit on either the men or the women who advocate them. A great many think that those doctrines have, at least, the merit of novelty; but we will show that such is not the case. Thus, for example, there is not a single " right" claimed at the present day by the most unblushing of our fair orators, but was claimed and enjoyed by the women of Sparta, nearly three thousand years ago.

Now let us pause for a moment, and learn what we can from this fact, for it is fully attested by the most reliable historians. Those authors tell us what the Spartan women were before and after those "rights" were conceded to them. They tell us that before they had any more rights than the women of other countries, they were equally distinguished for their industry and virtue; nor were there any more baautiful women of their time. In short, they were just such as those daughters of America are now, who worthily maintain the national character of the sex; for we hold that, if the woman's rights advocates be regarded as exceptions — what they really are — there are no women that possess the best and noblest characteristics of the sex, in a higher degree than our own. But what was the character of the Spartan women, after they had obtained their rights? what did they gain by their emancipation from the tyranny of man? It matters little which of the historians who relate the facts we consult; all bear testimony to the degradation brought on those excellent women by that very " equality before the laws " which is now so clamorously demanded by the advocates of woman's rights. The Spartan women had been at least as good as the women of any of the other Grecian states before they obtained their rights in the manner indicated; and so early as the time of Homer, the Grecian women had manners and customs which would do no discredit to the most refined and most virtuous ladies of our own time. The Homeric ladies wanted no rights; they enjoyed all they desired, and were content; and Thucydides assures us* that the modesty and delicacy so admirably and fully portrayed by the poet had subsisted in Greece for ages. Homer represents no indecent scenes in the relations of the sexes; on the contrary, the state of manners which he describes has never been surpassed. Andromache, Nausicæ, and Penelopé were but types of the women of the better class; yet they are regarded as models by the best modern and christian authorities. Certainly no women could be more feminine or more modest. Full of solicitude as Andromache is for the safety of Hector, in no instance does she attempt to go to see him without being accompanied by her maid; and never does her husband come home, but he finds her surrounded by her maids. Even Helen is everywhere represented by Homer as the victim of violence: nowhere as a depraved or faithless woman; and she never alludes to her abduction herself, but with expressions of deep regret and shame, and often bitter tears. Much as the suitors of Penelopé are condemned in the Odyssey, they make no indecent proposals to the wife of Ulyssees; they merely urge her to marry; and they do so solely on the ground that her husband is dead, and that there is no hope of his return. The very fact that all the states of Greece combined to make war upon Troy, to avenge the abduction of Helen, and compel her return, shows, at once, the high respect in which woman was held, and the odium with which "free love" was regarded.

The best authority on the manners and customs of the Spartans is Plutarch; indeed there is no better authority on any historical or biographical subject which he has treated. Plutarch agrees with all other ancient authors as to the exemplary character of the Spartan women before they got too many rights; and he tells us plainly how they lost this character. "They had, indeed," he says, " assumed great liberty and power *on account of the frequent expeditions of their husbands*, during which they were sole mistresses at home, and so gained *undue influence and improper titles*."† Aristotle informs us that when the women, once so exemplary that they were eagerly sought in marriage by the young men of all the neighboring nations, found themselves in the possession of

---

* Lib. 1. c. 3.　　　　　　† Plut., *in Lycurgus*.

their rights, even Lycurgus had to desist from the effort of bringing them under *sober rules*.* We have interesting evidence, in various forms, that they exercised quite as much power in the time of Pericles, as our own woman's rights ladies so loudly and persistently demand at the present day. Thus the historian informs us, that on Gorgo, the wife of Leonidas, being asked by a woman of another country how it was that those of Sparta were the only women in the world that *ruled the men,* her answer was : " *We are the only women that bring forth men.*"†

It is to this ascendancy, on the part of the women, that the Stagirite alludes, when he remarks that the surest sign of the decline of a nation is, to find its women ruling the men. But let us glance at some of the means by which this state of things was produced in Lacedæmon. Thus, for example, we are informed that " in order to take away the excessive tenderness and delicacy of the sex, the consequence of a recluse life, the virgins were accustomed to be seen occasionally *naked,* as well as the young men, and to dance and sing in their presence on certain festivals."‡

Lest it might not be sufficient for the young virgins to appear naked among the naked young men, and dance and sing in their company, the former were also encouraged to " indulge in a little raillery upon those that had misbehaved themselves."§ In short, both young and old of the ruder sex had to submit with as good a grace as they could to whatever treatment the ladies thought proper to give them.

But be it remembered that we cannot blame the Spartans for having deliberately agreed to their own degradation; that the "revolution" had been accomplished during their absence, when there were none to oppose the revolutionists but the non-combatants—all the varieties of the Miss Nancy fraternity—who, for various reasons, were as anxious for the change as the women themselves. Some will say, that at all events, the Spartan women must have gained courage in this manner, according as they lost the more feminine virtues; and that the service they must have rendered the state, in time of war, should be taken into account. To the casual observer

---

* *Politics,* lib. ii., c. ix.   † Plut., *in Lycurg.*   ‡ *Ib.*   § *Ib.*

this may seem plausible ; but we have the most satisfactory testimony that this is the best that could be said in its favor. It will be admitted that Aristotle is good authority on the subject ; and what does he tell us ?—"And as this boldness of the women *can be of no avail in any matters of daily life, if it was ever so, it must be in war; but we find that the Lacedæmonian women were of the greatest disservice in this respect,* as was proved at the time of the Theban invasion, when *they were of no use at all, as they are in other cities, but made more disturbance than even the enemy.*"*

There is no modern nation, need we say, in which women are treated with more deference than in the United States ; not only are all our women " ladies," but a large proportion of our men are quite willing even to wash the dishes for them. Yet a great deal of progress, if such it may be called, has yet to be made before our people look upon their wives and sweethearts as such superior beings as the Spartan women became at one time in the eyes of the Spartan men. It was the latter who were in need of rights in Lacedæmon ; only those who behaved themselves satisfactorily were allowed to keep company with the female members even of their own household. Even when a man got married, he could only expect to enjoy the society of his wife on particular occasions. Thus, we are told, that when the bridegroom staid a short time in his wife's apartment, on the night of his marriage, " he *modestly* retired to his usual apartment, to sleep with the other young men, and *observed the same conduct afterwards,* spending the day with his companions and reposing with them at night, not even visiting his bride but with great caution and *apprehension of being discovered* by the rest of the family."† Thus it was the men who were supposed to have modesty in the model republic of the ancient world, and not the women, after the latter had obtained their rights ! It may be said that this timidity, or high deference, on the part of the men, is not incompatible with delicacy or virtue, on the part of the women, although the naked exhibitions alluded to above may justify some

---

* Aristotle's *Politics*, b. ii., c. ix. p. 65.　　　† Plut. *in Lycurg.*

suspicion in that respect. But the historian leaves us in no doubt; we are at no loss to understand what female equality, or rather female preponderance, meant. We have already alluded to the failure of Lycurgus, according to Aristotle, to bring the Spartan women under "sober rule." But the law-giver was also a philosopher. Seeing that the men were willing to be ruled by the women, when they got used to the yoke, he thought it well to have the latter on his side; he suggested that it would be well to extend their rights. Accordingly, we are told that "he laughed at those who revenge with wars and bloodshed the communication of married woman's favors; and *allowed* that if a man in years should have a young wife, he might introduce to her some handsome and honest young man whom he most approved of, and when he had a child of this generous race, bring it up as his own," &c.*

It seems the "emancipated" ladies considered this excellent logic; the men may not have liked it so well, even in their degenerate state, but what could poor fellows do but submit, who dare not be seen approach their wives' appartments until they were sent for, or allowed permits, like servants! It was some consolation to the men, if they sometimes felt a little uncomfortable under this regulation, that they had the assurance of their great law-giver that the Spartan race would be vastly improved by it.

What a tremendous excitement has been created recently throughout Europe and America, even by the unfounded accusation of incest against the illustrious dead! But the model republic whose manners and customs our women's rights advocates would have us imitate, legalized that very crime. If a Spartan lady of this "enlightened" period had a son and daughter that happened to like each other, both the law and public opinion allowed them to get married.† Now let the reader bear in mind the reply of the modest Gorgo, when asked how it was that those of Lacedæmon were the only women in the world that ruled the men. What the good lady meant was, that because her fellow-countrywomen

---

* Plutarch *in Lycurgus*.
† See *Strabo*, Lib. x. See, also, Montesquieu *Esprit des Lois*, Liv. v., c. v.

enjoyed their rights in full, because they could form their own "affinities," because they could go about day and night, to teach the men, and take home with them any they happened to fancy, their offspring could not be otherwise than superior specimens of mankind. We may ask, in passing, has no such argument as this been adduced by our own woman's rights advocates? Do we hear nothing about "the rights of maternity?" Has no intimation been given by our peripatetic female orators and reformers as to the fine, strapping fellows all our young men would prove in due time, if the existing superstition and tyranny which restrain enlightened ladies from choosing their "affinities" were only set aside as they should?

None acquainted with the subject will deny that the whole matter was fully tested by the Spartans; nowhere else has the experiment been made on so large a scale. But how did the race exhibit improvement or superiority? Let the story of the Helots, even as told by their apologists, answer the question. Nothing is clearer than that in proportion as the women became licentious in the exercise of their "inalienable rights," the men became cruel and bloodthirsty. "The governors of the youth," says Plutarch, "ordered the shrewdest of them, from time to time, to disperse themselves in the country, provided only with daggers and some necessary provisions. In the day time they *hid themselves*, and rested in the most private places they could find, but at night they sallied out into the roads and *killed all the Helots they could meet with.*"*

Still darker is the picture drawn by Thucydides, and it is fully sustained in its worst features by the testimony of Aristotle. Not content with murdering their wretched, naked slaves in detail, in the manner indicated, Thucydides tells us that the Spartans selected such of the Helots as were distinguished for their courage, pretending that they wished to reward them. Under this pretext, they declared about two thousand free, crowned them with garlands, and conducted them to the temples of the gods. All were slaughtered in cold blood—not one was allowed to escape.

* Loc. cit.

Such was the improved race—such the model republic—whose example our advocates of women's rights and "free love" would fain have the modern world imitate !

If we turn to ancient Rome, we shall find the same causes producing the same results. In the time of the republic, the Roman women were celebrated for their truly feminine qualities, for their modesty and their virtue. The Cornelias and Cordelias were but types of the Roman matrons of their time. There is abundant evidence of this in the pages of both historians and satirists. Livy, especially, fully describes the women of the republic; and Tacitus, Juvenal and Horace describe them in contrast with the women who became "emancipated from the tyranny of men." Law after law was passed for their gratification, always at the instance of men who wanted to raise themselves to power by their influence, or by men who were nearly half women themselves. It was these two classes who were always their allies in their "aspirations for liberty;" and nothing is more plainly demonstrated than that just in proportion as they were successful, did the women of Rome become infamous. In order to determine the morals of a people from their historians, it is necessary to examine their whole works ; but it is different with the satirists. The latter direct their attention to particular vices which they think are most reprehensible, or most dangerous to the public welfare. That this is the course pursued by Juvenal is universally admitted; no other satirist, of ancient or modern times, combined in a higher degree the two essential qualities of honesty and fearlessness. Now let us hear a word or two of what he has to say in rsgard to his countrywomen, bearing in mind, in justice to his memory, that it is for no lack of respect or love for woman, that he utters those terrible denunciations against her; on the contrary, he does so because he is grieved at heart to see her so degraded, and wishes to warn posterity against the causes which produced that degradation. Juvenal, as well as Tacitus, shows that as long as the women attended to their domestic duties, and abstained from competing with men, they had no superiors anywhere. Alluding to the character of the women before their "rights" were acknowledged, or even thought of, the satirist proceeds : "Nor did hard toil and short nights' rest, and hands galled and hardened with the Tuscan fleece, and Hanibal close to the city, and their husbands mounting guard at the Colline tower, suffer their lowly roofs to be contaminated with vice.* Upon the other hand, he places, in relief, the cause of the change : "What modesty," he asks, " can a woman show that wears a helmet, and *eschews her sex, and delights in feats of strength ?*"† Is this different in the nineteenth century ? Can modesty or delicacy be expected from such modern ladies? The Roman dames, also, sometimes left their husbands to mind the babies, wash the dishes, etc. "But let her rather be musical," says the satirist, " than *fly through the whole city with bold bearing, and encounter the assemblies of men*," etc.‡ Sometimes they chose their own "affinities" openly, and travelled about with them. "Hippia, though wife to a senator, accompanied a gladiator to Pharos, and the Nile, and the infamous walls of Lagos."§ So licentious did the women become before very long after they obtained their "rights," that comparatively few men had the courage to marry at all. This is illustrated by the satirist but too faithfully. Purporting to address a friend, who is bold enough to venture, he proceeds : "Fall prostrate at the threshold of Tarpeian Jove, and sacrifice to Juno a heifer with *gilded horns*, if you have the rare good fortune to find a matron with unsullied chastity. * * * Is one husband enough for Iberena? Sooner will you prevail on her to be content with one eye."‖

But our female reformers will tell us that those whom we pretend to regard as their prototypes, were but ignorant, stupid creatures, who had no idea of colleges, seminaries, institutes, or even schools. But let us hear Juvenal, who was

---

* Sat. vi.

† Quem praestare potest mulier galeata pudorem.
  Quae fugit a sexu ?   —v. 252.

‡ Sed cantet potius, puam totam pervolet urbem
  Audax, et coetus possit quam ferre virorum.—v. 398.

§ Nupta Senatori comitata est Hippia Ludium
  Ad Pharon, et Nilum, famosaque moenia Lagi. — v. 82.

‖ Delicias hominis ! Tarpeium limen adora
  Pronus, et auratam Juaoni caede juvencam,
  Si tibi contigerit capitis matrona pudici.—Sat. vi., v. 47–49.

a scholar and a philosopher, as well as a poet and satirist. The "girl of the period" opens her mouth, the incessant cruelties of men are her topic, there is nothing can resist her eloquence and learning; "the grammarians yield; rhetoricians are confuted; the whole company is silenced; neither lawyer nor crier can put in a word, not even another woman. Such a torrent of words pours forth you would say so many basons or bells were being struck at once. Henceforth let no one trouble *trumpets or brazen vessels ;* she will be able singly to *relieve the moon when suffering an eclipse.*"

We think we have now fully shown what woman's rights really mean. If we turn to the great European nations of the present day we shall find that it is the women who enjoy most "rights" that have the most doubtful reputation at home as well as abroad. It is certain that no country in the world has presented nobler specimens of womanhood than France ; every intelligent person can recall the names of French ladies, who, in all the relations of life, have proved a credit to their sex. But if the history of these exemplary ladies be examined, it will be found that they were trained in a very different manner from the generality of their countrywomen. They did not get, nor did they give themselves, the habit of running about like men. Thus it is, that while Frenchwomen in general have everywhere the name of being lax in their morals, there are no more excellent teachers of youth, no more faithful and devoted wives, no more affectionate daughters, no kinder mothers than are to be found among the women of France. But although the ladies of France enjoy more rights than those of any other enlightened nation of Europe, not excepting those of England, they certainly do not enjoy as many rights as the ladies of America. Both the laws and public opinion favor the latter vastly more. In illustration of this we need only say that in every particular of any importance, Frenchwomen must render obedience to their husbands ; if they refuse to do so, they forfeit their protection. A French lady cannot even accept a donation or a legacy without the authority of her husband.* Yet, as we have said, they have more liberty than the women of any

---

* See articles 905 and 934 of the *Civil Code.*

other European country; at the same time, it is not pretended that they are equal to the men, for all, save our woman's rights advocates, admit that this would be impossible, and contrary to nature. " L'egalité rigorouse n'existe pas, il est vrai, entre l'homme et la femme," says an eminent French jurist, " mais cette egalité est *impossible* elle *n'est'ni dans la nature, ni dans la destination sociale de l'homme, et de la femme.*"

In England, as all know, the women live much more private than they do in France ; accordingly it is admitted by the most patriotic French authors that Englishwomen are more modest than their own countrywomen.* It is not because the women of England are naturally more virtuous, or more modest than those of France ; it would be a slander on a great nation to assert any such thing. No doubt climate has some agency in producing the difference ; but, beyond all question, the chief, if not the only cause is, that, while the women of France are pretty nearly "emancipated from the tyranny of man," the women of England are still more or less subject to that tyranny. It may be that it is because they do not know better that they seem to bear their yoke with so much resignation, and even apparent comfort. The law which allowed an Englishman to give his wife "moderate correction,"† with certain weapons,‡ is still on the statute-book, though now, like many another law equally rude, it is a dead letter. But even at the present day, a husband is empowered to lock up his better half in some safe room, if she misbehaves, and keep her there on bread and water until she exhibits becoming penitence.§ But the great English jurist, in reviewing the whole subject, fully corroborates the views of all other great thinkers of ancient and modern times. He shows that the laws constituting the "disabilities" under which English women labor are intended for their protection and benefit ; and that they do protect and benefit them, he thinks sufficiently obvious. "So great a favorite," Blackstone says, "is the female sex of the laws of England."

---

* As an instance, see Montesquieu, *Esprit des Lois*, Liv. xiv., c. xxvii.

† *Modicum castigationem adhibere.*   ‡ *Flagillis et fustibus acriter verberareu xorem.*

§ *Vide Blackstone's Com.*, B. I. II.

No intelligent, sensible person need be informed that we are not actuated in writing this article, by any hostility to the sex. Nor do we oppose their competing with men in the highways and byways of the world, on the ground of their being inferior to men either intellectually or morally ; indeed we have ever held that women are much better, morally, than men. They are more honest and more truthful, as well as more virtuous, and less disposed to the commission of crime. As to our depreciating their intellectual capacities, we think it will be admitted that we have always pursued the opposite course. And as a proof of our sincerity we could point to articles in different numbers of our journal, contributed by ladies, which are among the most brilliant contributions we have received ; and their authors would bear us testimony that we did not value them anything the less, pecuniarily or otherwise, for their being the productions of women. It is precisely, then, because we think highly of the sex in every respect, that we are opposed to those habits and practices whose inevitable tendency is to degrade them.

Even the woman's rights advocates admit that women are not as strong, physically, as men ; but we have shown that there are much more cogent reasons than this, why ladies who respect themselves, or their families, should attend to their domestic affairs as their mothers and grandmothers had done before them, and leave the voting, speech-making, office-holding, fighting, gambling, &c., to their husbands, brothers, and fathers.

Those who have a taste for intellectual pursuits, have ample opportunities for indulging it without any detriment to those qualities for which they are most esteemed and admired by the best of men — indeed by all men worthy of the name. It has afforded us pleasure, on many occasions, to remind our readers, in these pages and elsewhere, that there are no better teachers than ladies ; it must be admitted that in this pursuit, at least, they are quite equal, if not superior to men. In literature, art, and science, numerous ladies have distinguished themselves without in the least compromising their character for modesty or delicacy. In short, there is no intellectual pursuit to which they can devote themselves in private, or without having to work surrounded by men, to which they may not devote themselves, and with good prospect of success. But, whatever the pursuit may be—let it be intellectual or physical — in which the women have to be associated with the men, indiscriminately, no matter how exemplary may be the conduct of the latter, the former must necessarily deteriorate in their best womanly qualities.

We cannot, therefore, agree with those who think the medical profession a suitable one for woman, although we readily admit that no profession is more honorable or more useful. Altogether, independently of the incalculable benefit they render mankind in alleviating their sufferings, they have always occupied a high rank in the moral scale. But precisely because this is the fact there is no sufficient reason why a lady should endanger her virtue by attempting to become a physician ; for, disguise it as we may, there is danger in it. And surely those who claim to be equal to men, especially in the exercise of the reasoning faculty, and the government of their passions, should not pretend, if they lose their virtue, to throw all the blame upon the men! This would be illogical and somewhat inconsistent, to say the least ; and the day will come when the public will regard the matter in the same light, as it has long been generally regarded in Europe even in those instances in which the ladies losing their virtue have never pretended to be equal to men.

Be this as it may, most cheerfully do we admit that, far from being an evil, it were a positive good that women could be attended in all their diseases by learned, skilful, experienced and *modest* female physicians. But they could not; it is utterly impossible ! How are the learning, experience and skill to be obtained ? Can ladies, young or old, habitually attend clinical lectures with men—lectures delivered and illustrated by men necessarily in the plainest and most graphic language—and retain the natural delicacy and modesty of the sex ? Who that has ever heard the demonstrator of anatomy address his pupils a half dozen times' with the naked human body in view, would believe such a thing possible ?

Be it remembered that there is nothing liable to disease

which the student of medicine must not see. There is nothing which he must not examine—nothing which must not be fully described to him. Can any modest lady pass through such an ordeal, again and again, day after day, in the presence of men, without feeling that if she is not ashamed, *she ought to be?* Nay, if some young men so far forget themselves as to cry "shame" because she persists in witnessing such scenes, and listening to such descriptions and explanations, can she blame them much, on reflection, although all must admit that their conduct is ungentlemanly? It might be still worse if they suggested in her presence that she ought to be subject to an anatomical examination herself, in accordance with the theories of St. Hilaire and other medical philosophers. Then, if she does not expose herself in this manner, she cannot become a learned and skilful physician, and if she is not learned and skilful, or either, how can women more than men be expected to employ her and confide in her diagnosis or prognosis?

Finally, suppose her superior skill is universally recognized, will she be ready to go out at any hour, day or night, she is called, and willing to enter any place in which a sufferer may need her aid? If she is married, will her husband accompany her at night, or will she prefer to go without him, since his presence might suggest that, after all, there are some "rights" which she has not yet obtained? In short, view the matter as we will, it is surrounded with difficulties; it is in open conflict with modesty and delicacy. No doubt much good will be done by our female physicians ; but when the day of reckoning comes—when the question has been fully tested—we are convinced that the mischief resulting from the same will be vastly more.

But undoubtedly it is themselves and their friends, not their patients, our female doctors will injure most. We can assure them that no men will fancy them, except, perhaps, the class alluded to above, physiologically, or their brethren of the "free love" school ; and even these, however liberal they are in general in conceding rights, are not always to be relied upon. But if our female doctors would become teachers, or authors, then, if it

140

were not their own fault, they might claim the esteem of the everest moralist, as well as the love of the most fastidious admirers of those qualities, which, when refined by culture and intelligence, are the only true and lasting ornaments of the sex.

Since the above article was put in type, a tragedy has occurred to which we may allude, briefly, as affording a startling, if not new illustration of the most prominent views we have put forward in that paper. The only novelty we can see in the McFarland-Richardson affair, is the extraordinary course pursued by certain ministers of the gospel. Nor can we pretend that we are surprised at even this. That it is shameful, is but too true ; it should render its authors infamous in the eyes of every decent man and woman ; and yet we cannot say that we expected much better from Mr. Beecher. That gentleman may not, hitherto, have expressly justified adultery and made marriage a mockery ; but has he not for years been the zealous aider and abettor, directly or indirectly, of every "ism" whose obvious tendency is to strike at the foundation of the social system ?

It affords us pleasure to place on record the fact, that, with one or two exceptions, all our journals that are possessed of any influence have denounced each of the principal actors in the disgraceful scenes alluded to, as their outrageous conduct deserved. But they will have to denounce many more, and for conduct still worse, if possible, if women's rights triumph ; let those who doubt this interrogate Lycurgus and Plutarch, Tacitus, and Juvenal, for, thanks to the refining and elevating influence of christianity, no modern historian or satirist has yet witnessed the full development of woman's rights, as taught at the present day by various female associations, parliaments, &c., &c.

THE SEXES IN COLLEGES.

THE admission of women to our colleges and universities is, if not the most important educational problem yet to be solved, at least the most press-ing and the most clamorous for an immediate solution. It hangs closely together with the question of female suffrage, and, indeed, may almost be said to depend upon that ; for, if women are once admitted to vote, there will be little likelihood of their being long excluded from college classes, and if, on the other hand, the suffrage is still denied them, it will be largely on grounds which will be equally weighty against the reform in question. Still, the separation of the sexes in education has nothing to do with any alleged inferiority of the one to the other—hardly, indeed, with any difference in " sphere ;" for all agree as to giving women as good an education as men, and an identical one if they desire it. And in those institutions which are designed to complement college education, such as the university courses at Cambridge, no objection is made to the admission of ladies, and no mischief can result.

The subject of coeducation in colleges and universities must be re-garded from two points of view—that of the character and demeanor of the students, and that of their intellectual training. In the courses just spoken of, intellectual considerations are the only ones, as the students are supposed to be old enough and mature enough to look after them-selves. The lecturers have no responsibility but to give their best ; it is for the hearer to determine whether it meets his or her wants. But the college has higher aims than mere intellectual training—to turn out well-developed men, in both intellect and character ; and it is the essential feature of a college that it assumes the responsibility of the student's entire development. Any college, therefore, before making so radical a change as that proposed must satisfy itself that it is ready to assume this added responsibility ; that it feels prepared to turn out as good members of society, men and women, as it could men alone or women alone. The assumption that it is " natural" or " right in itself" has nothing to do with it ; the sole question is as to the results, and that not merely or mainly in securing good discipline and good lessons, but in producing manly men and womanly women, fitted to do the work of life in their generation. President Eliot, for the Faculty of Harvard College, frankly says that they are not prepared to assume this responsibility ; and, so long as this is the case, the question of duty is settled for them.

The colleges are distinguished from those institutions of higher culture which are able to make a certain provision for women, by the fundamental fact that they take the young man at the most critical period of his youth, and retain the entire control of him for a period long enough to form his character, and give his mind the training he needs in order to prepare him for the work of life. This is what the American colleges undertake to do, and, with all their defects, they may claim a fair degree of success; the college graduates as a class are not unworthy of the pains and expense that have been bestowed upon them. There are two other classes of institutions which appear to possess a considerable analogy to colleges in this respect—the high schools and the normal schools—both of which, in very large proportion, are composed of students of both sexes, and of nearly the same age as college students. In what essential point do these differ from colleges? It seems at first sight that the normal schools especially present a complete analogy to them, and that the entire success of the experiment in these gives good reason to expect equal success in colleges. It will be found, however, we believe, that this analogy is not complete. The normal schools lack the essential feature of the colleges. They are not established to make men and women, but school-teachers; the students are, on the average, not far from the age of the higher college classes, but they go to the school with the definite purpose of fitting themselves for a special work, not with the vague desire of being disciplined into manhood. The school authorities, to be sure, have their rules, and maintain more or less supervision over the demeanor of the students; but this discipline is wholly subsidiary to the professional training, not itself an end. And as to the high schools, they are simply the last and highest grade of our mixed common schools, touching upon the lower edge of the college course, as the normal schools do upon the upper.

And what is more essential still, the scholars of the public schools live at home and are under the care and responsibility of their parents, looking to the school only for intellectual instruction. Now, it is precisely here, where the colleges differ essentially from the high schools, that we find the weak point of college discipline. It is right that a time should come when the boy shall leave home and learn to rely upon himself, leaving behind him the constant and watchful control of his parents, and having in place of it only the indirect and general influence of the college. This is just what he needs *at the right time;* but it is in the impossibility of knowing in each individual case just when the right time has come that the dangers of college life chiefly consist. The boy goes from home, passes four years in the comparative freedom of college life, and leaves the college walls a man. Are we prepared to have our girls do the same thing? Many a boy is wrecked in his course, many a one stumbles and recovers himself; but a girl cannot retrace a false step as her brother can. For her, once to fall is ruin.

It is here that the peculiar difficulties of coeducation in colleges appear to reside; and it was from a consideration of these, no doubt, that Horace Mann, as we are told, insisted so strenuously upon the dormitory system as essential to success in a mixed college. That is, the freedom which young men enjoy with safety and profit will not do for young women of the same age and on professedly the same footing. In this he was probably right; a college will not undertake this peculiar responsibility for girls away from home, except by retaining a much more constant control than they care to exercise over boys. But is not this really admitting that not only a real equality of the sexes in college education has never been tried, but we are afraid to try it? If every girl lived under her father's roof, it would be different. There could then be no objection to mixed classes—none, that is, from the point we are now considering; it is in the fact that the college assumes a responsibility which it has not adequate means of maintaining that the danger lies; for we see no more harm in girls and boys meeting in the class-room and lecture-room than in sleigh-rides and parties.

We have spoken only of the moral aspect of the question, and that side of it which has to do with the special dangers arising from the sexual relation; because this is the first and most essential point of view in which to regard it. We have seen that the analogies from other kinds of educational institutions do not apply here, for the reason that the aim and the circumstances differ. No experience can be conclusive except where these are the same; we must, therefore, fall back after all upon the limited experience of Oberlin and Antioch, and other less known institutions in the West. With regard to these, it must be admitted that the evidence of experience is favorable in this point; we believe that they have been as free from scandal and moral danger as the average of institutions for girls alone—certainly far more so than many girls' boarding-schools. On the other hand, it cannot be denied that the community appears to have lost confidence in this feature of these institutions, as is shown in some interesting statistics lately given in a series of papers in the *College Courant*. We pass over those which relate to Antioch, for the reason that the financial embarrassments and suspension of that institution may be fairly presumed to have affected it in this respect. As to Oberlin, it is shown that the proportion of girls in the college classes has steadily decreased from one-fourth to one-fifteenth; that of the nine present members (against one hundred and thirty-five men), three belong to Ohio, all of these residents of Oberlin itself; while a separate "Ladies' Department" contains one hundred and seventy; and eight Ohio girls are members of the college classes of the distant and expensive Vassar College. These remarkable figures certainly seem to show a falling off of the demand for education in mixed colleges, from whatever cause it may be.

We suspect that the real cause is that the young ladies do not, after all, wish for the same education with young men; and while we fully believe that, if they do wish for the same, they ought to have it, we as fully believe that, in nine cases out of ten, they had better not have it. Very few girls can do, without breaking down physically, the intellectual work which their more robust brothers can safely undertake. And even if they could, we cannot but believe that a quite different training is required to fit the members of the different sexes for the diverse work that will necessarily fall to their lot. Where they feel called upon to undertake the same work, they should have the same training; but this is *profession* training, and we have already pointed out the wide distinction between the professional school and the college. In the professional schools we see no reason that much of the preparation for the same work should not be made in company.

We have not touched, however, upon a point which is made much of in arguments upon this subject—the mutual influence of the sexes in their coeducation. Apart from the serious moral dangers which we have already considered, there seems no doubt that, in regard to the demeanor of the students, the mixed colleges are under no disadvantage. More than this is often claimed—that the female influence is necessarily refining and elevating. But this depends upon other things. Nothing is more healthy for a young man at this critical age than the society of cultivated ladies. We do not know that we can say as much for that of school-girls. It is only by constant watchfulness that the intercourse of school-girls and boys can be kept from downright rudeness; so that we should say only that under good management the influence of the sexes may be good upon one another; under bad management, it will be unequivocally bad.

Intellectually, we should pass a different judgment. Girls as students are quick, faithful, and intelligent; but they have loose habits of thought, and are prone to be mere book-students. It is an unmixed good for them to be brought in contact with the freer and, at the same time, closer habits of reasoning of the boys; while their perfect knowledge of their *lessons* serves to stimulate their rivals to faithful application. Nor is there much danger of the influence being the other way, and each sex acquiring the bad habits of the other; for each recognizes the other's points of superiority, and the women especially feel that it is mainly from this masculine quality of mind the long supremacy of the male sex has resulted.

We have given the reasons which make us incline to the opinion that the experiment of mixed colleges is not likely to be a success. At the same time, it must be remembered that it is still an experiment, and whoever has real faith in it possesses so far a chief condition of success. We hope that trials will continue to be made, until it is an experiment no longer. We have so much confidence that it would be an intellectual benefit to women, that we should be sincerely glad if it should be found practicable to unite the classes so far as the studies cover the same ground. But whether this movement is to go on or is to die out by degrees, there is, we are confident, one condition to a successful union of the sexes in college classes—a policy of sympathy and trust rather than of suspicion. If it is safe for girls and boys to be together, let those who have the control of them be men who heartily believe so, and show that they believe it. If there is danger of mischief, the surest way to make the mischief come is to be constantly expecting it. Nobody expects girls to have the same freedom as boys when they are sent from home to be educated. They are of necessity subjected to rules and hours from which boys may safely be free ; and this circumstance, while it shows the futility of expecting a real and genuine equality of the two sexes in the same institution, has also this evil effect, that the girls who are promised equality of treatment, and expect it—ignorant as they are of the dangers of their new life, and ambitious for their sex—chafe against restraints which they would not mind if they were by themselves, and by this again become unwittingly the instruments of their own disappointment.

ANOTHER DELICATE SUBJECT.

The fact, which there is no denying, that there are to be found, amongst the female advocates of Woman's Rights in this country, some whose reputation is positively bad, and others whose reputation would bear improving, has not unnaturally brought some odium on the whole movement, and this odium is somewhat increased by the belief which many people entertain, that, owing to the chance of acquiring notoriety which the movement offers, the number of such women engaged in it is likely to increase greatly if it continue to spread. These charges the respectable agitators meet by a plea which is known to lawyers as "confession and avoidance;" that is, they say: "True, but what of it? You men, in your politics, have no hesitation whatever in associating on perfectly friendly terms with well-known profligates of your own sex, and think yourselves and your work none the worse of it. Indeed, some of your most famous statesmen have been men of dissolute lives. Now, chastity is a law of universal obligation, just as binding on one sex as on the other. We shall, therefore, not submit any longer to the imposition of pains and penalties for the violation of it on women to which men are not also exposed. If you wish us to be particular about the company we keep, you must set us a good example. Until you do so, we shall follow the good old plan of 'accepting aid from any quarter,' and shall admit everybody to our platform who is willing to adhere to our doctrine and preach it." This is the argument, too, which the Englishwomen who are engaged in the discussion of that savory subject, the Contagious Diseases Act, use freely, with the necessary modifications, and although as yet it is brought forward somewhat timidly in this country, and oftener in private than in public, we have little doubt we shall see it paraded before long as invincible, and large numbers of "strange women" securing under cover of it "spheres of usefulness," from which, under the present heartless social regulations, they are excluded. Some of the respectable section of the agitators are, however, conscious apparently that this view of the subject at least needs defence. Mr. T. W. Higginson, in a recent number of the *Woman's Journal*, utters a mild protest against bringing to the work anything but "clean hands," and deprecates the use of the platform for the repair of damaged reputations or the purging of old stains. Mrs. Stowe has also warned the brethren and sisters away from the discussion of matrimony and kindred subjects, feeling conscious apparently that the views of some of them on these questions can hardly be aired without giving offence. But, with all this, we believe we are right in saying, that from the doctrine that "chastity is a law of universal obligation," which there is no gainsaying, the champions of Woman's

Rights have deduced, or are fast deducing, the conclusion that one of the things they may lawfully do, in order to get these "rights," is to treat female violations of the law as no worse than male violations of it, and to disregard, as of male invention for the perpetuation of male tyranny, the old and universal usage which lodges woman's honor in her purity. In doing this, they are doing one of the things which make them in our eyes, and that of a large portion of the community, mischievous people, and mischievous in the direct ratio of their individual worth and influence, and in support of this view we shall resort once more to that plain speaking without which, as we have already said, it seems impossible to discuss this question efficiently.

Although it is true that chastity is a law of universal obligation, it is not true that men's guilt in violating it is as great as that of women, because the degree of guilt depends on the degree of temptation, which in the case of men is very strong, both from temperament and circumstances, and in the case of women very weak. Men's passions are fierce and active; women's, feeble and dormant. Moreover, the way in which the work of life has been divided makes men's exposure to temptation constant; women's, very rare. The race has, therefore, in forming its moral judgment on the quality of offences against sexual purity, always treated the man's guilt as less heinous than the woman's, and although this rule does occasionally work astounding injustice, and has called into existence that great blot on Christian civilization, the cold-blooded male seducer, it does in the vast majority of cases work what, we believe, is in the courts of heaven, as well as those of earth, recognized as substantial justice. The distinction has, however, a utilitarian as well as a purely ethical basis, and one no less important certainly. Like most other of the usages kept up by society for the regulation of the relations of the sexes, it has for its object the maintenance of the integrity and purity of the family. The maternity of a child is a physical fact, very difficult of concealment, hardly ever successfully concealed, and usually provable by many witnesses. The paternity of a child is, on the other hand, simply an inference which derives all its strength from the importance attached to chastity by the female sex. It rests simply and solely on the character of the mother. It is incapable of proof by any other testimony than hers. All that is known about it is locked up in her breast, and to weaken her scruples, therefore, is to throw doubts on the origin of all her children; or, in other words, to strike at the very roots of the family organization. If we had things so arranged, therefore, that a woman thought no more of violating her marriage vows than a man, we should have probably in a very large part of the world have either to give up the family altogether, or shut women up, as they once were shut up. The inference with regard to the paternity of children, therefore, has to be jealously guarded, not only because it is in the nature of things weak, but because it furnishes what is,

in the present state of human nature, the main or sole inducement to husbands to toil and accumulate for their wives and offspring. For, let it
never be forgotten, the husband must, except in an infinitesimally small.
number of cases, be everywhere the bread-winner. Children must always
look to their father for most of the arms with which they face the world.
Now there may come a time when, after having heard the requisite number
of lectures, and read the requisite number of tracts, a man will toil cheerfully for the maintenance and education of such children as his wife
may see fit to introduce into the household, without caring whether they
are his own or not. But we are still far away from any such consummation. As matters stand, brutal man will neither dig nor delve for the support of any children which he does not possess a moral certainty he has
begotten. He acquires this certainty through his confidence in his wife's
purity, and society helps to justify it by visiting her lapse from virtue with
the deepest of earthly damnations. To be sure, the arrangement does not
work perfectly; but then the world is full of imperfections, brethren.
We know you would have made a far better world if you had had a
chance, and it does seem a pity that so many things, and especially the
relations of the sexes, and the manner of perpetuating the species, should
have been settled without waiting for your appearance or consulting you.
But then, you must admit, it is the Lord's doing, and, if not as well done
as you could have done it, is at least unchangeable.

But we have another worse charge to make against this new manifestation of the rage for equality, and a more serious one. Instead of trying to level *up*—that is, to raise men to the female standard of purity—
the agitators are actually, and almost without blushing, trying to level
down—that is, to put women on men's lower plane. The necessity of associating with scoundrels, and of pretending not to know that they are
scoundrels, is to the best men a horrible necessity. Women are saved,
and to their own infinite gain, from having to undergo anything similar
with regard to the worst members of their own sex. We know there is
often cruelty in the exemption, but we know, too, that it is an
unspeakable support to virtue. It might, perhaps, have been better,
as we said some time ago, if matters had been so arranged that a
man might have thieves for his bosom friends, while entertaining a hearty
horror of theft. So also it might, perhaps, have been better if matters
had been so arranged that ladies might have prostitutes visit them freely
at their houses without losing a particle of their horror of vice. Providence has managed the affair differently. It has made, as is notorious,
the avoidance of bad company one of the greatest aids and one of the chief
conditions of right living. Women are fortunate enough to be able to
avail themselves of it in the cultivation of the greatest of all their virtues, and the most useful. It is now gravely suggested that they throw

this aid away, and display for the morals and manners of their fellow-women that beautiful indifference which their brothers and husbands show for the weaknesses of the Fisks and the Whittemores—that is, reduce us all to the same condition of moral phlegm, so that, when we go home in the evening sick and sad, after a day's work among male scallawags and cheats, we may meet our sweet Mlle. Cora Pearl, the distinguished Cocotte, and her friend Madame Dodo, the brilliant and public-spirited proprietor of the celebrated " never-failing No. 3 pills," coming out from a committee meeting in our back parlors.

We venture to affirm, however, that the moral standard which prevails among the women of the Western World, and the precautions they take for its maintenance, are among the most precious achievements of civilization—those of which mankind may most justly be proud. If we were asked to point out the most impressive indication of progress, we should unquestionably name, not the deliverance of women from the bolts, and bars, and veils of the harem, but the commission to their custody of their own purity, and the singular fidelity with which they have fulfilled the trust. We doubt, too, if anything has done half as much for the elevation of men as the lesson which every man learns from his earliest years from them of what is possible in the field of self restraint, and one of the very best things we know about men is the pains they take to keep the unseemly, or base, or degrading side of life from the eyes and ears of their wives, and daughters, and sisters. Women, it is true, have done little for the world by their minds ; but they have done an enormous deal by their manners, in exemplifying, day by day, virtues of which, in their absence, men would only dream. The next task to be undertaken by them is the introduction among men of their standard of virtue ; and not— even for the sake of shining in the edifying wrangles of the caucus and the court-room—the adoption of men's. The value of their contributions to politics is a matter of pure speculation ; if we were to judge from what they have done already, we should say it would be very small. The value of their contributions to morals, happily, is a matter of experience. There is no man to whom some woman has not proved a second conscience, and it will be a sorrowful day for humanity when we see men and women in the market-place and the legislature encouraging each other—to use the chaste language of a distinguished male Republican politician and philanthropist—" not to be too damned scrupulous."

SEXUAL SCIENCE.

BY THOMAS MEEHAN.

SCIENCE has had its say on most modern questions; but, in relation to the great movement for "women's rights," it has been singularly dumb. We are not of those who believe that science can solve every social problem. We want something decisive for political action; but science knows of no dividing line. We may, as a matter of fact, assert that there is day, and be as positive that there is night; but there is also a time when it is neither day nor night, — a twilight which some will class with one or with the other, according to the different optical power with which they may be blessed. It is the province of common-sense, not science, to set that matter at rest.

But though we would not appeal to science as an unerring guide in all the affairs of life, a knowledge of its leading principles will so expand our views and guide our judgment, that we are far less likely to err in our practical efforts to have things right, than if we go blundering along in the dim light of tradition and past experience. It may help us in this matter of the relations of the sexes. Let us see what light it will give us. And first, why are we created of two sexes? What separate purposes do these divisions serve? Separate sex is not confined to man. Nature will not answer us in this limited field. The division exists in high and low organisms; in the vegetable as well as in the animal world. Those who do not look far beyond men might answer that sex had for its object the continuation and reproduction of species or individuals; but this can scarcely be the leading object of nature, because in plants and the lower orders of animal life reproduction is carried on quite independent of any sexual organization. Many things, such for instance as some grasses and herbaceous plants, increase themselves year after year by underground suckers or shoots. In some cases all behind the leading point dies annually, and a new plant appears a short distance from the original starting-point. Take a potato, for instance; a thread-like production pushes from the parent-stem for perhaps a foot, and at the end appears the "potato." If this remain in the earth without disturbance, the thready connection would die, and the potato grow as before, gaining another foot, and so forth, until, after a period of twenty years, it would be twenty feet away from the starting-point, and have given birth to twenty new individuals. This may go on for an indefinite number of years, and for any thing we know forever, without any sexual agency whatever. In gardening we know how we can go on year after year continually reproducing a plant by grafts, cuttings, buds, off-sets, and other ways. The red Dutch currant has probably been reproduced in this way for many hundreds of years. In the lower order of animal life also the original will break apart, and each separate piece grow; and we may get even up to a crustacean where we find, that, though a broken-off limb will not reproduce the original, the animal can reproduce the broken limb. We see from these considerations that whatever was Nature's object in the creation of sex, reproduction was not the primary consideration.

There is one observàtion we may make as we go along, in regard to these modes of propagation, which may help us hereafter. Each individual born, so to speak, in this way, is for the most part an exact reproduction of the original. A graft from a seckel pear-tree produces a tree which bears seckel pears; and the red Dutch currant is the same currant still; and a bunch of fruit from one tree is just the same as if taken from the other. A sprig from the dwarf box-edging reproduces edging-box; and the tree-box produces in the same way the tree-growing kind. If Tom Thumb or Daniel Lambert could be reproduced in this style, there would be scores of large or small people so exactly alike that their own mothers would not know them apart. This recognition is unnecessary in plants and the lower animals. Each part can take care of itself as soon as it is detached from its parents. Here it does not concern Nature whether the mother knows its own child or not. But in the higher orders of animals, where identity is of the utmost importance in enabling a mother to care for her young, the races could not exist on the same principle of increase which marks the lower ones.

But we go back to the plant. Besides all its powers of reproduction by extension and division, it bears seed. Here, however, the results differ. They do not reproduce exactly the same plant. In a bed of seedlings no two are exactly alike; and it · is through this law that we have so many varieties of flowers in our gardens. The florists preserve the most striking variations, and destroy the rest. So in fruits. The seeds of the seckel pear will produce something like seckel, but not seckels exactly; and if we raise fifty trees from fifty seeds in this way, there will be fifty varieties, all resembling seckel, and yet all varying from one another. Hitherto botany has regarded the seed as created for the chief purpose of *distributing* the species or individual.

But although distribution is certainly more readily effected in this than any. other way, we have seen that it is not the essential difference. The production of variety, thus securing identity, is the leading office of the seed.

No doubt the close reasoner will stop us here. A tree can reproduce itself by buds and cuttings where identity is not necessary. If variation is to provide for identity, what is the use of identity to it? This is a case of *twilight*, before referred to. We suppose we are on the boundary here of a transition. All we can positively know is, that seed is not essential to reproduction, and that with the introduction of seed-variation dates its vigorous origin. We can further see, that, in the higher organisms without variation, identity, so far as mutual recognition is concerned, could not exist.

It is a self-evident proposition, that the first leading principle of all nature is the effort for *existence ;* and, as all organic beings can exist for only a limited time, the second grand object of its care will be *reproduction.* There can be little doubt but that every action of every living thing, and indeed the form of every living thing, is in some degree connected, more or less remotely, with one or the other of these grand objects of Nature. *We,* of course, have our own motives for what we do; and every animal is impelled in its conduct by some idea of pleasure or necessity. Plants we regard as unconscious, and probably they are; but they all act by laws tending to their own good in the same way as animated beings do. We do not stop to think of Nature as a whole. The individual seems rather a world unto himself, yet behind him and behind all is the one great idea, *nature ;* and this Nature only caring for its one self, — its self-existence, and continued reproduction. The principle of variation is only secondary, and subservient to the other two prior and greater aims.

There can be no doubt that Nature will throw around the great reproductive principle a greater measure of protection than she will around the mere incidents thereof. Thus if sustenance failed to carry along variation and reproduction together, she would let the first go. In this event, all that appertains to the division into sexes of the present order of things would disappear; and only those lower orders would exist which can extend themselves without it. And this is all in accordance with what embryologists tell us : that with the failure of nutrition, the last organs in the usual order of structure are the first to die away.

It would hardly be correct to call the reproductive principle in Nature the female principle ; and yet when Nature has advanced so far in the plant or the animal as to call for a division into sexes, it will hardly be denied that the female is in more intimate communion with this leading object than the male. The female must necessarily be the most favored of Nature. At the commencement of the division the female will be first provided for; and in the great struggle for life, all other things being equal, the chances will be largely in her favor. In plants the division into sexes is not made apparent until the flowering period arrives. Some are hermaphrodites; that is, they have stamens and pistils in the same flowers. Others are diœcious, or have the male flowers wholly on one plant, and the females on another. But it is seldom known, prior to flowering, which is the male plant or which is the female. Still the peculiar sexual principle in some cases, no doubt, pervades the whole plant, and exists long anterior to flowering; for a male or female plant once known will generally always remain so. Cuttings taken from either will be pretty sure to reproduce the same sexual flowers again, though not always; for the female silver-maple will not unfrequently put forth branches with male flowers. Still, as a general thing, sex is not determined in plants until near the flowering time ; and is, as has been said, never known until the flowers have actually opened. In those plants which bear male and female flowers separate on the same plant, it is then seen that the male flowers only appear on the weakest branches or branchlets. This is best illustrated by a pine or spruce tree. The female flower is that which ultimately becomes the pine-cone. The male flowers gather in small clusters, and are those which produce the dust (pollen) in early spring. The female flowers or cones only appear at the ends of the healthiest branches. As the tree grows, of course the branches now at the end in time become the interior, and are then shaded by those which go beyond them. Shade always tends to lessen the vitality of a growing branch ; and here we see that branches once strong and bearing female flowers, as soon as thus partially weakened by shade bear only male ones. An inspection of any pine-tree in spring will show, that though male flowers are sometimes borne at the base of the shoots bearing female flowers, weak shoots never bear any thing but male ones. This will be found the case in all plants of a monœcious character. In the common *ambrosia*, or ragweed, the male flowers are on a sort of weakened, half-dead-looking, raceme; while the females are situated in the best position for receiving the highest amount of nutrition the plant can bestow. Those who have examined this matter in plants, see the truth of the position in the vegetable world, that nature's highest efforts in the formation of the sexes are invariably in the female line.[1]

The same facts appear to us in the animal world. In the very first struggle with life the males get the worst of it. The vast majority of all the children who die under five years of age are males. As the sexes approach maturity, the terrible strain on the female system begins, and the numbers of males and females again nearly equalize. The amount of nutrition over and above that required to sustain life passes in the male to brain and muscle, to mere physical strength and intellectual capacity; but in the female, to immense nutritive power for the support of another human being. Man is physically stronger than woman; that is, in cases requiring an immediate concentration of power, he is her superior. But in *vitality*, if by that

we may understand the ability to endure circumstances tending to destroy life, he is below her. Not only can he not endure as much during the first five years of his life, but as an adult he sinks under pain that a woman would hardly faint with. Any of us can look around and see women with perhaps half a dozen young children which she must look after, in a continual series of routine, monotonous housework which she must attend to, now roasting at the oven, steaming over the wash-tub, or freezing at the clothes-line, and continually with the worry of crying children ringing in her ears; and all this for years and years, with ailing infants and sick older children, and perhaps even a male specimen of an older cast to whom she is expected to be a " help-mate " besides all this; altogether for months and months giving her but three or four hours of sound sleep per night. Where is the man that could endure it ? A year of such a life would kill the strongest of us. We find the same law of vital endurance outside of man. Cavalry officers in the late war found out the wisdom of selecting mares for arduous services ; and we all know what a miserably dull animal the unsexed ox becomes. This branch of our topic need not be further pursued. It has been shown that naturally the reproductive principle should be endowed with the highest attributes of vitality, and the few instances cited will show its bearing in the world of facts.

And now why is this intellectual superiority and greater muscular strength given to man ? If woman has greater endurance, and greater traits of general vitality, why not excel in all points ? It is simply because he is to use these for the

[1] For fuller details of this matter, see papers by the author in the Salem and Troy Proceedings of American Association for the Advancement of Science; and in Rec. of Phila. Acad. Nat. Sciences, 1869-70.

benefit of the female. In the wild state in which man first found himself, it would be impossible for the woman with her young child to defend herself from the continual elements of warfare then everywhere about. Wild animals would soon end the whole human race. Moreover, she could not leave her young at home to hunt for food. Man thus appears as an essential aid to Nature's great reproductive principle. He is the ruler, the planner, the protector, but not for his own sake, but all in the cause of a greater and more beloved power in the economy of Nature.

In the animals below man, we find pretty much the same law to prevail: that the male animal is physically and intellectually the superior only in proportion to the weakness or incapacity of the female or the progeny to take care of themselves at certain periods of their existence. In many birds, where the young is difficult to rear, either the male is much the superior of the female, or else monogamy prevails. In the pigeon, for instance, and similar birds, where the young require constant attention for some time, both male and female seem nearly balanced in qualities. In the barn-door fowl, where the young can take more care of themselves, polygamy prevails. The young of the duck can take care of themselves also; but here, although we do not find strict monogamy, we find the female and male birds much more equally matched than they are in the case of the barn-fowl.

When we come to fishes, we find no difference apparently in the physical or intellectual capacity of male or female. The young take absolute care of themselves, and the mother requires no protection. Questions of relative strength of the sexes, or of monogamy or polygamy in fishdom, are therefore of no consequence. Both have to take care of themselves, both have equally to fight with enemies for their own preservation, both have an exhaustive strain on their vital functions at spawning-time, and hence they are about evenly balanced in every way.

It is curious to observe how soon the male disappears from the scene when he can in no way serve the great female cause. In plants, no sooner does the pollen from the stamens fertilize the pistils than they drop away; while in some cases, the pine for instance, the female organs continue alive for a couple of years afterwards. In the hemp and the spinach the whole male plant dies some weeks before the female one. In some spiders the female devours the male before she proceeds to lay her eggs, and when she has no further desire for his companionship; and a large number of male insects die immediately on the exercise of their special functions. The females live to deposit their eggs or to rear their young. It is clearly to be seen that it is necessary they should have this extra power. The extra vitality is given them for this purpose. Still, the simple fact remains, that the female possesses greater vitality than the male.

From these and similar considerations, which those who wish to follow the subject further can pursue for themselves, we may conclude that woman worship is not a mere poetical fancy, but has its seat deep down in the heart of Nature. When the youth asserts his beloved to be his queen, swears eternal allegiance, and vows forever to be worthy of, and to serve her, he is really following but the dictates of Nature, who worships the female as ardently as he does. She is undoubtedly the most favored, and in elementary constitution at least, if not in actual form, must claim a place in nature long anterior to the origin of man in the sexual sense of this term. For theological purposes she may have been formed of the rib of Adam; for Mohammedan or Mormon uses she may be but the mere slave and creature of man, without even a soul to be saved except through his sovereign will and pleasure; but the religion of nature demands rather the sacrifice of the other sex to her eternal law.

It will not be difficult to apply these principles to the great woman question of the day. Man is the great acting, working force; all that appertains to providing or protecting is his place in nature. The gun, the plough, the ship, the sword, — the elements of force whatever they be, and the ballot which is to direct and control that force, — all these are the essential prerogatives of man. At the same time these laws and forces should be used for the interests of woman; and where they are not, man is not fulfilling the purposes for which he was created.

And this brings us again to our starting-point. Science will not solve every practical problem, because we want absolute laws; while the laws of nature run into one another. As a general thing, it is the male bird which does the singing and the female the hatching; but there be hens which crow, and birds of the male

persuasion which believe it to be a solemn duty to sit on eggs, and take the young under their protecting wings. These we can again compare to the twilight reasoning. One may assert it night, another that it is day; one that it is right in the hen to crow, another that it is not, — these boundary-line questions can never be solved. But the main question as to the natural duties and responsibilities, the relative rights and wrongs, of the sexes, these seem as clear as day and night; and, when clearly perceived, ought to render the subject of general legislation not so puzzling a question as it seems to so many of us.

In a special way there will always be men who will neglect their natural duties, and society itself may at times wander so far from the main purpose of its creation that its members may feel totally unable to perform duties which otherwise it would be their pleasure to do. Women left without natural protectors must take on themselves the duties of men in order to live at all. For all these aberrations from general law, special arrangements must be made. The only danger to society is when it takes the minor for the major proposition; seeks to adapt laws necessary to twilight, to every purpose of day and night; asserts the absolute equality of the sexes in every particular, instead of properly defining the main rights and duties of each, and endeavoring as far as the artificial state of society will permit to keep each sex to its own natural sphere.

Citizenship, its Rights and Duties,—
WOMAN SUFFRAGE.

Mr. President, Ladies and Gentlemen:

In presenting this subject for your audience, I have no apology to make for the importance of its consideration, since I believe that as the "best study for man is man," so the best study of the the citizen is citizenship; that is, his nature, status, and relationship to government.

But I am inexpressibly diffident of my ability to treat this subject, so important it is, with that degree of efficiency calculated, not so much to please as to instruct and benefit. I reprove myself for my temerity in attempting to discuss the subject of citizenship, connected as it is with law, although not a perfect creature of law, at the capital of the nation where laws are made and illustrious lawyers reside. These considerations have more than once baffled my determination to write on this subject, and now I only bring it before you, in the hope, that as a speck of mineral uncomely deposited in some rugged rock of disproportion and rude shape, sometimes arrests the attention of the scientific explorer and leads to vast discoveries of precious treasure, so a ray of truth may be uttered before I close this subject, which will arrest the attention of abler minds than my own, and cause this subject to receive that treatment which will ennoble and instruct in ages to come. But I am further urged to this endeavor by the information that among ancient nations—Grecian and Roman—the civic capacity and the civil duties of every citizen, were frequently brought before the public, and the citizens were instructed concerning them. These subjects formed a part of the education of the youth, so that men knew so well the value of citizenship that it became not a matter of indifference by the many, but pride in all, and no right was denied, or privilege rejected a Roman; but the invader was reminded, "I am a Roman citizen!"

This duty of the study of Citizenship is no less incumbent on *us* to-day as American citizens. But more especially does it become the important duty of every colored citizen, in public or private life, rich or poor, professional or non-professional. The doors of civil liberty, through which we were to gain access to the temple of our citizenship, it rights and duties, have been shut against us during more than two hundred years. Ninety and eight years have passed away since our common country sprung from the unjust embrace of the mother country into the family of nations; yet the greater part of this time a component part of civil society of government of the American nation—the African race—has been denied every avenue and every path by which it may obtain a knowledge of the beauty and value of its possession as citizens. We now, therefore, feel that, as much of this is now removed, and our rights are being acknowledged, and our privileges widened, we should inquire into the intrinsic elements of these possessions, so that undertaking them we may justly use them for the benefit of ourselves and our country.

The word Citizenship is derivative of the word Citizen. A citizen in the primitive and most comprehensive sense, means "one of the sovereign people," a constituent of society, and is synonomous with *People.* In common law it means "an inhabitant of a city." In American law it once meant (in the dark ages) "a *white* person, born in the United States, or a naturalized person born out of the same." And this definition. to the shame of our country and law literature, found its way into the books written by eminent lawyers and jurists for the use of students. Hence we find it in the widely circulated volumes of Judge Bouvier's Law Dictionary. Yet, happily, this was not the definition universally acknowledged or adopted; nor can it claim to have derived its justification from the Constitution of the American government. The most comprehensive and just definition of citizenship I have read, is to be found in the profound opinion of ex-Attorney-General Bates in the case of the "schooner *Elizabeth and Margaret,* of New Brunswick." This vessel was detained by the revenue cutter *Tiger,* at South Amboy, New Jersey; because commanded by a colored man, and so by a person not considered a citizen of the United States. The question propounded by Captain Martin of the *Tiger* ship to the Attorney-General, was: "Are colored men citizens of the United States?" The answer given was worthy the head and heart of the man who uttered it at such a time, when obloquy was the only recompense. But to-day it is complete. Truth is triumphant. The words of Senator Sumner, when writing in 1846 to Robert C. Winthrop, are truly verified: "Aloft on the throne of God, and not below in the foot-prints of a trampling multitude are the sacred rules of right, which no majorities can displace or overturn." Attorney-General Bates says: "A citizen of the United States, without addition or qualification means neither more nor less than a member of the nation. And all such are practically and legally

equal — the child in the cradle and its father in the Sentate. * * *
Prima facie every person in this country is born a citizen, and he
who denies it in individual cases, assumes the burden of stating
the exception to the general rule, and proving the fact which works
the disfranchisement," and, to cap the climax of the fulness of this
definition, the learned jurist continues: "I think no one will venture to deny that *women* and children, and lunatics, and even con-
vict felons may be citizens of the United States." Hence it is considered that the fact of citizenship is never changed, unless
by the violation and act of the individual. Once a citizen, whether
natus or *datus*, always a citizen, even to the uttermost parts of the
earth, and everywhere it should be protected with ·that fidelity
which is due from government to subject. Crime may disqualify the
exercise of the rights and duties of citizenship, but it cannot annul
or demolish the intrinsic quality itself. Citizenship is of the
earth, earthy.

The Constitution of the United States, as it at present stands,
with its amendments, declares, "that *all* persons born or naturalized in the United States, and subject to the jurisdiction thereof,
are citizens of the United States and of the State wherein they
reside." Hence, we find citizens as described by law, divided into
naturalized and natural-born citizen — a distinction which all
civilized governments recognizes — but the barrier against citizenship on account of race or color, has been left to be adopted by the
American government only. But the last remnant of this shame
and disgrace, as well as injustice, will soon, we hope, be wiped from
the records of our beloved country by the passage of a supplementary Civil-Rights Bill, now pending before Congress, and introduced into that body — the highest legislative tribunal in the land
— by our veritable friend and benefactor, the late Hon. Charles
Sumner: who has departed this life, and the like of whom we shall
not soon see again; whose name is a synonym for integrity, excellence in character, virtue, excellence in statesmanship, philanthropy,
the champion of the colored man's oppression, one of the icono-
clasts of slavery, the mighty destroyer of unequal laws; and,
above all, the friend of humanity. Mr. Sumner thus speaks of the
citizenship, rights and privileges of the colored citizen: "Ceasing
to be a slave the former victim has become not only a man but a
citizen, admitted alike within the pale of humanity and within the
pale of citizenship. As a man he is entitled to all the rights of a
man, and as a citizen, he becomes a member of our common household with equality as the prevailing law. No longer an African but
an American. No longer a slave, he is a component part of the
Republic, owing to it patriotic allegiance in return for the protection of equal laws. By incorporation of the body politic, he be-

comes a partner in that transcendent unity, so that there can be no injury to him without injury to all. Insult to him is insult to an American citizen. Dishonor to him is dishonor to the Republic itself. Whatever he may have been, he is now the same as ourselves. Our rights are his rights; our privileges and immunities, are his great possessions. Not only is he a citizen, but there is no office in the Republic, from the lowest to the highest — executive, judicial, or representative — which is closed against him He may be Vice-President; he may be President." *   *   *   In the light of this statement, we learn that the Civil-Rights Bill purposes to blot out all distinction, and make us equally citizens of a common country; for citizenship is an integral th ng, and bears no relationship before the law.

The political and civil equality of all men is derived from the origin of civil government.

Men in their natural and individual state of existence, uncontrolled by human legislation, found in their wants and fears, the necessity of organized society and government. Or, in other words, as expressed by Sir William Blackstone: "They discovered that the whole should protect all its parts, and that every part should pay obedience to the whole." Such was the idea that gave body and soul to our great government as organized by the fathers. Such should be the light by which our constitutional lawyers and jurists should read the Constitution, our *magna charta*.

This condition of society which I have just described as the beginning of government, necessarily in some degree restricts the natural liberty of men, made so by their consent. No act is law except by general consent, which is the ground of all just government. Violence and fraud can create no right. Hence the idea that was once entertained, that "this is a white man's government," is not only absurd, but false and discreditable Our race which has been shut out from just and equal participation in this government on account of color or race, has been thus governed by violence and fraud, for any restriction against its consent, and in denial of these liberties, was unjust, unconstitutional, and no part of a just and civilized government. Every man is absolutely free, until he enters into organized society or government, such as he chooses for his own good.

No one can fully discuss the origin of citizenship without adverting to the various views which have been entertained in this country, relating to the citizenship of the black man. Neither in our law books, nor in decisions of courts was there ever a just definition of citizenship of the United States. The Dred Scott decision was the most unjust. The intrinsic qualities and intent of citizenship, were constantly overlooked by prejudice. The fact that it was a part of man's being, an inalienable right, brought into the common brotherhood of man in the organization of society and government, was discountenanced, and in this country, until the fourteenth amendment to the Constitution was adopted, the question resolved itself into whether color or race could disfranchise a subject and it was so holden by a large number of citizens. But he who was once in bondage, whereby he was restricted in his liberty, denied his rights and deprived of his privileges, is now a free man, and decides upon his status as a citizen, his rights and privileges, as a component part of the Republic. It may not be inappropos to call attention, to how universally unjust man has been to his fellow in this respect throughout all ages. Might has always endeavored to trample right, and this, too, not only between whites and blacks, but also among races irrespective of color.

During the middle ages, how the tyranny and legal exactions of the Normans were exercised over their Saxon brothers, have only to be read to be understood. These so grew, that it was only when the rapacity and imbecility of John Lackland, manifested in his obsequiousness to the Pope of Rome, and in disregard for the rights of his subjects, had become intolerable, that at Runymede, A. D. 1215, the great principles of liberty, which set beyond further question, the equal, civil, and political rights of English subjects, were established; the essential clauses of which protect the personal liberty and the property of all freemen. "There is no part of the English Constitution," says Hallam, "so admiral as this equality of civil rights." But, for more than two hundred years the American negro has not been recognized in general as a citizen, yet from what I have already said, it is easy to discover that to-day he is no new citizen. He has always been a citizen by virtue of being a man, governed, when justly governed, by his consent, or not governed at all, but enslaved and oppressed. Neither color, nor race, nor condition of servitude, ever could divest the American, born in this country, of the title and capacity of a citizen. Neither has he new rights. He is an old citizen of the bone and sinew of this government, and in the new garb of his rights. He is the political peer of his white fellow-citizen, and his rights and duties fully understood and well performed, he undoubtedly comprises an essential part of the American body politic, its prosperity and permanence, so long as he remains in its midst. And thanks to the good results of time, which wears away the strongholds of prejudice and evil in all communities, and the indefatigable labors of our anti-slavery friends, — all directed by the providence of God, — that we are now in the exercise of our citizenship, and we have only to under-

stand our rights, then demand them; comprehend our duties, the
perform them.

Cicero says : "The *equality* of rights has ever been the object
of desire, nor otherwise can there be any rights at all."

RIGHTS OF CITIZENSHIP.

And now I come to the second division of my subject, namely,
the rights of citizenship.

Right, in its most comprehensive sense, is a "well-founded
claim." Man in his natural and individual capacity possesses what
is known in the Declaration of Independence as "inalienable
rights," which, in the law, is denominated absolute rights, which
are divided into the right of personal security, the right of
personal liberty, and the right of private property, and these
rights precede government·

The right of personal security consists in a person's uninterrupted enjoyment of his life, his body, his health, and his reputation.

The right of personal liberty consists in the power of locomotion; that is, moving one's person to whatsoever place one's inclination may direct, without restraint, unless by due process of law.
And, let me mention in this connection, that the law doctrine is,
any restraint without due process of law, is false imprisonment.
Then, when a colored citizen, or a white citizen, is hindered from
entering a car or hotel, or denied accommodation at an inn or public place of amusement, or is assigned, contrary to his will and
inclination, and in defiance of law, a separate place in any of these
places, he is in a strict sense, falsely imprisoned.

The right of private property consists in the free use of all we
have acquired in the nature of property, real or personal, tangible
or intangible — lands, houses, papers, moneys, articles of merchandise, and other property, to dispose of as he pleases, without
control or dimunition, save only by the laws of the land.

These natural rights which I have mentioned, develop themselves in proportion to the advancement of civilization, and the
extent of liberty. Yet all who enter into society, or the compact
of government, give up part of the control of their natural rights,
in consideration of receiving from government mutual protection.
And thus arises what is called civil rights.

These civil rights, or rights accruing from our relationship to
government as citizens, are expressed in the Constitution of the
United States, either in affirmative, or prohibotory language.
Chief among the rights of citizenship is that of *suffrage*, or the
exercise of the ballot in the choice of our representatives in the
affairs of government.

Suffrage is incidental to citizenship, but is not a necessary sequence, as is most erroneously supposed, — especially by the advocates of woman suffrage. This is seen in the fact, that the exercise of suffrage, or the right to vote, is always qualified and regulated by law, and many do not, cannot enjoy it. Suffrage is a privilege, or a qualified right, and not absolute. The claim to suffrage, whenever it is well founded, should not be denied or abridged. It was never a well founded objection to deny the colored race suffrage on account of color or race.

WOMAN SUFFRAGE.

The question of to-day is, whether sex is a valid objection against suffrage. Before entering fully upon this topic, I will continue to show that suffrage is a privilege and is to be granted. I do this in order to prove that the question of woman suffrage may be regarded, as to its fitness, by such as have authority to grant it. In Massachusetts, in 1779–80, the Constitution declared that " every *male* person, 21 years of age, resident of a particular town for one year, having a freehold estate or the annual income of £3, or any estate to the value of £60 shall have the right to vote." The constitution of North Carolina, adopted in 1776, declared that all *freemen*, at the age of twenty-one, inhabitants of the county twelve months, and who shall have paid public taxes, shall be entitled to vote." Thus we see that two States, each in its jurisdiction, discriminated in granting suffrage, one as to sex, the other as to condition. Nothing can more clearly prove that the right of citizenship and the right of suffrage are distinct and different. Yet it is tyranical to circumscribe suffrage by illegal or unjust requisitions or provisions, since it is the ark of a people's safety capacious enough to protect them from all wrong and oppression.

I will now briefly, but more directly ask your attention, while I venture my views on the all-absorbing topic, the "Woman Suffrage Question," or what is more commonly known as the right of woman to vote. It is pertinent to the subject of citizenship, and, as I said in my opening remarks, these views are offered only to induce further consideration of the subject.

A woman, born in the United States, and not a child of a foreign minister, or other unnaturalized foreign person, is a citizen of the United States, and if she is duly qualified, as provided by law, it is not the easiest question to answer why she should not be granted suffrage. It is said that suffrage is a *right* growing out of citizenship. If so, I answer, It is a well-founded claim. But how shall we determine this? I have already regarded it as a privilege to be granted, with a view to fitness and qualification of the applicant. Moreover, it is to be observed that government does not deal with the abstract; but with the concrete principles. Hence, I deem it proper by such as have authority, namely, legislators and judges in courts to determine the social expediency of granting woman the exercise of suffrage. And this is co-extensive in jurisdiction with the right to qualify the exercise of suffrage, in man by conditions as to property, education, residence, or the like.

I think sex is a good objection against woman suffrage. I look around me, on the fields of nature, and I behold among the sexes of the lower animals, distinction. Not inequality, but distinction. I also see in these distinctions, the hand of God pointing to fitness.

"The object of government is to promote the good of society." Is the exercise of suffrage by woman calculated to promote the good of society? Civil society is nothing but household society, well regulated, or, as it is sometimes called, domestic government, enlarged. The latter is the parent of the former. Is not fitness of duty, as to sex, plainly seen in domestic government? I do not expect the exceptions to be given me as an answer. Evil doubtless exists in government by man, but, in the language of Paley, "it is a defect in the contrivance, but not the object of it."

I may be asked whether the same argument used against woman suffrage could not have been made against the suffrage of the negro? I answer: The so-called well-founded claim used against negro suffrage, was based on *color*, and not condition, morally, socially, or religiously, and, I suppose for the reason, that the white race in these objections would have found many of its own which answered the objections as completely as the negro. But is not sex a better claim against the exercise of suffrage by woman, than color ever could have been against the negro? Does it follow because there have been excellent queens, female scholars in every department of learning, that woman is as virtuous as man, that a few women of exceptional natures, and especial training, seem fit to govern or legislate, that therefore the woman should enter the body politic as a voter? Should the exception to a proposition form the rule to govern it?

I must confess I am in favor of woman suffrage to the extent of my conviction that her claim is well founded, in the sense of not only being lawful but expedient and for the good of society.

But let men learn that this claim of woman, at the present time, is the outgrowth of men's misdeeds in government. Equality in rights, when secured, give no opportunity for extravagant privileges. The law, regarding the rights of woman in her security of property, and giving her equal protection before the law, needs reform. But why should woman enter legislative halls or attend the polls to remedy this?

It cannot be denied that woman was impliedly a party to the

contract in the organization of this government; if not, there is no right to govern her at all, or make her amenable to the laws. How shall we remedy this defective contract, or when? Shall the minority or majority justify the call? Few women ask for the exercise of suffrage. Shall the few govern the many?

The present status of society in government is the growth of nearly six thousand years. What effect will it have to introduce a new element, except we are certain that it will promote good? It is not strong enough, nor conclusive enough to say that woman has a *right* to vote. Can the naked rights of the subjects of the king of Dahomey, being men, enable them to partake in the affairs of civilized government? I use this as an illustration only of the principle of fitness. But the whole trouble is with man. He may well hang his head when he thinks he has so treated woman for all ages, as to be compelled to question her fitness to be a partner with him in the affairs of government.

Sir Edward Bulwer Lytton, in his novel, "The Student," in his essay on the "Spirit of Society in England and France," impartially adverts to this question. He says:

" Here we cannot but feel the necessity of subjecting our gallantry to our reason, and inquiring how far the indifference to what is great, and the passion for what is frivolous, may be occasioned by the present tone of that influence, which woman necessarily exercises in this country, as in all modern civilized communities. * * * In order to account for the tone that fashion receives. we have but to inquire into the education bestowed upon women. Have we (men) then instilled into them those principles (as well as private accomplishments) which are calculated to ennoble opinion. No one will deny that they (women) are the first to laugh at principles. which, it is but just to say, the education we have given them precludes them from undertaking. * * * Now, were it true that women did not influence public opinion, we should be silent on the subject. * * * But we hold that feminine influence, however secret, is unavoidably great, and owing to this lauded ignorance of public matters, we hold it also to be unavoidably corrupt.

" How often has the worldly tenderness of the mother been the secret cause of the tarnished character or venal vote of the husband."

I will admit that the times and circumstances in which men live and are surrounded beget their minds. It may be different with the women of the present day in this country. Is it so? Already women have proven their fitness, by a new education, and the advantages of civil contact for many callings, hitherto exclusively exercised by men. But even in these we see a peculiar adaptation for one thing, and not for the other. These remarks are made not to condemn the advocates of woman suffrage. They are the result of my honest convictions at the present time.

RIGHTS OF CITIZENSHIP, RESUMED.

Citizens have the right to be secure in their persons, houses, papers and effects against unreasonable search and seizure, as provided by the Constitution. A man's house is spoken of in law as his "castle," and he may protect it to the extent of the death of the invader. A citizen is entitled to a speedy trial for all offences charged upon him. He is entitled to an impartial jury of his peers. A citizen's political peers are all other citizens than himself, without regard to color or race. Hence a jury of white men exclusively, and thus because colored men are not permitted to be jurors, is not an impartial jury. This equality of citizenship before the law, is what every citizen should demand. It is fully provided for in the language of the Constitution, which says: "No State shall make or enforce any law which shall abridge the privileges or immunities of citizens of the United States. This is what the supplementary Civil-Rights Bill calls for. It purports to enforce the *equality* of citizenship — giving us our rights, and leaving us to perform our duties. The passage of this bill will be the source of great good, a national dishonor wiped from the brow of our country, and the development of untold strength and prosperity, by creating indissoluble ties among citizens of a common country.

All writers of just government recognize the principles of the Civil-Rights Bill and the authority of government in securing it. Thomas Paine in his dissertation on government, says: "The foundation of public good is justice, and wherever justice is impartially administered the public good is promoted ; for it is the good of every man that no injustice be done him, so likewise it is his good that the principle which secures him should not be violated in the person of another, because such a violation weakens his security, and leaves to chance what ought to be to him a rock to stand on."

In the declaration of rights as originally pronounced by the fathers in asserting the independence of the colonies, and framing a government by consent, we find the following, which is in perfect accord with the principles of the Civil-Rights Bill, and doubtles actuated its author: "Government is or ought to be instituted for the common benefit, protection and security of the people, nation or community, and not for the particular emolument, or advantage of any single man, family or set of men who are a part only of that community ; and the community hath an undeniable right to reform. alter or abolish government in such manner as shall be by that community judged conducive to the public weal.

13

Suffrage is the exercise of the privilege to vote, which is giving our voice, or manifesting our disposition by some symbol in the choice of some person to fill public office, as a representative of the people in the arrangement of the affairs of government.

This, although a privilege, is not a new one; and, in consideration of the length of time it has been exercised by civilized governments, it may now in general terms, be called a right. It was imperfectly exercised as early as the time of the Judges of Israel, when the people chose their rulers from among the most brave. It is declared in the Scriptures "that all the elders of Israel came to Hebron, and King David made a league with them in Hebron before the Lord, and they announced David King over Israel." In the days of Rehoboan, we find a more improved system of political organization in which the right of suffrage was more definitely exercised. When the people of Israel were about to elect Rehoboan king, they said unto him, "If thou wilt be a servant unto this people this day, and wilt serve them, and answer them, and speak good words to them, then they will be thy servants for ever." In other words, these people said we will elect thee our king. This system of choosing rulers by suffrage continued in all civilized liberal governments.

To the present time it is the distinguishing feature of a republican form of government and limited monarchies.

The right to vote and give expression to one's consent to be governed, is the foundation of a free government. It preserves the only true government because the people are governed by their consent. Hooker, the great divine, and author of ecclesiastical history of government, says "that all publiic regiment, of what kind soever ariseth from the deliberate advice of men seeking their own good, and all other is mere tyranny. This right of the people to have a voice in the choice of their representatives is further seen in the words of God to Samuel when the children of Israel desired a king. "Hearken to the voice of the people," is the injunction from God himself.

But all success in the exercise of our suffrage depends upon the right use of it. Let the law of right govern our actions, and we shall not fail. Honesty, sincerity, and truth should be the guide; efficiency the test. At the present time the colored voters, as a whole, are most susceptible to delusion.. Fellow-citizens, gather your leaders, from such as Plato recommends. He says: "If one man be found incomparably to excel all others in the virtues that are beneficial to civil society, he ought to be advanced above all." Yet, my fellow-citizens, beware of demagogues, white and black. This class

169

of men ruined the Roman republic. Do not make your votes a matter of bargain and sale, an auction, at which the highest bidder gets the article; remember that the African race in this country has yet to make a history of its own in every department of life—politics not excluded. Place your good men to the front, colored or white. Virtue has not her seat in the complexion, but in the immortal soul which is given to all men.

I would also warn in this connection against the practice of changing representatives because the next man wants office. This is detrimental to ultimate good, and creates no permanency. The best representative can have no successor while living. The principles of government are not learned in a day, neither are the defects of government to be ascertained in a year.

In concluding this division of my subject, let me suggest that no false pride be encouraged in the possession and use of our rights of citizenship. Rights are sacred possessions. We may pervert these rights by a bad use of them. The standard is justice. In the exercise of our suffrage, the safest means of securing justice for ourselves is being just to others. An honest colored citizen is nobler far than a dishonest white man, and vice versa. Let our measure of men be loyalty to virtue, which is honesty, justice, and integrity incarnate.

DUTIES OF CITIZENSHIP.

Duty, in its widest sense, is analogous to right, and is the higher degree of relationship in citizenship between man and man. Duty is inherent, and is that which we ought to perform in obedience to the laws of nature, and the teachings of a just conscience. Judge Bouvier defines it in law as "a human action which is conformable to the laws which require us to obey them." Duty differs from a legal obligation in that it cannot be enforced by law. God has created within us reason, that we may understand our duties, follow the laws which regulate them and perform them. Our duty, as individuals, is various in detail. It is our duty to eat and drink that we may live, to be temperate in order to preserve good health. These may be called our natural duties. There are other duties known as our moral duties, and others still, our civil duties. Our civil and moral duties are more nearly allied than our natural duties. Our civil duties are obligations resting upon us as members of society. Our civil obligations are expressed, our civil duties implied. The former accrue from the contract entered upon by all citizens as members of the body politic. And these duties are incumbent upon all citizens in no less a degree than individual obligations. When performed they tend to bind us together for the good of society and government. Our duties ramify all our doings—from those of our household to the most public performance.

In mentioning some of our civil duties, I will commence with parent and child. I have already stated that a child is a citizen. But it is not called upon to perform its duties of citizenship until arrived at a mature age, hence these duties rest upon its parent, as its natural guardian.

The first duty of a parent towards a child is maintenance. Puffendorf declares it to be "a principle of natural law, an obligation laid * * not only by nature herself, but by the parents own proper part in bringing them into the world; for they would be in the highest manner injurious to their issue if they only gave their children life that they might afterwards see them perish." In no manner does a parent perform a nobler act of civil duty than by a proper maintenance of his or her children. Some think that if they secure for their children food, shelter, and clothing, they have completed their civil and parental duties. Not so. The government of a household, in regard to the care and training of children, is more arduous than is generally supposed. Health and vigor of body is to be maintained by a judicious use of food and exercise. The manners and learning of children need a watchful eye, else, like a neglected plant, they either grow rank or wither and die. And far above all is the element of character which is the seed of a noble, useful, and virtuous citizenship. A wisely trained character in a child makes such a citizen as will, when a man, never stop in public or private life to ask what will society think of me if I do this thing or leave it undone. The question by which a man of character will test the quality of an action will be, Is it just and wise, and fitting, when judged by the eternal laws of right? I invoke such an education to such an end for all children. It is better than books.* Our greatest bane to-day is the uneducated condition of suffrage. Through this, many of the enfranchised race are made the dupe of designing politicians, and those of the white race seal their own oppression. Education is the bulwark of a nation. Its diffusion is a national duty. It produces national prosperity. The Prussian maxim is, "whatsoever you would bequeath to a nation must be taught in its schools." And this is verified in the fact that a pro-slavery education has given us, pro-slavery legislators, pro-slavery judges, preachers, and teachers; hence to-day, in the face of the civilization of the nineteenth century, an American Congress hesitates to do justice to innocent black children, who are to become active

* The Grecian law-giver, Lycurgus, declares ' children to be the possession of the State."

members of the body politic, and partake of the affairs of government, by placing them in common schools with other children of the white race. I foretell that, unless our children are permitted to enter public schools in common with those of every other race, there will exist enmity, ill will, and divided interests all the days of distinction, and, as such, ill calculated to prosper our country or elevate the people. Education is described as "a companion which no misfortune can depress, no crime can destroy, no enemy can alienate, no despotism enslave—at home, a friend;' abroad, an introduction; in society, an ornament." Who will reject it? Who will deny it?

After the education of the child, comes its means of livelihood. The time when the guardianship of the parent ceases is the great launching time of responsibilities and duties. The ship of life, if strong in its timbers, well manned by education and character, is then placed on the ocean of time, as allotted to man's existence. Well-balanced, and gradually trimmed by experience, it enters upon its course to encounter shoals and quick sands, and visit ports of fortune and adversity—and thus is a success or a failure. But a successful means of livelihood depends on the good training of the child, with few exceptions, and a wise and judicious course of practising it.

Various are the avocations of men. Some are farmers, others mechanics; others teachers, doctors, lawyers, and statesmen, and preachers of the word of God; and they are also what are called politicians. Each, in his own sphere, is necessary to the grand work of human happiness in individuals and in society. And the roads to learning these avocations should be open to all without distinction. In these the child is seen the father of the man.

Of politicians, I will say a word or two. An honest politician is a valuable member of any city or State. He is the sentinel, and in proportion to *his* fidelity to duty, does the safety of his fellow-citizens become firm or weak. But the politician, whose conscience is an article of merchandise, as is his vote, and whose cunning and artifice enter all his actions with his fellow-man, is little worse than an epidemic. So likewise the leader, who seeks self-aggrandizement at the expense of the people's highest interest, is a dangerous element of society. A true leader is a hero—he is self-sacrificing, and, none ought to be regarded as leaders until they have shown this qualification. To the colored citizen I would say make no choice of your leaders on account of color; but let your test be inbred loyalty to justice and equality. This, and this only, is the true guide for the colored man. It comprises all he needs. To

172

this the white citizen should adhere, for he is equally benefited.
Let me denounce the opinion held by some that colored men
should vote for colored men at all times and under all circumstances, and that a black thief is more tolerable than a white one.
Men ought not be measured by their color, but by their character,
their integrity. Where this is found, not even party ties should
operate adversely; and I pronounce *this* as a public, political,
virtue; yet where the colored man is equally honest, full of integrity, and efficient, and there is a majority of his race where he resides,
and he is a candidate for office, he ought to be chosen in preference
to a white man of like capacity, for the reason that, all other
things being equal, one of the majority is the only true representative. Representation follows number as well as political principles.

Another public duty and civil obligation is the exercise of our
suffrage as voters. Evasion or omission of this duty is recreancy
to our trust as suffragists as well as infidelity to a sacred privilege.
One vote may save a city, or State, or nation, from ruin. Who, by
his neglect, would like to bear the stigma of criminal in this
respect? Among the laws of Solon, the Grecian law-giver, "all
persons who, in public dissensions and differences, espoused neither
party, but continued to act with a blameable neutrality, were
declared infamous."

From politics, we will return to the means of livelihood, so
necessary to the prosperity of every citizen, and to the prosperity
of his country—let us learn to labor—all labor that tends to supply man's wants, to increase man's happiness, to elevate man's
nature, is honorable, and is a civil duty. None have a moral right
to consume unless he produces; and this is true alike of the rich
man and the poor, the black man and the white.

It is strange to see what little regard is paid by those in affluence to the rights of the laboring classes. Civil society draws a
line of distinction between the manual laborer and the laborer of
the head, as if they were not coequal. This is a civil distinction
that smacks of a false pride—an aristocracy upon a false basis.
Our railroads, which spread over our country like a net work; our
steam cars, our magnificent houses, our fine equipages, our clothes,
our paper, our pen, our cannon, our ships-of-war, our books of
learning, are all the result of manual labor, coöperating with
mental labor. This distinction, which is even carried into our
social circles, is the beginning of the breach between capital and
labor.

Labor should be facilitated by liberal legislation, and should be
respected. An honest manual laborer is the peer of any other
man, and his work as necessary as that of any other man.

The earth, the air, fire and water, God has given to man to contribute to his happiness by means of his industry. A race of people has only a standing among men in proportion to their education and industry, which comprise their civilization. Men are enslaved only when they are uncivilized—that is, uncivilized in art and science, in manners and religion Not even war is potent enough to enslave an industrious class of people. They may be conquered, reduced to poverty: their bodies may be kept in chains; but they cannot be reduced to servile servitude. Then industry is a safe guard against conquest, of mind, and depravity of race, as well as it is a sure means to social elevation. No people that have ever lived upon the face of the earth have elevated themselves to the stanard of social and civil equality with their superiors resting upon their rights alone. It is the duty of every citizen to widen the commerce of his country, and elevate himself and his race by industry. In plain language, let me say to you that if you desire to destroy exclusiveness by proscription, as practiced by the white race in this country; to mingle with them in churches, schools, hotels, inns, and other places upon a platform of perfect equality, socially, civilly, and legally, you must create an inter-dependence. Law inaugurates rights and protects them. Industry cements them, and renders them permanent.

We must encourage among ourselves artisans of every description, manufacturers, scientists, philosophers, merchants, lawyers, doctors, politicians, and statesmen like unto white men. The colored people throughout the United States, especially those having money, and those who are educated, must coöperate and establish workshops, be incorporated to the end of having steamboats, street cars, steam cars, dry goods stores, stationers, (there is not one in the District of Columbia, as there may well be.) And these institutions are not to be designed for colored people, but for the public. A good article will command a purchaser, a good workman patronage, education esteem and respect without regard to color. History fails to tell us of any other means by which a race of people has risen in the scale of civilization and equality among men having been once slaves. For slavery has been the lot of every weak race of people when conquered, and this without regard to color. All this, colored citizens, you must do, or your civil rights will be a myth.

But I cannot leave this subject without admonishing the white race in this country not to throw itself across the path of a struggling class of citizens—a part of the body politic with themselves. It is suicidal. The elevation of the colored race in this common country, and its con-association in all legitimate business with the white race is necessary to the safety, permanence, and prosperity

of the Government. This may appear extravagant; but, as the
whole is made up of all its parts, so the whole is imperfect, unsafe,
unsteady, and weak, without all its parts; and the man who would
debar his fellow-citizen from any opportunity to rise in the scale
of industry and education, is more a traitor than a patriot.

"No man," says a great author, w"hether he be a commander
of an army, or a leader in a State, has ever been able to perform
great salutary achievements without the zealous coöperation of
men." This is wise counsel for the white portion of the South,
who would expect to prosper without the coöperation of the colored
man upon a platform of equality.

Yet, let me state that this commonality of citizens, in the exercise of their rights and privileges, is by no means intended to
instruct against that necessary preservation and distinction of the
different races. For it is well to bear in mind that the confusion
of tongues at Babel seemed to have begotten the distinction of
races, and that neither war nor peace, religion nor heathenism,
civilization nor barbarism, wealth nor poverty, color nor creed, has
ever been sufficient to so absorb one race into another so as to lose
the origin of either. Nor is this a good argument why the colored
American should go to Africa. Man is nomadic. Moreover, if
the colored American should go to Africa because it is the land of
his forefathers, what right has the European, the Asiatic, or the
Australian in America? The right to locomotion is a fundamental
principle, as I have already shown, and cannot be circumscribed
or abridged by man. We, as colored people, should be unified as
to race interests, like unto the Germans, French, and Irish who
adopt this country, when such do not conflict with our duty as
citizens.

Art. III.—WOMAN, WRONG AND RIGHT.

BY REV. GEO. H. JOHNSTON.

The relation of woman to man and to secular life possibly engages more attention in modern times than in any other period of history. In our own and in other Christianized countries, her sphere in the family and in society is not a special question. Here she takes her position without let or hindrance, and impresses her own spirit and character upon them; and even where she has been reduced to slavery, as is so prominently the case in heathenism, ancient and modern, she has not failed in her seclusion and servitude, to mould the minds and hearts of her offspring. Sometimes she has allayed the rising anger of her husband and master, or roused his passions, and aided in forming purposes and plans, which, when carried out, laid the foundation of governments or compassed their destiny.

Occasionally, all along the course of history, she is seen stepping out of the limits of the home-circle and social life in its narrower sense, and her form, bold and defiant, looms up sword in hand, on the battle-field; or crowned upon a throne, she sits a queen, swaying the sceptre over a submissive people.

Her appearances in such positions are only sporadic and incidental, and not of continuous historical occurrence. These episodes in the trials and triumphs of the race are like meteoric flashes that, though uncertain in origin and indefinite in destiny, yet confront the student as sometimes brilliant, but always transient phenomena, in the onward flow of history.

In the field of letters, anciently, she was seldom heard, and then chiefly, almost exclusively, in sacred history; but in more recent times, she uses her pen in well-nigh every department of study, adding volume to volume, until her productions are like the leaves in the valley.

But woman is not content, in the present, to continue to move quietly in the circles, to which she has mainly devoted her life in the past. Grown impatient of restraint, she oversteps the boundaries of home and social life in the narrower sense, and although cheerfully accorded the right of cultivating her powers in the sphere of the fine arts, in poetry, music, painting, sculpture, and in literature; these, she insists, are too limited and tame for the right development and due exercise of the faculties of her nature. She will own no limits man does not acknowledge. Where he walks she may confidently tread, not only as his mate and companion, but also as his leader and guide. In civic life, in all its departments, in the forum, on the bench, in the legislative hall, in politics, she is, in our day, not only willing, as if impelled by the judgment of history, to act a responsible and equal part with the masculine constituency of the race, but she now claims these prerogatives with the lords of the manor, and insinuates, if she does not openly affirm, that she has been swindled out of her inalienable rights from time immemorial. This disparaging treatment she is in no mood longer to endure. Her conventions, organizations, circulars, addresses, indignant protests and resolutions flood the land. She is moving to vindicate her rights.

For awhile her claims to the walks of life apparently committed to man by his Maker, and so long well-nigh indisputably occupied by him, especially the legislative, executive and judicial departments, in the Family, the Church and the State, as also the interests of politics, medicine and theology, which he almost exclusively and always represented, were received with an air of incredulity, and an intuition, perhaps the inspiration of the Almighty, that she could not be in earnest in her apparent efforts to cross the boundaries thus defined and fixed, and now also sanctioned by the words, deeds and lives of a long catalogue of the noblest matrons and maidens adorning the historic page in Jewish and Christian times.

However, she wakes man up to the reality. The claim is earnestly and persistently made, reasons are given, and the argument follows in support of the new theories. Old men and matrons shake the head in doubt; the vast majority of them may be counted as denying the claims of these modern aspirants to indiscriminate public intercourse, position and place, and denounce their advocates as unworthy of confidence, and their theories as false. The younger classes of both sexes generally treat the efforts of the women-reformers with comparative indifference, and not infrequently with down right levity and practical jest. But it is not to be concealed, or denied, that the so-called Woman's Rights' movement has made its presence felt in a decided way already, in various quarters in the land. It has taken hold on many leading minds, wired its way to the ballot-box, gained admission into school boards, and assumes to expound the commentaries of Blackstone, and scruples not to minister at the Altar. The claims are put forward, the positions sought, and the posts accepted and occupied, not as so many concessions made by society, but as a solemn inalienable right, precisely in the plane of life, liberty, and the pursuit of happiness demanded by this new order of things. Neither is it assumed that woman ought to be permitted freely to move in every sphere in which man engages, and occupy it merely for the purpose of earning for herself and those dependent on her the means of support, and gathering, if prosperity smile upon her, the boon of a competent fortune. On no such utilitarian level as that does she put her claim. She advocates the existence of talents buried, possibilities and powers smothered, which, if permitted to be developed to even comparative maturity by exercise in all leading avenues of activity in which man has always stood so overshadowingly conspicuous, she would soon be able to demonstrate her capacity to the full satisfaction of her mate and lord, carry conviction to the hearts of the incredulous, stop the mouths of all who have spoken to her injury, resurrect her slumbering genius from the dust and comparative obscurity of the ages, and rear monuments of marble and brass, silver and gold that would transmit to the ages to come the exact quantity and true quality of her native powers. She insists that, hemmed in and bound by the chains which man has forged to limit her freedom, sanctioned by the conventionalities of society, and riveted also by the traditions and ignorance of the past, there is many a talented maiden and stately matron now sitting with clouded vision, hugging the delusive phantom of hope, who if their shackles were removed, and their liberty accorded them, "the rod of empire might sway, or wake to ecstacy the living lyre."

The consideration of a question of such far-reaching meaning, embracing the gravest interests of social and religious life, affecting as well the private as the public well-being of society and the age, challenges earnest thought, careful analyzation of the relations involved, and the calm dignity of disinterested judgment.

Turning to the oldest Record of history, we are reminded that in the beginning man was created male and female. Man's body is fashioned out of the dust of the earth in its crass condition, and by the inspiration of the Almighty, this workmanship is endowed with life, and all the faculties of an intelligent personality. For man, the culminating handiwork of God, Eden was provided, the proto-type of heaven, in the midst of which his eye rested with delight on the loveliness of nature yet free from the blightning curse of briers and thorns, and animal life frisking around him, looked into his face and acknowledged him as the rightful lord appointed by the Creator, to exercise dominion over all the creation, subdue the earth, and cause it to minister to his will and pleasure. To give him some right conception of his superior dignity and glory as compared with all the creation besides, the creature-world was made to pass before man in orderly procession to do obeisance to him; and he named them, not giving each *individual* a separate name ; but male and female as they passed were, in each case, designated by one name, as lion, horse, dove; and God gave him the sceptre of dominion, and charged him to be faithful in the administration of the great trust. Looking out upon the scenes around him, and contemplating the constitution of the animal world, he was struck with its diversity, and yet its apparent unity. Two and two, male and female, they passed him by; but somehow these two always seemed to be bound together as one. In the vegetable kingdom the same fact seemed also to be more or less prominent. Contemplating his own solitary condition, there heaved up in his bosom a spontaneous feeling, an impulse of his nature, that, however fearfully and wonderfully made, he needed a mate of like sort with himself to complement his nature, in harmony thus with the beauty and perfection of the natural world of which he formed such a distinguished part.

Man had scarcely discovered his onesidedness of nature, when the Creator, according to His purpose, completed His work by fashioning another creature corresponding to man and complementing him in all respects, the representative of His own image and likeness.

But, mark you, the body of woman was not, like man's, fashioned out of the gross dust of the earth; but the Creator took for its basis a rib of man, which indeed originally was itself dust of the earth, now wonderfully refined, however, in the process of creation; and this accounts for the delicacy of her physical organization as compared with man; and since body and mind have a relative correspondence throughout the universe, it is seen how beautifully delicate and high-toned is the mental and moral constitution of woman, thus filling out, with "softer lines and brighter shadings," the full conception of humanity in the first pair of the race.

The hand of the mighty Architect had just given the final touch of His pencil to this last, most beautiful piece of workmanship, when Adam, looking into the face of his mate, saw traits physical, mental and moral, necessary and intended to beautify and ennoble his manhood; and woman, looking into Adam's face, saw reflected those qualities adapted to strengthen and complete her womanhood; together they embodied the full conception of humanity, lacking nothing for perfect enjoyment, and endowed for the holy mission entrusted to their keeping.

"This is now bone of my bone and flesh of my flesh; she shall be called woman." God looked upon the work He had made, saw it was good, smiled upon His creatures, and set His seal irrevocably upon the instinctive declaration of man, that woman reflected the demands of his nature, and he the needs of her's, the two together constituting the unit of humanity; no more, no less; and so He gave His word to the living abiding fact: "And they shall be one flesh."

How could the two be one, in a generic sense, if each is one? If the male is a creation, wanting nothing, having no sense of incompleteness, acknowledging no lack, and desiring no associations to be supplied to strengthen and dignify his manhood, then it was a cruelty rather than otherwise, that another, intended to be a mate, should be provided and thrust upon him. The facts, however, sustain the wisdom of the events as they transpired. Man is an individual, a specific creation. He is created, he lives, he dies as an individual. The same is true, of course, of woman. As individuals, each has a separate, independent existence. No one will dispute that. But no single individual human being represents the full conception of humanity. This is broader and deeper than any merely individual human existence. Humanity is a generic conception and fact, and can therefore hold, not in any individual existence, separately taken, but in the conception of the race. Adam as an individual died, but humanity, as comprehended in the first pair, lives and abides forever.

This truth the Record itself requires as its own proper sense and meaning. "In the day that God created man, in the likeness of God made He him: male and female created He them; and blessed them and called their name Adam." "He called *their* name Adam;" the two individuals were so related in nature and constitution that together they comprehended substantially one fact, one creation, namely, *humanity*, whose concurrent life and character should ennoble and glorify the ages to come.

The argument is confirmed by remembering, that the word *woman* has the same root as the word *man*, only with a feminine termination: and the word "help-meet" here means, not only one who in an outward way assists another, but primarily that which corresponds to, complements, fills out, what is lacking in another, the very fact we are endeavoring to enforce. The union holds not in man nor in woman, but in their joint correspondence of nature, and their federal union. In the same connection, it is not said that He created them man and woman, but male and female; not *a* (one) male and *a* (one) female, but male and female. And afterwards "He called *their* name *Adam* in the day when they were created," because there was a common bond of life between them.

If there be valid ground for what we have now said, then it follows as a legitimate corollary, that marriage is a divine institution, sanctifying with its genial love and moulding power the Family, the Church, and the State, the living power behind the throne of history, whose law is love, whose standard is virtue and good-will, and whose mission is fidelity to God and honor and integrity in the bosom of the race.

Of course we here grant that man, in the course of history, has failed to recognize his right relation to woman; that he has oppressed her, ignored, from time to time, the true qualities and genius of her nature, made life an intolerable burden, filled her soul with groaning, her eyes with tears, and loaded her with coarse burdens grievous to be borne. All this is sadly true, true even to-day. But injustice and wrong in one direction does not justify a false claim and a wrong course of action in another, the infringement of an order established for the purpose of conserving the best interests of society, having its ground in the "eternal fitness of things."

It is contended over against the facts we have presented, that man's relation to woman as seen in history, as well in the history of Jewish and Christian civilization, as in the rougher walks of heathenism in its various stages, is, even in its best phases, substantially self-assumed, and that there is no good reason why woman should really, or apparently even occupy, in any sense, a dependent or subordinate position. It is said that she is just as independent of man as he is of her, and that she must only assert herself, and insist on a due recognition of her native character and rights to demonstrate her equality with him. She will own no sphere of active life as peculiarly her's, and acknowledges none as specially man's. Man is man and woman is woman, and that is all there's of it. In the race of active life she wants each sex to have an equal chance upon the same arena, without let or bar, and the one will show as much adaptability in every legitimate calling as the other, and win equal success and renown. Why should she be mainly limited to the retirement of home, she asks, and be expected everlastingly to prepare viands to delight the palate of her would be lord and master? And the very thought provokes a strong-minded woman, and stirs her up to engage in the holy cause of liberty and equal rights.

She insists that man's place is as properly his father's roof, or his wife's, as woman's is her father's roof, or her husband's. He may as properly superintend household affairs as she, if only he is brought to the work. Has not man left the primitive tent-life, so simple and beautiful in its appointments, and built houses, made furniture, woven carpets, moulded dishes and invented all kinds of furniture? Having invented and made all these goods and chattels, is it not presumable that he knows best how to manipulate their use? Let him keep the house in order and rock the baby then, while she prepares the briefs for the Quarter Sessions, or grapples with the five points of Calvinism. Do you say he would look awkward, out of his sphere? Who invented the magnificent emporiums of dress and dress-making, so prominent in the metropolis of every country? Who, chiefly, produced the thousand and one articles, useful and beautiful, that adorn homes, towns and cities, and beautify the persons of man and woman? If it is answered that man is largely their author, by what law then, human or divine, founded in justice and right, shall woman continue to be limited almost exclusively to the narrow boundaries of house and home, there forever to go from kitchen to dining-room, from bed-room to parlor, from garret to cellar, only to gratify man, to minister to his daily recurring wants, when she might as well herself have been prominent in all this history ? Is she not his equal? And does she not compromise her womanhood to submit to this restraint?

But, listen to her story; for she desires to be heard and heeded:—

What powers of endurance, she asks, has man not native to woman ? In what toil and privations, in what labors and sufferings has she failed to bear an equal part with man from begining to end? Where is the record of her failures?

Is she not also intellectually man's equal? Has he any faculties bestowed wanting in her mental organization? What achievements of mind are his that lay beyond her ability? What breadth of mental vision is his not also granted her by the same munificent hand?

Does she not also stand in the same plane morally? Is not her origin, her life, her destiny, the same with man's? If he is endowed with religious instincts, grapples with ethics and metaphysics, searches into the secret fountains of nature and of God, launches his bark to discover the boundaries of the temporal, and mounts to the throne of faith to compass the borders of the eternal, why may she not bear him company, or lead the way· even, in every domain of thought, in every flight of spiritual vision? What limits circumscribe her being that are foreign to his? No! The disparagement of woman, setting her back of man, and subordinate to him, is an assumption in the face of facts! It is a tradition of ignorance, founded in pretended inequality. It is a relic of heathenism, at war with truth and justice, a wrong long and patiently borne, now happily being seen and acknowledged in this age of greater light and progress. The time is come. Now then, let justice be done half the race, and it may be the better half, though the heavens fall! Stand out of the way, ye oppressors of woman!

Let her step abreast with man. Take off the cords that have bound her to the altars and fires of house and home through the weary centuries; open the avenues for active, independent work, and see what an age of progress and glory will be ushered in to bless the nations and herald the millennial dawn !

Sex, you say? Her sex? Woman's sphere? Her mission? A help-meet to man, to hold up his hands, to assist him in achieving the great purposes of life and being, and while doing that, crowning herself? Her natural delicacy of organization? Away with it all! I'ts only a notion !

There! Open the way for her! Let her out into real life ! Give her the coat and cap of the police, and as she goes her daily and nightly rounds, arrests the drunken and the profligate, frequents the haunts of vice and sin, learns to drink and to swear in order to efficiency in the service; it will call out and cultivate the finer feelings of her nature, and help her the better to fill the offices of a mother and the duties of home! Make her a delegate to the caucus, and let her learn the airs, and clothe herself in the incorruptible virtues of secular politicians, that she may adorn her womanhood ; and then, ticket in hand, let her take her stand in the crowd on election day and court the favors of the masses with the smiles and graces of her sex that she may be elected to some civic office! The experience thus acquired will adorn her intellectual and moral nature, and prepare her for her true mission in the world ! Let her occupy her place in the attorney's office, and at the bar, ferret out the doings and misdoings of business life; discover and bring to the light the ulcers and rottenness of the lanes and alleys ; expose the crimes of age, and unravel the sins of youth ; con over the lists of larceny, robbery, debauchery and murder, until she can identify herself fully with the interests of her clients ; let her study the calendar of sin and shame, comprehending the flagrant violation of every commandment in the decalogue ; give herself to the demands made upon her ; subject herself to crosses, excitement, fears, reproach, slander; let the public bandy her name, character and sex, until her

34

sensibilities are blunted, her constitutional delicacy seared, and the result will wonderfully fit her for the modest, high-toned, loving daughter; the amiable, considerate wife; and the tender-hearted, affectionate mother, who inspires her offspring with the beautiful and the sublime at every step of life !

Let us understand the question.

The so-called Woman's movement claims that there ought to be no distinction between the sexes before the law, civil or divine; that position and occupation ought in no wise to be determined by traditionary customs, or enforced by legal enactments; that distinctions in education and professions, position and mission in life are founded in imagination, having no basis in fact; and that sex ought not to be a question in education, either as to quality or quantity; nor ought it in any wise fix a relation of comparative dependence of the one sex on the other, as is now, and has been so common in society.

We reply, that the movement started in modern times by fanatics and errorists of both sexes, is founded in false premises, illogical and inconclusive in its reasonings, and damaging to her character in proportion to its success. She shrinks from the consequences herself that legitimately follow in its wake, and disowns, in her calmest moments, the new doctrines. Her sex, her organization, naturally so sensitive to every rude touch, her womanly instincts and intuitive love of retirement and the genial atmosphere of home, her native sense of the beautiful, and her sympathy with the sunshine and smile of infancy and childhood, disqualify her forever to move contentedly and happily in any other sphere than that which she has blessed with her presence and crowned with her virtues in the ages gone by.

The movement misconceives the true character of the race; does not understand the right relation of male and female to each other as originally constituted; disparages the beauty and perfection of humanity so wondrously brought to view in the creation; and excites friction and antagonism in the family and society, in the State and Church, whose consequences from first to last are of the most serious character. It is the author of an unholy spirit of rivalry between the sexes. It breeds discord in the family and home. It sets husband and wife virtually against each other. Instead of the husband being the head of the wife and the head of the family as by divine ordainment, woman is claimed to be in no sense subordinate, not even to her husband, and thus the family has not one culminating centre, the husband and father ; but it has two heads, the husband being the one and the wife the other. In accordance with this doctrine, of course the old marriage ceremonies must be amended or discarded, for they are based upon divine revelation ; and this is accordingly done. No strong-minded woman, knowing her rights, and daring to maintain them, will consent to "obey" her husband, and she will honor and love him just as long as she pleases, and no longer.

The divine order in the relation of the sexes does not intend or require a subordination of woman in any arbitrary, oppressive sense. The relation between them rests in the element of love ; and the subordination in the marriage relation is not one of arbitrary self-will, tending to oppression and slavery, but a subordination founded in nature and law—the law of love—whose soul is the very element of freedom, and whose life and discipline for both sexes, is contentment and the highest happiness. Where love reigns as the distinguishing characteristic between the sexes, sanctified by a sense of right relation to God, there is no sense of wrong, there can be no conception of wrong done by the one to the other, because this is precisely the relation which nature dictates, the divine fiat sanctions, and thus the demands of humanity are met and satisfied. This was the experience of the first pair ; and in a line of succession representing *God's people* down to the Christian era, although this conception of the normal relation of the sexes was by no means fully, nevertheless it was measurably realized. Apostate man, in the person of Cain, already on the threshold of history, introduced polygamy, whose slimy trail of sin and sorrow drew its votaries on the lowest level of social and moral degradation, and succeeded in fastening its virus upon the lineage of the true seed to their hurt. Apostacy is the mother of all the maladies that afflict society in every age; the foul fountain whence issue mire and dirt to blur and blast the body and damn the soul.

Of course heathenism wrongs woman always and everywhere, and wrongs man as well. Here she seldom rises to the dignity of her character, though there are some exceptions. But where the light of revelation shone, and the light was accepted as man's beacon to virtue and nobility, there are glimpses of her true position and dignity all along through patriarchal and Jewish history. Her social equality with man is most fully implied in the Mosaic record, and a high tone was maintained generally on this subject by the force of public opinion. "The wives and maidens of ancient times mingled freely and openly with the other sex in the duties and amenities of ordinary life." Miriam and Jephthah's daughter, the women in Saul's and David's time, Deborah and Hannah, Huldah, Noadiah and Anna, Elizabeth and the Virgin Mary, are examples in a period stretching over fifteen hundred years, of the social, literary and public distinction enjoyed by woman under the sanction of the divine economy. Social equality she has by inherent right and by divine sanction; in literary and public life she anciently had no connected history. From the date that the light of the cross begins to illuminate the twilight of the world with its effulgent beams, the old and first order of things in the social sphere is reasserted and gradually re-established. Polygamy and social degradation are met with the clear declaration of the Great Teacher come from God, "*In the beginning it was not so.*" That was the key-note for the redemption of family and social life to its original plane. As the leaven of Christianity is mixed in the meal of humanity, permeates its arteries and veins, infusing its spirit and quickening it with its glorious life, just so fast does the race rise in new vigor and strength. Here man is himself, woman has all her rights, society is virtuous and happy, and the race blooms and blossoms as the rose, fragrant with the dews of heaven.

Who are these woman's rights' representatives? Are they the ladies and matrons in the representative *Christian* homes on the Continent, in England, and in the United States? Do they embody the piety and virtue of female character in our principal American homes? They are a class of strong-minded women, discarding old-fashioned piety, and giving little countenance to any other; who, in a mood of insubordination to the instincts of their sex, seek to inaugurate manners and customs directly at variance with the best experience of history and the decrees of human nature. Their views of social life and of the marriage relation, of the sweet atmosphere of home with its blessed influences, are often of the poorest and lowest sort. They prate loudly of woman's wrongs, of the systematic injustice she endures in silence and obscurity, when, if she were lifted into the possession of all these dreamers claim for her, her inevitable degradation would only then properly commence. She would not only suffer in every distinctive faculty of her nature by contact with secular life in all its forms, but home, the true paradise of woman, would be invaded by influences that would gradually undermine the associations, and destroy the memories that cluster around it like a garden of sweet flowers, to beautify the age of infancy and childhood, and in which the foundation of solid man-and-woman-hood is laid.

Why, one may see their principles practically demonstrated. Among the more refined and literary representatives of this class, the trouble crops out in family feuds, coldness and alienation of feeling and affection, divorces and lawsuits, as seen illustrated every day in the New England and Western States, soils in which the new doctrines have taken root, and are bearing their fruit. The same principles may be seen in another form in the lower walks of life, though the morals here are often of a more substantial character.

Where the position is taken that not mutual concession, cooperation and union on the basis of a correlation of the sexes, but perfect independence of thought and action is to be cultivated and maintained among girls and boys, young men and ladies, men and matrons, and a constant watch kept lest the one should invade the rights of the other, there the tenderest throbs that heave the human bosom, the loveliest memories of home, and the dearest ties of society, would be gradually vitiated, if not sublimated into airy nothing !

The spirit here questioned and resisted crops out especially in the sphere of education. The effort of the Woman question is practically to eliminate all that is feminine in her, and to substitute masculine traits and qualities in their stead. Take away what is feminine in woman, and you strip her of her true glory. Woman is not inferior to man in her domain, nor is man superior to woman. Man in his sphere is a king; woman in her sphere is a queen; together as God made them they are like the dove and his mate, lovely themselves, and inspire a like spirit in others.

Co-education of the sexes is a special hobby with the new theorists. By co-education is meant, " that boys and girls shall be taught the same thing at the same time, in the same place, by the same faculty, with the same methods, and under the same regimen."* They practically say, " that boys' schools and girls' schools are one, and that that one is the boys' school." The curriculum of study for boys is well fixed on the basis of experience, and girls are expected to adopt their course as also the right one for them. Their sex, their organization, their mission, are all ignored by these visionary enthusiasts, as if these were idle dreams !

Where the views of these theorists prevail "education looks upon the girl as if she were a boy, treats her as if she were a boy, and trains her as if she were to have a boy's destiny." This false position is pressed by the enemies of sound social economy because it belongs to the system which they represent. If they can secure the acceptance of their theories by the colleges and seminaries of the country, succeed in inoculating

---

* Sex in Education: Clarke, p. 122.

them with their crude ethics, then the object of their dreams will be met, their ambition satisfied.

In the New England States and at the West, strenuous efforts are made, and they have in part succeeded, to put boys and girls, young men and ladies together in the same institutions, and give them the same intellectual, and as far as possible, the same physical training; and not the female, nor a medium, but the male standard is made the basis of the course of study best suited to develop the intellect of both sexes ; the ground is assumed, and the object is to show, that there is no difference between boys and girls, there ought to be no difference in their education, and there ought to be no distinction made between them in active life.

It is also claimed, that besides inculcating right principles on the relation of the sexes by this method, the mutual benefits to each sex by daily intercourse, are of vast account for a right knowledge of human nature, issuing in the happiest results. Intercourse of the sexes is a common instinct, but the shadow of home, and the judicious guardianship of parents or friends, and not the recitation rooms, the windows and corridors of schools, are best for the cultivation of those friendships between the sexes that look forward to the battle of life.

" The only difference between the sexes is sex; but this difference is radical and fundamental, and expresses itself in radical and fundamental differences of organization, that extend from the lowest to the highest forms of life. True progress is impossible without accepting and respecting difference of sex. That it is physiologically possible to diminish sex by an education arranged for that end, no physiologist can doubt ; nor can it be doubted that identical methods of educating the sexes, such as prevail in many of our schools, tend that way. One result of a school-system animated by such methods is to make a very poor kind of men out of women, and a very poor kind of women out of men. Fortunate for the Republic, if no illustrations of the truth of this remark could be found within its borders.

The best quality, noblest power and supreme beauty of the two sexes, grow out of their dissimilarity, not out of their identity. Differentiation is nature's method of ascent. We should cultivate the difference of the sexes, not try to hide or abolish it. When a gardener seeks to produce the best possible apple or peach, he selects one whose beauty or flavor is desirable, and cultivates the selected difference. Nature has selected difference of sex by which to give humanity its choicest beauty and quality. The perfection of one sex is unattainable by the other, and at present is rarely comprehended by the other. Each loves and reverences in the other what it has not and cannot grasp itself, and despises any imitation. Let education respect and cultivate nature's selected difference."*

The main objection to be fairly urged against this false attitude of the relation of the sexes, especially in education, is that the whole movement is substantially soulless. It is utilitarian from first to last. It represents material, worldly, temporal interests, and these only. It does not seem to have occurred to these new lights that woman has a soul that needs culture, as well as a mind and body that need education. They are at fault not only in social science, but their physiology, psychology and theology are just as lame and inadequate to the demands of the case. Education with them means the drawing out of the physical and intellectual powers to their full capacity. Only this and nothing more. They talk much of proper physical discipline. Some of the modern fashions in dress are handled with a degree of severity. The dress, they say, and fixings, tight and loose, by which the proper activity of the body is hindered, must be modified or discarded. Perhaps some of the paraphernalia now fixed on, crowded in, hung around, tucked up, or saucily waving in the breeze, might be dispensed with, for aught we know. This point, however, they press, not on any high moral ground, but because too much flummery is a hindrance to her in her race with man.

* The Building of a Brain : Clarke, pp. 52, 53.

Education involves vastly more than the discipline of the mind and body, a drawing out of all man's powers. This conception of education obtains, to a large extent, if not prevailingly; but it is false. The true symmetry of man-and-womanhood is not secured in this way. There is another element in the·human constitution that lies deeper than education under this view reaches, and that is the spiritual element, naturally shrouded in the garment of sin and death. True education must take this factor into the account. No developing of the mental faculties merely, either roots out or puts the evil propensity of man's nature under control, so that the spirit is free to pilot the human bark across the seas of science to the goal of glory. Education in its work of drawing out and strengthening the mind only opens new avenues for the spread of moral disease, if it have not the culture of the heart as its basis. "Moral evil does not issue from ignorance and false systems of education, but the reverse; ignorance and false systems of education issue from moral evil." History abundantly confirms the proposition. Education is a power; a power in the family, in the Church, in the State; a power to leaven, to sanctify, to ennoble every relation of life, on the condition here now and always absolute, that education brings man's will into right relation to the will of God, so that the moral nature, the power of evil being broken and held in abeyance, shall sit in the throne of knowledge, and so guide man not only with reference to the interests of time, but also of eternity. True education involves not only what man can do for man in the way of teaching, and what man can do for himself in the way of thought and learning, but it involves also what God has done, can do, and does for man. If it be true to the sacred interests which it represents, it must give its students a *basis* of strength morally, precisely in proportion to their intellectual attainments. The moral must always have the balance of power for normal man-and-womanhood, else education is more likely to be a curse than a blessing. Every school in this or any other land, resting in the theory that a systematic discipline of mind and body, without a substantial basis of Christian philosophy, can raise man and woman to true distinction and qualify them for the highest responsibilities of life, is rotten at the heart, and fruitful of the saddest consequences for society and the age. The moral power in man is the strongest element in his nature. To leave that in the bondage of sin and the devil, without compass or anchor, while the mind is disciplined, is only to leave him, though educated, at the mercy of powers within him, and foes without, to prey upon and destroy him.

It is a chief glory of our times that schools for both sexes are multiplying, and efforts are made to make them broad, thorough, proficient. Learning is becoming as common as the leaves of autumn. But it will be valuable only as the whole man is brought under the power of right education and culture. Christ and Christianity, faith and worship, the culture of the soul along with the education and discipline of the mind and body are fundamental. The old motto, "a sound mind in a sound body," must here be supplemented by the addition, and these developed in union with Jesus Christ, the true light and life of the world, a condition absolutely essential to sound education and a virtuous successful life.

Education is a great power; a power for evil as well as for good, depending entirely on the heart of man. If this be without a *standard* of interpretation, if Christ be not for it the first and last resort for illumination and guidance in the fields of knowledge and science, then, though man possess all learning, it will be for him without true sense and meaning. He may be full to overflowing; without a *reliable criterion* for the interpretation of learning it will be for him only a *chaos of facts*, leaving its possessor, like a Humboldt, in confusion and night.

"The earth is the Lord's, and the fulness thereof." The following thought is true. What will the study of the mineral kingdom profit if the student see not in it the Pearl of Great Price, the Rock of Ages? What is all the joyous beauty of the vegetable kingdom, with its towering cedars, mighty oaks, lovely landscapes decorated with grasses and adorned with flowers, if the Rose of Sharon and the

Lily of the Valley are left out? What does the giant strength and the instinctive wisdom of the animal kingdom signify, from the greatest to the least, if man fails to discern the Lion of the tribe of Judah? The student raises his eye towards the heavens, and surveys the incomparable panorama spread out to his vision. There are the Pleiades, the Bands of Orion, Arcturus with his sons, and Mazaroth in his season; but what does it all mean, if he see not also the Star of Bethlehem? We study history, trace the course of mankind, follow the nations in their rise and decay, map out the lines of civilization and barbarism, take up physiology, psychology and mental philosophy; but we find no perfect model in any age, among any people; our researches are unsatisfactory until we come to the man Christ Jesus. In Him we have a perfect model, a model physically, a model mentally, a model morally, a model in life, in death, in the resurrection, in the ascension, whose life is man's life, whose teaching is man's learning, into whose exaltation man may be lifted and glorified.

If woman is animated by the tenor and spirit of these principles, she will find herself, in every age, standing precisely, in her relation to man, to her own sex, to society, to the State, to the Church, to education, just where the noblest matrons and maidens have always stood. Circumstances, events in history, the necessities of the times, the demands for bread, may, and do now, as in the past, bring her voluntarily and involuntarily into walks of life more or less repugnant and incongenial to her nature. Necessity drives her into shops and factories, and she may legitimately, in exceptional cases, come into active public life and accomplish important work. In the work of education of both sexes in their youth, and of her own sex on to the end of the course, she moves in a legitimate sphere. Here she is eminentlysuccessful, because it is a part of her nature to train the young and beckon them on to noble endeavor. In the fine arts so congenial to her nature, because their element is the true, the beautiful, and the good, she has always manifested a special delight. In poetry, the lyrics of Deborah, Hannah, and the

Virgin Mary, are specimens of her genius, and stand unrivalled to this day. Monica, mother of St. Augustine, is a fair example among Christian matrons of that skill in training, and importunate pleading with God so sure to win success in the end. Here is a sample among the thousands present and past, where woman, in the hallowed precincts of home, moulds the hearts and lives of those who are the benefactors of the race. Monica is great in the greatness of her son. Dorcas, moving about the huts of the poor widow and fatherless, is in her appointed sphere while she ministers to the wants of these with her own hands. She accomplishes a nobler work for herself and the race, than she, who sword in hand on the battle-field strikes at the foe, or than she who stands at the bar, or occupies the platform. She is far nobler in the hospital, moving among the wounded and dying, an angel of mercy, with tender touch binding up the lacerated limb and bathing the brow of the dying warrior, than upon the field urging on the carnage. Florence Nightingale among the wounded, sick and dying, in the hospitals of the Crimea, achieved a more substantial fame than Joan of Arc clad as a soldier, infatuated with a wild spirit of heroism, joining the hosts of war and stirring them up for the strife. Offices of love and sympathy she can fill as only a woman can do it.

Home is the divinely appointed theatre of her activities. Domestic life is her native element; not as a servant or a slave, but beautiful as the rising sun, stately as a queen, pure in heart, amiable in life, inspiring man by her devotion to her mission, qualifying him for his work, and helping him on to the goal of the highest manhood. Outside of domestic life in its broadest and best sense, woman has no history, her life no meaning. Here, like the sun, her light is her own. Outside of the sphere called home, and the activities that have affinity with it, she shines with a borrowed light. In it her voice is heard, and her influence felt. Desiring to reach the public ear and to move the public heart, she does it most effectually in the life she leads, and in the principles she instils into those around her.   Does she want to vote ?   She votes through the "boys" and her father.   After she attains to her majority, she votes through her husband, and is perfectly satisfied with such an organ as that.   In his keeping the common wealth is just as safe as her own home, and there she dwells none daring to molest or make her afraid.

SOME ASPECTS OF THE DIVORCE QUESTION.

AS probably the best service that can be rendered just now to the discussion of the Divorce Question, this article will, after brief outline of the facts, aim to call attention to some aspects of the problem which deserve special study, but which have been too generally overlooked. It will, therefore, touch upon the more familiar phases of the subject only as they shall be necessary to its particular aim. The facts are given in somewhat fuller outline than the necessities of this discussion require, to meet the increasing demand for an accurate and comprehensive statement of them.

Connecticut granted 91 divorces in 1849, which, to use the customary and generally fair method of comparison, was probably one for each 35 marriages of the year. In 1878 the annual average for fifteen years had become 445, or one to every 10.4 marriages. Vermont granted 94 divorces in 1860, or one to every 23 marriages; and 197 in 1878, with a ratio to marriages of one to 14. Massachusetts granted 243 in 1860, or one to 51 marriages; and 600 in 1878, or one to 21.4. In New Hampshire there were 107 in 1860, and 314 in 1882. This latter year the ratio was one to 10.9; in the former it must have been about one to 31. Rhode Island recorded 162 in 1869, or one in 14 marriages; and 271 in 1882, the ratio becoming one to 11. There were 587 in Maine in 1880, probably one to at most 10, or possibly even 9, marriages. From such reports as other States give, a similar condition of things is found. The ratio of divorces to marriages in Ohio was one to 26 in 1865, while 1806 divorces were granted in 1882, or one to 16.8 marriages. In the two most populous counties of Minnesota the ratio of divorce *suits* to marriages rose in ten years in the one county from one to 29.3 to one in 22.9, and in the other from one to 19 to one in 12. For six years the ratio of divorce *suits* begun in Cook County, Ill. (Chicago), to marriage *licenses* issued was one to 9.5. In 1882 the ratio of divorces actually granted was found to be one to 13.4, which is almost exactly the ratio for the year before in Louisville. St. Louis granted " about 205 divorces" one year, and in the next 430 suits were entered. San Francisco divorced 333 married pairs in 1880, and 364 the next year. Making the estimate of nine marriages to the thousand inhabitants, there were actually granted in that city in the latter year a divorce to each 5.78 marriages! Yet counties in other States than California make as bad or a worse showing. Philadelphia, it is said, granted 101 divorces in 1862, 215 in 1872, and 477 in 1882.[1] There were 212 in New York City in 1870, and 316 in 1882. Complete returns show that New England granted 2113 divorces in 1878, and probably the number last year was still greater, notwithstanding important legislation which has reduced the number in some of these States. It is safe to say that divorces have doubled in proportion to marriages or population in most of the northern States within thirty years. Present figures indicate a still greater increase. No statistics from the South are yet collected, except those just given from Louisville and St. Louis, but the frequency of "spontaneous" divorces among both whites and blacks in some sections is well known. Probably legal divorce has increased since the war.

Some remarks on these statistics and the condition of things they represent will lead to those remoter considerations to which this article aims to call particular attention. This increase of divorces has quickly and surely followed a relaxation in the stringency of divorce laws. In Connecticut and Massachusetts, the numbers of divorces rose rapidly after the addition of new causes for which they might be obtained. In Vermont the

---

[1] Since this was written the Rev. Dr. I. E. Dwinell, of Redwood, California, in an admirable article in the *New Englander* for January, has shown that there were in a year in 29 of the 52 counties of California 789 divorces to 5849 marriage licenses, or one divorce to 7.41 *licenses*. The Bureau of Vital Statistics of New Jersey have just found that for the five years ending July 1, 1883, the courts of that State granted a total of 788 divorces, with a probable ratio to marriages of one to not less than 50. The divorces increased in the five years from 144 to 183. The explanation of these remarkable contrasts is largely in the difference in the statutes and procedure of the courts in the two States, the latter element being the greater factor.

transfer of jurisdiction from the supreme to the county courts worked badly. On the other hand, the restrictions of the facilities reduced the number granted. The repeal of the notorious omnibus clause in Connecticut, now followed by a like but greater change in Maine law, and the restrictions upon the remarriage of divorced persons, now made in Vermont, Massachusetts, and Maine, have tended to reduce divorces. Changes for the better in methods of procedure affect the granting of divorces by causing parties to withhold cases or to transfer them, if possible, to more lenient courts. Procedure is often bad. Personal service of the libel is frequently entirely evaded; and when printed notice of it is given, it is sometimes done in ways that defeat the design of the law. Instances continually come to light in which the proceedings are based on fraud, and occasionally all the papers have turned out to be forgeries even to the signatures of the officers of the court. Collusion between the parties themselves, or the so-called opposing counsel, is notoriously frequent. The celerity with which causes are often heard, and the frivolous evidence on which their decision is made to turn, add to the evil and to its increase. Competent authority asserts that fifteen minutes is the average time spent on a divorce suit in the courts of one State. There are many honorable exceptions to this haste, but probably no causes of any importance have so slight work done on them as divorce suits. A dozen families will be declared non-existent in half as many hours by a court that has spent a day or two on an issue involving five dollars and no principle of law worth ten minutes' thought. To any one who knows the care usually taken in this class of trials in European courts, the carelessness of the American system seems extremely reprehensible.

The consequences of the evil are too well known to detain us long. Probably in every county in Connecticut some person could be found who has figured in three or four divorce suits. Even the seducer has found the courts a pliant tho unwitting tool of his trade. And in the great cities many a young man is lured to marriage by some elderly female who gets a good share of his property and—a speedy divorce. At least two members of the last Senate of the United States and two former senators, one of them " a War governor" of his State and the other a foreign minister, were in the divorce courts within a period of six months. The recent case of an officer of the regular army is well known. He persuaded his wife to visit Europe, and then got a divorce on the ground of her desertion, and remarried. She, however, carried the affair to the courts, and the divorce was annulled. But he indignantly resented the criticism of the newspapers, and declared the public guilty of meddling in his domestic affairs!

The worst of the mischief, however, is found in the middle and lower classes of society, which furnish by far the most of the divorces, and whose ideas of marriage are fast changing. The statute-book, or the conventional life of those around them, affords their only rule of duty in this matter. The facilities for divorce are sometimes deliberately taken into the account of the risks of an unfortunate marriage, and so hasty marriages and speedy divorces are, each in their turn, both cause and effect. And below these classes there is a disregard of marriage, similar to that which has long prevailed in the South, that needs attention. In some New England manufacturing towns, the migratory workingmen, chiefly those of foreign birth, are found to desert their wives and children in one place to form a new alliance in another,—a custom which exists to some extent among the lowest classes in the cities and in back-country districts. Some of these people are learning to secure ends in a lawless way which they say the rich can afford to get in conformity with the legal and conventional arrangements of society. The revolt against the established social order will inevitably pass beyond economics to the Family. For the notions that lead to divorce and kindred evils have their full share in fostering class feeling in a society organized politically on a democratic basis.

The effect of the conflicting laws of the several States, in increasing divorces and multiplying their mischiefs, needs scarcely a word here. The uncertainties as to whether a marriage or divorce in one State is valid in another, the forcing of the *status* of marriage everywhere to the lowest level of any other State, the increased opportunities for avoiding that publicity which is here, as elsewhere, in the long-run a wholesome safeguard of society, and the cheapening of marriage and morality, are well-known evils. They are so apparent that we think them overestimated *relatively*, both in amount and in comparison with the mischiefs wrought by what may be called "home divorces." [1]

The moral statistics of our country are extremely meagre, and do not, therefore, afford a very wide basis for judging of the prevalence of sexual vices and their relation to the increase of divorces. If, however, we can trust to the official reports of Massachusetts and one or two other States, illegitimate births are rapidly increasing, tho yet far below the high rates of Europe. In some States their increase has kept pace with the increase of divorces. The diminishing size of the New England Family of so-called native stock is well known. The reported number of children of school age in Vermont and New Hampshire is scarcely three fourths as large as it was thirty years ago. The prevalence of criminal abortion and similar vices in some sections is already a subject of great concern. A committee appointed by a Western State Board of Health to investigate the former, express the opinion " that in the United States the number of women who die from its *immediate* effects is not less than six thousand per annum." More than one gynæcologist asserts that the records of his practice show that it is not maternity that sends him the larger number of patients, but the needless refusal of its responsibilities. The old plea that easy divorce keeps in check various forms of unchastity is discredited by such statistics as we have. For in Massachusetts, where the convictions of crime for twenty years have been carefully reported, it is found that convictions for the various crimes against chastity greatly increased in nearly all parts of the State with two exceptions. And these exceptions of two crimes in the city of Boston, when examined, were found to prove the gen-

---

[1] We are inclined to think that the truth, if it is ever discovered, will be found to be that after all allowance for "foreign divorces," that is, those obtained in States by outside parties who go to them or to their courts for the purpose, is made, the vast majority of divorces are granted to actual residents of the counties granting them. The opinions of the newspapers on the abuse of the conflicting laws are apt to be formed from the data furnished by cities, in forgetfulness of their having a small percentage of the entire population. It is the constant discharge of the evil into the community where the parties are well known that most poisons the social blood.

Since writing this note the last Registration Report of Massachusetts has appeared, containing confirmation of the opinion expressed above. Congress has also been asked to provide information on this point.

eral rule. The increase far outstripped that of any other class of crimes, and even of the divorces, which more than doubled in this period. It is significant that while the foreign-born population of Suffolk County (Boston) were charged with 39 per cent of all crimes, aside from crimes against the liquor laws, only 34 per cent of the crimes against chastity could be laid at their door.

After extended and careful inquiry, the conviction is forced upon us that there is strong probability that the period marked by the increase of divorces has witnessed a serious growth of many of the more dangerous forms of licentiousness. Some localities in New England have improved vastly within this century, but this is probably not true of very many others, while certain of the worst forms of licentiousness have made alarming progress. The lower moral tone in regard to these vices is very perceptible. The growth of the opinion that adultery is a mere peccadillo, especially among married women, is painfully indicative of this. Perhaps there never were among us finer examples, or more of them, of pure, well-trained households than at the present time. But for all this, the physician and student of social life discover in some quarters a standard of morals and immoral practices that were almost unknown a half-century ago. And that this has some connection with the increase of divorces must be apparent to every close observer. Beneath the surface the physician often detects causes of divorce which the lawyer and the judge seldom discover. Sex is a tremendous factor in this problem of Divorce.

We simply touch the fact here, of which more will be said, of the relatively weakened power of the Family and the substitution of the Individual as the centre from which most duties and relations are viewed and the work of life is done. The forces of society in this respect have shifted within a half-century to a very great degree. The work of life, of almost every sort, deals more with men, women, and children as Individuals, and less as members of a Family, through and in which some of life's problems find their only full solution. There is a growing independence of one another on the part of husband and wife, as well as of parent and child. The opportunities for separate employments, the property rights of women, and their higher education, are evidence of this.

It is apparent then, so far, that the increase of divorces has several causes, and is attended with certain other things that are either essentially bad or incidentally so. The loose laws of this country, and the still worse legal practice under them, are greatly to be blamed for this condition of things. The adoption of a few simple legal measures would undoubtedly reduce divorces one half, and this should be secured. But then the real root of the evil, in the condition of society that tolerates existing laws and makes their reform difficult, would be untouched. The hasty marriages—in part due to the ease of divorce—the apparent increase of licentiousness, the great decrease in the birth-rate of the so-called native population, and often in the first and second generation of the descendants of immigrants, the prevalence of infanticide and criminal abortion, certain physical changes in American women, and the displacement of the Family by the Individual, introduce elements into the problem which show the need of pushing our search for causes still farther. A study of the statistics of Divorce confirms this. New Hampshire increased her divorces almost three fold in twenty-two years, without any change in her laws during a much longer period. So, too, in Ohio, the northern counties generally have of late years twice the divorce rate of the southern counties. After all allowance for other causes, the chief one is found to be the prevalence of the New England stock in the northern counties. These were settled largely from Connecticut, but long before that State had many divorces. Some of the worst counties are those in which Mormonism took shape and other vagaries flourished.

A recent report of the Italian Bureau of Statistics enlarges our field of view. Tho the tables cover only ten years at the most, they are significant. The numbers are for each *thousand* marriages, except in some Catholic countries, where they note the separations. They show that the increase between 1871 and 1879 in France was from 4.46 to 9.14; in England and Wales from .98 to 2.17; in Denmark from 36.27 to 40.29. Between 1871 and 1880 Italy remained stationary; Belgium increased from 2.85 to 7.40; Holland from 5.20 to 7.35; Scotland from .11 to .29; Sweden from 4.96 to 7.50; and Roumania from 9.05 to 10.86. Switzerland has the highest figures in Europe,

12

but the increase began earlier and does not appear in these tables. Her rate is about 46, but in some cantons it is far higher. Other countries report for shorter periods. In Wurtemburg the increase is from 5.67 in 1876 to 12.25 in 1879 ; in Saxony from 21 in 1875 to 31.42 in 1878 ; in Thuringia from 14.33 to 17.48 in eight years ; and in Baden from 4.53 to 7.31 in seven years ; in Alsace-Lorraine from 4.46 in 1874 to 7.85 in 1880; in Hungary from 6.74 in 1876 to 10 in 1880; and in Russia from 1.33 in 1871 to 2.05 in 1877. Other statistics for England and Wales, France and Belgium, cover forty years, and fragmentary returns from parts of Germany go back about as far, while we have those of Sweden for fifty years. From these and the figures already given, together with other proofs which we cannot recount here, there is pretty conclusive evidence of a general increase of divorces common to this country and Europe. Apparently the divorce rate has doubled in those of the United States where we know the facts, and in most European countries within forty years at the farthest, and mostly within half that period. The increase is found in Protestant and Catholic populations, and even in Russia under the Greek Church, tho more among Protestants than the others. It takes place where the laws clearly lead to it, and also where there are no legal changes to account for the increase. The rate is rarely so high in Europe as in even the best of our States, while generally it is far below us. Europe, with high rates of illegitimacy and generally bad sexual morals, probably could not venture upon the American facility in divorce without disastrous results. The attempt of Switzerland to do this, certainly is unhappy. The crowding of Germans and others of foreign birth into the divorce courts of St. Louis, Chicago, Detroit, and elsewhere in the West is very likely the beginning of great mischief. A divorce system that was tolerable with the peculiar morality of New England before immigration and the hot social life of the last half-century began to tell upon our institutions, may prove simply unendurable now. It may possibly become as closely interwoven with society, and as corrupting, as slavery did under a somewhat similar change of conditions. The problem is already very complex. It practically includes the whole question of the Family, which is undergoing great and radical changes. The causes must reach far back and run deep. They seem as. pervasive as the atmosphere of modern life. The best attempts at a better public sentiment or wiser legislation must be grounded in a comprehension of all the forces at work. A sketch of a few of these forces, necessarily a meagre outline, is the chief aim of this article.

The decay of the system on which Ancient Society rested did more than prepare the way for Christianity. It sent down through the channels of the new religion some of those ideas which had powerfully contributed to the overthrow of the ancient foundations of society. Yet for all this, we must look for the great starting-point of modern social development to Christianity, in the new conception it gave of the dignity of individual life. But the conception received its greatest impulse from the Protestant Reformation. The times were then ripe for it to find better lodgment in the general consciousness of men. The necessities of the controversy with the Papal power led to a clearer grasp of the religious rights and authority of conscience. The old ideas of the relations of the Individual to the State and the claims of the Church had generally kept men from seeing some of the consequences of the Christian view of Man, and held them back from fields now familiar to all students of political science. But the turning of the mind to the individual conscience for the determination of religious duties has, in its varied applications, probably produced vaster results than any other single force in modern life. Then came the German, English, and other versions of the Scriptures, the Reformation in Scotland and England, the philosophical methods of Lord Bacon, the great political influence of Milton, the Puritan movement and its Revolution, and the Puritan and Pilgrim settlement of New England. To the same age with Luther belong the discovery of America and the printing-press.

In recent times, more than formerly, historians turn from the more strictly religious and political events of the last four centuries to take account of their social changes. These prove very great. A new world calling for conquest and settlement held out its glittering material prizes to enterprising populations, and afforded a refuge from the tyranny of Church and State, and a new field for the rights of oppressed consciences.

The human mind, quickened into special forms of activity by the very spirit and method of Protestantism, guided by Bacon and others to better observation, and spurred on by necessities, soon began to unlock the secrets of nature and bring from them that long series of inventions which are the wonder of modern times. Watt and Fulton, Arkwright and Whitney, Franklin and Morse were pioneers in a vast army that has transformed the old industries and created many new ones. The secondary effects of the modern factory, the railway, the printing-press, and the other appliances of steam, machinery, and electricity, are almost as marvellous as their more direct work. National barriers yield to them and populations are intermingled more thoroughly than was possible in ancient times. Great cities multiply, drawing into them the life of the country, and—what quite as deeply concerns us—sending back their own subtle influences. The factory takes the place of the home as the typical centre of labor, and even in agriculture, vast farms are tilled by those who neither own them nor live on them. It is in this country, where we are without privileged classes and some other historic institutions of Europe, that this modern material life shows at once its greatest strength and its weakness. We are in the centre of a mighty current. "The division of labor," the massing of people as mere laborers and of capital, and for a generation or more, the attempted treatment of wealth as little more than a struggle of individuals from sheer self-interest, with competition for its method and a devil-take-the-hindmost for the toiling multitude, have tended to the "differentiation" of the Individual in diverse ways. The modern factory is doubtless an improvement on the old domestic system of labor. Still that, and the modern corporation generally, have strong temptations to treat their workmen simply as individual laborers. The competition for a laborer tells against the Family. The liberty that seems to allow the wife, the mature daughter, and the young children to go into the mill sometimes falls short of real freedom. It is often at cost of the Family and of a nobler Personality. And from the side of the laborer come those numerous real or fictitious wants which the dissemination of knowledge, easy transportation, and the growing demand for social equality stimulate. With all his immense gains since his emancipation from feudalism, the laborer has lost some things that once held him to others for his good.

The political principle involved in the Protestant theory of individual responsibility, which had but slowly emerged from the ruins of ancient society and was choked hitherto by the Church itself, has steadily advanced. Some evil, as well as much good, has followed. The Individual has come into clearest light, the great glory of modern society. But the incidents of the process should be noted. The Individual has been separated out from Tribe and Clan. Feudalism has melted away. The old conception of the State is gone, for the Individual is no longer lost in the State, but has become the special object of its solicitude if not the very end for which it exists. The Family of the Hebrew and other Semitic races and the Aryan household of our ancestors have been put farther than ever from our modern notions by the growing idea of the Individual, while the simplest Family of nature and Christianity has felt the overshadowing of this great idea. Law has preserved for us the successive steps in this change. Sir Henry S. Maine has called our attention to the drift from *status* to *contract* and from the *Family* to the *Individual*. Tho the movement is of vast extent in time and reaches over all civilization, our own times and our own country afford the most numerous and the most powerful instances of its effects, since we have inherited the largest possessions of modern thought with fewer incumbrances from the past. The volume of our legal business is overwhelmingly concerned with contracts, and that based on pure status has correspondingly shrunk. Few men now begin their daily work fixed in a status larger than themselves, to which Religion, Custom, and Law have closely fixed them, inquiring only how they may fulfil the conditions of an almost purely personal service. Nearly everybody in an advanced community starts as one of many equals, asking what suits his own free choice best. He feels all mankind more than ever, but not in the old ways. He is now free, even a sovereign. The service he now knows, tho never so imperative, is simply the incident of the democratic idea. He is one of many sovereigns who respect each other's domain in order that all may retain their authority. The American scholar may have outgrown this view of life, but it is very nearly the working theory of the average man, whose notions must always be taken into account in any just estimate of our political system.

The laws concerning the property rights of women show many of these changes. In some of our States these have changed almost as much in this century as they did in Rome from the earliest times down to the last days of the Empire. Recent English law is equally sweeping. The emancipation of women in this respect seems well-nigh complete. However strong our sympathies with the movement may be we must not shut our eyes to the fact and its consequences. The relations between Property and Marriage are so close that this change in the law of the former inevitably affects the latter. The history of Law is very clear on this point. And this is but a part of an inclusive movement. The education of Woman of late proceeds mainly upon the assumption of her having a mere individuality in common with Man, or with a strong tendency to reduce the element of sex to a minimum. The demand for her enfranchisement, either as a right or on the ground of expediency, grows out of this way of treating her as an individual whose relations to society are less a matter of condition and more of personal choice. And this principle is carried into a sphere entirely her own. A partial loss of capacity for maternity has, it is said, already befallen American women ; and the voluntary refusal of its responsibilities is the lament of the physician and the moralist. It is true we have a protest against these tendencies from one of the advocates of the rights of the sex in a plea for "The Duties of Women," but it came late, and then not from an American.

But these changes are the crystallization into law of others more radical. For back of them and in them lies the ethical thinking of one or two centuries. The ethical systems current among English-speaking people for the last two hundred years should be studied for their subtle influence on the political and legal relations of the Family and the Individual. But here a paragraph must suggest the barest outline. Lord Bacon, as the leader of empirical thinking, gave a most effective stimulus to those who followed him. Hobbes, Locke, Hume, and others, and later Bentham, Mill, and their adherents, call to mind a

great school of more or less intense Individualism. With varying degrees of clearness and assertion, these writers conceived
of duties and social relations as determined from Self. Moral
and consequently Political relations were primarily of egoistic
origin. The native conservatism of the English mind and its
intensely practical character kept the advocates of these theories from pressing them to their political conclusions. But
French Rationalism felt no such hesitancy. Rousseau, deeply
indebted to Hobbes, and especially to Locke, as were many
French thinkers of the last century, and who knew Hume personally, made haste to push the theory into practical politics.
Finding the way prepared for him by other Frenchmen, and
availing himself of the need of something which Naturalism
promised to supply, and of the peculiar conditions of his country, Rousseau made his Social Contract the working basis of the
French Revolution and contributed powerfully to the ferment
of all Europe. While his ideas gave the death-blow to the divine right of kings and did much to set thought free from certain trammels, they gave an immense impetus to modern Individualism.

Our own country has stood in the very place to feel the
thought of this school most deeply from first to last. The settlement of New England began in a desire for the self-determina-
tion of both religious and political duty. Milton naturally had
influence with us. Locke was a well-known author who long held
a large place in our reading. The War of Independence was preceded and followed by earnest study of the ethical and political
writings of the times. It seems impossible, too, to escape the
conclusion that Rousseau and the French school considerably affected Jefferson and filtered down into the popular mind. The
exigencies of the new system of self-government; the problems
of legislation growing out of a union of separate colonies with
conflicting interests in a country forced to independent thinking and action by its whole history; the new conditions under
which they wrought, and the solution of novel questions in state
and national legislatures by men comparatively unskilled in
a knowledge of public law; the rise and triumph of the anti-
slavery reform, advocated and carried to success chiefly on the
ground of the rights of man as an Individual; and the bidding

of political parties for votes—have combined to help the growth of these ideas. The common-school system has led us to forget somewhat the work of the Family in education, and the sub-division of the political units in some States below even the town into the school-district has urged on the movement. Our close relations with England, and the natural retention and pro-pagation of inherited and imported ethical ideas long after they have been outgrown in the country of their origin, have left deep impressions upon our partially educated masses in whose hands lies so much political power.

And still farther back are some of the direct and indirect influences of the religious spirit and methods of our country. Protestantism finds here the fullest expression of its character, and here more of its peculiarities and excrescences appear. It addresses men chiefly as Individuals. Its call of duty singles men out. Each must examine its claims for himself, and with each rests the responsibility of obedience. Under the voluntary system of support religious bodies multiply and crowd each other until many a little township has from six to ten churches, with almost half its population living in utter neglect of all. In many of these churches nothing is heard or seen from one year's end to another's that is not an emphasis of the Individ-ual. The Family as such is quite overlooked. It is scarcely an exaggeration to say that the typical representative of an im-mense class claims the right to a church of his own choice within easy reach of his door in which his own views of doc-trine and life shall be duly expounded. And the neglect of all worship, and the vagaries that are neither Christian nor relig-ious, have been fed more or less from the same stream. Theo-logical methods, and dogmas too, have helped fill the springs. Current philosophies and ethics have necessarily affected religious thought and also been themselves shaped by it. Mechanical theories of inspiration, verbalism in the use of texts, an in-tensely intellectual method with its excessive reliance on analy-sis and definition, the controversial excesses of denominational rivalries and the consequent relative suppression of those larger views and grasp of vitalities that come from fuller faith in God and the kingdom of Christ, and which refuse their best forms of truth to the dissection and construction of a mechanical logic, must be held accountable for some unfortunate, tho unintended, results. The supposed necessities of "systems" have sometimes led to open denial of eternal life to little children, and to a hesitating recognition, where it has not been an utter suppression, of the Family. These, certainly, are some of the whirlpools and eddies in the stream of progress, whose very dangers are commensurate with its greatness.

The Family, more than any other institution, has felt this general movement. This is natural. For it is in the Family that one feels the earliest and latest pressure that makes him conscious of others beyond himself, and it is through the Family that the Individual touches the springs of society most surely and permanently. The interaction of the two is so close that each step in this " differentiation" of the Individual has told upon the Family. The political results of the movement may be more striking, but the domestic changes are quite as sure. The intenser phases of Individualism and frequent divorces have often been found together. Tho the Individual, as we use the word, of even the last days of the Roman Empire was not much thought of by the State, those were the times of every man for himself, with a go-as-you-please method that reminds one strongly of the modern notion. The life-giving spirit of the ancient Family, which perhaps was religion rather than the natural ties of blood familiar to us, had departed. Men did not, as formerly, find themselves within strong ethical bonds larger than those of their own making. Nature also proved too strong for an unnatural religion. Life, too, in a material age grew selfish and sensual. The marriage-bond, having lost the conserving force that came from the ancient religion, was too weak to resist the disruptive evils of the times, and divorces multiplied. So, also, the bursting forth of the French Revolution and a wild riot in divorce and vice came together, and a writer tells us that in Germany, during the dominance of an individualistic school of writers, " divorce in their circle had become an every-day occurrence," and adds to his list of names the assertion that " there is something unhealthy even in those who do not break through the barriers of society." Traces of the same alliance appear in England. But the connection in this country is more striking. Here the speculations of leaders readily become the practice of the people. The divorce rate is generally highest in New England and where her people have gone in the West. The curious facts about divorce in Ohio, already given, illustrate this. The very counties where Giddings, Wade, and Garfield lived, themselves men of great purity of character, have been about the worst for divorces in the State. The old champions of anti-slavery and "rights" have been noticeably forward in the past in making apologies for easy divorce. And then, as our political ideas find their way back to Europe through the closer intercourse of later years, they have quickened similar forces there. And there, too, the divorce rate increases. Laws may retard or hasten the movement, but they cannot account for the whole of it. It is "in the air" of modern life.

The unfortunate history of Divorce in this country reminds one of the insidious growth of slavery. The current was set wrong in part by the early Puritan dread of everything like ecclesiasticism. Marriage at the first was made a civil contract only; and a religious ceremony forbidden or discouraged. The absence of men from their families, and perhaps the frequent migrations to other colonies, led to somewhat liberal provisions for divorce. The religious regard for the sanctities of marriage made the purely civil treatment of it safe for a long time. But the War of Independence, the revolt against "the standing order," as the recognized church was called, and the attendant rise and spread of other Christian denominations—due to social as well as religious causes—some political discussions of the early half of the century, the anti-slavery reform, the introduction of the factory system, the railway, telegraph, and steam printing-press, vastly changed the conditions of our life. The cotton-gin and other agencies in their day did scarcely more in the South. Marriage laws have been improved in some ways, since the justice of the peace, and sometimes the minister, often made the service a joke, but those of Divorce have grown worse. The movement seems to have begun in Connecticut between 1840 and 1849, when the legislature of that State was the scene of unseemly raids from discontented married couples. The lax laws of the latter year gave it new impulse, and the progress downward, especially since 1860, has been rapid and

general. Western emigration and the license of new settlements, the conflicting laws of the several States, popular doctrines of rights, the War, easy transportation, cheap reading,
a growing demand for social as the consequent of political
equality, the pouring in of foreign immigrants often, tho not
always having a low sexual morality, and the importation
through foreign travel of certain European notions of chastity,
have all joined in their way to increase evils that sap the
Family.

There has been no fit advance in the law and doctrine of the
Family to meet these new conditions. In making the Individual the centre of effort, the Family has fallen into neglect or
been obscured under the conceptions of individualism. Treatises on the law of " Marriage and Divorce" or the " domestic
relations" abound ; the law of these *relations* is discussed ; debates wax warm as to whether these relations are those of
" contract" or " status," whether marriage is or is not a religious institution,—a sacrament, and so on. But discussions of
the Family by itself and as the true point of departure from
which to determine all laws of marriage and divorce are too
rare. The defect goes farther. The morals of sex are often
treated in text-books and in legislation chiefly on the assump-
tions of individualism. Licentiousness is held to be an individual
vice, like drunkenness or theft. Its dual nature and peculiar
relation to the Family, taking it out of the category of individual vices and demanding for it peculiar estimate and special
care, escape the mind. After its recognition of consent and co-
habitation as constituting marriage, law is quite as defective as
the text-books of morals. Massachusetts now ventures to punish a man who neglects to support his children, but his wife is
protected only by a divorce. New Hampshire last year granted
80 divorces for adultery and punished two adulterers. That
State deals vigorously with those guilty of "cruelty to animals,"
but it divorced 101 women for suffering "extreme cruelty"
without punishing a man, unless giving him the privilege to
marry a new victim be a penalty. The two great institutions
of Property and the Family have very different legal defences.
Property would almost perish under the scant protection
afforded the Family. The inherent difficulties in the latter case

215

are confessedly serious, but that does not mend the mischief nor account for much that is sheer neglect.

Mormon polygamy threatens the Territories. It is a challenge to civilization on the Family. Yet the debates of Congress rarely rise to the real issue. Slavery destroyed the Family in one race and corrupted it in another, but political reconstruction has not clearly made the home the centre of a great work the South has needed more than anything else. And but slowly have the relations of the Family to the problems of Indian civilization, pauperism and crime, capital and labor, been perceived by the many. And the call for uniform marriage and divorce laws, of which there is need enough, seems to be heedless of the vastness of the subject and its complications. There is no adequate and at all well-defined *political consciousness* of the family on which to draw for a successful grapple with pressing questions. And this is partly because the true Family of Christianity and Nature has not been wrought into the very structure of our society as was the case with the early Roman, or in fact Aryan family. Most of our utterances are little more than the reiterated platitudes of tradition. Modern thinking has not wrought in painful toil over the Family as it has done with the Individual and the State. But these great practical questions and those Sociology raises will soon compel us to look into the problems of Monogamy and the Family as we never have yet done.

Yet it is not reaction to the conceptions of the past that we need. Modern Individualism does not seem so much a retrograde movement as a pushing out of human society in one form unduly beyond others. It is not, therefore, so much a thing to be rooted out or cut back as something to be corrected and strengthened with its natural supports. It does not by any means, for instance, follow that the recovery or, better, the growth of the Family into its true place means the relegation of Woman to her old narrow life, nor the real repression of the Individual anywhere. The work we need is essentially constructive. The achievements of the Nineteenth Century for Woman may be outdone by future efforts in her behalf, tho the method of them be not just what some now think the only possible one. For her advance by her differentiation as an Individual, which is the method of the present, may, after carrying her along in the path of the advance of Man, leave her behind her true place through operation of the very process by which her recent elevation has been promoted. Woman as a fact in social science may be much too large for the form into which Individualism now would crowd it. The deepest meaning of her nature connects Woman with the Family, and that truth may compel both parties in the controversy to halt until we all get a surer hold of the full meaning and place of the Family in political society, and so in part readjust our theories of the Individual. And so, too, the work of our first century of separate national existence which has been largely given to the rights of man as an Individual, and now incorporated into the organic law of the land, may lead us to this very work for the Family by way of advance and not of retrogression. Constitutional amendments here, as there, best come far on in the work. The Twentieth Century will be soon enough to look seriously for a Constitutional utterance upon the Family. And then it may, like other amendments, simply prescribe a uniform basis of *State* legislation according to the natural rights of the Family. Constructive work, let me repeat, should be our aim if we would meet the demands of the case.

And do not the best signs of the times point in this very direction? Here and there a scholarly leader of Individualism secretly drops into silence until his thought finds a surer foothold, and its excesses in immorality have turned away others. Its limitations in political economy are increasingly apparent. A "social law of labor" is acknowledged, in which the Family, Religion, and our complex social life generally, are perceived to be contributing something to its problems that cannot be put into the categories of self-interest and sheer competition, nor yet be wholly dismissed to a separate department of "social economy." Educational questions compel us to see that no conventional system, like that of public schools,—however necessary to our political institutions,—can supplant or ignore the Family as a natural agent for the training of children ; and that, whether we send boys and girls to the same or to separate schools, it is impossible to educate them properly as mere Individuals in forgetfulness of sex—the profoundest single element of life. Perhaps the assertion of a recent writer is too strong, who says, " English ethical philosophy is no longer purely individualistic. Both theoretically and practically the disintegrating movement of thought completed its work and exhausted itself at the close of the last century. Modern speculation is reconstructive in its tendency. It endeavors to free itself of its inherited atomism and fit the individual into his surroundings." For the Revolutions of 1848 and other events in Europe and this country must be charged to its lingering life. But surely the tendency here is towards a larger comprehension of the relations of life in ethics and religion, in economics and politics. The vitality of the old systems, which naturally enough hold their ground in new soil after they died out of the older, evidently fails. Their expositions of ethics and theology will no longer pass. Politically we have got on a good distance. The late War practically ended some old debates. Social questions are coming to the front. It is seen that society is to be accounted for and its laws applied in ways that Individualism can neither supply nor explain. Indeed, it is our American *life* that calls for better forms of expression and continually throws off those which pinch its growth. Sectionalism and State rights that found no organic principle above and inclusive of them are cast off. The problem now is to find a fuller freedom of the parts in the harmony of the Nation. Ecclesiastical liberty founds and pushes churches on the voluntary system until Individualism in polity confronts us with the serious dangers of license, and the cry comes for readjustment. And the spirit of theological inquiry is a spirit of life, seeking to add to the real results of past methods that which will preserve and vivify all truth and righteousness. The historical method refutes Individualism at all points, and brings positive contributions to the solution of the problem of the Family. If it shows the power of Custom over Law, it also gives views of the way the thought of the times changes Custom itself, and impresses us with the momentous character of the work to be done for the Family.

Christianity has wrought the most important modifications of the Family in all its particulars, and it must continue to do so. But historic conditions have warped its influence over the Family on this side and on that, and they sometimes have passed off on Christendom, as its own, coin that has been debased with the alloy of earlier times. It is difficult, often, to avoid the conclusion that the Family—especially in the matter of Marriage and Divorce—has suffered so very much more from a naturalism, which is yet not according to nature, that in its talk of contract forgets religion, than it has from an ecclesiasticism that in a worthy zeal for the religious has neglected the natural foundations of the institution. Let any one turn to the words of Christ, especially in the Gospel of Mark, and he cannot fail to see how careful our Lord was, in recovering Divorce from the wretched conventionalism of the times to truly religious ground, to lay the foundations of Marriage, or rather the Family, on the solid ground of natural law. The old Aryan and other early societies seem to have builded on the Family, and by the power of Religion. But it was too largely, if we can depend on certain authorities, an artificial Family and a puerile religion. Nature was too strong for such a Family, and humanity too great and too sinful for such religions. But the better religion, perceiving how many things society suffered from the wild, selfish naturalism of later Roman law, has probably been over-cautious and slow to learn the best things Christianity has had in store for men. I must think we have assumed too readily that the present is simply a renewal of the old conflict between Status and Contract, between the Family and the Individual, between Religion and Naturalism, to be fought over again and in pretty much the same old ways. From this point of view the experience of the past is discouraging enough, so far at least as we have followed it. For "the society," says Sir Henry S. Maine, "which once consisted of compact families, has got extremely near to the condition in which it will consist exclusively of individuals, when it has finally and completely assimilated the legal position of women to that of men." And again, "the so-called enfranchisement of women is merely a process which has affected very many other classes, the substitution of individual beings for compact groups of human beings as the units of society." Contract, the Individual, and Materialism have confessedly gained ground as against their correlative ideas. Religion and political society undoubtedly need to put a controlling hand on the Individual; but to do this by reaching over the Family would be the repetition of an old mistake and the rejection of the very instruments best fitted to do the work. For it is in those ethical relations which a vigorous Family supplies that the Individual must find correction and the larger growth of the future. We must look for the remedy for Individualism not in the repression of the Individual, but rather in his growth through the Family and Society into a larger, better Personality. The "survival of the fittest" and the despair of Hartmann are the dogmas of men to whom Individualism is the final word in the philosophy of life.

It is to do a little towards showing how the Divorce Question lies in the very centre of the problems of Christian civilization as they have been gathering for centuries and as they exist in their most intricate and pressing forms in our own country that this article has taken its shape. "Sociology," says an eminent scholar, "is the coming science;" and in its sphere very likely may lie no small part of the next battle-ground between Christianity and unbelief. The Family is its fundamental element, and the Divorce Question is the vital point in the problem of the Family.

SAMUEL W. DIKE.

THE REAL RIGHTS OF WOMEN.

BY MRS. ROSE TERRY COOKE.

THERE IS so much said of late years about the "Rights of Women" that the phrase has become to some women a terror and a disgust; though a certain class have made it a war-cry, and attached to it a meaning and an importance alike unwarranted and unpleasant.

Those who thus clamor for their "rights" mean by that phrase, to express the matter succinctly, the rights of women to be men. It is useless here either to ignore or contend with their dogmas, for in the end they will inevitably expose their own futility and presumption. It would be simple folly to notice the effort of a botanist to transform all the currant-bushes in the country into oak-trees; and no man or set of men would attempt to train cats to the duties and offices of dogs : ridicule would extinguish their essays and contempt be their portion. The Creator who peopled the earth with various sorts of animals, and made it beautiful with forests and flowers, each bearing seed according to its kind, when he also created man to rule over them, made also a distinction in humanity. "Male and female created he them," and no puny struggles of the race can nullify his original purpose. But in all this clamor, and the just scorn with which the more rational portion of the race treat it, there has been little or no attention paid to the fact that women—as women—have certain rights of their own coexistent with their position in life, which are too apt to be ignored by the men with whom they are associated in any relation. Let us examine a few of these rights, which ought to be self-evident both to men and women.

First—A woman has a right to respect, as a woman, as long as she respects herself. It is true that it is difficult for men to do this when the spirit of the age is against such an opinion. We

find the newspapers full of skits at women : their folly, their ex-
travagance, their ignorance, their shortcomings as mothers, wives,
girls in society, especially mothers-in-law and "old maids," are
the theme of story and illustration everywhere. And it is not
women who write these stories or sketch these illustrations, but
men who have mothers, sisters, and wives of their own. Any
true and manly man should show respect to women for the sake
of his own mother—the mother who bore him at the risk of her
very life in cruel anguish and intolerable terror; who reared him
with a mother's patience through his helpless infancy and ungrate-
ful childhood : for this office alone should he respect the sex to
which he owes so much. And the man whose wife has borne
him a family of children should be branded by society as he is by
God if he treats that wife with less respect and honor than he
would the noblest and greatest among men. Yet the world
swarms with men who rob women of this inalienable right all
their wretched lives ; who treat their mothers and their wives
with contumely and cruelty. All women know this to be true,
and resent in their hearts the contempt of their husbands and
brothers and sons. This it is that drives them thoughtlessly into
a struggle to remodel the laws of the land through the doubtful
expedient of woman suffrage, through which they hope to reform the laws in their favor. A little calm reflection would show
them that any law is worthless that is not enforced by public
opinion or public and pressing need. Yearly our legislatures
enact laws that are daily broken. Who keeps the dog laws, the
liquor laws, the laws of trespass, and numerous other statutes ?
Laws deliberately broken are worse than useless ; they are the
seeds of rebellion and anarchy ; and no human law will help
women to abrogate divine edicts. The only hope of women lies in
the training of their sons : the boy who is taught from infancy to
obey and respect his parents will be worth more to the cause
of true "women's rights" than a whole code of legal enactments.

   Second—Women have a right to care and consideration on
the score of their physical organization. However eager and
voluble is the clamor of the "Women's Rights" party to be
placed on an equality with men, the very laws of Nature laugh
at such a reasonless demand. Can a woman, even an abnormally-
strong woman, do the hard, rough work of the world ? Can
women construct railways, canals, houses, sail ships, clear away

forests, become pioneers of civilization, or explore remote places of the earth ? Could a woman do what Stanley has done ? Could she even perform the labor of a common "navvy," who digs all day, week after week, year after year ? Every woman knows, if she would only allow it, that this is impossible. Men have an incontrovertible argument against this equality in "their dynamic reasons of stronger bones," and every man knows that women are "the weaker sex" by reason of their physical constitution : therefore I say that women have a right to care and consideration on this account. But do they get it ? Where is the man, among the working class especially, who will not let his wife, his mother, his daughter, or his sister overwork herself for his support or his aggrandizement ? The records of our lunatic asylums fully bear out this statement : one-third of their female patients come from farms, where they rise early and go to rest late, working incessantly through winter and summer, no matter what is their physical condition ; bearing and rearing children through it all ; uncheered by recreation, unsolaced by rest ; not so much considered as the herded cows or the stabled horses, for these animals cost hard-earned money, but a woman can be had for the asking, and worked like a slave without wages. It is a mistaken economy that deprives women of the kindness and care that should lighten their burdens and assuage their anxiety. Men assume toward them the attitude of the immortal Bagnet toward his capable wife,—

"I never saw the old girl's equal! But I never own to it before her. Discipline must be maintained !"

A few kind words, a little appreciation, even a frank acknowledgment of the work she has done, are like reviving balm to weak and weary women ; it pays to praise us—we are so foolishly fond of kind words.

> "A merry heart goes all the day ;
> Your sad one tires in a mile-a!"

And is not this small and easily-rendered wage, which benefits the giver as well as the receiver, a true right of every woman ?

Third—A woman has a right to her own religious opinions and preferences ; but how rarely is it accorded to her. The married woman almost inevitably leaves her own church and goes with her husband, whether he is a member of the church he attends or not. Daughters, too, come to years of discretion, whatever may be their opinions or their wishes, are almost always expected to go to church with their parents. Indeed, not long since I read a pamphlet in defence of a certain sect, of which the opening argument was that people should always go to church where their parents did ! This extraordinary reasoning, which in its full extent would render futile all endeavors to convert Romanists, Jews, infidels, or even hereditary heathen, to a better way than that in which their ancestors walked, is carried out in too many families to-day. It is as much a woman's right as a man's to select the denomination to which she will belong.

Fourth—Every mother-woman has a right to share in the decisions of the father concerning their children's education. It is impossible for a man engaged in the active business of life, separated from his children during the weekdays and not extremely intimate with them on Sundays, to understand their characters as well as the mother, who is their daily friend and guide. She knows how the timid and sensitive nature of one of her girls unfits her for fighting her way through a public school ; while the courage, alacrity, and self-confidence of another will thrive in such a conflict with others, and find its true level there. She knows that the dreamy, studious boy, who does not care for athletic sports or mathematical problems, but spends his leisure in the fields inspecting stones with his geological hammer, hunting for floral specimens, impaling rare and curious insects round the crown of his hat, is meant to be a professor of natural sciences ; while his sturdy, hearty young brother, always " trading " and " dickering " with his fellows, standing high in his arithmetic class, and with a keen eye for his just share in " treats," will be a successful merchant. To the unacquainted father these are generalized as boys and gir' , he is just as likely as not to insist on putting the naturalist into a dry-goods shop and trying to make a clergyman of the sharp boy ; and it is here that the mother's right to advise, and even insist, comes in ; it is the right of superior knowledge, and should be willingly conceded to her.

Fifth—A woman has a right to choose her own husband. To her belong all the consequences of such a choice. It is well to offer advice, to set before her the true character of the man she elects to marry, and thereby to clear your own conscience,—the only good result, as a general thing, of such advice !—but to attempt coercion of any sort is a fatal error. Marriage is the great disciplinary institution of the sexes, and its general trend and special detail cannot be averted or avoided by the average man and woman. To women a mistake in this matter is a mistake that involves portentous consequences, and no reasonable man or woman should be willing to take the great responsibility of directing or forcing that choice which will make or mar a whole life. The angelic young women in modern novels, who marry men they loathe to save a father or a brother from deserved shame or pecuniary ruin, are not and should not be the women of real life. " Thou shalt not do evil that good may come" is a divine truth, and ought to be impressed on the minds of our girls. But there is little danger that they will to-day indulge in such self-sacrifice; their end and aim are chiefly to " have a good time," and if they mistake the way to that end they learn a great and stern lesson, which may educate them for the eternal future. Therefore, as it is a purely individual matter, concerning the parties thereto far more than any one else, I contend that it is the inalienable right of every woman to select her own husband and take the consequences on her own shoulders.

Sixth—A woman should be allowed to choose her own physician. This seems on its face to be a trivial matter, but it is one that involves much suffering or much comfort, and is intimately connected with her health—that greatest of earthly blessings. For women, particularly in illness, are nervous, fastidious, and susceptible to odd impressions and strange fancies to an extent no man can comprehend. A sick man is cross or stupid ; if he is that *rara avis*, a patient sufferer, he is also silent and grateful ; but a woman fidgets, cries, exhausts herself with imaginary terrors and apprehensions, and looks forward to her physician's visits with disgust or delight, as the case may be. If she is so unfortunate as to dislike the aspect, the manner, the voice of the most skilful doctor to be had, he will do her little good : she will not tell him her symptoms ; she will resent his lightest touch ; she will probably refuse to take his prescriptions, or find some means of disposing of his pills and potions wide of their due destination ; while if she likes the face and speech of another, much less skilful it may be, his presence will give her comfort, allay her nervous exasperation, and soothe her terrors ; her pulse will grow quiet, her restlessness subside, and she will accept his doses with that faith in their efficacy which adds so much to the power of all drugs, and invests the tiniest sugary pellets with all-powerful virtues. It is the petty tyranny of many men to force upon their households physicians of their own choosing, who are objectionable to their wives or daughters : it would be for the good of such autocrats if they reflected that this procedure injures themselves in its reflex action, for it only prolongs the invalidism of the shrinking and suffering patient, and makes the bills, which even autocrats detest, far heavier than they like to pay. Therefore, for the sake of both parties it is best—would it be idle to add kindest ?—for women to be allowed this useful right, and to choose the presence that cheers them and the face they trust to medicine both mind and body.

Seventh—Every woman has a right to a home, unless stringent circumstances prevent. I mean to a home in the house of her husband or her father. This seems an unnecessary statement to many people; yet there are instances, numerous enough, where it applies. There may be a nominal home, where a wife leads such an unconsidered, down-trodden existence, so lorn and loveless a life, that it is no real home to her, but the dwelling of a captive in the grip of a tyrant ; a position where even her children treat her with cold contempt, and the very servants of the house ignore and despise her. Is this to be called a home ? Yet such there are ; some that I have personally known ; more of which I have heard. And there are parents who, for reasons they do not make known, exile their children from their houses ; often to please the caprices of other members of the family who do not desire to be bored or affronted by the offending member ; often for some freak of their own temper or perverted idea of their own unfilled demands. No idea of duty inspires or daunts them ; they do not reflect that they gave existence to these children and owe them unfailing patience and kindness to alleviate that infliction. To deprive a boy or a girl of the shelter and refuge and amenities of a household to which he or she has a birthright is an intolerable injustice, and one that seems impossible ; yet is not.

I once heard a man say to his wife, referring to the trouble his wayward daughter gave her (the daughter of his earlier marriage):

" I wish I could afford to send her away to school, and spare you this anxiety and trouble."

"Never!" was the energetic reply. "Not if you were worth millions. She is your child, and she has a right to a home in her father's house; it is my duty to make her home a shelter and benefit to her; and I will, at whatever cost to myself!"

Is not this the right thing to do? Is a man or woman ever cast into such piteous and unchristian exile as when he or she has "no place on the earth to call home," as I heard a woman say once, with a voice of mortal sadness?

Eighth—A woman has a right to the use and control of her own money, whether she inherits or earns it. There is a general feeling among married men that women ought not to have money of their own; that they should ask their masters for every cent they need. I have known a man to invest his wife's small portion, and make her come to him for every needed dollar, until, being a woman of spirit, she insisted on an allowance. I have known another to take the money left to his children, absolutely to be in their own control, and, without ever rendering them account, invest it in ways they knew nothing of and which proved greatly to their loss, long after they were of full age. They could not go to law with their father, as another set of heirs might have done, but had to bear this injustice and dishonesty as best they might. I have known still another, unfortunately executor of his father-in-law's will, to take money left his wife under that will and spend it as he pleased, so that when she needed and demanded it it was gone. And yet another who, being trustee of an estate from which his wife received a considerable annuity, never allowed her to have one cent of that income, though he was a rich man himself. Nor did he ever give her any money for her own use; she had a bill at the grocer's and the shoe-shop, but he bought her clothes without any reference to her wishes, and paid her dressmaker. I could multiply such instances till time failed me; they are the rule rather than the exception; and these are the humiliating and painful experiences that have driven women to arise and fight for the chimerical rights they demand, considering those the real way to amend the sufferings they do not exploit.

When men are ready to allow women their true and just rights, to remember the admonitions of Holy Writ,—"Husbands, love your wives and be not bitter against them"; "Likewise, ye husbands, dwell with them according to knowledge, giving honor unto the wife as unto the weaker vessel, and as being heirs together of the grace of life, that your prayers be not hindered" (significant latter clause !); "Husbands, love your wives, even as Christ also loved the church and gave himself for it"; "Fathers, provoke not your children to wrath"; "Fathers, provoke not your children to anger, lest they be discouraged,"—then the true rights of women will be achieved. We have much from pulpit and press to impress on us the duties of wives and children ; for it is men who preach and edit; but all duty is of its own nature reciprocal, and the other side of these family obligations is just as stringent as that commonly preached and written about.

Looking over the social, the conjugal, the parental status of the sexes in this age of progress, it is sad to see that the true rights of women are so frequently ignored and set aside. It is true we owe the delay of our restoration to these God-given privileges greatly to those "freedom-shriekers" who forget their position and their womanhood, who leave their families neglected and their homes forsaken to rant on platforms and usurp pulpits ; the women who demand suffrage for themselves when as yet they are too weak and ignorant to use so mighty a weapon, and try to reverse the creative ordinance that did not make the race all men. These idle and reasonless demands react on the more sensible and faithful part of their own sex, and give men, who are so apt to be deluded by "glittering generalities," the idea that all women are fools.

I can but close this attempt to show that we women have some rights that ought in the name of religion and humanity to be respected, but, alas ! rarely are, with repeating what Mrs. Siddons said to Samuel Rogers when once her proud soul was sore at seeing honors heaped upon a brother-actor which she knew she better deserved herself, yet never would attain,—

"I hope, Mr. Rogers, that one day justice will be done to women !"

ROSE TERRY COOKE.

THE PRESENT LEGAL RIGHTS OF WOMEN.—II.[1]

THE woman has outstripped the man, it would seem, and will soon stand with whip in hand, ready to pay him back for the alleged hardships and slavery of the past. Would it not be well for her, ere she cries for more, to contemplate the extent of her present domain? Perhaps the disinclination on the part of men to extend to her the right of suffrage is caused by the insatiable voracity that she displays. Yet mankind has gone very far in this direction, also, and it is doubtful if either the friends or foes of the doctrine are aware of the large area invaded by it. Mr. Hamilton Wilcox, in a small pamphlet entitled "Freedom's Conquests," has compiled data which show that some form of woman's suffrage exists in one hundred and nine states, territories, and provinces, in all parts of the world. These cover an area of over fifteen million square miles, with an aggregate population of nearly three hundred million souls—a population as great as that of North America, South America, and Africa combined, and nearly as great as all Europe. In England, Scotland and Wales, women, unless married, vote for all officers except members of Parliament ; and some of them now hold offices as school directors, aldermen, and city councilmen, and a bill has now been introduced to give them, whether married or single, the absolute right of suffrage. In Ireland they vote for poor law guardians ; in some seaports for harbor-boards, and in Belfast for all municipal officers. In Sweden woman suffrage is substantially the same as in England, and it exists to some degree in Austria-Hungary, Italy, Finland, British Burmah, Madras, Bombay, Russian Asia, New Zealand, Victoria, New South Wales, Queensland, South Australia, and in about two thousand islands, including the Isle of Man, Tasmania, Sardinia, Sicily, and Pitcairns. In fourteen States of this country women may vote for municipal officers, and at school elections, and in some of them may hold office in school districts. In Washington Territory, until lately they could vote at all elections and

[1] See first article on this subject in THE AMERICAN of September 20.

hold office, serve on juries, and act in other manly capacities. But here, as well as in Montana and North and South Dakota, the experiment has not proved satisfactory to the majority of men, and, by a large vote, the woman suffrage amendments were rejected from the constitutions of the applicants for Statehood. This would seem to show a distinct retrograde movement on the part of those who have heretofore been in the van of the army of women's rights; and the fact may afford unpalatable food for those hungry innovators who violently call for more.

In Kansas, however, full municipal suffrage has been granted to women, as well as the right to vote upon the privilege of selling liquor. Over forty thousand female votes were cast at the last election, and five cities of that State have elected women to the highest municipal offices, where they are said to have performed their duties with excellent judgment, and to the entire satisfaction of the citizens. The Maine Legislature, at the last session, refused, by a vote of ninety to forty, to grant women suffrage at municipal elections, and the legislatures of Massachusetts, Vermont, New York, Michigan, and Iowa, have all rejected similar bills. In the States and municipalities, however, in which the privilege has been granted, there has been considerable chance for sociologists to study its effects. Experience seems to show that, unless there is a moral issue involved, women are not prone to exercise their right of suffrage; but in Kansas they have proven themselves not only voters, but politicians, as regards the liquor interests. They are the relentless enemies of the drinking saloons, and the vast majority will not tolerate departure from moral purity. Professor Goldwin Smith is alarmed at the prospect in England, and thinks that men will gradually come under the power of women, who will tyrannize over them and degrade them. Certainly their actions do not seem to show that lack of individual opinion that was predicted by so many wise ones before experience proved the contrary.

The interference of the legislatures seems necessary to remove the trammels of woman's condition; but, so far as the common law is concerned, the refusal to allow women to hold office is based more upon might than right, and the same may, perhaps, be said of the suffrage privilege.

When the military service, which was so great a feature of the early feudal system, gave way under the influence of agriculture and trade, the rights of women in property began to be recognized. At first, it was only those who could bear arms who succeeded to the Feudatory; but, when the system changed to a civil rather than a military plan, feuds began to be known as *feoda impropria*, and descended to either male or female heirs. It was then that women, having the right to inherit the property of their ancestors, were recognized as the rightful possessors of such offices as were inheritable. In early times it was much doubted whether a female descendant could receive and transmit the title to the Crown, but trouble on this score was evaded by various statutory settlements of the succession upon male and female heirs. So far as a woman may be said to possess a common law right to the throne, it must be looked upon as an exception to the general rule. It has been held, in England, that she may hold any office not strictly judicial. The matter of her fitness was less considered than her right of property in the office, and the former question was avoided, on the ground that she might act by deputy.

The first recorded case of a woman holding an important office, is Isabella de Clifford, who acted as sheriff of Westmoreland county in the 13th Century, and sat upon the bench with the judges, and signed the official papers of her position. At various times since women have acted as marshals, great chamberlains, constables, jailors, and foresters.

This right of women to hold office is as much law here as in England, despite some decisions looking to the contrary, and as ministerial officers they are entirely eligible. Their privileges have been seldom exercised, it is true, but if they can secure elections at the hands of the majority, the courts will be compelled to protect them and enforce their rights. There has, however, been a refusal on the part of several States to admit them to the Bar; but this denial has been promptly cured by acts of the legislatures. The courts of last resort in Wisconsin, Illinois, and Massachusetts decided against the admission of the weaker sex, on the ground of their want of fitness for the office, the dangers to the sex from the associations of the life, and general lack of common law authority. So, too, the Court of Claims at Washington refused to admit them, as did the Supreme Court of the United States; but these decisions were also rendered of no avail by Congress. Much was said by the judges, in these cases, concerning the common law disabilities of women, but a critical examination of their reasoning in support of the views expressed shows that it is the result of judicial bias rather than the outcome of the common law. In many of the States this has been recognized, and women have been admitted to practice the profession without question. Among others are Iowa, Missouri, Maine, District of Columbia, Michigan, Pennsylvania, and Connecticut.

It is impossible to ignore the fact that women are successfully invading all the professions; the doors of the leading colleges have been thrown open to them, and thousands have been graduated with honor, and are pursuing with masculine force and good fortune the pathways they have chosen. Yet with all these privileges, "the shrieking sisterhood" still cries for more. When universal suffrage is granted to them by the legislatures, and society admits female trousers without jeers, will there still be something for the agitators to inflame over? Will it be, as Professor Goldwin Smith fears, that women, finding themselves the superior animals, will transform the world into a land of Houyhnhnms, and by tyranny and oppression change mankind into Yahoos. The safety of the household has been looked upon by the student of political economy, in all ages of the world, as the one thing above all to be jealously guarded. To keep the home circle free from the strife of the dealings of men—a place where peace may be found from the turmoil of the world, and the energies recruited, must to every one seem desirable. To allow women to make contracts as if unmarried involves liabilities to all manner of controversies, lawsuits, and disturbances. Who can say what estrangements, losses, calamities may occur, if the peace of the home is thus to be invaded by all the harness of the daily battle, and women are to be taken from their natural duties to learn the sharp ways of the world?

It is questionable whether our ancestors did not appreciate the necessities of domestic relations more truly than the agitators and legislators of to-day. It has generally seemed to the social philosophers that the family was more closely knit together by the power of the husband over the property of the wife; that dissensions were far less likely to arise, if there was one to whom the wife and children looked for counsel and support, and whose duty it was to stand at the head of the little assemblies as its commander. The system was not devoid of faults of various kinds, as must ever be the case with all human devices; but the remedy offered does not seem to be free from disturbances quite as bad. The power to create trouble often brings it about, and even now sociologists claim that there is a marked deterioration in the peace and security of married life; and the vast increase in the number of divorces throughout the country seems to bear them out in their views.

It is a question of much interest whether the independence given to married women, by the numberless statutes passed in their favor, and the extension of their social and political privileges has not been the cause of this weakening in the strength of the marriage relation. If so, legislators may well pause, and the women who are so persistent in advocating further advances, should look beyond the polls and into the family circle. The happiness of their sex, and the stability of the whole social fabric lies in the peace of the household.

SAMUEL WILLIAMS COOPER.

WOMEN AND WOMEN.

BY ELTON ELIOT.

LL over the world," said Lady Mary Wortley Montagu, "I have met with but two kinds of people—men and women." "In America," says the foreign tourist, "I have met with but one kind of woman—the Northern woman." He writes about her, describing her as an American woman, forgetting that the Northern states do not form the whole of America, nor the women there all the women in the country.

There are two distinct kinds of women in America—the Northern woman and the Southern woman. There is a Western woman, of course, but her characteristics do not seem so distinctly marked as are those of her Northern and Southern sisters.

The Northern woman is apt to be dogmatic, is self-reliant and self-opinionated, believes in herself and expects other people to believe in her. She feels herself competent to give an opinion on all subjects, from the tariff to the proper disposition of the household garbage. Her mind is alert and active ; it takes a wide range, and we are not astonished to find her discussing social purity, the cleaning of the streets, political reform, the dramas of Euripides, and meteorological and astronomical science.

While, in the Southern acceptation of the word, the Northern woman is not hospitable, she is fond of society. She is never too old to enjoy balls and parties, the play, and the opera. Domesticity is not one of her virtues. Northern women are gregarious. They like to meet each other at clubs and listen to each other talk, even though they may learn nothing new. There are few fields in which the Northern woman does not show her activity. She shows herself in the literary world through the medium of books and newspapers. There is a "woman's page,"

231

and there are magazines devoted to the "cause" of women, and the marvel is how women of high aspirations can content themselves with the drivel hashed up for their edification, for the Northern woman *is* a woman of aspirations. She is charitable, after a fashion, but her charities are too much hampered by rules and regulations.

The young Northern woman comes under the head of "the arrogant young." She knows as much at sixteen as her mother does at sixty. She is impatient of home restraint, and wishes to set up what she calls "a bachelor establishment" where she and her friends can lead lives apart from the maternal eye. She is ready to undertake anything, from the editing of a newspaper to delivering a lecture at "Sorosis." She has but little respect for her seniors, considering her young wit superior to their old wisdom, and her manner is what an Irish boy called "bossy." Her respect for herself is unbounded, her instinct of politeness small, and her "push," when she is bent on succeeding in any avocation, wonderful.

The Southern woman has been thus depicted by Gail Hamilton. What Southern woman recognizes herself in this picture? "Many instances have been given to show how far more unreasonable, intense, malignant, vulgar, and venomous is the hatred of their country, shown and felt by Southern women, than that evinced by Southern men. It is very commonly said that they have done more than the men to keep alive the rebellion. The coarseness and impropriety of their behavior have been relatively far greater than that of the men. Has anyone ever suggested that the narrowness, the utter insufficiency of their education, the state of almost absolute pupilage, bedizened over with a gaudy tinsel of tilt-tournament, chivalry, in which they have been kept, absolutely incapacitating them for broad views, rational thinking, or even a refined self-possession in emergencies had anything to do with it?"

Can prejudice and ignorance go any farther than this? The Southern

woman is essentially refined, and e̶ under the most aggravating circu stances, the sweet perfume of ref ment and politeness clings to her a When insulted, as she often was Northern soldiers, she never laid her dignity of manner, never railing for railing, was never coa never unladylike. A Southern wo would rather hear herself call "perfect lady" than to be told th she was the greatest genius exta There is something repulsive to very nature in coarseness and vulg ity, and to be unladylike is somethi more than a fault in her eyes—it i sin.

The Southern woman is domest hospitable, and fond of society S is decidedly not "clubable," as J Johnson said. Of the many South women residing in New York, co paratively few are club members. S likes to entertain her friends in h own house, and believes it to be mistake to exclude men from a gathe ing of women. For this reason she not in love with women's clubs, an she clings to the old-fashioned ide that women may possibly learn som thing by associating with men. It not by being apart from men, tha women will rise to their highest alt tude of intelligence. It is by min ling with them, as they did in th French salons. Women's minds e panded by intercourse with men wh did not disdain to converse with the on art, literature, science, and pol itics. Said George Eliot, "I have no faith in feminine *conversazion* where ladies are eloquent on Apollo and Mars." One salon such as France knew has done more for the menta improvement of woman, more for broadening her views, than all the women's clubs extant. Men sat on the throne of France, but it was the women who ruled—ruled through men. There are a few women's clubs at the South, and perhaps in time there will be fewer, when all the women of that section awake to the knowledge that there can be no possible social improvement upon the old-time re-unions of the men and women.

of the South, where womanly refinement and politeness was met by manly deference and chivalry of manner.

Before the war, the ideal home of America was at the South. Unbounded hospitality prevailed, peace and comfort ruled, and the hand ever ready to extend to the stranger never failed to give a warm pressure of welcome. Society, too, was refined and charming; it was not simply a glittering and hollow show, where every woman tried to eclipse every other woman in the glitter of her diamonds and the sheen of her satins. It was a reunion of intelligence and good feeling, brightened by vivacity, and made delightful by agreeability.

In society, the Southern woman strives to please others; she likes to hear herself called "agreeable." The Northern woman does not possess the Southern suavity of manner. She prefers pleasing herself; she has no idea of "hiding her light under a bushel," to please any one. She is decidedly not conciliatory; to use an old proverb, "fair words don't butter her parsnips;" and, while clever, the aim of her life is not to win golden opinions, especially from men, whose presence in the world she by no means considers necessary. At the South there is no antagonism between the men and women, and no striving after place and power on the part of the latter. No shrieking for more freedom; no craving for the ballot. The Southern woman has never felt that she was an oppressed downtrodden creature, kept out of the lofty sphere in which God and her own abilities intended her to shine. She has met with no opposition in taking up her work in her own way, whether it be the raising of a public monument or the writing of a book. As a rule, she is contented with the existing order of things, even though her Northern sisters accuse her of being anti-progressive.

Professor Erastus Everett, in his lecture, "A Sugar Plantation of the Olden Time," thus speaks of the Southern women, praising their "quiet industry," and declaring that they were "the most pure, beautiful, and virtuous" he had ever met; that they ap-proached nearer to Solomon's description of a virtuous woman than any other class of women he had ever seen or read of; and this praise—for praise it is, and high praise, too came from a New England man.

These women were not longing after a "career." To make home a haven of rest and peace was their highest ambition. In their eyes home had a sacred signification. They adorned it by their graces; they sweetened it by their gentleness; they sanctified it by their virtues; and they threw the comforting arms of love and sympathy around the inmates. Nothing that tended to elevate, refine, and give comfort to home was beneath their striving after. Hospitality reigned supreme, and the stranger within their gates was welcome to the best they had. They never cast longing looks at the presidential chair, nor sighed for the time when the power to vote would be theirs. They did not seek to guide the Ship of State over the stormy waters of debate; neither did they believe that their assistance was required to help Hercules to drag his wagon out of the mire. Southern domestic life was as beautiful as one of Claude Lorraine's sunny landscapes.

The Northern woman is by nature a reformer; the Southern woman believes that what was good enough for her grandmother is good enough for her. She does not believe that there can be an improved edition of Martha Washington, Mrs. John Adams, Mrs. James Madison and other women of the Revolution—women men delighted to honor, and who exercised a most salutary influence over home and society. The Northern woman sees much to sweep away with her besom of destruction. She would depose man and reign in his stead. She would perform duties for which nature and education has not fitted her. Give her power to make the laws and you would soon see an era of honesty, of fair dealing, of matrimonial felicity, and a general well being. The Southern woman would prefer obeying the laws to making them; and she does not care to call indignation meetings to discuss the depravity of man, his

233

tyranny to woman, and his general good-for-nothingness. Mr. Gladstone declared in a speech that the world was too large and too bad for any one club, one organization, or one community to reform. "Home is a little place, and there a good woman can make a heaven, rear a throne, and reign a goddess." A Persian ambassador asked the wife of Leonidas why such honor was paid to the women of Lacedaemonia. "It is," she replied, "because they have entirely the forming of the men." They certainly did not form the men by lashing them with their tongues, nor will the women of to-day reform men by the same process. The Northern woman does not confine her reforms to dress, nor to cooking, nor home matters. She goes outside of this to "assail the gray preeminence of man" in the political world, the municipal world, and every other world in which man was once the monarch of all he surveyed. Like the Princess of Tennyson's poem, she is ready to dare all, to do all

"To compass our dear sister's liberties."

When Mr. George Seney was asked why he gave so much money to Wesleyan Female College, of Georgia, he said, "To honor my mother, to whom, under God, I owe more than to all the world beside. I admire the Southern women. There are possibilities in the Southern women not equaled anywhere else on earth." What were these possibilities? Not the courage which enables women to fight men in their own arena. Not the activity which seeks to circle all the earth with its energy; not the fearlessness which undertakes to wield the battle-axe of contending political parties. The possibilities of which Mr. Seney spake was the ability to recognize the wide-reaching influence of home, and all that the word meant. The Southern women have intellectual possibilities too, as well as domestic, which is proved by the books they write. It has been said of the women of the days of chivalry, "They were distinguished for courtesy, affability, and grace; while, at the same time, they cultivated all useful arts which were

proper to their sphere;" and the same may be said of the Southern women. Mr. Jefferson Davis declared that "if asked what his sublimest ideal of woman should be in time of war, he would point to the dear women of his people as he had seen them during the recent struggle. All they had was flung into the contest—beauty, grace, passion, ornaments; the frivolities so dear to the sex were cast aside; their songs, if they had any heart to sing, were patriotic; their trinkets were flung into the public crucible; the carpets from their floors were portioned out as blankets to the suffering soldiers of their cause; women bred to every refinement of luxury wore home-spuns made by their own hands; when materials for an army balloon were wanted, the richest silk dresses were sent in, and there was only competition to secure their acceptance. As nurses of the sick, as encouragers and providers for the combatants; as angels of charity and mercy adopting as their own all children made orphans in defence of their homes, as patient and beautiful household deities, accepting every sacrifice with unconcern, and lightening the burdens of war by every art, blandishment and labor proper to their sphere,—the dear women of his people deserved to take rank with the highest heroines of the grandest days of the greatest countries." This picture differs from that drawn by Gail Hamilton, and will be recognized as a truer likeness.

If it depended on the Southern women to keep alive the fires of woman suffrage, the flames would have gone out long ago. Few are the Southern women who have been won over to this cause, and yet the most earnest, the most eloquent of the lecturers on the right and the desirability of woman to vote is a woman of Southern birth living in New York, who is regarded by the women of her own section as an erring sister. Her followers are, with few exceptions, Northern women; for, as a class, the Southern women do not care to appear as debaters and fighters in the political arena. To deposit a ballot is a small affair, and this is only one act in the drama. This done, and women must sit on juries, hold office, and go to Congress. While Bellona mounts the war chariot, Mars stays at home and presides over the cuisine and the nursery.

The Northern woman, to use her own word, is more *advanced* than the Southern woman. That means that she has adopted certain views and ways that do not find favor with her Southern sister. Much of the so-called prog-ress of the present day is turbulence, restlessness, a desire for change. There is a false glare that blinds the eyes to all that is sweet, tranquil, and lovely in the life of woman. It is not that the Southern woman is incapable of receiving new ideas and new theories; but, before adopting them, she must be convinced that they are an improvement on those which have hitherto swayed her life and made her what she is, "The angel in the house."

FOIBLES OF THE NEW WOMAN.

WHEN woman revolts against her normal functions and sphere of action, desiring instead to usurp man's prerogatives, she entails upon herself the inevitable penalty of such irregular conduct, and, while losing the womanliness which she apparently scorns, fails to attain the manliness for which she strives. But, unmindful of the frowns of her observers, she is unto herself a perpetual delight, calling herself and her kind by the epithets "new," "awakened," and "superior," and speaking disdainfully of women who differ from her in what, to her judgment, is the all-important question of life—"Shall women vote or not?" To enumerate her foibles is a dangerous task, for what she asserts to-day she will deny to-morrow. She is a stranger to logic, and when consistency was given to mortals the New Woman was conspicuously absent. Her egotism is boundless. She boasts that she has discovered herself, and says it is the greatest discovery of the century. She has christened herself the "new," but when her opponent speaks of her by that name she replies with characteristic contrariety that the New Woman, like the sea-serpent, is largely an imaginary creature. Nevertheless, in the next sentence, she will refer to herself by her favorite cognomen. She has made many strange statements, and one question she often asks is, "What has changed woman's outlook so that she now desires that of which her grandmother did not dream?"

Within the past forty years woman has demanded of man much that he has graciously granted her. She wanted equality with him, and it has been given her in all things for which she is fitted and which will not lower the high standard of womanhood that he desires for her. This she accepts without relinquishing any of the chivalrous attentions which man always bestows upon her. The New Woman tells us that "an ounce of justice is of more value to woman than a ton of chivalry." But, when she obtains her "ounce of justice," she apparently still makes rigorous demands that her "ton of chivalry" be not omitted. Woman asked to work by man's side and on his level; and to-day she has the chance of so doing. The fields of knowledge and opportunity have been opened to her; and she still "desires that of which her grandmother did not dream," because, like an over-indulged child, so long as she is denied one privilege, that privilege she desires above all others. She has decided that without the ballot she can do nothing, for, in her vocabulary, ballot is synonymous with power.

The New Woman is oftentimes the victim of strange hallucinations. She persists in calling herself a "slave," despite her high position and great opportunities; and she maintains that, because she cannot vote, she is classed with lunatics and idiots,—until those who are weary of hearing her constant iterations of these themes feel that, if the classification were true, it might not be unjust. Still, it has not been clearly shown that withholding the ballot from woman, in common with lunatics and idiots, necessarily makes her one. Women and cripples are exempt from working on roads; does it follow that all women are cripples? Is a woman a bird because she walks on two legs? This hackneyed cry about lunatics and idiots, which has been uttered by nearly all writers and speakers favoring woman suffrage, appeals to prejudice rather than intelligence. If the would-be female politicians—ignoring woman's great opportunities, especial privileges, and the silent testimony of countless happy wives,—choose to consider themselves "slaves," and to announce whenever they speak that they are classed with lunatics and idiots because they are denied the ballot, they are certainly entitled to all the enjoyment they can get out of the delusion. Sensible people know that such statements are false.

The New Woman says that a "mother's prerogative ends at the garden gate"; but common sense replies that no mother's prerogative ends there. A mother's prerogative is to govern and direct her child; and there is no child that does not carry through life his or her mother's influence. Let that influence be good or bad, it is always present. Any mother can make, if she will, her power over her child "stronger than the seas of earth, and purer than the air of heaven"; and she needs no especial legislative act to accomplish her work. If woman does not make the laws, she trains and educates those who do, and thus is indirectly responsible for all legislation.

The plea which these women make, that they need the ballot for the protection of their homes, is self-contradictory. Has the New Woman never heard that "to teach early is to engrave on marble"? If she would devote some of the time in which she struggles to obtain the ballot to rational reflection on the influence a woman has over the pre-natal life of a child, and would then consider what a mother may do with a plastic human life,—say during the first seven years of its

existence and before it goes out to be contaminated by the evil influences of the world,—she would then find that ballots are not what
women need for the protection of their homes. But the faculty of
logically reasoning from cause to effect has never been characteristic of
the New Woman.

She laments because government is deprived, by lack of equal suffrage, of the "keen moral sense that is native to women as a class."
Since all the people in the world are born of women and trained by
women, it is difficult to see how government, or anything else, lacks
woman's "keen moral sense."   Can women make no use of their moral
sense without the ballot ?

It is a chronic grievance with the New Woman that she is taxed
without representation.   She scorns to be represented by the sons she
has reared, or by the men who come under her immediate influence.
These she pronounces unworthy and considers incapable of doing her
justice.   But when she is told that, if women vote, they should also
bear the burdens of war in case of necessity, she replies with her usual
inconsistency, "She who bears soldiers need not bear arms."   She has
not the aversion to being represented by men on the field of battle that
she has to being represented by them in legislative halls and at the
ballot-box.   She greatly deprecates man's selfishness and tyranny, as
exhibited in human history.   But she has come vaunting into the
arena with "woman's clubs" and "conventions" and "leagues" and
"tribunes" and "signals."   If a periodical be not wholly devoted to
women, they demand that it must at least have its "woman's column"
wherein they may chronicle the most insignificant acts of the sex.

The New Woman tells us that the present century is her own;
and, indeed, she approaches the truth in this instance.   She has
promised us a "Woman's Bible," and she has shown that even the Infinite Father does not escape her jealousy, for she has discovered that
we should pray to a "Heavenly Mother" as well as to a Heavenly
Father.   She informs us that the Pilgrim Fathers are no more, and
adds, "There stepped on Plymouth Rock, on the bleak shores of New
England, thirty-two women accompanied by sixty-nine men and children."   At expositions she must have a "woman's building," wherein
she may glorify the work of her brain and hand.   No work done by
man can be placed beside hers for examination or competition.   Surely
she furnishes a noteworthy example of modesty and self-abnegation
for the benefit of the tyrant man!

An illustration of the New Woman's fallacious judgment is shown by her belief that all opponents of equal suffrage are controlled by brewers and liquor dealers. " Sold to the liquor interest " is the cry she always utters when she detects a note of opposition. Now, it is entirely probable that some may object to the extension of the franchise to women and, at the same time, lead thoroughly temperate lives and work for the promotion of temperance. The word temperance means more than total abstinence from intoxicating drinks, and the New Woman has not yet proved that a vote by a woman means a vote for temperance principles.

" Woman's vote will purify politics." This is her favorite cry. Not long since a prominent equal-suffrage lecturer, while earnestly setting forth this claim, and enlarging on the shameless manner in which men conduct elections, declared that woman's chaste and refined influence was the only thing that could change the present undesirable condition of affairs. She was not ashamed, however, to relate, before the close of her lecture, that, a short time previous, her sister had induced the family's hired man to vote for a certain measure by presenting him, on the eve of election, with a half-dozen new shirts, made by her own hands. The absurdity of this incident reached a climax when it was noticed that, in a large audience of women, few saw anything wrong in female bribery. The fair speaker omitted to inform her audience whether or not this was to be the prevailing mode of political purification, when one half of the burdens of state rest on female shoulders. But, as women never lack expedients, some purifying process, less laborious than shirt-making, may soon be devised.

The New Woman requests that the opponents of equal suffrage open their " dust-covered histories " and therein read of examples of famous women of the past whose lives forever silence all arguments against granting the ballot to woman. Let it be remembered that the New Woman's greatest grievance, since her earliest advent, is the lack of woman's power. Without the ballot woman can do nothing. " Bricks without straw,—that has been the doom of woman throughout the ages," is her disconsolate wail. An extremely brilliant New Woman rarely makes a speech without saying, " Women will enter every place on the round earth, and they will purify every place they enter." With these statements in mind, by all means let the " dust-covered histories " be opened so that we may see the " bricks without straw " which the women " without power" have made, and the manner in which they have purified every place they have entered.

Catherine de Medici prevailed on Charles IX of France to give the order for the massacre of St. Bartholomew. This crime, which she boasted of to Catholics and excused to Protestants, greatly increased her power, which she used unscrupulously, even conniving at the murder of her own son when she considered him an obstacle to her advancement. She died amid the fierce strife of wars, which she had caused, her use of political power having been only an injury to the world.

Madame de Maintenon, using the power which she so long exercised over Louis XIV, instigated the Revocation of the Edict of Nantes. Its most odious features were her especial work. She had been false to her native creed; and she was determined that her fellow Protestants should be equally false. She drove from the shores of France many of its best and most intelligent people. All the bloody history of that period was the result of one woman's work.

During the reign of Louis XV of France the court was under the absolute dominion of women, yet none of the instances of ancient and modern immorality presents such an astounding display of individual and national corruption as do those of the time when Madame de Pompadour ruled the king of France. She did nothing for the alleviation of human wretchedness during those twenty years of power and splendid opportunity. She was largely to blame for the evils in church and state which caused the revolution and overturned all in one common ruin. It may be urged that no good woman would have been raised to power by such means as she accepted; and consequently no good could be hoped for from her. But she and her successor, Madame Du Barry, furnish proof that there are women whose advancement to high positions would only increase evil influences; and there are many such who would quickly seize the enlarged opportunities of suffrage, while many good women, engrossed with home cares, would be indifferent to the ballot.

Woman's record in the first French revolution was one of cruelty and horror. The "Patriot Knitters," as they were called, could shriek or knit according to the requirements of the case. They could also urge men to deeds of violence; and could themselves do violent deeds. Carlyle said that these women had exchanged the "distaff for the dagger." If they had kept the distaff and let the dagger alone France would have lost nothing in the way of political advancement, and might have been spared much of her horrifying history. There was an entire absence of any political purification in their influence.

There is no name in history of which women boast more than that of Queen Elizabeth, always quoting her in evidence of what women might do, could they be intrusted with affairs of state. Froude, in summing up his exhaustive work on the time of Queen Elizabeth, wrote :—

" The great results of her reign were the fruits of a policy which was not her own, and which she starved and mutilated when energy and completeness were needed. She was remorseless when she ought to have been most forbearing, and lenient when she ought to have been stern. She owed her safety and success to the incapacity and divisions of her enemies, rather than to wisdom and resolution of her own."

Humiliating as it may be to those women who clamor for a voice in national affairs, the historical truth is, that the splendors of the Elizabethan age were due to her ministers, Burleigh and Walsingham.

Catherine II of Russia is also a great favorite with the New Woman. One of them has said, " Next to the great Peter, she was the ablest administrator Russia has ever known." In the life and reign of Catherine II, Empress of Russia—she who became such through the murder of her husband, in which crime she had borne full well her share,— there is but little to admire or emulate. She was unquestionably a woman of great talents and energy, but her morals were no better than Madame de Pompadour's.

These examples and many more may be found in the " dust-covered histories." But, if the New Woman will read history with honest eyes, she can never find that women have ever lacked power ; neither can she prove that in the past they have purified all the places they have entered ; what authority, then, has she for the statement that they would purify every place they may enter in the future ? Woman was endowed by her Creator with marvellous power, and, from the time of our first parents until now, that power has been a " savour of life unto life, or of death unto death," as has been eminently manifested in the teachings of history and the experience of human life.

The New Woman has a mania for reform movements. No sooner does she descry an evil than she immediately moves against it with some sort of an organized force. This is very noble of her,—if she have no other duties to perform. It would be more gratifying if her organizations met with greater success ; but alas ! her efforts, mighty as they are, usually represent just so much valuable time wasted. The evils remain, and continue to increase. She disdains to inquire into the cause of her numerous failures, and moves serenely on bent upon reforming everything she imagines to be wrong. When she gets the ballot all will be well with the world, and for that day she works and waits. But if the New Woman or any other woman neglects private duties for public works, her reform efforts are not noble, but extremely unworthy of her; for the " duty which lies nearest " is still the most sacred of duties. Possibly the many *Mrs. Jellybys* of the present day and the undue interest in " Borrioboola-gha " may have something to do with so much being wrong in the average home and with the average individual. When we read of women assembling together, parading streets, and entering saloons to create, as they say, " a public sentiment for temperance," it is but natural to ask, What are the children of such mothers doing in the meantime? And it will not be strange if many of them become drunkards for the coming generation of reformers to struggle with. The New Woman refuses to believe that duty, like charity, begins at home, and cannot see that the most effectual way to keep clean is not to allow dirt to accumulate.

The New Woman professes to believe that all women are good and will use their influence for noble ends,—when they are allowed the right of suffrage. This theory is extremely pleasant, if it were only demonstrable; but here, as elsewhere, it is folly to ignore the incontrovertible facts. Woman cannot shirk her responsibility for the sins of the earth. It is easy for her to say that men are bad; that, as a class, they are worse than women. But who trained these bad men? Was it not woman? Herein lies the inconsistency of women—striving for a chance to do good when the opportunity is inherently theirs. It is only when they have neglected to train the saplings aright that the trees are misshapen.

It was the New Woman's earliest, and is her latest, foible that woman is superior to man. Perhaps she is. But the question is not one of superiority or inferiority. There is at bottom of all this talk about women nature's inexorable law. Man is man and woman is woman. That was the order of creation and it must so remain. It is idle to compare the sexes in similar things. It is a question of difference, and the " happiness and perfection of both depend on each asking and receiving from the other what the other only can give."

> " For woman is not undevelopt man,
> But diverse : could we make her as the man,
> Sweet Love were slain : his dearest bond is this,
> Not like to like, but like in difference."

Sentimental and slavish as this may sound to many ears, it is as true as any of the unchanging laws governing the universe, and is the Creator's design for the reproduction and maintenance of the race.

ELLA W. WINSTON.

WOMAN AND THE REPUBLIC.

CHAPTER I.

INTRODUCTORY.

THE introduction to the "History of Woman Suffrage," published in 1881–85, edited by Elizabeth Cady Stanton, Susan B. Anthony and Matilda Joslyn Gage, contains the following statement : " It is often asserted that, as woman has always been man's slave, subject, inferior, dependent, under all forms of government and religion, slavery must be her normal condition ; but that her condition is abnormal is proved by the marvellous change in her character, from a toy in the Turkish harem, or a drudge in the German fields, to a leader of thought in the literary circles of France, England, and America."

I have made this quotation partly on account of its direct application to the subject to be discussed, and partly to illustrate the contradictions that seem to inhere in the arguments on which the claim to Woman Suffrage is founded. If woman has become a leader of thought in the literary circles of the most cultivated lands, she has not always been man's slave, subject, inferior, dependent, under all forms of government and religion; and, furthermore, it is not true that there has been such a marvellous change in her character as is implied in this statement. Where man is a bigot and a barbarian, there, alas! woman is still a harem toy; where man is little more than a human clod, woman is to-day a drudge in the field; where man has hewn the way to governmental and religious freedom, there woman has become a leader of thought. The unity of race progress is strikingly suggested by this fact. The method through which that unity is maintained should unfold itself as we study the story of the sex advancement of our time.

Progress is a magic word, and the Suffrage party has been fortunate in its attempt to invoke the sorcery of the thought that it enfolds, and to blend it with the claim of woman to share in the public duty of voting. Possession of the elective franchise is a symbol of power in man's hand; why should it not bear the same relation to woman's upward impulse and action? Modern adherents ask, " Is not the next new force at hand in our social evolution to come from the entrance of woman upon the political arena ? " The roots of these questions, and consequently of their answers, lie as deep as the roots of being, and they cannot be laid bare by superficial digging. But the laying bare of roots is not the only way, or even the best way, to judge of the strength and beauty of a growth. We look at the leaves, the flowers, and the fruit. "Movement" and "Progress" are not synonymous terms. In evolution there is degeneration as well as regeneration. Only the work that has been in accord with the highest ideals of woman's nature is fitted to the environment of its advance, and thus to survival and development. In order to learn whether Woman Suffrage is in the line of advance, we must know whether the movement to obtain it has thus far blended itself with those that have proved to be for woman's progress and for the progress of government.

I am sure I need not emphasize the fact that, in studying some of the principles that underlie the Suffrage movement, I am not impugning the motives of the leaders. Nor need I dwell upon the fact that it is from the good comradeship of men and women that has come to prevail under our free conditions, that some women have hastily espoused a cause with which they never have affiliated, because they supposed it to be fighting against odds for the freedom of their sex.

The past fifty years have wrought more change in the conditions of life than could many a Cathayan cycle. The growth of religious liberty, enlargement of foreign and home missions, the Temperance movement, the giant war waged for principle, are among the causes of this change. The settlement of the great West, the opening of professions and trades to woman consequent upon the loss of more than a half million of the nation's most stalwart men, the mechanical inventions that have changed home and trade conditions, the sudden advance of science, the expansion of mind and of work that are fostered by the play of a free government,—all these have tended to place man and woman, but especially woman, where something like a new heaven and a new earth are in the distant vision.

To this change the Suffragists call attention, and say, " This is, in great part, our work." In this little book I shall recount a few of the facts that, in my opinion, go to prove that the Suffrage movement has had but little part or lot in this matter. And because of these facts I believe the principles on which the claim to suffrage is founded are those that turn individuals and nations backward and not forward.

The first proof I shall mention is the latest one in time—it is the fact of an Anti-Suffrage movement. In the political field alone are we being formed into separate camps whose watchwords become more unlike as they become more clearly understood. The fact that for the first time in our history representatives of two great organizations of women are appealing to courts and legislatures, each begging them to refuse the prayer of the other, shows, as conclusively as a long argument could do, that this matter of suffrage is something essentially distinct from the great series of movements in which

246

women thus far have advanced side by side. It is an instinctive announcement of a belief that the demand for suffrage is not progress; that it does array sex against sex; that woman, like man, can advance only as the race advances; and that here lies the dividing line.

How absolute is that dividing line between woman's progress and woman suffrage, we may realize when we consider what the result would be if we could know to-morrow, beyond a peradventure, that woman never would vote in the United States. Not one of her charities, great or small, would be crippled. Not a woman's college would close its doors. Not a profession would withhold its diploma from her; not a trade its recompense. Not a single just law would be repealed, or a bad one framed, as a consequence. Not a good book would be forfeited. Not a family would be less secure of domestic happiness. Not a single hope would die which points to a time when our cities will all be like those of the prophet's vision, "first pure and then peaceable."

Among the forces that are universally considered progressive are : the democratic idea in government, extinction of slavery, increase of educational and industrial opportunities for woman, improvement in the statute laws, and spread of religious freedom. The Woman-Suffrage movement professed to champion these causes. That movement is now nearly fifty years old, and has made a record by which its relation to them can be judged. What is the verdict?

CHAPTER XII.

CONCLUSION.

In the opening of this volume I have given it as my opinion that the movement to obtain the elective franchise for woman is not in harmony with those through which woman and government have made progress. I have spoken of the marvellous forward impulse that has marked the passage of the last half-century, and have mentioned the growth of religious liberty, the founding of foreign and home missions, the extinction of slavery, the temperance movement, the settlement of the West, the opening of the professions and trades to women, the progress of mechanical invention, the sudden advance of science, the civil war, and the natural play of free conditions, as among the causes of this impulse. I have pointed out the fact that the Suffrage movement has nearly reached its semi-centennial year, and has made a record by which its relation to these progressive forces can be judged, and I have appealed from the repetition of its claims to the verdict of its accomplishment.

In the second chapter I have considered the

growth of republican forms the world over, and endeavored to show that the dogma of Woman Suffrage is fundamentally at war with true democratic principles, and that, practically, woman suffrage has been allied with despotism, monarchy, and ecclesiastical oppression on the one hand, and with the powers of license and misrule that assail republican government on the other.

In the third chapter I attempt to prove this further by a study of the origin of the Suffrage movement, and by its relation to the Government of the United States. I try to refute the two propositions which it has put forth as solid resting-ground for woman's claim to the elective franchise in this land—"Taxation without representation is tyranny," and "There is no just government without the consent of the governed." I have also set forth the difference between municipal and constitutional suffrage, and shown that the extension of school suffrage, so far from being a stepping-stone to full suffrage, affords another evidence that such full suffrage is unprogressive and undemocratic. It is held that regulated, universal manhood suffrage is the natural and only safe basis of government.

In the fourth chapter I consider the early relation of the Suffrage movement to the causes of anti-slavery and temperance. I also discuss the attitude of the Suffrage leaders during the civil

21

war, and indicate that the Suffrage movement was not patriotic, and was a hindrance to emancipation and reform.

The fifth chapter treats of the connection of the Suffrage movement with the change that has taken place in the laws, and it contains a synopsis of the present laws of New York regarding women. From this study it appears that the Suffrage movement did not originate the change in the laws; that many changes most vigorously urged by its associations never have been enacted; and that change of laws has not been so much sought as a voice upon change of laws— the fact being, that the vote *per se* has been urged as the panacea for all woman's wrongs.

The sixth chapter deals with Woman Suffrage and the trades. It shows that this movement was not instrumental in opening the trades to women; that the conditions of industrial life are not changed in such essentials as would involve a change of sex relation to Government; and that, so far from altering the basis of government, industrialism has introduced new problems of such grave import that security in the enforcement of law is doubly necessary. It shows, furthermore, that socialistic labor has been naturally the friend of Woman Suffrage, while the safer and sounder organizations have extended sympathetic help to woman.

The seventh chapter discusses the connection of Woman Suffrage with the professions. It aims to show that here, too, suffrage has not been necessary to gain, for women who were fitted to hold it, an honorable place; and, in regard to the places they have not yet entered, it is held that the impulse must come from within. It is argued that, in the professions, as in the trades, Suffrage effort has hindered more than it has helped, and that in the West its practical working is the most damaging thing that has attended woman's real progress.

The eighth chapter considers the connection of Woman Suffrage with education. Its conclusions are, that not education, but coeducation, was the persistent demand of Suffragists, and that woman's advancement in college and university was wrought out by the impulse gained from women who opposed the Suffrage idea, and made practical by men to whom also that idea was repugnant. It is suggested that women who could prepare and defend the ignorant Suffrage Woman's Bible have no right to utter a syllable in protest of the educational ideas of men and women who are competent to speak on the subject, and whose verdict has been, on the whole, for separate study during collegiate age, wherever such could be afforded, while it is not disputed that coeducation has its place and its uses.

The ninth chapter presents Woman Suffrage in its relation to the church. It first discusses, briefly, a few points in the Suffrage Woman's Bible, published in New York in 1895. This is a commentary on such passages in the Pentateuch as relate to women, and the title "Rev." is prefixed to four names of editors on its title-page. This book, or rather a book of which this is the first instalment, was promised by Suffrage writers and speakers from the beginning. It is considered to contain the consummate blossom of the mind that first expounded the Suffrage theory— the mind that grasped it as a whole, in its full meaning and intent, and never has wavered in expression as to its ultimate object and the means by which that object is to be sought. This chapter sets forth, in few words, the present writer's view of woman in the creation, and of St. Paul's attitude toward woman. The chapter further discusses woman's early preaching in this country, and shows that it has not been such as to build up religion or the state, but has been such as to suggest that, while the possibilities of her nature tend to make her supreme in capacity to point the way to higher regions, it also contains qualities that may render her peculiarly dangerous as a public leader.

The tenth chapter, entitled "Woman Suffrage and Sex," alludes briefly to the social evil, and then discusses the Suffrage ideas in regard to sex as explained by both their older and more recent writers. It discusses the disabilities of sex in relation to the suffrage—the difficulties in the way of jury duty, police duty, and office-holding —and draws the conclusion that the fulfilment of such necessary work of the voting citizen is practically an impossibility for woman, and has been found to be so in the Western States.

The eleventh chapter has for its title " Woman Suffrage and the Home." It sets forth the belief that the Suffrage movement strikes a blow squarely at the home and the marriage relation, and that the ballot is demanded by its most representative leaders for the purpose of making woman independent of the present social order. It argues that communism is the natural ally of Suffrage, and that, as homes did not spring out of the ground, they will not remain where men and women alter the mutual relations out of which the institution of home has slowly grown.

The general conclusion of the book is, that woman's relation to the Republic is as important as man's. Woman deals with the beginnings of life; man, with the product made from those beginnings; and this fact marks the difference in their spheres, and reveals woman's immense advantage in moral opportunity. It also suggests the incalculable loss in case her work is not done or ill done. In a ruder age the evident value of power that could deal with developed force was most appreciated; but such is not now the case. It lies with us to prove that education, instead of causing us to attempt work that belongs even less to the cultivated woman than to the ignorant, is fitting us to train up statesmen who will be the first to do us honor. The American Republic depends finally for its existence and its greatness upon the virtue and ability of American womanhood. If our ideals are mistaken or unworthy, then there will be ultimately no republic for men to govern or defend. When women are Buddhists, the men build up an empire of India. When women are Mohammedans, the men construct an Empire of Turkey. When women are Christians, men can conceive and bring into being a Republic like the United States. Woman is to implant the faith, man is to cause the Nation's faith to show itself in· works. More and more these duties overlap, but they cannot become interchangeable while sex continues to divide the race into the two halves of what should become a perfect whole. Woman Suffrage aims to sweep away this natural distinction, and make humanity a mass of individuals with an indiscriminate sphere. The attack is now bold and now subtle, now malicious and now mistaken; but it is at all times an attack. The greatest danger with which this land is threatened comes from the ignorant and persistent zeal of some of its women. They abuse the freedom under which they live, and to gain an impossible power would fain destroy the Government that alone can protect them. The majority of women have no sympathy with this movement; and in their enlightenment, and in the consistent wisdom of our men, lies our hope of defeating this unpatriotic, unintelligent, and unjustifiable assault upon the integrity of the American Republic.

NEW YORK, *March*, 1897.

THE UNQUIET SEX

THIRD PAPER—WOMEN AND REFORMS

By Helen Watterson Moody

NOT long ago, a man, a busy and successful editor, who has an unusual way of ruminating facts until he gets all the significance possible out of them, said to me, "Have you ever thought of this?—there are in this country at the present time an unusual number of capable and conspicuous women, at the head of distinguished political or educational movements and reforms, or administering unpaid public offices with great tact and charm, and with some helpfulness. Now, if one were fully to inform himself as to the station in life of these busy persons, he would find, I think, that they are, almost without exception, either women of great wealth, having, consequently, abundant leisure and the power to destroy it, childless or unmarried women, or self-supporting women whose business interests are supposed in some way to be forwarded by publicity."

Yes, I had thought about it in a desultory and unproductive fashion.

"Well, go on thinking about it and you will find conclusions ahead of you somewhere, if I am not mistaken."

I did go on thinking about it, and he was not mistaken, but the first conclusions I arrived at (by the pleasant Hibernian process) were questions. Which is cause and which effect? Is it public service for public service's sake or for publicity's sake? Is it not possible with leisure and the consciousness of money-power to develop a kind of epicureanism in reforms as in the other pleasures of life? Are we in danger of making a fad of what must be really a very solemn undertaking, when one considers that a reform is necessarily a readjustment of creation, and that if it comes to anything more than an experiment in reform, it must be about as serious a matter as creation itself? I have not yet answered any of these questions satisfactorily

to myself. Can anybody give me a ray of light?

So much for the first conclusions, which, as you see, were no conclusions at all, and perhaps the second were like unto them, for the one serious matter I settled with myself was that I did not agree with my friend as to the limitation of this taste among women for public affairs. So far as my own observation goes, most women have it, to-day, to a greater or less degree, and have had it, with different manifestations, ever since the days when their Puritan fathers and husbands pushed into reforms, having not yet taken the time to push out of the wilderness. Those early days of transcendentalism in New England must have been glorious times for the reforming instinct, when, as Mr. Lowell says, there was "no brain but had its private maggot, which must have found pitiably short commons sometimes," and in which it is evident that women were deeply involved, from the very nature of the reforms themselves.

These dealt not only with the establishment of communities, where, as one chronicler has it, "everything was to be common, except common sense," and with a reversion to labor upon land, which was declared to be only work in which men could lawfully engage, but there were those who wished to do away with yeast, and eat unleavened bread, fermentation being considered an unholy and unwholesome process; there were persons who attacked buttons as allies of the devil, and other means of locomotion than legs, and marriages, and miracles, and the ordinary courtesies of expression—from all of which it is indubitably to be inferred that many of the prophets, even then, were of the unquiet sex.

Now, the desire for reform is by no means to be decried, since it must make an essential part of the working capital of every earnest man or woman. Heaven

The Unquiet Sex

The Unquiet Sex 117

forbid that any word of mine should be interpreted as remotely casting levity (which is worse than casting discredit) upon any attempt on the part of anybody toward that strenuous reach to "exceed one's grasp" which is "what a heaven's for." Only since we women (I see no derogation in acknowledging it) are by that entire physical and mental organization generally known as temperament, more inclined to extremes in all things than men are, it appears wise to me that we should suspect the desire for reform whenever we can see that it has passed onward from that latent quickening heat which warms the ovum of thought to life, into the open excitement which will hopelessly addle it. To be able to sit down beforehand, to a cool and impartial scrutiny both of the animating spirit of our reforms and their objective and subjective results, seems to me wholly necessary, before we can be sure that we are not undertaking reform for reform's sake alone, or that in the high and unselfish purpose which is prompting us, we are not losing some adornments of character which seem to me greatly worth keeping.

It may or may not be worth comment that during the early days of reforms in this country there were more men reformers than women, but that later on, dating, perhaps, from the Civil War, the number of reforms instituted by women is the greater. Perhaps this bears out my editor's suspicion that leisure and wealth and the power it buys are at the bottom of half our reforms, as well as of half our mischiefs. At any rate, the number of public affairs we poor women have to look after nowadays must be either exceedingly gratifying or exceedingly disheartening, according to one's point of view. We seem to have the health of the country wholly in our hands (at least, one is inclined so to fear, contrary to what one has been taught to believe about microbes and bacteria, to say nothing of an all-wise Creator whom we used to credit with some sense of responsibility for the world He has made); we have kindergartens, and the Alaska Indians, and sanitary plumbing, and doing away with distinctions of sex in work, and the introduction of patriotic teaching in the public schools, and the higher education of parents, and dress reform, and

many more things of like gravity, which, like the apostle, I have not time to speak of now.

Now, very likely all these things are good to do, and to be—and to suffer, too, if one is able to "drink fair" in the matter of reforms and to take as well as offer an appropriate opportunity for improvement. But it seems to me most essential that we should not lose what the Germans call Uebersicht, in our zeal, and that we should remember, however necessary it may be to the world alone that a social or political reform should be instituted, it is surely of much more importance both to the world and the reform—to say nothing of ourselves—that the reformer herself should be sane and pleasing—particularly pleasing. For here, my friends, I stoop to plead the cause of unreformed feminine nature. I have never been able to see why any one of us should be ashamed of a desire to please—even to please men. Could woman's desire go farther, on the whole, even in post-mortem vanity than the epitaph Mr. Lowell was so fond of recalling, "She was so pleasant?" For myself, in honest confession, I would rather be pleasant than be President, and St. Paul defend me if I imitate his humble example and speak these words as a fool!

One of the regrettable things about the reformatory instinct is its persistence. If one could only be occasionally a reformer and anon come back to one's quiet and passive provincialism, the case for the reformers would be proved at once. But a taste for reform is like a taste for the luxuries of life — one seldom gets over it. This in the case of women is particularly to be deplored, because there is likely to result a habit of mind and behavior more or less egoistic, downright, declaratory, and dead-in-earnest, while most of us still like our women as Sairey Gamp liked her porter —"drawed mild." Why not? Is there any advantage, in the nature of things, in severity and strenuousness over mildness and serenity? Can we be certain that the latter have not a surer vitality of their own? It is to the meek and not to the strenuous that the inheritance of the earth was promised, and at least it is to be conceded that in mildness and serenity is to be found the antidote to the strain and tension which the acceleration of the age puts upon us all. Possibly here is still another mission for women—or will be, when we get the composure to consider it : that of ranging ourselves with the calm and leisurely forces of nature which the hurry of modern life has not yet been able to alter, and which even the American must accept until he finds some way to change his constitution, or to do away with it altogether and live on the by-laws, as one American statesman used to say he did. The American may have discovered how to digest badly, but he has found no way to digest both well and quickly.

All this misbehavior on the part of men is bad enough, but it seems to me infinitely worse when it comes to women, for I do not see how it is possible to evade the conclusion, as indicated by the supreme functions and most imperative duties of women, that they were meant to live closer to nature than men were, to be a very part of its great orderly processes, and to have the inestimable privilege of sharing, if they will, in its simplicity, its largeness, its tranquillity, its unconscious patience. If this be true, and I like to believe that it is, it seems to me most essential that in our desire to perform one set of duties, we should not lose sight of another still more important set, that we should keep our sense of perspective, and not mistake, even in reforms, the false need for the real one ; that we should be able to discriminate between the righteous necessity for fundamental adjustment and a mere desire to relieve our feelings.

" Is reform needed? " asks Walt Whitman. " Is it through you? The greater the reform needed the greater personality you need to accomplish it." Let us see. Is reform needed? Not always. A number of men and women, all good and wise, may meet together and, discovering a great evil or a real abuse, may decide that something ought to be done, and set about doing it at once. Yet it by no means follows that because things are out of joint no duty remains but to set them right. It is not quite enough that a reform should be desirable or even necessary ; it must also be inevitable. And when it is inevitable it "hath a way " of its own. It seems then to be set in motion by an inner spiritual vitality rather than from any mechanical and outside force. And when

the reform is accomplished, it is usually to be observed that it seems to have moved with a curious—almost a human—perversity, never in the obvious or direct line toward its end, but, bringing up its re-enforcements from unexpected quarters, its march has been through a series of zigzags, leading sidewise, backward, anywhere, but along the simple straight line upon which our convictions have settled as the one practicable method of approach. The genius of reform, like the genius of the German sentence, seems to be for " yawing and backing, for getting stern foremost and for not minding the helm." Nothing better betrays this delightful sense of humor in the spirit of reforms than that reform, at once the most complicated, the simplest, the most long-suffering, most endeared to the hearts of women—dress-reform.

It is hardly to be supposed that the dress-reforming spirit is a product of modern times, since we find the necessity of it enjoined upon women as far back as Bible times, but for present purposes it is sufficient to go back to forty years ago, when the women of this country began to look timidly and tentatively (much as the little fish in the fable looked at the fly on the hook) toward the mere possibility of such changes in the garments they wore as should conform them, in some degree at least, to the demands of beauty or health or convenience or adequate bodily protection. A few women, looking at the matter quite simply and directly, and conceiving, therefore, that dress-reform was a matter solely of individual and private concern, shut themselves into the privacy of their homes, snipped and sheared and stitched industriously, coming forth at last to shock the gaze of a waiting world with a curious hybrid garment, neither male nor female, lacking the stern practicability of the masculine garb, lacking also all the sweet appeal of the flowing feminine line, lacking even that long " petty-coat," without which, as the acute Mr. Pepys observed, " nobody could take them for women." It is not strange that the reform received a blow, then and there, from which it staggered along unsteadily, upheld only by the occasional enthusiasm of a business-like prophet, or a Rainy Day Club, or a Woman's Congress (where it crept in with other more popular and less necessary reforms) until about three years ago. Then, without any seeming movement, without declaring itself at all, suddenly, like light at the creative fiat, it *was*. And it *was*, not through any tempest of organization, or any whirlwind of enthusiasm, but through the still, small wheels of the bicycle, bringing forth the one thing that was necessary and had been lacking all the time—reason enough. What a regard for health or beauty, or convenience, or individuality, or comfort had never accomplished, the desire for pleasure brought at once. To-day the short skirt, the comfortable blouse, the well-protected ankle, make up a costume as respected and as non-committal on the streets of a great city as on the golf-links of the most remote hills. Dress-reform need go no farther in accomplishing its own ends, though it is certain to carry with it half a dozen linked reforms, more or less desirable. Given reason enough, you see—specific and immediate need—and any reform is inevitable, but in the absence of sufficient reason it is as impossible to accomplish a reform as it is physically impossible (to use one of Mr. Mallock's illustrations) to knock a man down unless he gives you a sufficient motive for doing so. There is no doubting that reforms are sometimes necessary ; that the world is full of affairs which are not righteous, and that many of them should be set straight; just as there is a restful certainty that these surely will be set straight in their own ripe time. But it by no means follows that you and I are necessary to their reformatory conduct. I have sometimes wondered whether we women, conscientiously anxious as we are not to play the shirk in all questions of serious import, have not come to overrate the responsibility of the individual in the simple possession of convictions and powers. For it is not always inevitable, even in the stern deductions of the moral world, that because one has the ability to do fine things, nothing remains but to be constantly about their discharge. To be always living " at the top of one's voice " does away both with the logic and the distinction of the performance. I like to think that each one of us has a right, if she wishes it, to a sense of unexpended power and to the ample self-possession that comes with it, just for their

own sweet sake, if she happens to prefer these to a more ostentatious and ambitious self-expression. And as for convictions, perhaps an advance in ethics may some day lead us to suspect that convictions were meant to be serviceable mainly as springs of action, and to govern us in our relations with others, rather than for promiscuous circulation among our friends—who may also happen to have convictions of their own. Possibly, too, we have been over-advised as to the peculiar responsibility for morals which is generally supposed to attend upon the possession of petticoats. Whatever the Turveydrops of the moral world may have to say about the necessity for elevating moral deportment on the part of "wooman, bewitching woman," I have never been able to see any indubitable intent in nature herself toward binding them over to any higher moral standards than she does men. Both men and women seem to me to be compounded of the same average morality, though with certain unlike manifestations, largely the result of circumstances and opportunities. I see no special cause for believing that the average woman under like temptation would do very differently from the average man—a belief which is not lessened by Bishop Potter's recent accusation before the Women's Auxiliary of the Civil Service Reform Association, that they put their relatives into office whenever they get the chance, "without any evidence that they are fitted to fill the places they applied for." Possibly women were intended by their Creator to stand for the reformatory interests of life, but I think there is not, as yet, sufficient evidence thereto either in the nature of things or of women to warrant any special abrogation of other distinct and more familiar duties in favor of interests mainly moral.

And even if we had as a sex displayed that special aptitude for managing public affairs which has distinguished a few of us, we are still, most of us, as the division of labor adjusts things at present, either too busy or too tired to undertake them. It must be quite clear to those who are watching the trend of modern life with any interest as to its results, that we women are taxing ourselves to the point of physical distress and mental superficiality. We are carrying the heavy end of creation. We seem to desire to impress ourselves and the world at large with the great virtue that consists in getting tired. I wish, instead, we might arise to such an appreciation of our physical worth and dignity as would make us as ashamed of exhaustion (except under extremest provocation) as we should be of any other equally grave physical immorality. And as for the extreme busy-ness in which we rather glory to-day, what is to be said of it except that it is no more worthy of respect than any other departure from nature, and that it argues not so much for general ability as for the specific inability to exercise a wise and proper selection in the affairs of life? Somewhat, also, does it indicate a lessened sense of personal dignity, in that we permit ourselves to be whipped like slaves through each day with the scourge of many duties.

I suppose the end of reform is the betterment of the world at large, and with that in view it has always been surprising to me that so little attention has been given to the part played in this general betterment of creation by mere happiness. I believe it is Mr. Stevenson who says that the duty of being happy is the most underrated duty in the world. And in spite of all we may wish or assert to the contrary, there is indubitable evidence that happiness, up to date, at least, has a basis in physical well-being. I suppose one of the reasons why the reformers of the earth have not been notably delightful persons to live with is because they were either too busy or too tired to be happy. And yet a happy man, and especially a happy woman, is a radiating focus of reform, for such a person possesses that gentle and diffused persuasiveness which leads us into willing good endeavor, simply because it displays to us the good taste of enjoying fine behavior.

But however true this may be, there will still be some of us whose taste is for the purple of heroic action ; who would rather give themselves to public benefaction than to private happiness, as also there will be some whose splendid abilities will give them to command both. For these there may be a not unfriendly suggestion in occasionally recalling the remark of the sage Mr. Birrell, that there is "a great deal of relativity about a dress-suit." There is also a great deal of relativity about reform, and it is the failure upon the part of many reformers to understand this which makes the pathos and the humor and the satire of so many reforming movements, in themselves noble and uplifting. The social structure being not a thing of mechanical parts, but a living growth, it is impossible even to lop off an excrescence without drawing blood from the whole body. It is with reforms as with everything else in the world that is an evolution and not a manufacture—you cannot get one end, which you may want, without getting the other end, which you will probably not find so desirable. It was, as Mr. Lowell says, the inability of Don Quixote to discover for himself what the Nature of Things really was, or of accommodating himself to it if he had discovered it, which makes the work of Cervantes an immortal commentary on "all attempts to re-make the world by the means and methods of the past and on the humanity of impulse which looks on each fact that arouses its pity or its sense of wrong as if it was or could be complete in itself, and were not indissolubly bound up with myriads of other facts both in the past and the present. . . . Don Quixote's quarrel is with the structure of society, and it is only by degrees, through much mistake and consequent suffering, that he finds out how strong that structure is, nay, how strong it must be, in order that the world may go smoothly and the course of events not be broken by a series of cataclysms. . . . 'Do right though the heavens fall,' is an admirable precept so long as the heavens don't take you at your word and come down about your ears—still worse, about those of your neighbors. It is a rule rather of private than public application, for, indeed, it is the doing of right that keeps the heavens from falling."

THE COLLEGIATE EDUCATION OF WOMEN.

A SEMI-CIVILIZED condition of mankind educates its men or rather its men of certain castes, and leaves its women in ignorance. There is always then on the part of the men a lack of respect for the women. The women on their part grow up to be idle and frivolous, and remain childish. Unable in any degree to be the mental companions of the men, they are despised. Again the men, unaffected by any ennobling influence from the women, are brutal. In Turkey, for example, the young boy treats his mother with marked disrespect, and in this only follows after his father.

262

To no one can such a condition of the sexes be more abhorrent than to the New-Churchman. He is taught that man and woman are absolutely equal before the Lord and that, unless they regard each other as equals, there can be no true marriage. The child must respect its mother just as highly as it does its father. The word of admonition from the one must come with the same weight as from the other. The mother's influence must be exercised to the full in every orderly family, or the children will lack something important to their moral welfare. It is a common saying that great men have had great mothers. It goes without saying that any nation which neglects to place its women on an equality, morally and intellectually, with its men, will suffer from a dearth of great men and must sink into a brutalized condition.

The teachings of the New Church, while they insist upon the equality of the sexes, do not fail to explain that beautiful symmetry of distinctive character which makes true marriage possible. As the two hands could not unite if they were in form identical and not symmetrical, so man and woman, if not wonderfully adjusted from creation in their characteristics, could never form that indissoluble bond of which it is written that God has joined them together. While each is created in the image and according to the likeness of God, a truly united pair of human minds form one still more perfect image and likeness of Him. In that distinctness of mental form which promotes so perfect a union, neither is inferior to the other, but they must unite in mind and life on the basis of perfect liberty and equality. That marriage is sometimes a failure through the lack of high motive on one side or on both, does not in the least destroy the ideal conception of man and woman presented in our faith for the ultimate realization by and beatification of Christian lives.

It is undoubtedly in the direction of an improving humanity that we now see attention given to the higher education of woman, which is of course necessary if she is to fill her right place in the community. Obviously her advance must be as steady as that of man, or the best results of his progress will perish with each generation and not be transmitted. At this point, however, while the plans for woman's higher education are in their formative stage, two paths are presented to those who have control of the courses of training. One path, which is at present perhaps the more easily pursued, gives woman an education identical with that of man, places her in the same institutions with courses of study already fixed upon when there was no thought of her participation, and stands for the doctrine that, except as to physical characteristics, the two sexes are alike, and can successfully exchange the duties of life.

The result of this mode of training is seen in mannish young women, ambitious to excel in everything but as matrons of families — a life which they abhor — and justifying the criticisms of those who take the ground that college training disqualifies a young woman for her best life. While the qualities of woman are so innate that it is by no means true that the woman's colleges are spoiling all the young women, there is some ground for the complaint which is made, and we are glad that there is so much anxiety on this point.

But all the time there is another path of advanced mental training which recognizes the beautifully distinct qualities of woman and seeks only to secure their best development, and we have been much pleased to see this view clearly expressed in the inaugural address of the new president of Wellesley College for women. Caroline Hazard, a woman of noble presence and in the full strength of mature youth, is known as a historical writer of accuracy and also as the beneficent supervisor of a large manufacturing village which has grown up about the mills belonging to her family. Her strength of mind had already shown itself, but in her inaugural she displayed true womanly modesty and affection. After speaking of the changed conditions under which women live, she said : —

The order of nature does not change. Yet nature's law is growth, and with that growth the position of women has changed, and with that change the cultivation of the individual becomes more important. The problem is not simply that of bringing children into the world, but what kind of children shall be born, what kind of a mother shall be educated; or, if the highest development of motherhood is denied her, how shall she take her place in the world, a useful and honored member of the community, having children of her spirit. For I take it the eternal feminine is simply this: It is the power of love which has its throne in a good woman's heart. Call it altruism if you like, call it the Mother sea, found a philosophy or a system of speculation upon it — it is simply this endless capacity of love and devotion which Mary of Bethany showed when she sat at Jesus' feet.

Granted then, that this is at the root of woman's life, that every woman child who comes into the world has this great gift and responsibility, that this is her contribution to human life, with what reverence, with what awe, should we approach her, to make or to mar! Sentimentality and mannishness, like Scylla and Charybdis, stand on either side.

She went on to point out that there have been solitary learned women all along, but this is not what is now wanted, and she indicated how necessary is the broad scholarship which will control its environment and make life noble, and then she spoke of the delight of learning practical wisdom, and said : —

This highest gift of heaven, this gift which is good in God's sight, woman is peculiarly fitted to receive. If the deep, abiding fountain of love in her heart is her greatest element of strength, then indeed she has a true and vital spark of the divine life in a peculiar sense. It is her great task to interpret the divine spirit in terms of every-day life. What countless men, the best of the world's leaders, have acknowledged their debt to their holy mothers! There have always been men to speak with tongues, and there must always be women to interpret. How close, then, to the source of all life must we women press, lest the light that is in us should turn to darkness!

Her closing words were most emphatic : —

It is because I believe with all my heart in the holiness of life, that I stand here to-day. I believe that women have an increasingly important part to play in that life. With enlarged opportunities come increased responsibilities — responsibilities as yet unadjusted to unaccustomed shoulders. It is to cast my mite into the treasury of the world's experience that I come. Wellesley has always stood for the high and ideal things of life. It is because I believe in divine life among men, in the direct and personal connection of each soul with its Maker, that I dare to take up the great work you are committing to my care. Humanity without divinity is of the dust that perishes. Humanity joined to divinity can compass the impossible. Therefore on this day, at this solemn hour of accepting a trust, I speak not of knowledge, wide and profitable as is that great field, but I speak of wisdom, the gift of heaven, which must descend like gentle rain to fructify and fertilize, or there can be no harvest fit for the nourishment of man.

It is interesting to note that President Eliot, of Harvard University, in following with an address of congratulation on behalf of his institution, approved of the distinctive work of woman set forth in the address of Miss Hazard, and predicted that important good results would follow from her wisely-conceived endeavors; and it is also interesting, though to be regretted, that President Thomas, of Byrn Mawr College for Women, has seen fit, in a public address, to reject this principle of woman's dis-

tinctness from man, and to assail the views expressed at Wellesley after a manner which, in its excitability, is certainly truly
feminine and not a little unfortunate as illustrating the very defects of the unmodified education for women which Presidents
Eliot and Hazard had deprecated as harmful to women.

She is reported to have said that the argument of President
Eliot, —

. . . would not be worthy of a serious reply had it not been thrown deliberately by the President of one of the greatest of American universities, as a
gauntlet in the face of an immense audience, most of whom were directly interested in the education of women students. It only shows that, as progressive as one may be in education or other things, there may be in his mind
some dark spot of medievalism, and clearly in President Eliot's otherwise
luminous intelligence, women's education is this dark spot. He might as
well have told the President of Wellesley to invent a new Christian religion
for Wellesley, or new symphonies and operas, a new Beethoven and Wagner,
new statues and pictures, a new Phidias and a new Titian, new tennis, new
golf, a new way to swim, skate, and run, new food, new drink. It would be
easier to do all this than to create for women a new science of geometry, new
Greek tragedies, new chemistry, new philosophies; in short, a new intellectual
heaven and earth.

The account of her remarks concludes with saying, —

After thus answering President Eliot, President Thomas quoted Dr. Taylor of Vassar and Professor Palmer of Harvard, who do not agree with President Eliot in finding any essential difference between the masculine and the
feminine mind.

Both these women are sincere and the work of both will be
tested by its results. Who can doubt that the wise womanliness
seen in President Hazard's address will in the end prevail, and
that the result of her work and of that of all who truly understand woman's nature will be most beneficial?

T. F. W.

When the College is Hurtful to a Girl

BY S. WEIR MITCHELL, M.D., LL.D.

Author of "Hugh Wynne," "Characteristics," etc.

IRST, let me state my creed. I believe that, if the higher education or the college life in any way, body or mind, unfits women to be good wives and mothers there had better be none of it. If these so affect them that they crave merely what they call a career, as finer, nobler, more to their taste than the life of home, then better close every college door in the land. In thus speaking I do not refer only to the married life. A vast number of women who do not marry come to have, at some time, charge of households or of children not their own. This surely is the natural life of woman. I say the like of men. It is their natural place to meet the outside cares of life, and whatever of dissipation, mistakes or indolence unfits them to endure and to labor in their proper sphere is as much to be deprecated as is anything which makes a woman hate the duties of home, or renders her, as she may think, superior to their claims.

I have seen in my long medical career a great number of women, and men too, who have been prevented by ill health from being in life either useful or pleasant to themselves or to others. Very often these failures have been due to neglect of or inattention to obvious matters of diet or exercise, to lack of correct self-estimates, tendencies to gauge endurance by the standards of more vigorous people. I see women fall into ill health, too, from self-devotion unintelligently guided, from emotional causes such as rarely injure the lives of men, from lack of willingness to yield to the just demands of their own physiological conditions, from such defects of character as make it hard to set aside with decisiveness worry and the frictions of life. As to the larger part of these failures of character which work so much ruin, let me say a word in passing. They begin in childhood, and are usually the fault of want of intelligent discipline. To teach children habitual decisiveness, thoughtful patience, self-restraint, kindness, endurance, is not hard at the plastic age. These qualities do not need high intelligence. They are moral characteristics ; if won in youth they assist much in making the later and large use of the mind easy and safe, and are vastly protective when we come to face the inevitable shocks and disasters of existence.

I BELIEVE that most women would be wiser, better, and therefore happier, for larger intellectual training. Is it to be desired for all women? By no means ; nor for all men. Just what it should be is another matter. For most women, who are to live the ordered and usual lives of women, it should be such as cultivates tastes which bring intelligent joys into the midst of any life whether its lot be care-filled struggle, or ease and luxury, whether its fate be to live single, or to marry.

But before we go further let us pause and reflect. You come here, and for what? To acquire knowledge? Why? What we have not, what is hard to get, what few attain, is apt to be overvalued. I have found many young women, and some men, prone to overrate the uses and the joy to be had out of the mere knowing of what others do not know. This idea becomes a sort of possession : it owns you, not you it. That is what possession means.

I go a step further. Knowledge, with power to use it for the begetting of other knowledge, has its evils, or may have. If it become an overmastering passion, even in genius, it may be satisfied at a cost beyond its worth. Would you see what it can do? How in one with a really splendid intellect it can destroy happiness, obliterate the moral sense and substitute for love of family the extreme of selfishness and even contempt for the decencies of existence? If so, read the story of Sonia Kovalesky, and remember it is not needful to be a genius in order to be morally hurt by the greed of learning. I wish only to call to your minds the danger which may arise out of the excess of a relatively good thing.

If you can learn any branch so as to liberalize your soul and give to joy fresh wings, well and good ; but to do this through acquiring a language as dead as Greek or Anglo-Saxon is a task beyond the possibilities of most folk.

I want you, therefore, to be clear as to what you want and why you want it. Are you to be a teacher? That is one thing. Are you to have a home life which involves no use for the sharply defined knowledge which is to be in turn a source of knowledge? Then think a little of why this or that science is desirable.

"IT IS of no moment to her own worth or dignity that a woman be acquainted with this science or that ; it is of the highest moment that she be trained to habits of accurate thought ; that she should understand the meaning, the inevitableness and the loveliness of natural laws." It is no less of use that history should broaden her sympathies, and sociology enlighten her conscience. If the character is dulled in the seizing of learning — nay, if it be not built up, confirmed and enlarged, then give us for this world's use the nobler heart and the less tutored brain. Let then the woman while training her mind use for this such knowledge-getting as may help her thereafter to enlarge her views of life.

Character is, after all, the true business of life. If we are here for any visible purpose it is this. And so comes up the question as to whether you can get the silver and not let fall the gold. In a word, what perils does the woman run who at the time of maturity breaks away from home to live among strangers and acquire knowledge? I do not say that ill *must* come of it ; I do say that it *may*, and it is your business to be sure that it shall not.

A man at college gets contact with men, larger views, acquaintances, education (either general or special), training for law, physics, business, engineering — what not. Possibly many of you have the desire or the urgent necessity to be able to teach, to study medicine, to do some form of literary work. Take care. This seems to release you from obligations as to home duties and cares, from household vexations, the looking after children, those of other folks or your own. But this is not so in the life of fact. Few women of those who do not marry escape the need to assume some of these natural functions. Most folks think vaguely of home as meaning marriage, husband, wife, children ; but for me, its foremost and most beautiful human necessity is a woman ; and, indeed, this is of her finest nobleness, to be homeful for others, and to suggest by the honest sweetness of her nature, by her charity, and the hospitality of her opinions, such ideas of honor, truth and friendliness as cluster, like porch roses, around our best ideals of home. It is instinctive, and civilization kills our instincts. Man has none left ; woman yet has, and natural duties also ; he has none which are implacable.

I WISH all women, before they go to college, to have a sensible competency of common household knowledge and of all a house needs where means are small. As to this, the French are more wise than we. Their training for the work of teaching is most severe and systematic, but these foolish people ask some curious questions of women before they will examine them at all as to the science required for admission to the École Normale. Why should not we, too, insist upon these preliminaries? The primary and grammar schools demand a certain amount of knowledge as to sewing, cooking, etc., and these are elaborately set forth in the programs. These matters are much insisted upon in those who enter the Écoles Normales.

In these higher schools are taught care of the house, heating and lighting, care of furniture, of stuffs, of linens, the art of washing and ironing. Cooking is most elaborately dealt with, and a host of other such things ; bookkeeping as applied to the household, hygiene, and care of the injured in the minor accidents of life. Finally, there is the hygiene of the nursery, care of children, and again sewing and the making of garments. As for the scientific studies which occupy the rest of the time, I have read them with thankfulness that I am not a girl in an École Normale.

I saw last year three unhappy men. Two at least were gentlemen of unusual attainments. All married sweet girl graduates. None were rich men. All three were uncomfortable because their wives had no more idea of household management than they. One declared, in fact, that he had to run the house himself. His wife did know the romance literature and was a fair Grecian. The wife of another found no interest in the care of an economical house, and said : " Where was now the good of her mathematics : she had not time for them." I could not tell her, nor could he. As a fact her lack of time was due to lack of knowledge.

Of a hundred men of eighteen years almost all will be fit to stand the trials of college work ; of a hundred women, far fewer. How many cannot I do not know. I have often stopped women who wished to go to college, thinking them physically unfit. It is very rare that I have to give a similar verdict as to young men. If I had my way, every college for man or woman should follow the example of Amherst : an entrance examination as to physical conditions should be inexorable and complete.

❦

YOU understand that I now speak of both sexes. I do not mean that, because in man or woman the heart is unsound, or the eyes abnormal, or the general health below par, such persons should be excluded. Far from it. I would shut out but a few. My plan would only insure that fore-knowledge and after-thoughtfulness which make for success and prevent disaster. Indeed, the regular life of college for the student who accepts the rational consequences of imperfect physical conditions is often a source of improved health and not of disease.

And now the student takes up the life of systematic study. What then? How is she to get the best out of the training, and keep or better her physical health? First of all, do not conclude that the whole mass of you can assume the man's standard as to what you do in the way of mental labor. It will be at your peril. Some of you can. There are days for most of you when to use the mind persistently is full of danger. You are women, not men. She who forgets it is foolish ; she who persistently and intentionally ignores it is worse. The debts of despised Nature roll up with interest, and at last here is an inexorable creditor. Your very goodness betrays you. Women have terrible consciences and decline to waste time as so many young men do and have done : this present preacher among them. Hence, women at college work harder than men ; out of their eagerness arise disregard of physiological limitations, the tendency to shirk play and exercise for study, the cutting short of meal leisure, and the robbing of sleep to add to the hours of the day.

The man yearns for exercise ; he gets it at all cost, and gets hunger with it. Women do not so eagerly crave it, and have their way. Nor can they violate the laws of health which are good for both sexes, and not suffer more and longer than men. Trust me, I am right. Do not try to be men when you are women. Keep your honest pride of sex. Be regular as to hours of sleep. Dismiss the day work and do not lie thinking it over. If you are feeling your work get a rest at dusk, and after the mid-meal. Above all, be punctual at meals and do not take a book or the thought of work to table, or talk shop there. This is a first-class platitude. I find in some women that afternoon tea is a serious evil. Girls go from one pleasant room to another, and by and by are really tea tipplers. Be careful as to this excess.

There are certain symptoms which tell any watchful worker that something is wrong in the method or amount of his or her work. The brain slave is beginning to rebel ; you are tired at midday ; you cannot get to sleep at night, or you wake too early, or are restless, and wake and sleep, and wake again. Take care. These are Nature's first signals of alarm. Stop and think -- there is need. Do not delay and fight it out ; get more rest. Shorten the work hours. Take milk or soup between meals and at bedtime. If these simple helps fail, stop. Quit work. Get some physical labor. I would rather be a healthy waiting-maid than Professor Minerva with a yellow skin and a lazy liver. There are times when if a tired woman does not lie abed and read a novel she is a goose, and will howl for it some day, if geese can howl. I have seen many, many breakdowns of college women, and always it was from being primarily unfit, or else it was from after-disregard of wise regulations and the working too long when unfit for work.

Again there are times when, as at examinations, you will feel the anxieties and worries competitions engender. Take care ; this is a season which presents me with emotional neurasthenics, with hysterical breakdowns in health.

Even in childhood the examination time furnishes an increase in the number of choreal cases. I rather incline to think that I would have no examinations, except the final one, in my ideal college ; perhaps not that. Examinations such as I hear of are cruel and destructive.

❦

WILL you think it queer if I say a word as to dress from a man's standpoint? If you want to see ill-dressed people the worst are women doctors, platform ladies, college professors (men), and the folks generally who are overvaluers of learning. In the effort to dress the mind I pray you not to forget the body. I never saw a professional woman who had not lost some charm. There comes a little hardness, less thought as to how prettily to do or say things ; affected plainness of dress ; something goes. It seems to me a duty for men and women to seem as well as to be gracious in dress and manner. Are the women who become learned necessarily in peril of partial loss of what makes the social life agreeable? I do not know. American men are the worst dressed in the world, and I do not want to see our women fall away as to this because they are too intent on mere learning. As to all these matters I may be talking folly ; I do think there are some such risks.

And now as to your idle hours. Keep them sacred. Guard the seventh day as free from work. Cut off brain labor an hour before bedtime. Read verse then, or a novel. I do always, and have read every endurable one you ever heard of, and many not worth reading at all. A fine brain clearer is a novel which captures attention, and almost as good as a cold bath to sweep out the thoughts of the day. If you work in summer let it be an hour or two after breakfast, and no more.

You ought to want to be reasonably learned, but you should as eagerly desire not to forget what makes life agreeable ; nor should you fail to keep touch of its practical aspects. Very learned folks run some risk of undervaluing what is outside of their own studies. This is what we mean when we say they are narrow-minded. But the narrow who lose touch of the wide activities of life are uninteresting, and no one has a right to be uninteresting.

For many women, as for men, the learning won at college goes for nothing. With a man it has been a mind training for life work. For this class of women it is—shall I dare to say it—useless. The freedom of college life is gone. Here are restrictions, simple duties. The result is, and I have seen it over and over, discontent. The man goes out into a larger life ; yours narrows to home functions. This is what I so much fear.

And here, too, comes in the wild craving for what girls call a career, and if these women do or do not marry, the result is the same—neglect of duty, ungratified ambitions, discontent ; and so what was meant to make life fuller ends in lessening the sum of happiness. This is not always so ; nor need it be. I am told that a smaller portion of college graduates marry than do women not so cultivated. If this be true there is something wrong ; for surely the completeness of life for man or woman is in marriage. Is it that men do not like highly educated women? Or is it that these fail to attract, not from this cause, but owing to some of the other reasons I have mentioned? Is it not true that some college graduates are inclined to think of marriage as of a thing beneath them? If so they have lost something of the naturalness of the truer life.

❦

ONE word before I close. You are here in competition with men. I do not like that. The professor expects of you virile standards of work and results ; you are, therefore, as I think, in an atmosphere of peril, and unless you live as reason counsels, for some of you life here will leave you certain regrets. The exceptional successes and vigor of the rare few serve but to lure the mass of women into the belief that the continuity of work of the man can be imitated with no more risks than are his. Time, I know, will teach a larger wisdom in work.

I hope I have not been extreme nor brutal. It is so easy to criticise, and yet I have said no word which is not the outcome of a rather sad experience of the disorders of women too ambitious to be thoughtful as to health, too eager to compete with men, to remember they are women. I see the wrecks come ashore to sail the seas of success no more. Is it any wonder I wish to warn those who are sailing or about to sail on treacherous seas?

268

RETROGRESSION OF THE AMERICAN WOMAN.

BY FLORA MCDONALD THOMPSON.

I HAVE not encountered the ghost of my great-grandmother, but something akin to it which has startled me no less. I have been face to face with the American woman of little more than half a century ago, who rose to greet me from the dusty pages of De Tocqueville's "Democracy," and who, by the light of contrast, has caused me to gasp with astonishment, beholding the degeneracy of her end-of-the-century descendant.

M. De Tocqueville, you will recall, came among us before the first woman's rights enthusiast had sounded her war-cry in the land. American woman's suffrage was not; co-education was not; the industry of woman was not in trades and the professions, but supplemented man's in the home. Also, when De Tocqueville came among us, it was soon after the "three days' revolution" in France. He was very alert to observe every operation of the principle of democracy as it might be applicable to the conditions of his own people. He believed that on the operation of that principle the happiness of his own country and the destinies of the civilized world depended. Thus it was with a great love of liberty and with jealous discernment of all that opposes its highest realization, that he "explained with a pencil of light" the successive steps and more important features of our development as a nation. A contemporaneous American critic of his production wrote: "He exhibits us in our present condition a new and, to Europeans, a strange people."

A strange people we are to ourselves, as we look backward to De Tocqueville's picture of us; and, compared with the American woman of De Tocqueville's time, the modern American woman is something more than strange. She has changed not alone with respect to outward form and manners, but in the whole under-

270

lying principle of her development she has so far departed from the ideals then logically set forth as indispensable to the continued growth of our national greatness, that the American woman of to-day appears to be the fatal symptom of a mortally sick nation.

De Tocqueville thus expressed his fundamental notion of woman's political importance:

"No free communities ever existed without morals; and as I have observed, morals are the work of woman. Consequently, whatever affects the condition of women, their habits and their opinions, has great political importance in my eyes."

Fancy representing to the heralds of woman's suffrage that the political future of woman is in mere virtue, that the greatness of woman is to be good, without reference to being President or even to being a school trustee!

Adhering to his original point of view, De Tocqueville enters into a minute analysis of the American woman in the character and relation of wife, and supplies a standard measured by which the retrogression of the sex becomes so clearly apparent as to be all but reducible to an arithmetical equation.

"In the United States, the inexorable opinion of the public carefully circumscribes the married woman within the narrow circle of domestic interests and duties, and forbids her to step beyond it. I by no means suppose, however, that the great change which takes place in all the habits of women in the United States, as soon as they are married, ought solely to be attributed to the constraint of public opinion; it is frequently imposed upon themselves by the effort of their own will. When the time for choosing a husband is arrived, that cold and stern reasoning power which has been educated and invigorated by the free observation of the world, teaches an American woman that a spirit of levity and independence in the bonds of marriage is a constant subject of annoyance, not pleasure; it tells her that the amusements of the girl cannot become the recreation of the wife, and that the sources of a married woman's happiness are in the home of her husband. As she clearly discerns beforehand the only road which can lead to domestic happiness, she enters upon it at once and follows it to the end without seeking to turn back."

Side by side with this vision of wifely excellence known to De Tocqueville, and to my great-grandfather, I place the history of Oklahoma, South Dakota, Newport! So far from the modern American wife steadfastly pursuing the road to domestic happiness without ever turning back, divorce statistics have determined that the actual number of American women, during twenty years, who set out on the road to domestic happiness and did turn back, or were sent back, is 328,716. Of this number 67,685, or about one-fourth, turned back from causes involving immorality of woman, and in more than half the given instances of marriages dissolved for this cause, the law fixed the blame on the wife.

A danger De Tocqueville perceived to threaten men, in consequence of the virtue the young democracy imposed upon American women, has been unexpectedly averted:

"I am aware that the education of young women in America is not without its danger; I am sensible that it tends to invigorate the judgment at the expense of the imagination, and to make cold and virtuous women instead of affectionate wives and agreeable companions to man. Society may be more tranquil and better regulated, but domestic life has often fewer charms. These, however, are secondary evils which may be braved for the sake of higher interests."

Courageous philosopher! My poor, inevitably self-sacrificing great-grandfather! The eminent virtue of your American woman was inseparable from the perfection of a great republic; and for the discomfort it brought upon man, the latter would receive a reward—in heaven and pure politics! How is all this changed at the end of the century! What the effect upon "higher interests" is to be is a question that coming years will answer; but so far as austerity of virtue is concerned, the American wife to-day may put a man quite at his ease.

The stupendous stride this country has taken in the development of depravity since De Tocqueville held us up to the admiration of the world is forcibly suggested by a statement he makes concerning American literature and its treatment of women and morals:

"In America all books, novels not excepted, suppose women to be chaste, and no one thinks of relating affairs of gallantry."

From what, then, have you sprung, all you unnumbered hosts of American erotic writers, and all you scandal-monging daily papers of the United States? I know. Your morals and your manners are a disorder that American *nouveau riches* have contracted in travelling abroad—to Paris and other places; and, once in the blood, the disorder has been transmitted to posterity. When De Tocqueville wrote, Western gold mines were locked in the bosom of the earth; the great Chicago hog was unborn; American enterprise had not penetrated the wells of commercial cunning from which stock is freely watered; Americans were still hard at work making fortunes, and not at a loss how to employ them, and earnest toil rather compelled virtue than deferred the opportunity of vice—an opportunity we realize to-day along with our boasted prosperity.

That the economically ideal organization of the American family has been overthrown by the aggressive spirit of the "new" woman appears with amazing clearness, placing De Tocqueville's view of the equality of the sexes in the United States of the earlier time in contrast with the facts of to-day:

"In no country has such constant care been taken as in America to trace two clearly distinct lines of action for the two sexes, and to make them keep pace one with the other, but in two pathways which are always different. American women never manage the outward concerns of the family or conduct a business or take a part in political life; nor are they, on the other hand, ever compelled to perform the rough labor of the fields, or to make any of those laborious exertions which demand the exhaustion of physical strength. No families are so poor as to form an exception to this rule."

Directly to the contrary to-day, over seventeen per cent. of the whole number of persons employed in all occupations are women. Furthermore, the United States Commissioner of Labor has found the number of women so employed to be constantly increasing, and that at the expense of men; the percentage of increase of women, in every given instance, showing a corresponding decrease of men. In this connection, still another suggestive fact appears in the statistics of the United States Department of Labor. In proportion as women advance in men's industries, and thus cause the retirement of men, the latter engage in domestic labor and personal service. The American woman competes with man, not alone to his disadvantage, but to his degradation.

Involved with this chaos in the industrial order, revolution with reference to sex constantly advances in the domain of American politics. We have woman's suffrage to some extent existing in a number of States and in several Territories of the United States, and absolutely unrestricted woman's suffrage in four States—making a total of almost three-fifths of the whole number of States in the Union which have in some way yielded political power to woman. Also we have the American woman clamoring for every office in the gift of the people, from President to police-court justice. Supporting and furthering this anomalous economic development of the American woman is a universal system of education, founded on a theory which assumes not alone equality of the sexes, but identity of rights and opportunity. In short, we have realized precisely the condition De Tocqueville describes as existing in the misguided minds of certain people in Europe, who, according to him, "confounding together the different characteristics of the sexes, would make of man and woman beings not only equal but alike. They would give to both the same functions, impose on both the same duties and grant to both the same rights; they would mix them in all things—their occupation, their pleasures, their business. It may readily be conceived that by thus attempting to make one sex equal to the other, both are degraded; and, from so preposterous a medley of the works of nature, nothing could ever result but weak men and disorderly women."

Further defining the admirable state of equality of the sexes originally prevailing in the United States, De Tocqueville says:

"Nor have the Americans ever supposed that one consequence of democratic principles is the subversion of marital power, or the confusion of the natural authorities in families. They held that every association must have a head in order to accomplish its object, and that the natural head of the conjugal association is man."

Certainly, this picture of wifely submission would move modern American women to scorn and their husbands to hollow mirth. Common experience anywhere in the United States to-day proves its absurdity as applied to the existing family order, and I have found, in a recent labor report of the State of Massachusetts, token of the anarchy and confusion involving "natural authorities" of the American family that is both formal and formidable.

The Bureau of Statistics of Labor of Massachusetts—Massachusetts, the State which is the greatest pride of American civilization—presenting facts concerning the earnings of heads of families, officially publishes a category of "husbands of heads of families." In this analysis of the situation there are recorded in Massachusetts eighty-five "husbands of heads of families."

Concluding his view of the happy organization of the family in America, De Tocqueville says: "I never observed that the women of America consider themselves degraded by submitting to conjugal authority. It appeared to me, on the contrary, that they attach a sort of pride to the voluntary surrender of their own will, and make it their boast to bend themselves to the yoke, not to shake it off. Such, at least, is the feeling expressed by the most virtuous of their sex."

Remembering what De Tocqueville conceived to be woman's contribution to political greatness—the morals of a country—and bearing in mind that the greatest moral force proceeds from self-immolation, the logical success of the old-fashioned American woman must be admitted.

"As for myself," says De Tocqueville, "I do not hesitate to avow that although the women of the United States are confined within the narrow circle of domestic life, and their situation is in some respects of extreme dependence, I have nowhere seen women occupying a loftier position, and if I were asked to what the singular prosperity and growing strength of the American people ought mainly to be attributed, I should reply—to the superiority of their women."

Considering the new form of superiority of the American woman at the end of the century—a superiority which is greater than all the domestic virtues, a superiority that boasts of feminine independence, a superiority that immortalizes woman and demoralizes man; considering this modern superiority of the American woman, one looks curiously to the future and asks, What of its effect upon our national character and standing?

FLORA McDONALD THOMPSON.

The Restless Woman

By His Eminence, J. Cardinal Gibbons

HAT woman was created to fill certain well-defined places in this world no one familiar with her physical, moral and mental make-up can doubt. That many women of to-day show a tendency to think slightingly of those privileges and responsibilities which have come down as the best inheritances of their sex is a fact which faces us on every side in this country of ours. It is more the case here than in any other nation, I regret to say. It has spread in the last few years like some great epidemic, until it has, to a distressing extent, affected the whole system of society and home government.

Modesty and gentleness, those two sweet handmaids of womankind, seem to have been laid aside by many, and masculinity and aggressiveness have been given their places.

The spirit of unrest has found easy victims in thousands of American homes, until the social condition which presents itself to-day, even among the best and most cultured classes, differs essentially from the standards heretofore held as inviolable. It is a sad and a dangerous change which confronts us. Its shibboleth would seem to be : masculinity is greater than motherhoood.

I wish I could impress on American women the dangers that attach to such innovations. I wish I could show them, as they appear to me, the ultimate results of participating in public life. It has but one end — the abandonment, or at least the neglect, of the home. And when the influence of the home is removed life loses one of its most valuable guides, and government its strongest ally — indeed, its cornerstone.

You remember, perhaps, what a great General of ancient times said: " Greece rules the world, Athens rules Greece, I rule Athens, my wife rules me, and, therefore, my wife rules the world." Nor is the illustration overdrawn. The woman who rules the domestic kingdom is in reality the ruler of all earthly kingdoms.

As I have said before, I regard woman's rights women and the leaders in the new school of female progress as the worst enemies of the female sex. They teach that which robs woman of all that is amiable and gentle, tender and attractive, and which gives her nothing in return but masculine boldness and brazen effrontery. They are habitually preaching about woman's rights and prerogatives, but have not a word to say about her duties and responsibilities. They will draw her from those sacred obligations which properly belong to her sex, and fill her with ambition to usurp a position for which neither God nor Nature ever intended her.

While professing to emancipate her from domestic servitude, they are making her the slave of her own caprices and passions. Under the influence of such teachers we find woman, especially in higher circles, neglecting her household duties, gadding about, at rest only when in perpetual motion, and never at ease unless in a state of morbid excitement. She never feels at home except when abroad. When she is at home, home is irksome to her. She chafes and frets under the restraint and responsibility of domestic life. Her heart is abroad. It is exulting in imagination, in some social triumph, or reveling in some scene of gayety and dissipation. Her husband comes to his home to find it empty, or occupied by one whose heart is void of affection for him. Then arise disputes, quarrels, recriminations, estrangements, and the last act in the drama is often divorce.

I speak the sober truth when I affirm that, for the wrecks of families in our country, woman has a large share of the responsibility. In so many instances she seems to have entirely forgotten, or purposely avoided, the place she is called upon to fill. She looks to material greatness in man as her guiding star. She wishes to do what men have done, and are doing. She enters this field, foreign to all her faculties and her strength, and seems to think she is living up to a higher standard than was ever before permitted to her kind. But if she stopped a moment to consider, could she find a mission more exalted, more noble or more influential than Christian wifehood and motherhood ? That makes her the helpmate of her husband, and the guide and teacher of her sons and daughters, rather than a stumbling-block in the way of all.

If woman would only remember that her influence over a child the first few years of its life can have greater effect, and produce wider and more lasting results, than her whole life given up to walking in the ways of men !

Where are the men that have achieved triumphs and have not owned that the debt was largely due their mothers? What know we of the mothers of the world's greatest men, save that most of them were faithful to their holy station and true to the high privilege of motherhood — the most divinely sanctioned and the noblest of all earthly positions ?

Christianity set its enduring seal on this Queendom in Bethlehem centuries ago, and the woman who seeks a higher sphere will not find it among men, or even in earth.

But the tendency of the times is altogether apart from such things. Women must be independent, and masculine. They must even indulge in all the sports formerly classed as masculine. They take to these not as occasional pleasures, but as constant pursuits. I see no harm in a woman's taking part once in a while in a game of golf, or any other outdoor exercise that befits her station. She is not to be housed like a plant, and never allowed the benefits derived from fresh air and moderate exercise. Any proper outdoor pursuit should be encouraged as an occasional recreation, but as a regular avocation it must be condemned. For pleasures that become habitual are no longer mere recreations, but serious occupations.

Then consider the woman who must join a club, or perhaps two or three clubs. These will require her presence or attention several hours of the day. How can she do all this and at the same time fulfill the duties of domestic life? After the labors of the day the husband rightly expects to find a comfortable home, where peace, good order and tranquillity reign. But his heart

276

filled with sadness and despair if he finds the partner of his bosom attending a club, or neglecting her household duties for those of some semi-political or social organization.

There is another phase of this great question which I resents a most dangerous aspect. When the home is abandoned, what follows? The substitution of flats and hotels as residences, where, instead of having a home in any sense of the word, women are merely escaping the responsibilities and the cares of domestic life.

♣

But if domestic life has its cares and responsibilities —and what life has not?—it also has its sweetness and its consolations, its joys and its benefits, that are infinitely superior to anything that can possibly be obtained in hotels or flats. It is manifest that hotels do not furnish the same privacy and the same safeguard against questionable associations that are supplied by the home.

I am glad for their own sake that American women generally do not exercise the privilege of political suffrage. I regret that there are those among our American women who have left their homes and families to urge on their kind the need of suffrage. I hope the day will never come when in this land all women will be allowed to register their votes, save, perhaps, in municipal elections which come near to the home, and might, therefore, properly be influenced by those who should be responsible for the home.

Who enters the political arena is sure to be soiled by its mud. As soon as woman thrusts herself into politics and mingles with the crowd to deposit her vote, she must expect to be handled roughly, and to surrender, perhaps wholly, at least in part, that reverence now justly paid her. The more woman gains in the political arena the more she loses in the domestic kingdom. She cannot rule in both spheres.

The model woman is not she who takes up all the "ologies" and scientific studies. She is not the woman who is constantly seen and heard in public places, the woman who insists upon entering all branches of trade and commerce, and pursuing all lines of thought, who wanders restlessly through the world.

The model woman, thanks to Christianity, is she who is thus sung of in Holy Writ: "Who shall find a valiant woman? far and from the uttermost coasts is the price of her. . . . She hath looked well to the paths of her house, and hath not eaten her bread idle. Her children rose up, and called her blessed: her husband, and he praised her. . . . Beauty is vain: the woman that feareth the Lord, she shall be praised." Proverbs xxxi.

♣

American women, your husbands are the sovereigns of America, and if you be the sovereigns of your husbands, then, indeed, you would rule the nation. That should be glory enough for you. We are more governed by ideals than by ideas. We are influenced more by living, breathing models than by abstract principles of virtue.

The model that should be held up to American women of to-day is not the Amazon, glorying in her martial deeds and powers; not the Spartan, who made female perfection to consist in the development of physical strength at the expense of feminine decorum and modesty; not the goddess of impure love like Venus, whose votaries regarded beauty of form and personal charms as the highest types of womanly excellence. No, the model that should be held up before you and all women is Mary, the mother of Christ. She is the great pattern of virtue, and all that goes to make the perfect woman alike to maiden, wife and mother.

Co-Education in Colleges

I.—A Man's View

By W. A. Curtis

IT would seem as if co-education were still on trial and that not yet had the popular verdict been rendered. A decade ago we thought it had completely vindicated itself. College after college was opening its doors to women; and to-day, west of Pennsylvania and north of Mason and Dixon's line, there are more colleges exclusively for women than exclusively for men. Indeed, Wabash and Notre Dame in Indiana, and Kenyon in Ohio, are the only men's colleges in the region. A decade ago we believed that opposition to co-education would soon entirely fade away. To be sure, we were far from believing that all colleges would open their doors to women, but the attitude of even the colleges that steadfastly proclaimed their intention to remain exclusively male colleges was not one of condemnation of co-education. Rather was it the wish for the preservation of local customs, the adherence to old traditions, a resistance to any sort of innovation and change in the pleasant old monastic life that linked them not only to the past of their own institution, but to the past of all universities back to Oxford, Paris, Salamanca, and Padua.

But within the past few years there has been a change in the attitude toward co-education, a strong change in the attitude of the male students everywhere, and here and there a reflection and response to this attitude on the part of faculties and trustees.

Here and there this has taken concrete form; now as discrimination, ostracism, proscription, and even downright insult of the women students by their male compatriots, now as restriction upon their numbers and onerous disabilities intended indirectly to restrict their numbers, imposed by faculties and trustees. For years

Cornell male students have ostracized their women. College women are rarely seen at the swell balls of the year, "imported" girls furnishing the necessary partners for the scornful men. The University of Michigan some time ago began to follow Cornell's example, and a later imitator, the University of Wisconsin, goes into the importing business even more than Michigan. Two years ago, at the University of Chicago, the girls made a protest because they were no longer invited to the university functions and the boys went beyond the quadrangle for their girls. At the University of Minnesota the Greek-letter society girls will tell you that they have harder work each year keeping up their membership, for the reason that so many Minneapolis families now send their daughters to women's colleges or keep them at home. In all of these universities brothers discourage their sisters from attending. The reason they give is that they do not like to see their sisters descend from the pedestal they occupy at home and lose the glamour that surrounds them anywhere but within college walls, to see them put aside, notwithstanding beauty and accomplishments, girls far their inferior, but who have the indisputable claim to homage that they are "imported." Indeed, I am prepared to state, and have the support of my fellow hardened alumni, that the girls of my Alma Mater are far more lovely than the girls the students import and ask us to admire. The chillness of our response does nothing but convince them that we are fogies and no connoisseurs, and the fact that the Supreme Court, sitting *en banc* as invited guests at the great function of the year, the junior ball, has year after year rendered a decision favorable to the college girls, has no effect upon the importers.

279

Rather do they think that our judicial system needs altering.

Some of our colleges have shown something more than a passive opposition taking the shape of social non-intercourse. Barbaric acts have been committed in colleges both East and West that have caused us to ask if American chivalry were dead. Rising almost to riots, demonstrations have occurred in some of our institutions that have made the whole country blush. Had some decadent Latin country been guilty in like manner, not yet would these things have passed from our national remembrance, and the speaker and writer descanting upon Anglo-Saxon virtues would have pointed many a moral with them.

Leland Stanford Junior University—what a dreadful name, with all due respect to that mighty institution, precursor and precedent for such Philistine titles as John B. Stetson University, George H. Smith College (colored), and others to follow—has passed a regulation that the number of girls must never be more than thirty-five per cent. of the total number of students. Colby is mooting a similar regulation. At Northwestern a year ago, for the first time, the number of girls in the senior class of the college of liberal arts, or academic, as they say at most colleges, equaled the number of boys. A trustee at the alumni banquet said that the number of girls must be restricted, that the university was becoming a woman's institution. He was cheered to the echo. The trustees and Dr. James, the new President, are in favor of reducing the proportion of girls. A late remark of Dr. James to the effect that co-education is still on trial at Northwestern has flashed all over the country. At Northwestern, of all places! The university where it has hitherto been proclaimed the most successful, and where hitherto the trustees have been regularly accused of spending more money on the girls than on the boys!

Though Northwestern, on the northern borders of Chicago, is a threatening point, its rival on the south side of the city is the present storm-center of the co-educational question. The University of Chicago has actually banished co-education. The various co-ordinate branches that carry on the university government have voted and revoted to segregate women.

At this institution there are three legislative bodies or houses, which correspond somewhat to the National Senate and House of Representatives. The Board of Trustees forms the highest of these. Members of the Faculty compose the others. Among them, these bodies have considered the matter some time, and the removal of the girls has been decided upon. They are to have separate classes, separate buildings, a separate quadrangle. Dozens of woman's clubs passed condemnatory resolutions; the alumnæ of the University and the Association of Collegiate Alumnæ protested. The press was severe. The public expected to see the University retire from its position and rescind the obnoxious edict, but though it wavered for a while, it now stands firm.

The professors assign as the principal cause of the edict the fact that the young men neglect their studies because of the girls, and that particularly they are inattentive in the class-room because of looking at the girls. This sounds rather strange in view of the complaint of the girls that the boys show them no attention. It sounds strange in view of the fact that no one alleges that the girls neglect their studies because of the boys and are prone to inattention in the class-room because of making sheep's eyes at them.

In a discussion of a question like this one must give opinions and cannot give statistics. The Germanic habit of piling up appalling heaps of statistics, which has accompanied the Germanizing of our educational methods down to a Germanizing of our pronunciation of English, has about driven individual opinion from our modern discussions. Inferences from phenomena of human nature inspire little respect. Only deductions that are but sums of columns of figures are now convincing. Nevertheless, I am going to exercise my Yankee prerogative and proceed to make some inferences.

The action of the University of Chicago faculty is a response to a sentiment of the male students. Were they to attempt to show that better work was done in exclusively male or female colleges, they would ignominiously fail. Their contention that class work suffers finds nothing to rest upon. It is, then, a response to the voice of the male in the University of Chicago, which is the voice of the university men of America, which is but the first peeping of what shall presently be the voice of all the men of America! For this is no educational question, no university question, this attack upon co-education. It is a social question, a fundamental question of the most serious character, whose subterranean fires slowly gathering have broken through the crust in the weak spot of the universities, but shall soon belch everywhere. This is no university matter, this eruption of hostility to woman, for hostility it is, naked hostility, in its ungenerous and unchivalric expression. It is man, face to face with the fact that woman in this twentieth century is not his ally, his helpmeet, his wife, but his competitor, his rival, and that of all the meeds, the prizes, the rewards of life that she cheats him out of, it is the supremest prize, herself !

Once woman doubled our joys and halved our sorrows. She now halves our incomes and doubles those seeking employment. Declaiming against the injustice of paying her half what a man got, in her blindness to the fact that the man got twice as much in order that he might give her half, she has succeeded in getting her rate of compensation raised somewhat, but his has descended to meet it. And so, some assert, result the unmarried and unhappy thousands of women and the unmarried and hardly less unhappy thousands of men, so the increase of the social evil, so the weakening of the National stamina that assails a nation where family life is passing.

Blindly, unconsciously, rudely, unchivalrously, yet with a righteous purpose at bottom, though he know it not, the college man strikes at co-education. In the college he sees woman serving an apprenticeship for active life in the world. Every girl who stays at home tacitly admits that she hopes and expects to be a wife. Talk with a college woman. She will, just as a man, tell what she " is going to do " when she graduates. There is no tacit admission that she expects or hopes to be a wife. She is preparing for a life of competition with the man. She is preparing herself to assist in a state of things which brings it about that neither she nor any other woman may be the wife of the boy she sits beside in class.

Other women enter active life; not all

college women do by any means. But you can nowhere else put your finger on a whole class who are likely to do so. The college boy does not object to the college girl because she is learned. If neither she nor any other woman were ever to be part of a system that prevents him from having a wife at all, or defers marriage until his head is bald, his joints stiff, and romance dead within him, he would rejoice in her attainments. But now he talks of the womanliness of the girls who stay at home. He prates of this. He harps upon it pitifully. " They are different." He finds a charm in them. Their dream of life is solely of him. The college woman may include him as a possibility in her dream, but he is only a part of it and not a probable or essential part. The college woman is not responsible for the present condition of affairs. She did not create it. Numerically, she is not a large factor. But she is a sure factor, and the college man, obeying one of those strange psychological waves that sweep over a nation and make all blind, unconscious agents in a great change, a great reform, is trying to save her from herself. Cruelly, sometimes even dastardly ; unseeing the end, unknowing what urges him, from Colby of Maine to Leland Stanford Junior of California, from Wesleyan of Connecticut to the University of Wisconsin, he is striking at the inversion of a natural order, at the destruction of what makes life most dear, striking the defenseless woman, too, doing things to make one weep, yet to save that woman.

Co-education will not pass. All that it ever was it is and shall be. But the competition of woman with man will pass. In just such measure as woman has increasingly driven man out of his wonted employments, in such degree has our national courtesy departed, in such degree has the opposition to co-education grown. The movement of which this college agitation is the forerunner, the social movement which has first had its expression in the field where plainly could be pointed out cause for a deplorable effect, will soon become general. The question removed from the colleges, the balance of life restored, the college man of the future, as the college man of past years, will rejoice in the culture and learning of this college girl, who, no longer his rival, his com- petitor, is his wife. Toward this happy outcome of it all we look forward with hopeful eyes. But the poor girls of the last decade, and the poor boys, it is too late for them, too late!

THE WOMAN PROBLEM

I. SHALL WOMEN VOTE?

A STUDY OF FEMININE UNREST—ITS CAUSES AND ITS REMEDIES

By *Ouida**

Author of " Under Two Flags," " A Dog of Flanders," etc.

🌱

EW things can appear more curious to a dispassionate observer than the foam of discontent seething up amongst women at the present day. Any discontent, if it be strong enough, will produce revolution; but a not uncommon result of revolution is a recoil into a more despotic absolutism than any that existed before the rebellion. It is possible that such a result will follow on the present revolt of womankind; meantime, coupled with another equally prominent feature of their sex in the present time, it is certainly one of the most curious of our social phenomena. We have studied it as such with some degree of attention, and we have come to the conclusion that, despite the prominence of its school, it is not altogether so original as it believes, and it does not very clearly know what it actually aims at and requires.

"Equality with men," we are answered. But this is exceedingly difficult to define. Of course it is perfectly easy to pass jests upon, and concoct witticisms out of, such a subject; they suggest themselves by the million. The harder effort is to avoid the attractively and facilely ludicrous side of the subject and write upon it seriously. All jests apart, it is something difficult to define—this equality with men that is the female cry of the hour. If equality in privileges be taken, equality in

* Mlle. Louise de la Ramée, better known as Ouida, the brilliant novelist, wrote these two papers more than twenty-five years ago and sold them to this magazine with the stipulation that they should be withheld from the public until after her death. She passed away in Viarreggio, Italy, January 25, 1908, and we are now free to give to the public these extraordinary documents which, in her characteristic chirography, have remained in the editor's safe so many years—passing uninjured through the great fire of 1899. The first paper is quite prophetic of the world-wide interest now obtaining in the question of woman's suffrage. The second presents a serious and startling philosophy of an evil as wide-spread as it is appalling. On both these grave questions, it will be understood, Ouida spoke for herself, and not as a mouthpiece for this magazine.   THE EDITOR.

liabilities must be enforced also. Are women to go to this extreme?—to become soldiers if they become surgeons; to become sailors if they become statesmen? We doubt if they are prepared to reach this length; but unless they are, the desire for " equality with men " is only another phase of the desire for every privilege and the exemption from every penalty.

We can thoroughly sympathize with the impatience of a clever woman at seeing herself excluded from an arena of public life in which some masculine fools and many masculine mediocrities succeed. We are fully prepared to admit that here and there may arise a woman of such brilliant abilities that she would be fully capable of governing an empire or manœuvring an army. But such women come once in five centuries; and this question is not of exceptional, but of all, women. The equality demanded is not for the few, but for the many. It is of the admission of the many to its rights and exercises that we have to treat; not of the admission of the two or three great women who may adorn a century, and who, be it noted, generally contrive to do well for themselves and rarely are participants in the cry of which we have heard so much in late years. Where real genius appears it levels sex: but this is at all times rare, in women rarest, and it is of the vast mass of " the general " that we speak. Maria Theresa, Catherine, Manon, Roland, Hypatia, Corinna, Sappho, will always make their own mark on the world's history; but the plea now raised is for the admission of all women—on the simple score of womanhood—to the possession of the paths and thrones of men.

Now, if sex be the pure physical accident that some psychologists affirm, it is certainly hard that it alone should confer such oft-un-merited superiority on those who, happily for themselves, chance to be males. Yet, if the " accident of sex " has not thus bestowed superiority, how comes it that the world has had no female Phidias, Tacitus, Plato, Cicero, Euripides, Plautus, or Thucydides? Women reply: " Because we have not been educated." There is some truth in this; a long succession of such emasculating education as the female sex has received generation after generation must tend greatly to debilitate and enervate the intelligence. But again the very fact that they have not insisted on better education, have not obtained it for themselves, is a proof of integral difference if we avoid the needlessly offensive term of inferiority.

In the prehistoric ages, in the times of the lake-cities and the dwellers in caves, we know that men were markedly inferior to the beasts of the desert and the saurians of the swamps. Against the enormous animals and serpents then existing men did wage continual and most unequal war, continually being vanquished and eaten up by these fearful creatures against which they possessed neither weapons nor armor commensurate with the huge tusks of the mastodon, the impenetrable hide of the rhinoceros, the jaws of the crocodile, the talons of the tiger and the bear.   Yet the issue was that in the end the originally weaker but integrally superior race ultimately conquered, subjugated, and from many parts extirpated the stronger; and by force of reason reigned alone.   In the same manner we conceive that women—had they been superior to their males as were their males to the beasts, by mind that overcame matter—would have conquered for themselves some sort of supremacy, or at any rate that equal position from which they now complain they have been perforce kept out, in the many hundreds and thousands of years that have seen them upon the earth.   If they had, of a truth, been possessed with a thirst for that learning and attainment which they assert has been so long denied them, could anything have drawn them back from its gratification?   If they had been born with a passionate craving for pure knowledge, could the schools have barred them out through all these centuries?   We cannot think so.

That women should, however tardily, awaken to a desire for greater intellectual light is of the utmost promise.   Education cannot confer genius, but it can do an infinite work in the refinement, the strengthening, and the enlightening of the mind; in the banishment of prejudice and in the correction of illogical judgment.   In view of the manifold superstitions, intolerances, and ignorances that prevail in the female intelligence, and of the fearful influence which these in turn bring to bear upon the children committed in such numbers to their charge, no crusade that can find favor with them, towards a New Jerusalem of Culture, can be too eagerly encouraged.

When we reflect on the enormous weight which the woman's influence has on the growing child; when we consider the incurable superstitions, the unreasonable fables, the illogical deductions, the warped and stifled prejudgments, which millions of young boys learn in education and religion at their mother's knee in infancy—it is impossible to overrate the invaluable consequences of any introduction of *geist* into the minds of women.   But for the backward pressure of woman—woman ever conservative, ever *réculante,* ever wedded to form and to precedent and to tradition—the world of men would have forsaken many a *cultus* built on fable, many a dominion of priestcraft, many a limbo of worn-out and oppressive credulity.   The evil mental influence of women is fully as great as can be the good moral influence of the best of their sex. Wars hounded on; fetters freshly riveted; the withes of dead beliefs binding down the free action of living limbs; the pressure of narrow ties, and of egotisms deified to virtue, forcing men aside from paths of greatness or of justice—all these, and much more, are due to the baneful intellectual influence of women.

It is from his mother's hands—she meanwhile believing that she holds to his lips the waters of life—that the awakening reason of the young boy drinks in the poisons of priestcraft, of religious fear, of illogical belief, of credulous bias; poisons that cramp and numb the mind which thus receives them; and which, if ever they be expelled in after years by wiser thought, still will not quit the soul in which they have sunk without pangs and throes of pain and reluctance. The poet writes with facile and fluent beauty of the benignant influence on later life of the early teachings of the mother, of the purifying and elevating effect that the memories of these early impregnations of the spirit exercise in after-time: doubtless there is truth as well as sentiment in this; but we believe that a considerably greater truth may be traced on the opposite view of the same question, and that in countless instances the evil done unconsciously to budding minds by the weak and superstitious lessons, given in all good faith by women to the offspring who take their dictum as a law divine, is incalculable and retards in an immeasurable ratio the progress and the liberties of the world. Therefore, we repeat, everything that can be done for the extension and the fortification of female intelligence is invaluable. We fully agree that women cannot too thoroughly receive the same intellectual culture as men, but we doubt if the manner in which they now agitate the subject will produce this result, and we also doubt if they have at all fairly considered the issue and the consequences of this movement.

The cry for "equality with men" is much the same thing as the roughs' cry for equality in government. In both instances the rights of citizenship are demanded; but the responsibilities of citizenship are shirked. The woman demands the exercise of political power, the rough does the same, but as the rough will not relinquish his enjoyment of lawlessness and license, so the woman will not relinquish her claim on social deference and social precedence. He is to remain a rough in his privileges of drinking, stone-throwing, and slang,—she is to remain a woman in her privileges of etiquette, homage, chivalry, and beauty; but both, surrendering nothing, are to receive a full and free grant of all electoral and representative rights; both are to be able to reverse the decree and invade the domain of those who, exercising political power, do also bear the burden of political responsibilities. Now as the vast body of educated and respectable men do resist this monopoly as proposed by the rough, so it is scarcely wonderful do they also resist the mononoply as proposed by woman. Briefly the case stands thus: an enlightened and honorable man must submit to be jostled and trampled by the one, and must stand aside deferentially with hat in hand for the other, and is only in return to have invaded and snatched away the few civil superiorities to both that he has hitherto enjoyed. Who can say that this is just?

If roughs and women be henceforth to rule (as rule they must through their overwhelming numbers if admitted to any share in governmental power), both should be prepared to make the sacrifices required; the one to surrender the vice and ignorance and dishonesties of their careers, the other to surrender the courtesies and suavities and securities of their position. The question of the former we leave to politicians; it is with the latter alone that we are concerned. And it is precisely this sacrifice that women will not make: we have known many vehement upholders of " women's rights " who claim for their sex the title to be politicians, physicians, anything that they choose, but we never knew one of them who would endure the suggestion of waiving in consequence the feminine demand for deference, homage, and all the graceful amenities that men have paid to women through the generous concession of the stronger to the feebler being. Yet what can be more absurd or more unjust than that women should bully their way into their national parliaments, share in the public administrations, fight in the rough and tumble of public contests, and take the place of men in every profession and pursuit, yet all the while claim the *pas* by virtue of their sex and exact that abdication in their favor which has been conceded to them out of reverence for the very inequality they so scornfully repudiate.

Herein, we conceive, lies the whole radical weakness of the present hue and cry raised by women: *i.e.,* the demand for everything with the resolve to concede nothing; the desire for admission into public life combined with total ignorance of all that public life exacts so heavily from its disciples. Women are prepared to rant loudly of their wrongs, and to agitate for an equal share in the government of their nations; but they are in no sense prepared to relinquish the pleasant privileges conferred on them by the present position of their sex, and to lay down the silver sceptre of their present social station. They desire to keep their feet still standing on the dais.of their old womanly royalty, whilst they reach their hands upward to pluck down the iron crowns of public and political honors.

It is not astonishing that in such an effort they overbalance themselves. If they are to fight at all, they must fight fairly, but this they show no inclination whatsoever to do. They are to be throned on the stone throne of the Acropolis, but all the while they are not to quit the rose aisles of their Armida's garden—such at least is all we can infer from their present attitude and outcry. Nor does it seem to occur to them that there is anything anomalous in the demand. And it is a little ludicrous to observe that in America, where the clamor for female rights is raised most loudly, there also are courtesy and obedience and subserviency to women, *as women,* exacted in the most ridiculously exaggerated manner. For a woman to state that she has the right to knock you out of your seat in Congress or Parliament and occupy your place herself, yet that she has also the right to expect you to give up your seat in a railway carriage and stand for her accommodation throughout a journey of hours, is a form of oppression as absurd as it is illogical. The strength that can achieve the political conquest and the weakness that can exact the social courtesy cannot possibly be leashed together. A woman must choose between the two: either she must " leave the one and obey the other, or she must forsake the one and cleave to the other." It is impossible that the two forms of right, so totally and irreconcilably distinct, can ever be conceded to her.

We wish that this absolute necessity of choice could be enforced upon the sex at large, for it were idle to deny that women are becoming extremely ill-contented with the position that they occupy, and the best thing for them and for mankind would be that they should be led to consider the subject impersonally and rationally if possible.

It will be conjectured that we do not ourselves apprehend that women have so very much of which to complain, or that their position is in any sense so intolerable as they regard it. We avow that it is so: we think that women are on the whole very fairly placed, and that the remedy for all that is vexatious lies chiefly in their own hands. The influence of women is already very great, and, although indirect, can be almost infinitely extended. We have no sort of prejudice on this subject: we know well that there are women who make splendid financiers, scholars, authors, and even mathematicians. We doubt not that the numbers of these would increase largely were the crucial test of examination by male examiners more generally brought as the criterion and the incitement of female studies, were the abilities and aspirations of brilliant women not so continually crushed out by the foolish fear of publicity in which they are brought up, and by the endless monotony of either domestic commonplace or fashionable frivolity. We are certain that if women were in early youth led to take keen interest in some one study, science, or pursuit, their lives would be infinitely happier, and the man who brought daughters into the world would not be guilty as he is now of mercilessly adding to the already overgrown numbers of the most useless animal in all creation. We cannot picture to ourselves a creature more deeply to be pitied than the father of grown up and growing girls who has to spend all his income on the brainless heads and the countless dresses of a tribe of young women who, at their best, can only be got rid of in marriage, exacting as their dower what cripples him no less than did their maintenance. With all these beliefs, therefore, it can scarcely be doubted that we earnestly desire to see women of more use and more capable of self-support than they are now (although we confess to a keen dread of the increase of mediocrity and commonplace that will probably attend the first deluge of women into any art or profession); and we are perfectly convinced that the world will be infinitely benefited if other means of livelihood are opened to them. But it is precisely because we attach so much vital and widespread import to the mental improvement of womankind that we do infinitely regret to see a cause so good and unassailable mixed up with cries so vague and often so preposterous as those we hear so often anent " female rights."

We cannot see what there is to prevent women attaining to the highest mental elevation if they are personally capable of doing so. True, the foolish and almost useless system of female education does all it can to retard the growth of female talent. The whole mode of instruction is vitally and utterly wrong. Still, it is almost as wrong in masculine schools; and we cannot think that if women genuinely desired high culture and fine attainment they would find any difficulty in obtaining both. Wherever a woman has genius enough to " dare greatly " she invariably finds the means to do greatly also. We know of an English princess—mother of a great English statesman—whom Arago declared to be as consummate a calculator as he himself, yet here the eminence was won simply from pure love of science, and the study pursued against many temptations of high rank and worldly honors. There is nothing to prevent women from being great painters, greater composers, great poets, great students, even great architects, great astronomers, or great classicists, if they develop the genius, the patience, and the unwavering purpose needed for all greatness. When they have more largely shown greatness in these forms of intellectual splendor, it will surely be time enough to claim a place wherein to display the additional intellectual capabilities that are developed in legislation and in all forms of political life. We are not denying that it may ultimately prove possible for women to attain all the eminence that we have mentioned: we only say that it is unwise and unreasonable to raise a clamor for the one arena denied them whilst there are still so many gladiatorial contests open in which they are free, but decline to engage.

MODERN THOUGHT

There are three phases of modern thought, which however they may differ in other respects, all unite in their
earnest advocacy of woman suffrage, namely, Progressivism,
Socialism and the propaganda of the Industrial Workers of
the World.

The modern progressive party, through its public tactics,
however it may urge on the side, certain tentative and wholly
theoretical economic measures, makes this doctrine a leading
one in its claim for public support. Socialism has put it forward as its first demand in every platform which it has issued
for the last quarter of a century. The "Industrial Workers of
the World" is a comparatively new party, ostensibly devoted
to the interests of the working people and the equal rights of
all, both men and women. It is in fact Socialism gone to
seed; that is Socialism which has reached its last and reproductive stage, the stage wherein talk gives place to action.
It is therefore as might be expected, more pronounced in
theory than any of the old parties.

The Chicago Tribune of December 1st, 1912, has an editorial entitled "Emotional Unionism" describing the Industrial
Worker whose companionship it is evidently a little ashamed
of, in which he and the movement which he represents are
set forth in the following terms.

"When a national organization, nation-wide in its scope,
inscribes the word revolution upon its banner, its leaders,
theories and literature become of public interest, the Industrial Workers of the World is such an organization.

"The extent to which the activity of the I. W. W. is regulated by emotion, passion and prejudice, rather than by clear
thinking is evinced by its literature. The entire literature
of this movement which promises to right all the wrongs of
humanity by means of revolution over night, consists of half

a dozen pamphlets. Each of these represents the central idea that employers and employes have nothing in common, and the workers should aim to wrest all control of industry from the hands of its present possessors. All the I. W. W. leaders are swayed by emotion rather than reason. They are men of no education or have a smattering of education, which is worse than none at all. They are men who have sprung from the most desperate, the most hopeless strata of the working class. The program of the I. W. W. with its direct means of getting even with society, appeals to these men largely because it offers an opportunity to wreaking vengance.

"There is another important feature about the I. W. W. agitators. The majority of them, in fact almost all of them—are men without family ties. They know of no responsibilities or obligations," which of course includes the repudiation of marriage and the home. "'The majority of them are absolutely' non-moral. This emotional unionism with its recklessness, open appeal to vengeance upon industry, upon their employer, is just the sort of unionism which the great masses of unskilled workers who have real grievances against present industrial conditions, understand most easily. The I. W. W. by devoting itself entirely to these unskilled and exploited masses, bids fair therefore to become the vortex of industrial turmoil in this country."

Thus far the **Tribune**. The question that we now desire to ask is, Why is it that these three classes, the Progressivists, the Socialists and the I. W. W.'s all base their proposed Social reform upon Woman Suffrage, or to use the most euphemistic language at hand, "equal work, equal pay and equal political privileges for both sexes."

And first let us notice that **there are** three classes and what they stand for. Progressivism in general regards marriage and the institution of the Home as a mere social incident, founded upon any present whim or desire. It thus opens a wider door for divorce, and attaches little opprobrium to the breaking of the relations between the sexes, whatever may be the consequences to such children as may have been born of the sexual relation. It encourages the labor of woman in fields hitherto regarded as the express heritage of men, as mill work, factory work, commercial enterprises and the like, to the robbery of female employments, which call for womanly traits; and instead of curbing these growing inclinations of the day, and encouraging womanly virtues, it scoffs at the home and lures girls more and more into the life of cafes, restaurants, hotels, places which all tend to bring about equality between men and women and the adoption of masculine habits, even in such personal matters as smoking, drinking and the like.

Socialism is quite as publicly advocated, makes even a more scornful jest of marriage and the home and has been for more than fifty years, corrupting the American mind on the matter of those well-known virtues of patience, honesty and upright rule, upon which our government was founded.

The I. W. W. has attracted attention within the past few years, and largely by the importation of such foreign words and ideas as "sabotage," which may be understood as the wooden shoe of the peasant kicking down the institutions reared by intelligence and spiritual aspiration to strengthen and solace the soul of man, or "syndicalism" which we of an earlier time knew by the more easily understood term of governmental communism, making its way to the front of the "advanced" system of modern thought, a growing multitude forging itself into a mass of immoral citizens ready to substitute a bullet for the ballot; and here let us say, that while a person without intelligence may innocently be unintelligent, a person who is "non-moral" must necessarily be immoral, because to be without morals is necessarily an immoral quality.

These advocates of modern thought range in their sphere of action from the highest to the lowest human beings, but each and every class of them founds itself from the beginning to the end upon the one doctrine of Woman Suffrage. And why? For two reasons. In the first place that all human beings, men and women as well, may be equal upon the material plane, equal as workmen, equal in opportunities, equal in political privileges. It is an egregious folly and mistake, born of ignorance and low ideals, to imagine that political privileges are withheld from woman because she is not capable of exercising them, however unsuitable they may be to her physiological make-up. They belong to man together with his physical and intellectual strength, because in no other way can he be the equal of that bright and spiritually minded creature whom God made in the beginning to be his help meet and equal,—the mother of the race.

For a second reason, this reversal of Woman's place in Nature, this placing her upon a forced and unnatural equality with man, promises to the unthinking multitude a solution of certain economic difficulties, of which a true observation and reason shows at once the folly and the absurdity. The quieter and more thoughtful of the race see in the elevation of the child through a truer education and mothering, the rising up of a new contingent of both men and women, to whom a better sense of the real objects of Nature from the first, shall come; the work of constantly elevating and purifying the unselfishness of the race, and giving to the world a new sense of the honor and the glory of the spiritual as above the material side of life. And this is a work to be done by woman and woman only. She may, indeed must, have the cordial and unselfish co-operation of the father of the race but he alone can never accomplish without her intuition and direction, the work which it is given her by Heaven to do, and which increases in amount and value with each generation and to which the attention of the philanthropist is called in this age as never before. It is a work which joins the two sections of the race in a tender and elevating co-operation and gives a new meaning to the old prophecy, "And a little child shall lead them."

Chicago, December, 1912.

Issued by the Illinois Association Opposed to Woman Suffrage.

1523 Dearborn Avenue, Chicago.

Our Perilous Waste of Vitality

Transcribed from
Literary Digest April 1912

We have often been warned that the hurry and rush of modern life is a grave danger to humanity, individually and racially. The warning is given in a particularly clear and outspoken way by Dr. Max G. Schlapp, head of the department of neuropathology in the Cornell Medical School, in an article entitled "The Enemy at the Gate," contributed to The Outlook *(New York, April 6). Not only is Dr. Schlapp a specialist in the diseases of the nervous system, but he also, as volunteer examiner of children brought before the Children's Court in New York City, has had an unusual opportunity of observing the relation between delinquency and mental defectiveness. The statistics he cites are but illustrative examples selected from a large number of tables of figures collected by him from official sources. The substance of his article is thus briefly stated in the editorial pages of* The Outlook. *He holds:*

"That the strain of modern industrial life is having an effect upon men, and especially upon women, that can be traced biologically; that it is such as to impair the vigor and the faculties of a great proportion of children that are in these days being born into the world; that the effect is seen in injury to motherhood, in a reduced birth-rate, in an increase in the proportion of the mentally defective, the mentally unbalanced, and the delinquent; and that the resultant conditions are such that only by a radical change in the present tendencies can modern civilized peoples be saved from going the way of the Greeks and the Romans."

Dr. Schlapp's figures are striking but not unfamiliar. The "emeny" of which he warns us is "the tension of modern life," embodied in our industrial and social systems. Its results, he tells us, are criminals, imbeciles, and defectives in all grades of life, high and low, indicating no less a calamity than the breakdown of the human race. Not only are criminality and mental deficiency increasing all over the world, but births are decreasing. True, science has also decreased the death-rate, but it can not continue to do so indefinitely. Says the writer:

"With the birth-rate then falling as it has been falling in the most advanced countries of the world, the end either of the present-day civilization or the end of all becomes apparent. It is not alone because fewer children are being brought into the world that we have cause for grave concern for the perpetuity of the races. It is not alone because children are not coming in sufficient numbers, but because the number of defectives born has grown alarmingly, and is constantly increasing in proportion to each 1,000 of population. This is the awful menace. The power of human thought and action is shackled before it. We may modify it, check it in places, but we can not exterminate it by any process known to us now, or that seems at this time likely to come to us, unless we can change the temper and reduce the intensity of our modern industrial and social life."

The physical mechanism by which the strain of modern life produces and must inevitably continue to produce such dire results is thus sketched by Dr. Schlapp:

"The fertilized egg of a fish is composed of a single cell. The single cell has the faculty of dividing itself, making two perfect cells. These two perfect cells have the faculty of dividing themselves, making eight. These eight perfect cells have the faculty of dividing themselves, making sixteen. These sixteen perfect cells have the power of dividing themselves, making thirty-two. This is the normal process to infinity of numbers, and this is the proportion in which the cells multiply until the fish is grown. These cells in the forming fish divide again into groups, each group having a special function. Thus there will be skin-cells, muscle-cells, gland-cells, blood-cells, brain-cells, and, most important of all to its species, sex-cells. Anything that interferes with the development of these cells in the precise proportions in which they must grow will affect the type, and, instead of a fish, there will be a monster.

"Human beings are in no sense differently developed from birth. From inception children pass throught the same process as the fish from the egg until they reach manhood and womanhood.

"When overwrought women have disturbed within themselves the processes of nature, they impart a disturbance to their offspring, and, as in the case of the fish, instead of the development of a normal human being, there is one distorted in body or mind, or in both. It is fundamental that the female must be quiescent. It is fundamental because of the basic difference between the male and the female cells. The female cell is quiescent. Its normal development depends upon this state.

"Latter-day women, driven by the strife of the elements within them to enormous exertions, are asking in what way women are inferior to men and are attempting to demonstrate their equal physical endurance. It is not a question of equality at all. It is one of physical difference in the sexes which forbids women from performing either factory labor or disquieting tasks."

We are kept alive and kept in proper balance by a great number of vital processes, some of which were not recognized until the investigation of recent physiologists had called our attention to them. The so-called "ductless glands," each manufacturing its own peculiar product and pouring it forth into the blood, are now known to be indispensable to the proper workings of the human machine. Distrubance of any one of them is fraught with quickly apparent injury. Without one of these products the nerves fail; loss of another may weaken the brain; lack of a third may take away all coordination in the growth of members and organs.

"These are simple illustrations of the necessity of maintaining the balance within the body. The busy man, working with all his driving force for twelve or fifteen hours a day, using either his brain or his body to excess—it makes no difference which—

is drawing to whatever group of nerve-cells that he is directly employing in his labor more than their quota of nerve energy. The other body-cells are not supplied, and the sapping begins. The glands that secrete the juices of the stomach are not supplied and, the stomach being unable to do its work, dyspepsia comes. This overworked man may have liver complaint, because the liver, not getting its proper nerve impulses, can not functionate properly. No group of cells ever perform their functions without direct nerve impulses. The liver, the stomach, the skin can not act normally unless normal nerve impulses come to them . . . .

"Leaving the facts as they are, let us, entering the field of conjecture, inquire what is to become of us? It might be satisfying to know, and, again, it might be disquieting. I am inclined to believe that only experience—the experience not only of the individual, but also of the race—changes the course of human affairs; that therefore industrialism and its allies will continue to weaken the people of the modern world until they will no longer be able to respond to the call to extreme effort. By that time, unless other peoples, not weakened by this fever, take the place of supremacy away from us, men will find it possible to spend strength that is only sufficient for their daily needs, and the rebuilding of our race should begin. It is possible, however, that long before that time sincere and wise men and women, possibly the churches, will undertake, before it is too late, to teach mankind that it has been misguided, and that is it not God's will that men should be put upon the rack in order that there may be created new and useless wealth. Possibly the multitudes of men will be taught to smite the industrial monster that is warping the generations to come, and, scorning the menace of it, will take time for peaceful pleasures and for recuperative repose; and women, relieved of those burdens and turning from those ambitions that have weakened their distinctive powers, will be restored to that manner of life which will enable them to rejuvenate the race."

THE IRRESPONSIBLE WOMAN AND THE FRIENDLESS CHILD

By IDA M. TARBELL

Author of "The Tariff in Our Times," "The American Woman," etc.

ONE of the first conclusions forced on a thoughtful unprejudiced observer of society is that the major percentage of its pains and its vices result from a failure to make good connections. Children pine and even die for fruit in the cities while a hundred miles away thousands of barrels of apples are rotting on the ground. Famine devastates one country while the granaries of another are bursting with food. Men and women drink themselves into the gutter from sheer loneliness, while other men and women shrivel up in isolated comfort. One of the most pitiful examples of this failure to connect is that of the irresponsible woman and the friendless, uncared-for child.

There never at any time in any country in the world's history existed so large a group of women with whom responsibility and effort were a matter of choice, as exists to-day in the United States. While a large number of these free women are devoting themselves whole-heartedly to public service of the most intelligent and ingenious kind, another larger number recognize no obligation to make any substantial return to society for its benefits. The heaviest burden to-day on productive America, aside from the burden imposed by a vicious industrial system, is that of its non-productive women. They are the most demanding portion of our society. They spend more money than any other group, are more insistent in their cry for amusement, are more resentful of interruptions of their pleasures and excitements; they go to greater extremes of indolence and of uneasiness.

The really serious side to the existence of this parasitical group is that great numbers of other women, not free, forced to produce, accept their standards of life. We hear women, useful women, everywhere talking about the desirability of not being obliged to do anything, commiserating women who must work, commiserating those who have heavy household responsibilities, and by the whole gist of their words and acts influencing those younger and less experienced than themselves to believe that happiness lies in irresponsible living.

Varieties of Feminine Irresponsibility

Various gradations of the theory of which this is the extreme expression show themselves. Thus there are great numbers of women of moderate means, who by a little daily effort can keep comfortable and attractive homes for themselves and their immediate families, and yet who are utterly regardless of outside responsibility, who are practically isolated in the community. They pass their lives in a little round of household activities, sunning and preening themselves in their long hours of leisure like so many sleek cats.

There is still another division of this irresponsible class, who build up frenzied existences for themselves in all sorts of outside activities. They plunge headlong into each new proposition for pleasure or social service only to desert it as something more novel and exciting and for the instant popular, appears. Steady, intelligent standing-by an undertaking through its ups and downs, its dull seasons and its unpopular phases, they are incapable of. Their efforts have no relation to an intelligently conceived purpose. With them may be grouped those women who, by their canonization of the unimportant, construct heavily burdened but utterly fruitless lives. They laboriously pad out their days with trivial things, vanities, shams and shadows to which they give the serious undivided attention which should be bestowed only on real enterprises.

There are others who seek soporifics, release from a hearty tackling of their individual situations, in absorbing work, a work

299

which perhaps fills their minds but which is mere occupation—something to make them forget—not an art for art's sake, not labor for its useful fruits, but a protective separating shield to shut out the insistent demands of life in the place, where they find themselves.

All of these women are rightfully classed as irresponsible, whether they are moved by vanity, indolence, purposelessness, social blindness or most pitiful, a sense of the emptiness of life unattended by the imagination which reveals the sources from which life is filled. No one of them is building a "House of Life" for herself. They are building gimcrack palaces, gingerbread cottages, structures which the first full blast of life will level to the ground.

Neglected Youth at Woman's Door

These women are not peculiar to city or to country. They are scattered nation-wide. You find them on farms and in mansions, in offices and in academic halls. In startling contrast there exists almost under the very eaves of the roofs which shelter them a vast and pitiful group of friendless children,—the deserted babe, the "little mother," the boys and girls running wild on side streets in every village in our land and in every slum in the cities, the factory child, the shop girl who has no home. Let us remember that a goodly percentage of those at work have homes and that they are engaged in a stimulating, if hard effort to "help," that they have the steadying consciousness that they are needed. Nevertheless this mass of youth is on the whole in an unnatural position—an anti-social relation.

Society can never run rightfully until all its members are performing their natural functions. No woman whatever her condition can escape her obligation to youth without youth suffering, and without suffering herself. One of the crying needs of to-day is a crusade, a jar, which will force upon our irresponsible women the friendless children of the country, give them some sense of the undeniable relation they bear to them, show them that they are in a sense the cause of this pathetic group and that it is their work to relieve it.

True, for a woman there is nothing more painful than putting herself face to face with the suffering of children. Yet for many years now we have had in this country a large and increasing number of women who were going through the daily pain of grappling with every phase of the distressing problems which come from the poverty,

friendlessness and overwork of the young. Out of their heartbreaking scrutinies there have come certain determinations which are being adopted rapidly wherever the social sense is aroused. We may roughly sum up these conclusions or determinations to be these:

It is not necessary or endurable that children grow up starved and overworked, that boys and girls be submitted to vicious surroundings, that talent be crushed, that young men and young women be devoured by crime and greed. Youth, its nurturing and developing, has become the passion of the day. This is the meaning of our bureaux of Child Labor, of our Children's Courts, our Houses of Correction, our Fresh-Air Funds and Vacation Homes, our laws regulating hours and conditions, our Social Settlements.

Men and Women Shirkers

At its very best, however, legislation, organization, work in groups, only indirectly reach the base of the trouble. These homeless babes and children, these neglected boys and girls, these reckless shop and factory girls are generally the pain and menace that they are because they have not had, as individuals, that guidance and affection of women to which each has a natural right. No collective work however good it may be can protect or guide these children properly. Rightfully they should be the charge of that body of women who are unhampered, "free." These women have more, or less, intelligence; they have time and means. They owe society a return for their freedom, their means and their education. Nature had made them the guardians of childhood. Can they decently shirk the obligation any more than a man can decently shirk his duty as a citizen? Indeed the case of the woman unresponsive to her duty toward youth is parallel to that of the man unresponsive to his duty toward public affairs. One is as profitless and parasitical as the other.

The man who has no notion of what is doing politically in his own ward, who does not sense the malign influences which may be working in his neighborhood, in his very street, perhaps in the next house, who has not his eye on the unscrupulous small politician who leads the ward by the nose, who knows nothing of the records of the local candidates, never goes to the primaries, this man is one of the most dangerous citizens we have. It is he who makes the machine possible. If he did his work the governmental machine, which starts there with him, would be sound. It would be begun by honest men interested in serving the country to the best of their ability, and on such a foundation no future solidarity of corruption could be possible.

The individual woman's obligation toward the children and young people in her neighborhood is very like this obligation of the man to public affairs. If is for her to know the conditions under which the children, the boys and girls, young men and maids, in her vicinity are actually living. It is for her to be alert to their health, amusements and general education. It is for her to find the one—and there always is one—that actually needs her. It is for her to correlate her personal discoveries and experiences with the general efforts of her community.

This is no work for an occasional morning. It does not mean sporadic or even regular "neighborhood visiting." It means observation, reflection and study. It has nothing to do save indirectly with societies or groups, or laws. It is a personal work, something nobody else can do and something, which if it is neglected, adds just so much more to the stream of uncared-for youth. How is it to be done? Have you ever watched a woman interested in birds making her observations? She will get up at daylight to catch a note of a new singer. She will study in detail the little family that is making its home on her veranda. From the hour that the birds arrive in the spring until the hour that they leave in the fall she misses nothing of their doings. It is a beautiful and profitable study and it is a type of what is required of a woman who would fulfill her obligation toward the youth of her neighborhood.

"What Were the Women Doing?"

Could we have such study everywhere in country and town what tragedies and shames we might be spared! A few months ago the whole nation was horrified by a riot in a prosperous small city of the Middle West which ended in the lynching of a young man, a mere boy, who in trying to discharge his duty as a public official had killed a man. Some thirty persons, *over half of them boys under twenty years of age*, are to-day serving terms of from fifteen to twenty years in the penitentiary for their part in this lynching.

Their terrible work was no insane outbreak—analyzed it was a logical consequence of the social and political conditions under which the boys had been brought up. In a

pretty, rich, busy town of 30,000 people, proud of its churches and its school, *eighty saloons* industriously plied their business—and part of their business, as it always is, was to train youths to become their patrons.

What were the women doing in the town? I asked the question of one who knew it, "Why," he said, "they were doing just what women do everywhere, no better, no worse. They had their clubs; I suppose a dozen literary clubs, several sewing clubs, several bridge clubs and a number of dancing clubs. I think they cared a little more for bridge than for literature, many of them at least. They took little part in civic work, though they had done much for the city library and city hospital. Many girls went to college, to the State Institute, to Vassar and Smith. They came back to teach and to marry. It was just as it is everywhere."

Another to whom I put the same question, answered me in a sympathetic letter full of understanding comment. The mingled devotion, energy and blindness of the women the letter described, spoke in its every line. They built charming homes, reared healthy, active children whom they educated at any personal sacrifice—all within a circle of eighty saloons! To offset the saloons they built churches—a church for each sect— each more gorgeous than its neighbor. It was in building churches that they showed the "greatest tenacity of purpose." They had a large temperance organization. It supported a rest room and met fortnightly to pray "ardently and sincerely." How little this body of good women sensed their problem, how little they were fitted to deal with it, my informant's comment reveals. "You doubtless remember the story," the letter runs, "of the old lady who deplored the shooting of craps because, though she didn't know what they were, 'life was probably as dear to them as to anybody.'"

"It was just as it is every where." Busy with self and their immediate circles, they went their daily ways unseeing, though these ways were hedged with a corruption whose rank and horrible offshoots at every step clutched the feet of the children for whom they were responsible.

Intensive Gardening in Youth

Perhaps there is nothing to-day needed in this country more than driving into the minds of women this personal obligation to do what may be called intensive gardening in youth. Whether a woman wishes to see it or not she is the center of a whirl of life. The health, the happiness and the future of those that are in this whirl are affected vitally by what she is and does. To know all of the elements which are circulating about her as a man knows, if he does his work, the political and business elements in his own group, this is her essential task. That she should adjust her discoveries to the organizations political, educational, and religious, which are about her, goes without saying, but these organizations are not the heart of her matter. The heart of her matter lies in what she does for those who come into immediate contact with her.

Her business firmly established in her immediate group should grow as a man's business does in the outer circle where he naturally operates. It will become stable or unstable exactly as trade or profession becomes stable or unstable. Every year it should take on new elements, ramify, turn up new obligations, knit itself more firmly into the life of the community. With every year it should become necessarily more complicated, broader in interests, more demanding on her intellectual and spiritual qualities. Each one of the original members of her group gathers others about himself. In the nature of the case she will become one of the strongest influences in these new groups. As a member goes out she will project herself into other communities or perhaps other lands, into all sorts of industries, professions and arts. Her growth is absolutely natural. It is, too, one of the most economical growths the world knows. Nothing is lost in it. She spreads literally like the banyan tree.

The Woman of Fifty with Nothing to Do

Yet in spite of this perfectly obvious fact there are people to-day asking with all appearance of sincerity: what a woman of fifty or more can do! Their confining work in the home, say these observers, is done. A common suggestion is that they be utilized in politics. This suggestion has its comical side. A person who has nothing to do after fifty years of life in a business as many-sided and demanding as that of a woman, can hardly be expected to be worth much in a business as complicated and uncertain as politics, and for which she had had no training. The notion that the woman's business is ended at fifty or sixty, is fantastic in the extreme. It only ends there if she has been blind to the meaning of her own experiences; if she has

never gone below the surface of her task—never seen in it anything but physical duties; has sensed none of its intimate relations to the community, none of its obligations toward those who have left her, none of those toward the oncoming generations. If it ends there she has failed to realize, too, the tremendous importance to all those who belong in her circle or who touch it of what she makes of herself, of her personal achievement.

A woman of fifty or sixty who has succeeded, has come to a point of sound philosophy and serenity which is of the utmost value in the mental and spiritual development of the group to which she belongs. Life at every one of its seven stages has its peculiar harrowing experiences: hope mingles with uncertainty in youth; fear and struggle characterize early manhood; disillusionment, the question whether it is worth while, fill the years from forty to fifty, but resolute grappling with each period brings one out almost inevitably into a fine serene certainty which cannot but have its effect on those who are younger. Ripe old age, cheerful, useful and understanding, is one of the finest influences in the world. We hang Rembrandt's or Whistler's picture of his mother on our walls that we may feel its quieting hand, the sense of peace and achievement which the picture carries. We have no better illustration of the meaning of old age.

Family and social groups should be a blend of all ages. One of the present weaknesses of our society is that we herd each age together. The young do not have enough of the stimulating intellectual influence of their elders. The elders do not have enough of the vitalizing influence of the young. We make up our dinner party according to age with the result that we lose the full fine blend of life.

The notion that a woman has no worthy place or occupation after she is fifty or sixty, and that she can be utilized in public affairs, could only be entertained by one who has no clear conception of either private or public affairs—no vision of the infinite reaches of the one or the infinite complexities of the other. Human society may be likened to two great circles, one revolving within the other. In the inner circle rules the woman. Here she breeds and trains the material for the outer circle which exists only by and for her. That accident may throw her into this outer circle is of course true, but it is not her natural habitat, nor is she fitted by nature to live and circulate freely there. We underestimate, too, the kind of experience which is essential for intelligent citizenship this outer circle. To know what is wise and needed there one should circulate in it. The man at his labor in the street, in the meeting places of men, learns unconsciously as a rule, the code, the meaning, the need of public affairs as woman learns those of private affairs. What it all amounts to is that the labor of the world is naturally divided between the two different beings that people the world. It is unfair to the woman that she be asked to do the work of the outer circle. The man can do that satisfactorily if she does her part, that is if she prepares him the material. Certainly, he can never come into the inner circle and do her work.

Equality Not Likeness

The idea that there is a kind of inequality for a woman in minding her own business and letting man do the same, comes from our confused and rather stupid notion of the meaning of equality. Popularly we have come to regard being alike as being equal. We prove equality by wearing the same kind of clothes, studying the same books, regardless of nature or capacity or future life. Insisting that women do the same things that men do may make the two exteriorly more alike—it does not make them more equal. Men and women are widely apart in functions and in possibilities. They can not be made equal by exterior devices like trousers, ballots, the study of Greek. The effort to make them so is much more likely to make them unequal. One only comes to his highest power by following unconsciously and joyfully his own nature. You run the risk of destroying the capacity for equality when you attempt to make one human being like another human being.

The theory that the class of irresponsible women considered here would be fired to unselfish interest in uncared-for youth if they were included in the electorate of the nation is hardly sustainable. The ballot has never succeeded in preventing irresponsible men. Something more biting than a new tool is needed to arouse men and women who are absorbed in self—some poignant experience which thrusts upon their indolent minds and into their restricted visions the actualities of life.

In all fairness I think it should be said that the recent agitation for the ballot has served as such an experience for a few women, particularly in the East. Perhaps for the first time they have heard from the suffrage platform of the "little mother," the factory child, the girl living on $6.00 a week. They have done more than espouse the suffrage cause for the sake of the child, they have gone out to find where they could serve. Let us be glad of every agitation that extends the sense of social obligation.

If there were to-day some way of forcing the idle and the self-absorbed women of upper New York City, who at the first touch of the summer's heat fly to the country or to Europe, to see with their own eyes the thousands of little children who, almost at the very doors of their closed mansions, must for weeks of this coming summer, swelter and often die, we might hope to open many a dull heart, give light to many a blind eye.

It is a new knowledge of that tide of life which breaks at her very gate and through which, in every great city, she must pass every time she leaves it in carriage or car, that the irresponsible American woman needs, if she is to discharge her obligation to the uncared-for child. To force these facts upon her, to cry to her "you are the woman,—you cannot escape the guilt of the woe and crime which must come from the neglect of childhood in your radius"—this is the business of every man and woman who has had the pain and the privilege of seeing something of the actual life of the people of this world.

(It is with "The Woman and Democracy" that the next articles in this series will deal)

303

The Renaissance of Woman

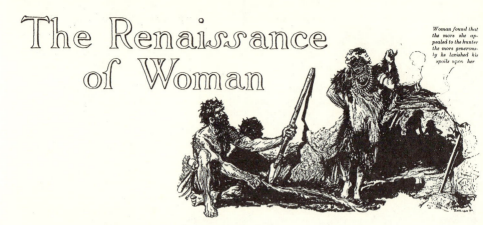

Woman found that the more she appealed to the hunter the more generously he lavished his spoils upon her

By ARTHUR STRINGER

ILLUSTRATED BY WALTER J. ENRIGHT

W OMAN'S history, the finger of the anthropologist points out, begins with her as a beast of burden. From the beast of burden she evolves into a domestic animal, and from the docile work animal again she becomes a slave. Her era of enforced servitude, we find, again merges into an era when she is man's servant, and as time leaves her mate less and less in need of her personal labor, she finds herself transformed into something akin to the house cat—with the implied obligation, of course, that she must continuously please her master.

Woman's history begins with her as a beast of burden

For a good many centuries now woman's first and last resource has been to please man. With the passing of feral life, man, the hunter and fighter, found himself taking up more and more woman's primitive occupations. He became the grinder of meal, the maker of cloth, the tanner of hides, the purveyor of food. To these new tasks he brought that ingenuity and inventiveness which countless ages of predatory warfare had imposed upon him. He perfected machinery and organized experience. He practically elbowed woman out of all industrial pursuits. In his blind male efforts to lighten her labors he succeeded in divorcing her from the actualities of economic conditions. In doing so he left her dependent on his own initiative and activity, and the greater this dependence the more flattering was the thought of it to him. He protected her. She became his possession. Woman, finding herself with no resource except to appeal to her possessor's imagination, was coerced into a display of those attributes which would most effectively and permanently placate a somewhat capricious master. In other words, she was compelled to make the most of her power to charm. She acquired the dazzle habit. And as mating became more competitive and man became less responsive to her natural and elemental appeal, she realized the advantage of ornamentation, of adding factitious value to her person by the things with which she adorned it.

O UT of this was born the parade instinct in woman, an instinct which under the operation of natural laws primarily belongs to the male. It is the male, as a rule, that carries the fine feathers, the intimidating mane, the dazzling coloration. But in the case of man the male has been content to let the female usurp this parade function. He has also relegated to her the use of ornament, since in beholding his mate heavily

adorned he may still revel in a keen if somewhat vicarious pride of possession. For in primordial times, it must be remembered, the personal possession of orna-

ment (whether it was the leopard skin or the eagle's wing or the zebra's tail) stood as the concrete evidence of courage and skill. The male hunter who possessed most of these things was the person to be most admired. He needed no further guarantee of his strength and craft. But woman, even in those early days averse to social extinction, found that the more she appealed to the hunter the more generously he lavished his spoils on her and the more readily he sought her society.

SHE also, during her hours of meal pounding and hide scraping, made another discovery. Since man's work by day was the eager quest of the spoils of the chase, since his pursuit of them was racial and instinctive, she realized in her tentative and inarticulate way that she might increase her attractiveness in his eyes by identifying with her own body the things which he himself so passionately sought. Toward her, hitherto, he tended to turn only in his hours of idleness. So she added to that acquisitive body of hers the brighter and better portions of his chase trophies. In other words she cunningly put a second string to the sex bow. She gradually tangled the issues of love and work. She sought to make man like her, not for her body alone, but for the riches with which that body came adorned to him.

Clothing, which was primarily worn for warmth as hunger drove her and her mate farther and farther away from the earlier equatorial plains, was accordingly converted into a medium of ornamentation. Woman became crafty enough to see that even a leopard skin could be worn at a tilt so insouciant as to make her more appealing to the eyes of man. So she made that skin do more than merely conserve calories: she made it add to her sex attractiveness. She translated dress into a decoration. And she awakened to the fact, once her mate had been won, that the paraded possession of many leopard skins marked her as the wife of a great hunter.

When the leopard skin was supplanted by fabrics manufactured from the interwoven hairs from animals, or from the twisted fiber of plants and the larva covering of worms, and was further embellished with bright stones and metals dug from the ground, woman's burden of splendor may be said to have firmly established itself. How heavily that burden of splendor has weighed on her none too robust shoulders is evidenced in even more things than the industries which depend on woman's dress and on her passion for decoration. It is more conspicuously evidenced by her projection into an era presumably civilized of many of the practices and traits peculiar to barbaric times. By this I mean not altogether the mere use of ingenious devices for the distortion of the body, the use of mineral dyes for the coloration of skin surfaces, the dissimulative additions to headdress and stature, and the artificial emphasizing of those lines and areas which have come to be associated with sexual allurement, but more woman's persistent preoccupation with self-adornment and self-exploitation during those long eras when her more restless-minded mate was laboriously organizing knowledge, evolving what he called Science and adapting invention to some ever-new economic and social exigency. During that time, which must always be known as the Dark Ages of woman, she insisted on idealizing ornamentation, precisely as her shriller-voiced sisters are to-day insisting on idealizing the ballot. The tragedy of her dilemma lies in the fact that it was not forced on her by man but by conditions over which man himself had no control.

WHEN primitive man had killed off his big game and ceased to be a hunter, he had to take more and more to his own roof tree, side by side with the woman. There he took more and more a hand in her work, changing the nature of it through his natural cunning, systematizing it so that it emerged from a means of sustenance into a source of wealth. Arrogating this wealth and what it brought him to himself, he left woman dependent on him.

When desirous of a mate he could purchase one or, grown fastidious, could leisurely pick from his own tribe the one who most appealed to him. And, henceforward, to appeal to man became the tragically primal duty of woman's career. Just how immured she remained in this ignobly simple task is reflected in the fact that, outside of sex intrigues, she had left behind her so little history that the unequivocally great women of recorded time could be inscribed on a sheet of paper no bigger than this printed page. That these great women were in a way desexed women, it might be unfair to contend; but that most of them, from Sappho and Aspasia to Catherine and Jeanne d'Arc, and on again to Rosa Bonheur and George Eliot and Carrie Nation, have been marked by attributes and habits distinctly masculine is a matter beyond dispute.

THAT man, so proud of his mastery in even pagan times, should meekly have allowed woman to strip him of all his fine feathers seems at first an anomaly. The greater response to stimulus, the greater excess of activity, the greater physical strength—these were always his. Yet these were the very things which both mediately and immediately led to his bodily denudation. When he became a coworker with woman, success in his new field as a food producer and cloth maker supplied him with a new instrument for attracting or holding her admiring attention. He began to crave her admiration, not for what he wore but for what he was able to achieve. His labor, becoming more and more skilled, carried with it such unequivocal evidence of energy and efficiency, such plain earmarks of the older "chase" superiority, that he could lapse into

Man in beholding
his mate adorned
may revel in
pride of possession

bodily somberness without resentment. To stand a hero in the eyes of woman, of course, was always his greatest stimulus. His old aggressiveness did not desert him; he merely changed his rôle. His new watchword of worth became efficiency. And woman, endowed with her protective cunning, a not ignoble cunning which the maternal instinct first imposed on her for the protection of her young, responded to this new phase of her mate's activity by stimulating it, by showing a marked preference for the man of accumulated riches, whether in bearskins or bank notes. She fanned his protective instincts by insisting on the oak and ivy relationship. She accentuated his sense of mastery by pretending to a greater inefficiency than was really hers; and vestigial remnants of this attitude we still see in her studiously dwarfed feet, her blanched hands, the deliberately encumbered limbs, the atavistic scream of fear, the gratuitous tendency to faint which met its twilight in the mid-Victorian era.

THEN came the bitter and ironic *dénouement* of the entire racial tragedy. Man made woman dependent upon him, and then proved himself incapable of her protection. Not only was he left to reckon with the problem of the unmated, but through the conditions which his own inventions brought about he found himself largely unable to support offspring. The female of the species was compelled to reenter industrial life.

Man, in the meantime, had made his world a man's world. He had shut woman outside the walls of his working life, leaving her only the consolation of her primary biological function, yet all the while confronting her with the tragedy of being played on by stimulations without the ability to translate them into action. That she was compelled, during those Dark Ages of her history, to exaggerate the embroidery of life into a semblance of life itself may be recognized as her misfortune, but never as altogether her fault. If she were conscious of the higher fields into which man's occupational pursuits were carrying him, of how organization and efficiency and industry were converting him into a specialist, she must also have been conscious of the fact that man had deprived her of her rights by giving her too little and not too much to do. And now, in the day of her renaissance, she has not entered the trades and professions until man's neglect of his paternal responsibilities and his inability to extend adequate protection to her and her offspring compelled her to do so. It is a disturbance of basic attributes, and, like all such disturbances, it involves a sense of shock. Woman is insisting on her freedom, on newer rights, and through that very insistence she is paying for them. While she somewhat shrilly proclaims that a single woman to-day can often be of more economic service than a mother, her very reentrance into occupational pursuits has necessarily diminished her reproductive powers, consciously through her reluctance to interrupt those pursuits, and unconsciously through the expenditure of her nervous energy and the gradual defemination of her character. She will talk of Mendelism and announce that while in Japan they are discussing the differentiation of workers and breeders, in America the movement is being effected without discussion.

The perpetuation of the race, apparently, is to be left to the idler, to the more luxuriously environed woman who has not yet encountered the normalizing effects of honest labor, who, being doubly parasitic, still accepts the gifts of life without weariness and service rendered, who still carries into her so-called refinement a thousand and one relics, subliminal though they be, of barbaric ages and practices. Daily in her idleness we may see her reverting to that love of caste and custom, that fondness for esoteric ritual, that excessive and irrational decoration, and that deliberate malformation of the body, that adeptness at deception, and that tendency to edacity, which so clearly marked her pagan ancestor.

That pagan ancestor, however, at least was compelled to look biology in the face. And woman, new as she may call herself, and new as her ideas may seem, cannot rise above the cold logic of biology. In the sum of her highest aspiration must fall the recurring decimal of racial duty. The reasons are plain and sane why she must in one respect remain elemental. In this she is not her own mistress. Childbirth must, in its way, always compel her rebarbarization. Her ideal and her duty as the essential conservator of human life is something which no exigency and no economic condition can alter. Her first duty, as Herbert Spencer put it, is to become a good animal.

DEFINITE as this reproductive privilege and sacrifice actually is, with its eternal call for tenderness and loyalty and serenity of soul, it has been momentarily blurred by woman's twentieth-century invasion of industrial life on the one hand, and her unassimilated consciousness of social emancipation on the other. Man is still dynamic and katabolic; woman, static and anabolic. Man with his inventions denatured her primal occupations. She in return seems to promise to denature her womanhood by elbowing a way into work, often unfitting her for offspring. For woman, from the childhood of the world, was never averse to being a burden bearer. But in fighting for recognition of function she has sometimes impaired function itself. Her very bitterness of protest, like her earlier deceptive instincts, were forced on her. Her craft and dissimulation are the fruit of thwarted powers and harsh treatment. Her very charm, her forlorn placatory tact, is the result of that tyranny which prompted her always to move by indirection. It was man himself who made her oversolicitous of approval—for once she had to please to live—equipping her with an aptitude of manner to conciliate a wayward and choleric mate; since barbaric woman's power to foretell her master's mood, gathering from a tone or look the coming outburst from which she must effect her timely escape, was the means of perpetuating her type.

And the type, for good or ill, with all the heritage of all its earlier days, must endure, although industrial labor means defemination and childbearing means a relapse into animality. For when woman refines herself beyond the nobilities of this animal instinct and obligation, she merely refines herself and her nation out of existence.

II

THE PROBLEMS

DR. FRAZER'S encyclopædic work on *Totemism and Exogamy* (1911) is a monument of wonderfully patient research, of masterly marshalling of evidence, of transparent fairness of criticism and of acute reasoning. It is impossible for one who is a mere biologist to offer criticism of such a work without recognising the danger of falling into many errors, and of stumbling into pitfalls which only a trained anthropologist can avoid. It is, however, precisely as a biologist, and with full recognition of the dangers ahead, that I venture to present certain aspects of the problems he has set forth which, so far as I know, have not been definitely expressed.

I am prompted by two reasons : in the first place, as I have already stated, the origin and the subsequent association of these two primitive customs as set forth by Dr. Frazer, appear to me to indicate that they afford evidence of the working of an elemental war of the sexes which, both for biological and for social reasons, is of great interest at this stage of our own history. In the second place, I am impelled to doubt certain of the conclusions Dr. Frazer has drawn. I feel that he has somewhat unduly neglected the biological aspect of the problem; that in discussing the origin of savage customs which he maintains are of such vast antiquity, he has overlooked the effect of that crude physiological impulse which, in view of the power it exerts to-day upon us, we may reasonably conclude must have exerted much greater influence long ages ago on the actions of those whose descendants are still savages; while he has demanded too much exertion of that human ' intelligence, deliberation and will' which is essential for the theory he advances.

If, therefore, my criticisms are just, some doubt must be thrown on Dr. Frazer's conclusions; I do not suggest that solutions of the chief problems are here afforded, but I think it is possible some light may incidentally be thrown upon them which will help towards a clearer idea of their essential nature. It is this end which my friend Dr. Frazer has at heart and it is this which every one who knows him must be assured is the sole aim of his great labour, so I am cheered by the knowledge that whatever errors I may fall into will meet with the generous criticism he never fails to accord to all who, with this aim in view, thrust themselves across his track. And indeed I am justified in this hope, for already he has supplied me with frank criticism of certain points advanced in a preliminary draft of a portion of this work which I submitted to him, and has set me at liberty, indeed has requested me to make full use of the notes and letter he has written. This I shall gladly do in the following pages, and, in order to differentiate between quotations from his book and from these papers, shall refer to the latter as MS.

In considering the problem in the aspect from which I propose to present it, it is necessary to bear in mind the biological constitution of the society dealt with; and this, it seems to me, is very generally neglected.

In the first place, I am struck with the fact that while all societies are compounded of two fundamentally different elements, the power and the effect of only one of these elements is, as a rule, seriously considered by anthropologists. The vast majority of anthropologists are men, and men are notoriously incapable of analysing the Female mind. But societies are compounded of Males and Females, and it seems to me very questionable whether anthropologists are not sometimes, perhaps frequently, entirely mistaken in their interpretation of facts which have their origin in, or bear upon, the habits, customs and beliefs of a society in which the Female element is a powerful factor. Thus, in dealing with any social problem we must not only consider the Male, for we are dealing also with the Female, mind; and no matter how primitive the society may be, this Female aspect of the subject, these Female feelings, these Female interpretations of cause and effect exist, exert drastic influence, and must not be ignored.

If there is one thing more than another emphasised by the study of reproductive physiology it is the essential differences between the Male and the Female. The reproductive system is one of the two most primitive systems of organs possessed by all living things. The digestive system is necessary for the life of the individual, the reproductive for the life of the species, and all the other systems of organs—excretory, vascular, nervous, muscular, skeletal, sensory—are called forth and built up in accordance with the needs which arise for the more efficient discharge of both these two primitive systems. But, and this is of great moment, one of these two primitive systems, the reproductive, is not only structurally but functionally, fundamentally different in the Male and in the Female ; and since all other organs and systems of organs are affected by this system, it is certain that the Male and Female are essentially different throughout. Some of these differences are glaring and forceful, others infinitely subtle, hidden differences, and the most remarkable are not due to structural differences but to profound divergence of function. The origin of them all is to be traced without doubt to the overwhelming influence, either of the forces which induce the activity of the reproductive system, or to the products of that activity ; it is by such means that all the tissues of the body are bound together and drilled subservient to sex.

What these forces are is a problem with which I have long concerned myself, but this is not the place, and indeed I am not prepared now, to discuss it. It is enough perhaps to say that, so far as I understand the matter, the origin of the stimulus is the same for both sexes, but its effect is very differently expressed in the Male and in the Female of all animals ; and further, that such difference is wholly due to difference of function in the two sexes. I feel very sure that the effect of this profound divergence of function is greatly underrated as a rule, and that neglect to recognise it frankly must result in disastrous consequences both to savage and to civilised communities alike.

Sometimes the bare fact that the Female mind contributes to primitive beliefs and helps to shape the customs and laws of a people, is clearly admitted. Thus Dr. Frazer writes (vol. iv. p. 64) : ' If we ask what in particular may have suggested the theory of conception which appears to be the tap-root of totemism, it seems probable that, as I have already indicated, a preponderant influence is to be ascribed to the sick fancies of pregnant women, and that so far, therefore, totemism may be described as a creation of the feminine rather than of the masculine mind ' ; and again he remarks (p. 63), certain ' maternal fancies appear to be the root of totemism.' Dr. Frazer is, I believe, the only one who has ever drawn attention to the effect of Female influence in this connection, and in my opinion it is a very important generalisation.

It is perhaps true that the effect of these forceful sex influences is specially marked in the Male during the breeding season, in the Female during pregnancy. ' Maternal fancies ' are undoubtedly strong. But it must be clearly recognised that the difference between the sexes is not confined to these brief periods, it is a constant, inherent difference, and, as we advance in the scale of organisation, will probably be found to be always acting with greater force, as a wedge driven ever deeper by social necessities and laws, and separating the essential nature of the two sexes further and further apart.

To speak of this difference between the sexes is to talk of a fact so self-evident that it will seem to many quite unnecessary to draw attention to it, but I feel very sure that, so far as the woman is concerned, such evidence as is usually deemed sufficient for the purpose is but gleaned from the most superficial layer of an infinitely complicated hidden structure, of the constitution of which we, as men, are profoundly ignorant. Moreover, it seems certain that the actual influence of the woman is in direct proportion to the secrecy with which her characteristic differences are guarded ; the less they are recognised the greater is their power. Patent facts are easy to reckon with ; it is the unknown which disturbs all one's calculations.

Such differences are not confined to civilised peoples, they are represented in the lowest savages. Civilisation has no doubt given rise to more delicate shades of divergence, but the main functions of the one sex are equally opposed to those of the other sex in all animals ; and it is these main functions, these inherent differences, which are responsible for an enormous proportion of the misunderstandings common between men and women ; responsible for the disregard the Male constantly shows for the Female, for the antagonism evinced by the Female towards the Male. Such disregard and antagonism is not necessarily wilful, it is inherent, and I am convinced is, as a rule, but vaguely recognised by the offender.

As an example ;—A girl of fourteen years was asked what she would like best in the world, and she replied in the most natural manner, she would like to marry and have four children, then she would like her husband to die and she would bring up her family. This is a striking instance of the inherent Feminine attitude towards the Male before love is introduced. Once the children are produced, the mother desires freedom to bring them up. The Male is no longer desired by her when once the productive stage of her life is over ; he then occupies only a subordinate place in her life work, and is, in fact, from a sexual point of view, only a nuisance to the woman when that time comes. Such a feeling is constantly to be found in women, though they themselves often do not recognise the force which is driving them ; they only have a feeling which, as a rule, they are ashamed to confess, but it is actually the same feeling which this girl, speaking of her natural instinctive desires, thus plainly expressed.

At the same primitive stage of civilisation the Male will look upon a woman primarily from a sexual point of view, secondarily, no doubt, as a worker for his benefit; and when, either temporarily or permanently, she fails to attract him sexually, he will look around for another woman to take her place. Such instinctive desires are a quality of the sex. I refer here, of course, to passion as distinct from love. But my view does not demand that savages are devoid of affection; love for one woman is not destroyed by passion for another; society may declare that constancy is the sole gauge of love, but love is naturally distinct from passion; it is only in accordance with social laws that the two are merged together.

Thus it is not only the Feminine mind which is different from the Male mind; it is the whole Female organisation, her inclinations, feelings, and intuitions which are different. It is the woman's biological necessities, and all the various forces which conduce to their satisfaction, which, though complementary to those of the man for a period in their joint lives, are quite different from, and eventually become diametrically opposed to, his needs and to the natural forces which drive him.

I venture to think Dr. Frazer has not sufficiently considered this aspect of the problem, and, if I mistake not, it lies at the root of both exogamy and totemism. As a man I cannot hope to define the subtle Female differences which tend to thrust the sexes apart, but as a biologist I think it may be possible to indicate certain directions in which that power is evinced, even, perhaps, certain cumulative results thereof.

It is such reflections which impel me to think the biological aspect of various anthropological problems is often insufficiently considered. Dr. Frazer appears to hold a different view. He remarks on ' a weakness which has of late years vitiated other speculations as to the growth of human institutions. It attempts to explain that growth too exclusively from physical and biological causes without taking into account the factors of intelligence, deliberation, and will.' Inquirers, he says, ' forget the part that human thought and will have played in moulding human destiny.' And again : ' In particular, the science which deals with human society will not, if it is truly scientific, omit to reckon with the qualities which distinguish man from the beasts ' (vol. iv. p. 98). Now these remarks are surely applicable to the interpretation of the *development* of laws and customs which have proceeded in accordance with that intelligence, deliberation and will which is peculiar to man. But his strictures are directed specially in this place against one who has attempted to assign a biological reason for the *origin* of a custom, and that is a very different matter from its development. The custom in question is that of exogamy, and Dr. Frazer finds that certain tribes inhabiting Central and Northern Australia, the most primitive human beings living to day, ' practise exogamy in its most rigid form ' and yet are ' still ignorant of the fact of physical paternity ' (vol. iv. p. 99).

Now it is surely a very remarkable fact that such

primitive people, people who, Dr. Frazer believes, are so void of intelligence that they are ignorant of the result of sexual intercourse, should have stringent regulations against endogamy, elaborate rules regarding exogamous mating, unless this habit of exogamy had grown through vast ages, very slowly, bit by bit, until it has come to be ' exogamy in its most rigid form.' And if that is so, the custom must have arisen many ages ago, when these people were possessed of appreciably less power of ' intelligence, deliberation and will ' than they now have, at a time, in fact, when they were governed by instinct in such matters, even as we are to-day in the same and in some others ! ' The abhorrence of incest, which is the essence of exogamy,' he says, has grown through a long series of ages ; ' there is no evidence or probability that the aversion is a thing of recent growth, a product of advanced civilisation,' while it is fair to suppose it has ' everywhere originated in the same primitive modes of thought and feeling ' (vol. iv. p. 153).

But a people who, at the present time, have no domestic animals, who are ignorant that a seed if planted will grow, and live altogether on the products of their hunting skill, must, some thousands of years ago, have stood at the very dawn of human existence ; and a custom so elaborate as the exogamy practised by these primitive savages must indeed have been of growth so slow that it is easier to believe it had its origin in instinct, that is, feeling, or an instinctive method of satisfying feeling, rather than in any other quality more nearly approaching reason or thought.

If there is any probability in the truth of this suggestion of the origin of the custom, one cannot fail to look with great suspicion on the statement that the abhorrence of incest is the essence of exogamy. Such horror may quite possibly have subsequently come to be a factor which helped to consolidate the law, but, if the custom arose in accordance with instinct—and I believe I can advance evidence which makes that view highly probable—horror is not the essence of the matter, rather is it founded on a definite sexual instinct, inclination, or feeling.

Dr. Frazer's elaborate and ingenious arguments, advanced to show that it is possible that the ' intercourse of near kin was thought to render the women of the tribe sterile and to endanger the common food supply by preventing edible animals from multiplying and edible plants from growing ; in short, that the effect of incest was supposed to be sterility of women, animals and plants ', may, as he says, be ' an effect rather than the cause of its prohibition ' (p. 157). But if so, on what grounds does he found his belief that abhorrence of incest is the essence of exogamy ? Dr. Frazer is so imbued with the importance of the effect of human intelligence on the customs of a people that, in spite of the admitted antiquity of this habit, he wholly disregards the bearing of any other influence upon it. It seems clear to me that such belief in the evil resulting from incest, where it exists, must be the effect of experience, since it can only have been learnt from experience, and such experience must be denied to those savages in Central Australia who practise exogamy while they do not recognise the consequence of sexual relationship.

Dr. Frazer, however, is apparently not prepared to accept such a view. He writes me (MS.) that he denies experience has anything to do with the matter, since the belief seems to be that the intercourse of near kin among human beings *ipso facto* sterilises animals and plants; and this, he says, is far from being a fact of experience, it is an absurdity, a mere superstition.

For my part, I do not recognise the relevance of such objection. If there is a belief that incest amongst human beings causes sterility in animals and plants it must be a superstition of secondary growth; it can have nothing to do with the main problem and it is, I think, an error to allow such adventitious matter to divert attention from the main question.

Incidentally one may remark that ' a mere superstition ' is not perhaps so far removed from experience as Dr. Frazer seems inclined here to believe. A vast proportion of superstitions have their origin in an attempt to account for, to explain phenomena which are not understood ; and no doubt the habits, customs, necessities, and experiences of a people influence the trend of thought which determines the character of a superstition. This very superstition which Dr. Frazer calls an absurdity may indeed be so accounted for. At first sight it is not easy to imagine any cause for imagining connection between the fertility of the human members of a tribe and that of the wild animals which surround them ; but, as a matter of fact there is such cause for connecting the two phenomena, for those natural conditions which influence the fertility of a savage tribe affect also the breeding powers of the animals in their neighbourhood. This fact cannot have escaped the notice of the wise men of the tribe; tradition will hand it down for it is of vital importance to them, it concerns the food supply. They do not understand the forces which so act on people, animals and plants alike, but they see clearly there is connection between them all, and they assume that the common result is due to some act of their own. There is, I imagine, no more common origin of superstitious belief than the conception that man is himself responsible for the results of natural law. Amongst peoples much more highly civilised than these savages the spirits of thunder, storm, and fever are supposed to work evil on a people because it is believed that their behaviour has in some way offended the spirits. Thus in the case quoted by Dr. Frazer, while the savage explanation of the fact is absurd the fact itself they have rightly learnt from experience, and so, if they believe that intercourse of near kin induces sterility amongst themselves, they may be considered logically entitled to believe it also affects the fertility of the animals and plants living around them.

To return to the main point, Dr. Frazer concludes (vol. iv. p. 160) regarding exogamy : ' Considering everything as carefully as I can I incline, though with great hesitancy and reserve, to think that exogamy may have sprung from a belief in the injurious and especially the sterilising effects of incest, not upon the persons who engage in it, at least not upon the man, nor upon the offspring, but upon women generally and particularly upon edible animals and plants.' In view of what is said before, this appears to me to be a very astonishing conclusion ; but, Dr. Frazer adds, ' If that is not the origin of exogamy I must confess to being completely baffled, for I have no other conjecture to offer on the subject.'

In the following pages I will venture to suggest another explanation, not one which primarily concerns intelligence, deliberation and will, but one which has its origin in those natural biological laws which influence habits and customs long before connected thought is efficiently exercised. I cannot doubt it is to such an age, to such a primitive state of society, to such an elementary condition of human faculty we must revert in order to conceive of the forces which are responsible for the origin of such a custom.

Regarding totemism and Dr. Frazer's derivation of it from a primitive theory of conception which presupposes ignorance of the part played by the father in procreation ; although I shall suggest another theory of the origin of the custom, my main

c

endeavour will be to show that ignorance of the result of sexual intercourse is not a primitive condition but is acquired by superstition, originating in the Female mind and accepted by the Male.

This custom appears to me to be the first evidence we have of the assertion of woman in society. It arose with her and results in part in raising her status in society ; she becomes through its agency of much greater importance to the community, and the power she thereby acquires she never again wholly loses. At the same time it appears that any permanent influence she subsequently gains may be traced to the same source—which is essentially, reverence for the mysteries of maternity ; and, so far as I am aware, on no matter wholly divorced from maternity and the rearing of the child has the woman ever succeeded in establishing herself permanently as of essential, of irreplaceable, value to society.

The treatment by the Male of this purely Female scheme is a circumstance of much interest. It demonstrates in a remarkable manner the fundamental difference in the natural characteristics of the Male and the Female ; it shows how that difference results in the ready absorption of Female ideas by the Male ; and it shows how his placid acceptance of the woman's claims is followed by his eventual assumption of control by means of laws which he formulates and administers.

There is one other matter to which I shall devote some attention, and that is the belief in the transmission to the unborn child of maternal impressions.

Dr. Frazer is disposed to attach some importance to this belief in connection with totemism, and the evidence I have to offer on the subject may be regarded as not unfavourable to such views. At the same time, as Dr. Frazer fully recognises, the fundamental question of the possible influence of a mother on her unborn child has not been definitely answered by biology, and I do not claim here to answer it.

IN THAT great and inspiring movement toward a full democracy, which has been going on in this country for one hundred and fifty years, the American woman has had her full share. At the beginning she saw that she must democratize her attitude toward life and all her ways if she was to keep up her end of her partnership with man. She set out right bravely. But she met at once, as man did in his efforts to democratize industry and government, the tenacious ideas of the past. Customs, habits, religious interpretations and social conventions centuries old obstructed her. It became a fight with her, as it did with the working man, the liberal-minded intellectual man and the progressive statesman.

Opposition always develops the aggressive natures in a body. The opposition to the democratization of the lives of American women soon aroused a powerful if small body to open revolution. By the middle of the last century they had formulated their grievances, prepared their program and were in active campaign.

Now up to this time the American woman had not questioned her partnership in society with man; her efforts had been directed to the democratization of their mutual life. But the new aggressive movement attacked the partnership by attacking the partner. It declared that the reason woman was having so much difficulty in applying the new ideas to her life was that her partner was interfering with her. Of course these aggressive ladies overlooked the fact that man was himself having a great deal of difficulty in working out his ideas; also that their own most bitter opposition came from women.

PHOTOGRAPH BY
MISSES KELLEY & WILSON

MISS TARBELL

WHERE WOMEN HAVE IMITATED MEN 〰️〰️❋〰️〰️ What the aggressive movement amounted to was a repudiation of that division of labor which men and women had worked out in the past. Man had always been the recognized producer and protector, woman the conservator and educator. She declared now that this division was a clever invention of his for keeping her in an inferior place; that if she was to realize a greater freedom, happiness and usefulness it would be by entering his peculiar field and by applying his peculiar methods.

For some sixty years this imitation of the activities of man has been an active force in the life of the American woman. What has been the result of these experiments with man's life? Take the matter of education. In the last sixty or seventy years tens of thousands of women have been students in American universities, colleges and technical schools, taking there the same training as men. In the last twenty years the annual increase of numbers has been amazing: more than ten thousand at the beginning of the period, more than fifty-two thousand at the end. More than eight thousand degrees were given to women in 1910, nearly one-half as many as were given to men. Fully four-fifths of these woman students and graduates have worked side by side with men in schools which served both equally.

Here then is a great mass of experience from which it would seem that we ought to be able to say precisely how the intellects of the two sexes act and react under the stimulus of serious study; to decide definitely whether their attack on problems is the same, whether they come out the same.

Although he would be a rash observer who would pretend to lay down hard-and-fast conclusions as to the mind of woman at work, certain generalizations on the whole may be safely made from our experience with co-education.

One of the first of these is that at the start the woman takes her work more seriously than her masculine competitor. Fifty years ago there was special reason for this. The few women who in those earl?

days sought a man's education had something of the spirit of pioneers. The girl who enters college nowadays has rarely the opportunity to be either pioneer or martyr. She is doing what has come to be regarded as a matter of course. Nevertheless today as then, in the co-educational school, she is more consciously on her mettle than the man. Her attention, interest, respectfulness, docility, will be ahead of his.

"IF I HAD TAKEN MY WIFE'S ADVICE" 〰️〰️❋〰️〰️ It will at once be apparent that she carries the larger stock of *untaught* knowledge. In the classroom she will usually outstrip him in mathematics. It is an ideal subject for her, satisfying her talent for order, for making things "come out right." Her memory will serve her better. She will know less of abstract ideas, of philosophies and speculations. They will interest her less. The chances are that she will be less skillful with microscope and scalpel, though this is not certain. She will show less enthusiasm for technical problems, for machinery and engineering; more for social problems, particularly when it is a question of meeting them with preventives or remedies.

In the first two or three years after entering college the girl will almost invariably appear superior to the men of her age, more grown up, more interested, surer of herself, readier. But by the time she is a Senior, look out! The chances are she will have less interest from now on with men's business and more with her own. In any case she will rarely develop as rapidly in

NO MODERN WRITER HAS PERHAPS SO SANELY AND STRONGLY POINTED THE WISE WAY FOR THE MODERN WOMAN AMID THE PRESENT UNREST AS HAS MISS IDA M. TARBELL IN HER VIGOROUS ARTICLES IN "THE AMERICAN MAGAZINE," AND IN HER RECENT BOOK, "THE BUSINESS OF BEING A WOMAN," PUBLISHED BY THE MACMILLAN COMPANY. THE EDITORS OF THE LADIES' HOME JOURNAL FELT THAT THEIR READERS WOULD ENJOY MISS TARBELL'S WHOLESOME ANALYSIS OF THE "WOMAN QUESTION," AND ACCORDINGLY HER VIEWS, ADAPTED FROM HER ARTICLES AND BOOK, WILL BE PRESENTED IN SUCCEEDING ISSUES.

THE EDITORS.

324

his field from this point as he is doing. He becomes assertive, confident, dominating; the male taking a male's place. He discovers that his intellectual processes are more scientific than hers, therefore he concludes they are superior. He finds he can out-argue her, draw logical conclusions as she cannot. He can do anything with her but convince her. Things are so because they are so.

And the chances are the girl is right in spite of the irregular way she got there. Something superior to reason enters into her operations—an intuition of truth akin to inspiration. In early ages women unusually endowed with this quality of perception were honored as seers. Today they are recognized as counsellors of prophetic wisdom. "If I had taken my wife's advice!" How often one hears it!

WHEN WOMEN SUCCEED
⋙✳⋘

One more important fact has come out of our great educational experiment: The college cannot rub femininity out of and masculinity into a woman's brain. The woman's mind is still the woman's mind, although she is usually the last to recognize it. It is another proof of the eternal fact that Nature looks after her own good works.

But it takes more than a college course to make an efficient, flexible and trustworthy organ from a mind, masculine or feminine. It must be applied to productive labor in competition with other trained minds before you can decide what it is worth. Set the man-trained woman's mind at what is called man's business, let it be what you will, what about her?

Here again there is ample experience to go on. For seventy years we have had them with us—the stern disciples of the militant program. Greater fidelity to a task than they show it would be impossible to find, a fidelity so unwavering that it is often painful. Their care for detail, for order, for exactness, is endless. Dignity, respect for their undertaking, and devotion to professional etiquette they may be counted on to show in the highest degree. These are admirable qualities. They have led hundreds of women into independence and good service. Almost never, however, have they led one to the top. In free fields, such as merchandising, editing and manufacturing, we have yet to produce a woman of the first caliber—that is, daring, experimenting, free from prejudice, with a vision of the future great enough to lead her to embody something of the future in her task.

In every profession we have scores of successful women, almost never a *great* woman—and yet the world is full of great women. That is of women who understand, are familiar with the big sacrifices, appreciative of the fine things, farseeing, prophetic. Why does this greatness so rarely find expression in their professional undertakings?

The answer is no doubt complex, but one factor is the general notion of the woman that if she succeeds she must suppress her natural emotions and meet the world with a surface as non-resilient as she conceives that of man to be in his dealings with the world. To do it she incases herself in an unnatural armor. For the normal, healthy woman this means the suppression of what is strongest in her nature, that power which differentiates her chiefly from man, her power of emotion, her "affectability" as the scientists call it. She sacrifices the most wonderful part of her endowment, that which, when trained, gives her vision, sharpens her intuitions, reveals the need and the true course. This superior affectability crushed leaves her atrophied.

The common characterization of this atrophied woman is that she is "cold." It is the exact word. She *is* cold; also she is self-centered and intensely personal. Let a woman make success in a trade or profession her exclusive and sufficient ambition, and the result, though it may be brilliant, is repellent.

She gives to her task an altogether disproportionate place in her scheme of things. Life is not made by work, important as is work in life. Human nature has varied needs. But the woman sternly set to do a man's business, believing it better than a woman's, too often views life as made up of business. Her work is her child. She is as fiercely jealous of interference in it as she would be if it were a child. It is hers, a personal thing to which she clings as if it were a living being.

Here is the chief reason why working with women in the development of great undertakings is as difficult as coöperating with them in the rearing of a family. It is also a reason why they rarely rise to the first rank. They cannot get away from their undertakings sufficiently to see the big truths and movements which are always impersonal.

Brilliant and satisfying as her triumph may be to her personally, woman frequently finds that it is resented by Nature and by society. She finds that Nature lays pitfalls for her heart, cracks the ice of her heart and sets it aflame, often for absurd and unworthy causes. She finds that the great mass of unconscious women commiserate or scorn her as one who has missed the fullness of life. She finds that society regards her as one who shirked the task of life, and who, therefore, should not be honored as the woman who has stood up to the common burden. When she senses this—which is not always—she treats it as prejudice.

ANTAGONISM TO MILITANT WOMEN
⋙✳⋘

As a matter of fact the antagonism of Nature and society to the militant woman is less prejudice than self-defense. It is a protest against the wastefulness and sacrifice of her career. It is a right-saving impulse to prevent perversion of the qualities and powers of woman which are most needed in the world, those qualities and powers which differentiate her from man, which make for the variety, the fullness, the charm and interest of life.

Moreover Nature and society must not permit her triumph to appear desirable to the young. They must be made to understand what her winnings have cost in lovely and desirable things. They must be made to realize the essential barrenness of her triumph, its lack of the savor and tang of life, the multitude of make-shifts she must practice to recompense her for the lack of the great adventure of natural living.

And they see it, many of them before they are out of college. The girl abandons her quest. In the early days she was likely to be treated as an apostate if, instead of following the "life work" she had picked out, she slipped back into matrimony. I can remember the dismay among certain militant friends when Alice Freeman married. "Our first college president," they groaned. "A woman who so vindicated the sex." It was like the grieving of Miss Anthony that Mrs. Stanton wasted so much time having babies!

But this growing suspicion that the attempt to enlarge woman's life by imitating man's methods and activities is unsound is pretty well obscured by the growing feeling that the woman has a narrowing and undesirable part in the partnership with man. There are various points at which she claims it fails. It is antagonistic to personal ambition. It makes a dependent of her. It leaves her in middle life without an occupation. It keeps her out of the great movements of her day—gives her no part in the solution of the ethical and economical problems which affect her and her children.

IS WOMAN PAYING HER WAY?
⋙✳⋘

Now is the woman right in crying down her share in the human partnership? Certainly if the cultivation of individual tastes and talents to a useful, productive point is out of question in the woman's business, if it is not a part of it, something is weak in the scheme. Something is weak if the woman is or feels that she is not paying her way. Both are not only individual rights, they are individual duties as well.

Moreover she is certainly right to be dissatisfied if, after spending twenty-five years, more or less, she is to be left in middle life, her forces spent, without interests and obligations which will occupy brain and heart to the full, without important tasks which are the logical outcome of her experience and which she must carry on in order to complete that experience.

But what is the truth about it? Is there no possibility of developing the work which Nature and society have laid upon her into a profession dignified, beautiful and satisfying?

Ida M. Tarbell

THE "BRUTE IN MAN" AS AN ARGUMENT
AGAINST FEMINISM

THE "most absurd and danger-ous vagary of a restless age," is what William T. Sedgwick, Professor of Biology and Public Health in the Massachusetts Institute of Technology, calls feminism. If rebellious women, he says, persist in their agitation for social and political equality with men, a "rough male power" will arise which will place them "where it chooses."

HE TELLS FEMINISTS THEY HAD
BETTER BE CAREFUL

If rebellious women, says Professor William
T. Sedgwick, persist in their agitation for social
and political equality with men, a "rough male
power" will arise which will place them "where
it chooses."

"With all sense of chivalry, of tenderness, of veneration, gone," the Professor gives warning (in the New York *Times*), "and nothing but fleshly desire left, the status to which that masculine strength may relegate woman will be a subjection in fact and not merely in theory." "There is," he asserts, "no dodging this hard, cold fact: man possesses always the brute strength; strip him of his chivalry, his tenderness, and his respect for womanhood, and you leave naked, unfettered, and unashamed his more brutal appetites toward woman."

Of course the Professor does not think any such horrifying thing is really going to happen. The feminist movement, he is confident, will soon exhaust itself. It is not normal men and women who are responsible for it, but the "mistakes of nature"—"the very masculine women, aided and abetted by their counterparts, the feminine men." To quote further:

"If the feminists are allowed free sway there will be a total destruction of wifehood and the home, a total destruction of all the tender relations and associations that home involves, but there will never be a relegation of man to a subservient position, there never will be a society in which women will rule men. Granting that they have no other superior quality, men possess the dominating brute strength, and in the last analysis government rests on force. Argument on this point is superfluous."

Perhaps, after all, this liberty which some women are clamoring for is in reality, Professor Sedgwick thinks, only the "privilege of seeking sex adven-

ture." He sees real peril in such an adventure:

"Sex adventure of this sort by any considerable number of women would be a costly enterprize for the sex. Rooted deep in man is brute instinct. This is now held in abeyance for most men and guided by a sense of chivalry that is instilled into m 's very marrow through his relation with mother, sister, wife and daughter. Wipe out that sense of chivalry—as it would be wiped out by any considerable 'sex-adventuring' on the part of women—and there is danger that man will simply retrograde into a sex pirate. He is and always will be the stronger physically and economically. And woman, if she is to survive in a time when male protection and chivalry do not exist, will be obliged to yield him what he demands."

Professor Sedgwick's views have met with quick response from at least one man of scientific training, who pronounces his opinions medieval, insulting and fatuous, not based on scientific evidence but on personal prejudices. "It is an affront," writes Dr. Frederick Peterson, of Columbia University, "to the great body of able and dignified women who are supporting the suffrage movement for the betterment of the whole race." As for the "feminine men" who support the feminist movement, Dr. Peterson remarks:

"In the company of Plato, of Abraham Lincoln, of John Stuart Mill and Condorcet, of Herbert Spencer and Condorcet, of William Garrison, Wendell Phillips and Bernard Shaw we need not be ashamed. If these are types of 'feminine men,' we may rest content to wear the label."

The most trenchant reply to Professor Sedgwick is that of Charlotte Perkins Gilman in *The Forerunner* (New York). She pronounces his whole argument fallacious, and refers ironically to the perils he discerns in the brute strength of man:

"To see man by 'brute strength' killing the mammoth, taming the elephant, exterminating the mosquito, turning single roses to double, devizing steam engines and aeroplanes, casting out smallpox, painting pictures, composing music, weaving silk, teaching school, is interesting enough; but when it comes to government—the art, science and practice of government—there indeed we see 'brute strength' triumphant.

"Julius Cæsar and Napoleon by brute strength achieved their position; Washington and Lincoln by brute strength held theirs.

"The brute strength of the Greek Church governs the submissive millions of Russia—soldiers and all. The hundreds of millions of Chinese have no brute strength or they would govern us at once.

"The brute strength of our magnificent army is all that gives us our power in the world; and in the army, of course, the men with the most brute strength are officers—must be, to be obeyed."

Concerning man's power over woman, Mrs. Gilman continues:

"Fearing that he did not speak plainly

enough in the earlier part of his article, Professor Sedgwick repeats at length, with buttressing quotations, the basic fact that women cannot move about freely in the world, or do anything safely outside the home, on account of constant danger from this vast reservoir of brutality in man, which he now only with difficulty restrains as a reward for her submission."

If this were the case, Mrs. Gilman says, it would be time for women to carry firearms and begin to drill. But the "brute in man," she adds, with crushing finality, is a bugaboo, "merely nonsense, like the rest of Professor Sedgwick's article."

FEMINISM AND SOCIALISM

I

WE have now for the first time in the history of democracy, a demand for the ballot for its own sake and because someone else has it. Men have been riotous for the ballot, and fought for it, but only as a means of redressing specific grievances, or for the protection of one class from another. The rich oppressed the poor, and therefore the poor insisted on a voice in the government. The white man oppressed the black, and therefore the ballot was given to the black, but without avail, because he would not fight for the rights conferred. The ballot in the hands of the militant suffragettes would not be futile for any such reason.

Of course more or less effort is made to rest the demand for woman suffrage upon her need of self-protection, or the need of the community for her especial talents politically expressed. As to the former, all legal disabilities of women have been removed by men, and if some women say that the work is not complete, other women say it has been carried to excess, and all must admit that if any legal disabilities remain, revolutionary methods are not needed to extort their removal from men who have already removed most of them.

More effort is made to show that the community is in dire need of legislation and administration for which women alone are competent. The ambition of women to "mother" the community rises with their aversion to mothering anything else, and their determination to do municipal housekeeping is declared when they are in revolt against domestic housekeeping, and their writers are admitting that they do not keep house very well, that they have never managed to solve its problems, and that they run away from housekeeping as much as they can.

In their present state of what their champions describe as slavery they have succeeded in abolishing the canteen at military posts, so that, instead of drinking beer under orderly surroundings, the soldiers go to saloons just outside the reservation and drink whiskey and consort with gamblers and harlots. Many women's interest in the ballot is due entirely to the conviction that if they had the right to vote they could secure the universal prohibition of liquor selling, but legislation against the liquor traffic has been going on for over half a century, in recent years it has been advancing rapidly, and there is a great gulf between the enactment of legislation and its enforcement, of which men have had plentiful experience, but of which women show little apprehension.

The humanitarian legislation in which women are showing especial interest, curtailment of the hours of labor, the exclusion of young children from industries, the safeguarding of women, has been going on for many years. It had attained large proportions before Feminism became formidable. Men had practiced philanthropies of every sort before women became a political factor. Women regard children — other people's children — as particularly their charge, and there are many very rich women: yet it is a man who for many years has been providing pure milk for the babies of New York's East Side, and reducing the infant mortality.

Some of the women themselves recognize that a person's fitness to use five talents must be judged in some measure by the use made of one, and that on this scale of efficiency woman has not demonstrated her ability to set right what man has permitted to go wrong. As Feminism is not a science, with text books and authorized exponents, but a movement, we must seek the explanation of its meaning in the speeches, books, and magazine articles of its

champions, and we may also take the testimony of
women who are not its advocates. Helen Watterson
Moody's little book of essays, *The Unquiet Sex*, was
published several years ago, before Feminism had become
rampant, and it shows no sympathy with the demands of
some of her sisters for "emancipation." In regard to
woman's use of one talent which might reasonably influence our judgment of the need of five or ten fields for
her superior "insight" and "tact" and "unselfishness,"
Mrs. Moody says:

> We women have been wearying ourselves in the rush after a
> superficial knowledge of many things, and particularly of the
> subjects that have especially engaged the attention of men, in
> order that we might become their political peers, and reform
> their political abuses. Yet in the management of that one
> kingdom that has been ours from the beginning, we are harking
> back to the Middle Ages and the institutions which modern
> society cast aside long ago. Like the King in the story, our
> Queens want to "go out governing by the day, or week," while
> the kingdom that has always been theirs rests in its primitive
> state of anarchy and disorganization. . . . It might appear to a
> profane observer of the situation, that, until women shall have
> given evidence of some small political sagacity, some desire for
> reform, and a very little capacity for organization in that
> department of the world's sociology with which the home is
> concerned, there is no glaring injustice in denying them a share
> in the government of the country.

Rheta Childe Dorr is an active Feminist, and much more
recently than Mrs. Moody wrote her essays, she told the
world *What Eight Million Women Want*. By way of
evidence that they ought to have what they want, she
says:

> The housekeeper clings to her archaic kitchen, firmly believing
> that if she gave it up, tried to replace it by any kind of co-
> operative living, the pillars of society would crumble, and the
> home would pass out of existence. Yet so strong is her in-
> stinctive repugnance to the mediæval system on which her
> household is conducted, that she shuns it, runs away from it
> whenever she can. Housekeeping as a business is a dark mys-

tery to her. The mass of women in the United States probably hold, almost as an article of religion, the theory that woman's place is in the home. But the woman who can organize and manage a home as her husband manages his business — systematically, profitably, professionally — well, how many such women do you know?

This is supposed to prove how much industries and civic administration could be improved by enlarging the field of a woman's activities. Mrs. Dorr continues:

Even when she has had some instruction in household tasks, she almost never connects cooking with chemistry, food with dietetics, cleanliness with sanitation, buying with bookkeeping. She is an amateur.

Her use of the last word is not unique. A woman who has attained fame as a dramatist says in the Sunday magazine of a New York newspaper:

We've evolved a new type, the woman who wants to do nothing to justify her existence. The country is full of such negative creatures. They are restless, discontented, uninterested in their husbands' affairs, ready to accept everything from them without giving anything — in short, grafters. Or, say, amateur wives, instead of professionals. They are spoiled and lazy, and lazy women are a danger to the community.

Professor Vida D. Scudder, Feminist and Socialist, says (*The Yale Review*, April, 1914) "Women are not handling the servant problem well; not nearly as well as their husbands handle office boys and clerks." Perhaps these strictures upon housekeepers are not just, but the fact that women make them when we are being told that politics and industries can never be well managed till women have a larger share in their direction, is of some significance.

As Mrs. Dorr is a Feminist, it is of particular interest that she thinks the attitude of mistresses to servants calls loudly for reform. In support thereof she quotes from

Miss Kellor's investigation into domestic service, that in one house the servant's room was "a little den partitioned off from the coal bin. In another place the maid was required to sleep on an ironing board placed over a bathtub. One woman planned her new three-story house with attic windows so high that no one could see out of them. When the architect remonstrated, she said: 'Oh, those are for the maids; I don't expect them to spend their time looking out.'"

II

It is not necessary to examine in much detail the reasons given for demanding the ballot, or the uses to which it will be put, for the ballot is only the first step in Feminism. The Countess of Warwick, who came to the United States in 1912 to give a series of addresses in advocacy of socialism, was met in New York by the corps of reporters, to whom she said in reply to some inquiry about the relation of window smashing to the higher life:

The ballot in itself means nothing. What prompts the fight for the ballot in England and America is a fight for sex independence, a fight women are making — and which eventually they will win — because woman, given economic independence plus the ballot, will then be started on the road toward her right to exact a recognition of the fact that she is entitled to exercise her God-given impulses quite as much as a man is.

"Votes for women," says Edna Kenton, *Militant Women — and Women, The Century*, November, 1913, "is near and insignificant compared with the stretches that lie beyond that first, simple step. . . . Of the Feminist movement, so-called, suffrage is a tiny part."

A good idea of Feminism may be found in *Adrian Savage*, a novel by "Lucas Malet." As we have fiction in our sociology, we need not be surprised to find sociology in our fiction. Adrian Savage asked Anastasia Beauchamp

why Gabrielle, who was very friendly to him, still kept
him at a little distance. She replied that it was the
Spirit of the Age, the Spirit of Modernity. Of this she
said:

"Whether Modernity is veritably the highroad to the state
of human earthly felicity its exponents so confidently — and
truculently — predict, or not rather to some appalling and final
catastrophe, some Armageddon and Twilight of the Gods,
appears to me in the existing stage of its evolution, open to the
liveliest question. . . . Among all the destructions and recon-
structions . . . of which Modernity is made up, one change is
very real, and has, I sincerely believe, come to stay, I mean the
widespread change in thought and attitude of my sex towards
yours."

"Feminism, in short," said Adrian. "In short, Feminism,"
replied Anastasia.

Gabrielle was hesitating between Feminism and marriage. Under the influence of the former she made a little
excursion into the unconventional, and visited René Dax
in his studio, unattended. Her experiences there did not
encourage her to push her explorations farther, and in
due time she yielded to the dictates of her heart. "Lucas
Malet" says of the process:

Her nature was too rich — let it be added, too normal and
wholesome — for the senses not to play their part in the shaping
of her destiny. She had coquetted with Feminism, it is true; but
such appeals and opportunities as Feminism has to offer the
senses are not of an order wholesome natures can accept. To
Gabrielle those appeals and opportunities were, briefly, loathsome; while in her existing attitude, an exclusively intellectual
fanaticism — such as alone can render advanced Feminism
morally innocuous — no longer could control or satisfy her.

Some thirty years ago there was a woman's society in
Washington bearing the fanciful name of "Wimodausis,"
made up of the first syllables of four terms of relationship.
The Feminists have got beyond the family, and stand
forth as individuals. So a report in a Philadelphia newspaper says:

124   The Unpopular Review

"Women are getting tired of being ladies' aid societies to
men, and having only a wife-and-mother point of view on life.
They want to have a human being point of view to fall back
on." This, briefly, was the sentiment expressed in an address on
"Legislation," made yesterday before the New Century Club,
by Mrs. J. Frederick Howe, of New York.

So in addressing the College Women's Club in New
York, Anna Garlin Spencer said, as reported in the newspapers: "We have the old patriarchal ideas of the family.
The individual is the unit of civilization, and not the
family." Her later statement that "the family is the
basic social institution, but not the unit of society," only
indicates a desire to bridge over the gulf between the
present, and what the Feminists expect to accomplish.
The change in the relations of woman to man of course
involves her economic independence, and this phrase we
encounter constantly in Feminist literature. There is
more in it than appears on the surface. As Olive Schreiner,
in *Woman and Labor*, sees it, a wife and mother who is
supported by her husband is earning her living by the
exercise of her sex functions. Charlotte Perkins Gilman,
prolific author of books and speeches, points out pleasantly
the analogy between wifehood and prostitution. Edna
Kenton is not far behind. She laments:

How many of the younger women in industry lapse, with
their marriage, into the old parasitism, and fall back gladly
into the old dependence, the old getting of bread by their sex
functions.

"Parasite" is the general term applied by Olive Schreiner to wives and mothers who keep house and do not dig,
or weave, or perform other labor for wages. The idea
is not entirely new. Mary Wollstoncroft, a Feminist
before Feminism became a movement, wrote of the
married woman: "She must not be dependent on her
husband's bounty for her subsistence during his life, or
support after his death." Her idea of the relations of men

and women was that which is inseparable from this dogma of the economic independence of woman; but her application of it did not bring greater happiness than that which is often found in relations sanctioned by church and state. Her latest biographer, G. R. Stirling Taylor, says:

> The woman who agreed in the theory of her mate, that love should not be fettered by forms and sacraments, had now discovered that the theory did not fit in with the facts, and the facts made her just as tyrannical as any lawful wife could be.

Molly Elliot Seawell (*The Ladies' Battle, The Atlantic Monthly,* September, 1910), regards the economic independence of the married woman as impossible, and her inevitable economic dependence as one of the two decisive objections to woman suffrage. She says:

> The second basic principle against woman suffrage — that one voter cannot claim maintenance from another voter — would deprive married women of any claim for support from their husbands; and in all questions concerning women, wives and mothers must be considered first. From the beginning of representative government it has been recognized that when a man acquires a vote he gives up all claims to maintenance, except upon public charity. . . . Under the present dispensation the status between husbands and wives is, practically, that the husband has the vote, and the wife has the property. In lieu of a vote the law has given the wife enormous property privileges, which of course are totally inconsistent with the possession of a vote.

Economic independence is already attained by a considerable number of single women. No ballot is necessary to secure their admission to any trade, or business, or profession. The effort is made to popularize woman suffrage among working women by assuring them that it would increase their earnings, which is the common dishonesty of the stump speaker and the agitator. In her study of the results of woman suffrage in Colorado Dr. Helen L. Sumner says:

The economic effect of equal suffrage during the first dozen years of its existence in Colorado has evidently been slight. The only clearly demonstrable results, indeed, appear to have been the opening up to women of a few avenues of employment, such as political canvassing and elective offices, and the equalizing in most public positions of their salaries with those of men doing the same work. But the positions are graded, and men are given the best-paid places. The average wages, even of women teachers, are still decidedly lower than those of men teachers. Considering the slight influence which equal suffrage can be clearly demonstrated to have exerted over the public employment of women, it would be surprising if their enfranchisement could be shown to have had any marked effect on their employment in private industry. As one woman said in answer to the question in regard to the effect of equal suffrage on the wages and conditions of employment of women: "It is the same old story of demand and supply in the commercial world."

The equalization of the pay of men and women would result in enormous injustice, unless men were at the same time relieved of obligations now imposed on them by custom and law. Women who can discuss other features of their "slavery" with moderation lose control of themselves when they touch on what seems to them the intolerable oppression of smaller pay for equal work. Yet the equity is so palpable that it seems incredible that intelligent and reflecting women can be insensible to it. Even in woman suffrage states a man is held legally liable for the support of his wife and children. Society condemns the man who marries before he can support a family, but a woman is not condemned for marrying with nothing but the clothes she stands in.

If the pay of men and women is to be equalized, let their obligations be equalized. We shall presently see that this is one of the aims of the Feminists, but it involves changes in the constitution of society little understood by multitudes of women whose only idea about the ballot is that it would enable them to shut up the saloons. Yet twenty-one years of woman suffrage has not given Colorado a prohibitory liquor law.

The economic independence of married women in general is impossible without social and moral changes of the most revolutionary character. Maternity, even reduced to its present proportions, is a disability to a bread winner. Not many women could live with their husbands and children to the age of 35 or 40 and then go out into the world and find places in the industrial procession. Any man who has lost his place when over 35, and has tried to get back into the industrial army, can tell the women a good deal about this. But women who have been widowed in middle life, without resources, do not need to be told.

III

At this point Feminist and Socialist join forces. No one can have failed to be impressed by the large socialist section of the suffrage parade in New York in the fall of 1912, and the huge socialist meetings in connection with the suffrage convention in Philadelphia directly after. Prof. Vida D. Scudder, in *The Yale Review*, says: "It is noteworthy that the socialist was first among political parties to give woman an equal voice with men in public affairs. . . . A suffrage plank, moreover, has always been in the socialist platform." May B. Samuel quotes, in *The Philadelphia Ledger*, a letter from Katherine Dallett Smith, of Los Angeles, of which the following is the last sentence:

At an assembly of men and women here recently an Eastern man asked what had been the result of woman's suffrage in California, and it was unanimously conceded that so far the only result had been to strengthen the socialist party, and to double the expense of the elections.

Mrs. Rossiter Johnson, in *The New York Times*, discussing only the political ends of Feminism, says:

Strange as it may at first thought appear to many, woman suffrage, if carried to its ultimate conclusions, could not but

destroy those same sacred institutions which socialism aims at
with continually increasing frankness. . . . Mormonism introduced the suffrage into the United States in Utah; and since
then no large body of thinkers has adopted the idea, save the
socialists. Mormonism gave suffrage to Idaho. In California
and Washington four-fifths of the women were opposed to the
idea, but it was forced upon the statute books by the votes of
socialistic men.

Mrs. Johnson shows how large a vote the Mormons have
in the eleven states which "have shown a stronger tendency toward suffrage than any of the others." As the
Rev. Dr. Anna Shaw lately declared that no bad man ever
favored woman suffrage, it may be assumed that her
opinion of Mormons is highly favorable.

In taking leave of the students of Vassar College Dr.
Taylor said: "There have been introduced many new
ideas, particularly in a political and social way. Woman
suffrage and socialism have been most conspicuous."

In *The New York World*, June 21, Mrs. Carrie Chap-
man Catt said of the English militants: "Among others,
the militants are closely in touch with the revolutionary
branch of the socialists."

Were the coincidence of Feminism and socialism nothing more, it would be unimportant. It is important because both are antagonistic to the private family. The
"thorough" element does not deny it, and the half-
Feminists who wish to vote only because men do, or in
order to close the saloons, have not sufficiently considered
the wide vista opened out by Edna Kenton and other
Feminists, after the trifling first step of the vote shall have
been taken.

If the economic and moral systems of socialism could be
separated, as the "parlor socialists," in the phrase of
President Taft, imagine, there would be little importance
in the fact that all socialists are Feminists, and most
Feminists are socialists. But the economic and moral
systems are inseparable. They are combined in the statement of a woman professor in a college for women, in a

speech in Boston during the Lawrence strike, that wages will be too low so long as there are any surplus earnings to divide among the owners of the mills. They are combined in a form more destructive of society in the fact that socialism is equally hostile to the private family and to private property, because the private family is the strongest reason for private property. William Morris and E. B. Bax, in their book on socialism say:

> The family . . . ignores quietly its real reason for existence, its real aim, namely protection for individualist property by means of inheritance. Its aim is the perpetuation of individual property in wealth, in workman, in wife, in child. . . . The present marriage system is based on the general supposition of economic dependence of the woman on the man, and the consequent necessity of his making provision for her, which she can legally enforce. This basis would disappear with the advent of social economic freedom, and no binding contract would be necessary between the parties as regards livelihood; while property in children would cease to exist, and every infant that came into the world would be born into full citizenship, and would enjoy all its advantages, whatever the conduct of its parents might be. Thus a new development of family would take place on the basis, not of a predetermined, life-long, business arrangement, to be formally and nominally held to, irrespective of circumstances, but on mutual inclination and affection, an association terminable at the will of either party.

Professor Vida D. Scudder, who lately preached in *The Hibbert Journal* a refined and ladylike sort of socialism, was unable in her article on *The Social Conscience*, April, 1909, to blink entirely the domestic changes involved in the millennium that she looked forward to, but treated the matter as daintily as possible:

> The fate of purity in the socialist state is a great question. Quite possibly it may have a harder struggle to maintain itself than it does even today. The reaction from individualism may bring here a serious result. Theories of free love, have, of course, absolutely nothing to do with economic socialism, in spite of a foolish confusion of thought in some quarters; nevertheless, one foresees that, as the idea of the sacredness of prop-

erty shrinks and dwindles, one inferior and adventitious support to the monogamic marriage may be withdrawn.

After a farther study of her socialist text books, Professor Scudder admits that there is some excuse for the confusion of thought which a few years earlier had seemed so foolish to her. She admits in *The Yale Review* that many socialists from Bebel down have identified socialism and free love. There are persons hardy enough to deny that Bebel advocated free love, but after this admission it is hardly worth while to cite the evidence. But the important thing is not that some persons identify socialism with free love, but that the most authoritative socialists we have oppose the private family because it is inconsistent with socialist economics. In *Woman under Socialism* Bebel leaves no doubt in the mind of any intelligent reader what he means, and he cites a German woman writer to the same effect; and he gives the reason for the dissolution of the family:

In future society there is nothing to bequeath, unless the domestic equipment and personal inventory be regarded as inheritance; the modern form of marriage is thus devoid of foundation and collapses. The question of inheritance is thereby solved, and socialism need not concern about abolishing the same. No right of inheritance can arise where there is no private property. Woman is, accordingly, free, and her children, when she has any, do not impair her freedom.

The Feminist would break down the family in order to give economic independence to woman; and the socialist would give economic independence to woman in order to break down the family. The latter would abolish theft by repealing the Eighth Commandment, and the former would abolish adultery and prostitution by abolishing the Seventh. Both concur in attacking the Tenth because it affirms the private family and private property.

Why should any of the women who are following the Feminist leaders balk at the moral side of socialism? The Countess of Warwick said in an interview:

Women have forever been held down by the man-imposed rules of so-called morality (and morality has nothing to do with the subject) and now they are revolting. The fight for the ballot is one manifestation of the revolution. Marriage will be revolutionized through economic independence of women, plus the ballot.

Edna Kenton says:

The militant campaign in England, has made clear the evolution among women of a moral code of their own, set up for themselves, of themselves, without regard to the wishes of men. . . . For nothing that has been termed woman's morality is hers.

Ellen Key, in *Love and Marriage*, describes an exalted moral state in which there is no marriage without love, and no love without — a substitute for marriage; in which all desires will be gratified — so long as they may be experienced — and the old love may be dropped like an old glove when the new one is encountered. It is not necessary, and in the case of young persons it is not even desirable, that permanence should be intended in the association of men and women. How can persons tell whether they will love the present objects of their affection next year, or next week, or to-morrow morning?

The issue between any civilization with which we are acquainted, and Feminism and socialism, is whether the social unit is the family or the individual. If the former, then the present constitution of society is fundamentally sound, and it is only needed that men and women should improve in their characters and dispositions. If the individual is the unit, the family is doomed.

Ellen Key and other apostles of Feminism believe that the permanent interests of the community demand that every restraint be removed from individual desire. The underlying question is whether the important thing in the union of men and women be its emotional character, or its exclusiveness. Society has got along tolerably well where the emotions were negligible, but nothing that we have any record of warrants the supposition that civilized society could exist where there was no regard for exclusiveness. In *Romantic Love and Personal Beauty*, Henry T. Finck says:

> Romantic love is a modern sentiment, less than a thousand years old. . . . Not till Dante's *Vita Nuova* appeared was the gospel of modern love — the romantic adoration of a maiden by a youth — revealed for the first time in definite language. Genius, however, is always in advance of its age, in emotions as well as in thought. . . . It remained for Shakespeare to combine the idealism with the realism of love in proper proportions. . . . Like Dante, however, he was emotionally ahead of his time, as an examination of contemporary literature in England and elsewhere shows. But within the last two centuries love has gradually, if slowly, assumed among all educated people characteristics which formerly it possessed only in the minds of a few isolated men of genius. . . . Romantic love, it is well known, hardly exists in France as a motive to marriage, being systematically suppressed and craftily annihilated. Nevertheless, as many observers attest, the French commonly lead a happy family life.

France is not so different from other European countries as Mr. Finck's specification of it would imply. In *The Lighter Side of Irish Life*, "George A. Birmingham" tells us that marriages in Ireland are usually happy, and rarely defiled by unfaithfulness. But they are generally arranged by the families. His explanation is of vast significance in any discussion of marital happiness:

> The probability is that as most of our people marry without romance, so they marry without illusion. The woman accepts wifehood and motherhood as a man accepts his profession, knowing that life is not a rose garden. The man accepts his wife without supposing that he is going to be mated with an angel. Somewhat less is expected in the marriage of arrangement than in the marriage of passion, and therefore, in the great majority of cases, somewhat more is obtained. Into the marriage of passion the man and woman rush with blind eyes, to recover sight afterward, and with sight, too often, disillusion. Into the marriage of arrangement they go with eyes very widely

opened, and are, therefore, all the better able to close them afterward when closing is necessary for domestic peace.

In this sentimental age we are losing sight of the permanent interests of mankind in the temporary pleasures of the individual. Perhaps it is the decreasing birth rate that makes us indifferent to posterity. We have come to exalt pleasure above duty, obligation, and the public welfare. We are trying to make everything amusing. We exaggerate the importance of satisfying every desire, and under the growing influence of Feminism we are stimulating our emotions. We are feeling instead of thinking.

THE FEMINIST PROGRAM

AS one burden after another is laid upon the shoulders of women in the warring countries, the Feminists rejoice exceedingly. Their latest triumph is that women are digging subways in Berlin, by night and day shifts, ten feet below the surface of the street. Dr. Anna Shaw, speaking of how the cause of suffrage is being aided by the war, says:

> Women have come out from their homes as never before, and they are doing all those things which men have done and which the men have insisted the women could not do. They are acting as police, as letter carriers, as hack drivers, working in the fields, garnering the crops, and busied at countless tasks which have always been confined to the field of masculine activities. Now that women are freed from the shackles of convention, they will stay so, and the governments of the different countries will not be able to push them into the background when the war is over.

But already in England the evil results of "woman's coming out from the home" are being seriously felt. The English people were naturally inclined at the beginning of the war to pride themselves on the splendid way in which women rose to the occasion, willingly undertaking anything from munitions work to tram conducting. But when the country began to settle down to war conditions, and to realize that an intense and terrible struggle for national existence opened up more problems than that of carrying it on from day to day, thoughtful people realized with misgiving that the nation would suffer if the women, in order to do war work, must neglect work which none but women can do. The misgivings were proved well founded when infant mortality jumped in six months to the highest rate in years. Commenting upon this alarming condition, an English writer says: "Unless drastic steps are taken to remedy this evil, posterity

will have harsh things to say of a generation that allowed
its women to do men's work to the neglect of the duties
which nature and the nation's interests alike called upon
them to perform. The first call on women ought to be
for women's work. Just as maximum efficiency is not
secured by sending skilled munition workers into the
firing line, so it will not be secured by taking women
from indispensable service which they alone can perform."

Even prominent suffragists are beginning to realize and
to admit the falseness of the outlook on life which under-
lay their movement. We are told that one effect of the
war has been to silence — almost — those English agitators who never tired of sneering at political opponents
who held that the well-being of the nation required that
the majority of women should find their main scope in
motherhood and the home. That numbers of women are
compelled to earn their livelihood away from home was
not denied; but the contention was that the home and all
that went with it, particularly motherhood and the care
of infant life, called for the first attention of women who
claimed to be interested in their sex. The jeers that could
always be relied upon at certain meetings to greet the
reference to "woman's sphere being in the home," are
no longer heard. In their place England has witnessed
a splendid campaign to promote the welfare of motherhood and infancy.

Suffragists assume that the world would profit if woman's
activities and interests became the same as those of men.
This is one of the most unsound of many unsound suffrage
arguments. It implies of course that the part of the world's
work which has naturally fallen to women is less important
and less likely to develop the individual than the part
which has naturally fallen to men. But how can the relative importance of these two halves of the world's work
be decided, since both are absolutely essential? As the
race would cease if either sex should break down, argument

as to which is superior seems absurd. That woman would develop better under masculine conditions of life is a totally unsupported theory. Woman cannot become man — she can only become a poor imitation. She develops best along the lines of her own aptitudes and instincts. To suppress these, as Miss Tarbell has well said, is to rob not only women but the world. When the powers and qualities peculiar to woman become atrophied, human society is the loser.

No work in the world is more important for the welfare of society than the care of young children, and this is woman's job. That babies need their mothers' care — that institutional life for infants is a disastrous failure — is the decision of experts in every country where the question has been studied. It is the Feminists alone who dispute this decision, and who still advocate the discredited theory that the proper sphere for women, except for a very short period before and after childbirth, is outside the home. The most striking recent exposition of the up-to-date theories of Feminism is contained in a book called *Feminism in Germany and Scandinavia* by Katherine Anthony. Miss Anthony is a member of the Woman's Political Union and of the Woman Suffrage Party of New York City. Her preface is dated from New Fairfield, Conn., and was evidently written before the recent overwhelming suffrage defeats in New York, New Jersey, Pennsylvania and Massachusetts. In it the author says:

> The suffrage movement in this country is approaching a successful climax; the hour glass must be turned promptly, otherwise the continuity of the Feminist advance will be broken and the acquired momentum squandered. These chapters from the work of the other Feminists may offer some suggestions as to the activities which should engage the collective attention of the American woman movement when it has been released.

Again she says:

> People are just now beginning to discover that Feminism means more than suffragism, that the ballot for the ballot's

sake is not the whole meaning of the suffrage agitation, that the political demands of women are inseparable from the social, educational and economic demands of the whole Feminist movement.

This is direct confirmation of the statement frequently made by anti-suffragists that suffrage is only the first step in the Feminist Program. The author continues:

To the American observer there is much food for reflection in the outspoken Feminism of the continental movement. One sees very little evidence of truckling to narrow-minded criticism.

In Germany, she tells us, there are various branches of the woman's movement. There are the socialist-feminists, the Bourgeois-feminists, the conservative feminists, the modern feminists, the radical feminists, the Christian feminists, the neutral feminists, the young feminists, the suffrage-feminists, and the feminist-feminists. One of the things against which their leaders rebel is the "superisolation of women in married life." "Man has enslaved them well," we are told. "They will not even hear of freedom. He has separated them well. They are angry with the stronger ones of their own sex."

The woman movement in America and England, Miss Anthony tells us, has largely taken the form of an agitation for Votes for Women. In Germany and Scandinavia, however, it is known as the Muttershutz (motherhood protection) movement, the objects of which are, apparently, to make the State, instead of the husband and father, responsible for the support of mother and child, and to standardize illegitimacy. There are 180,000 illegitimate children born in Germany every year; in Sweden 18,000; and in little Norway 5,000. This convinces the Feminists that the institution of marriage is a failure. That the failure lies with the mothers who have not trained their sons and daughters aright seems scarcely to occur to them. Our author says:

According to the church and the state nothing can be wrong with the form of sex union known as legal marriage; but ac-

cording to the woman movement and the Muttershutz movement something *is* wrong with the institution of marriage.
The Muttershutz movement . . . not only demands the abolition of proprietary rights in marriage, but questions the eternal
validity of monogamy.

It insists that the union without marriage must be accepted and recognized. Our author quotes the following:

There is one radical method which would bring our ideas
back upon the right track, and many a sincere friend of the
cause must have already wished it, — that illegitimate births
might occur right often. For rights and laws, as they are, were
not revealed by an unalterable cosmic order but framed by the
temporary majority. And the majority is always right — even
when it is wrong! Every century has a different law, and one
need not be a Utopian to assume that, after so and so many
decades or centuries, the ideas of illegitimate motherhood
hitherto cultivated may be transformed into its exact opposite.
The more illegitimate births there are to record, the nearer
comes that time.

To the writer just quoted monogamy merely happens
to be the present fashion in conservative circles! The
human need of the child for two parents — a father as
well as a mother — is something to which the Feminist
in her sex-conceit, closes her eyes. She is blind also to
the fact that the ideal of monogamy — of lifelong marriage — stands for much more than the emotion of youthful passion. It rests on the purpose of seeking another's
good, — "for richer, for poorer, in sickness and in health;"
the gradual adjustment of personalities, the companionship of ideas, of pleasures and of griefs form its basis.
This basis is so vital to the success of sex relations that the
Feminist attack on "the eternal validity of monogamy"
is fortunately not likely to meet with permanent success.

On account of the great number of surplus women in
Europe "the men who wish to evade the burdens and
responsibilities of lifelong marriage find it easier to do so,"
our author tells us.

The Feminist Program   323

In the colonies, on the other hand, the situation is reversed. The men form the majority of the population and become the competing sex. The women may make the terms of the sex union and exact the topmost price, lifelong support. It is clear that the surplus women gathered together in the centers of European civilization cannot exact this topmost price, even if the woman movement had not taught them to question the morality of a marriage for a support.

To Miss Anthony the spiritual side of monogamy evidently does not exist. To her mind, the woman who marries, simply sells herself, and drives a hard bargain.

"From the time of Luther," she tells us, "until the beginning of the 20th century the monogamic marriage was the highest ideal of sexual ethics, but at that time an organized movement began which encouraged skepticism toward the Lutheran sex code, and championed the victims of this code — the unmarried mother of the illegitimate child."

This new movement was called "The New Ethics." Many of its followers protest against the exclusive adoption of the monogamic marriage as an ethical standard. This is the kernel of the new ethics. "The right to motherhood" and the naming of all children after the maternal line in order that the illegitimate child should be at no disadvantage in this regard, are other "ethical" ideas freely advocated by this movement.

Still another is in favor of the "uniform title." (Einheits-Titel.) The original intention of the uniform title was the protection of the unmarried mother. In her case the epithet "Fräulein" invites the social persecution and the social revenge to which she is always exposed. To shield her, groups of women began to repudiate for themselves the title "Fräulein" and to assume the title "Frau." Frau Rosika Schwimmer, Secretary of the International Woman Suffrage Association, who campaigned for the Ohio suffragists in 1914, and who originated the "Ford Peace Ship" idea and carried it to its logical conclusion, is an unmarried woman who has assumed the uniform title.

A little clear thinking will show that all these "ethical" ideas do not touch the root of the matter. So long as the mother of sons in the well-to-do classes considers it only natural for her boys to seduce girls of the working class, and so long as the mothers of these girls also consider this situation one to be accepted, so long will it be the *mothers* of Germany and Scandinavia who are a failure and not the institution of marriage.

Thomas F. A. Smith, in his book *The Soul of Germany*, says that immorality in Germany is not only widespread, but that it is tolerated and laughed at. On proceeding to the university or obtaining a lieutenant's commission, the young Teuton looks around for a "Verhältnis" and will have no difficulty in forming one with a shop girl, waitress, daughter of a small tradesman or official, even a family governess. He incurs no other obligation than paying for entertainments, excursions and the like. During his premarital years he may form many such irregular acquaintanceships. No German would think of forbidding him his home on that account. His Don Juan proclivities may form a delectable subject of conversation for ladies over cups of coffee. The German girl's moral sensibilities never, according to this writer, lead her to reject a husband who had devoted ten or fifteen years to the primrose paths of dalliance; and when she becomes a mother she neglects her opportunities to combat these conditions, since she fails to instill better principles into her sons.

If the Feminists are undertaking to reform public opinion in regard to the matter of sex union why not reform it along the lines of increased individual responsibility and self-control, rather than in trying to remove every safeguard, social, moral or legal against illegitimate relations? The statute books may be filled with a thousand decrees that the illegitimate child shall have every privilege which the law can grant, but these can never make up to the child for the lack of the natural family life, which is its right. Instead, however, of attempting to raise moral standards and improve these appalling conditions, the Feminists urge that the standards common among "lower class" women be accepted by women of all classes.

Fritz Berolzheimer, in a book called *Morality and Society in the Twentieth Century* says on page 293:

Free love, formerly common in the lower classes, is now frequent among better class girls. This has not been caused by temptation, but it is the widespread acceptance of the doctrine, so diligently proclaimed in certain quarters, of the right to love, and because of the rejection, as oldfashioned, of the usual estimate placed upon chastity.

Such are the fruits of Feminist teaching.

That the theory of Feminism is poisoning our literature as well as our social life and that women writers are on the whole the worst offenders, no one who is conversant with recent American fiction can doubt. We have "progressed" along this road rapidly since the Feminist movement became strong, but Germany is still ahead. In 1907 she was already so far advanced that George Sylvester Viereck, whose own verses are certainly not without erotic tendencies, denounced in scathing terms the extent to which this tendency had developed in modern German literature. He said "Surely there is something rotten in the society which tolerates this sort of thing and applauds it." And he suggests that a great war may be needed to do away with this poison in German life.

It is small wonder that Karl Lange, the anti-feminist writer, is moved to say in his *Monatsblatt* for Dec. 1915:

May God grant that from our great need a new recognition of the value of marriage, honorably fulfilled, may arise; therein would lie the surest hope of rooting out the moral diseases which in the years just preceding the war threatened the downfall of our race.

Miss Anthony in her chapter on "State Maternity Insurance" tells us that such insurance in Europe forms one of the most significant chapters in the history of the changing status of women. It recognizes maternity as a service to the state, and entitles the wife to claim support, nominal though the payment may be in the initial stages of maternity insurance, from some other source besides her husband. She claims that this recognition is one of the most substantial gains of the German and Scandinavian woman movement.

On the other hand, she says, the foreign Feminists have no desire to stress the economic valuation of maternity to a degree which would mean the denial of the mother's right to work, or her exclusion from the ordinary wage-earning occupations. But they do maintain that her hard-won and dear-bought economic independence shall not be sacrificed as a condition for maternity. Henrietta Fürth, a prominent Feminist,

Whose demands are tied down to the essentially practical, merely asks that the mother shall be reimbursed for the wages she loses, and for a period of six to eight weeks following her confinement, and eight weeks preceding it. Along these lines the emancipation of the mother from sex slavery becomes a practical and feasible prospect and not a Utopian dream.

It should be noted that this Feminist program is identical with the ideals of the Socialists. The fact that Feminism is simply Socialism in its relation to women has not been sufficiently dwelt upon. Rheta Childe Dorr, in her book entitled *What 8,000,000 Women Want*, Chapter III, pages 70 and 71, speaking of the woman suffragist in Germany says:

She is a Suffragist because she is a Socialist, because woman suffrage, and indeed, the full equalization of the laws governing men and women are a part of the socialist platform in every country in the world. The woman member of the Social Democrat party is not working primarily for woman suffrage. She is working for a complete overturning of the present economic system, and she advocates universal adult suffrage as a means of bringing about the social and economic change demanded by the Socialists.

This is a clear and convincing statement of the relation of the two movements. Miss Anthony continues:

Many people, women especially, dislike the thought that child-bearing and child-rearing should be associated with any schedule of money payments. The mother's care of her child is something whose psychological and spiritual value is inestimable; it is admittedly one of the greatest cultural influences. It is a tremendous contribution, but it cannot be bought. All this, of course, is very true. But . . . after all we live in an economic world and not in a Paul-and-Virginia paradise!

Again she says:

There is, indeed, no question but that the child-bearer should be protected against all preventable disease and accident, and that the responsibility for such protection rests upon the state. The persistent neglect of this duty is not justifiable by any reason; it is but the lingering influence of an oriental fatalism which invented the myth of the curse of Eve. This myth has taught men to stand aside and regard with complacent neutrality this immemorial battle of woman with nature, and woman herself to submit to many preventable evils.

The rank injustice of this statement is apparent, as it is perfectly well known that the tremendous scientific advance in the care of women at childbirth is almost entirely the result of patient study on the part of men.

Our author adds:

The economic helplessness of the child-bearer has, to some extent, been relieved by the introduction of state maternity insurance. This put an end to the complete dependence of the mother and child upon the father. The far-reaching significance of this slight economic victory can be appreciated when we remember that the original enslavement of woman resulted from her weakness and defenselessness at childbirth. It is one of the deepest ironies of our civilization that the woman in childbed has for her sole economic shield and protector the being who once used just this occasion to conquer and rob her.

At what period of history was it the custom for a man to rob the mother of his children during her days in childbed?

Miss Anthony maintains that the successive steps towards state-supported childhood should not result in causing the individual father to fade into the background; but just how the Feminists expect to keep alive in the husband and father a sense of responsibility for wife and child after the state has undertaken their care and support is not explained. As this sense of responsibility for wife and child is the most steadying and civilizing influence in the life of men, to do away with it, as the Feminists plan to do, is to take a long step backwards toward barbarism.

The Feminists demand insurance for all mothers, legitimate or illegitimate. They consider the proposal that married women should be excluded from the factories as "Utopian." They quote Henrietta Fürth, herself the mother of eight children, as saying "There has never been a time yet when motherhood was a lifefilling vocation." The married woman who does not work outside the home they disdainfully label the Nur-Hausfrau (the housewife only). Of her it is said that "her economic and legal subjection is complete."

Dr. Kathe Schirmacker, one of the Feminist leaders, holds that the economic dependence of the married woman spreads its "baleful influence" over the economic position of the whole sex. She claims that it is because women's work in the home and for the family is not valued in terms of money-wages, their work outside the home is poorly paid.

The woman is accustomed to working in her own home for nothing, and she is not able to place a sufficiently high value on her services when they are performed outside the home for an employer. The economic independence of the unmarried woman is constantly hampered and impeded by the economic dependence of the married woman.

This is again straight Socialist doctrine, which the Feminists have accepted without revision. It is to be remembered, however, that there are some leaders of the woman movement both in Europe and America still sane enough to sound a warning note regarding economic independence, and to call attention to its appalling results. Mrs. Florence Kelley, Vice-President of the National American Woman Suffrage Association, says that "such statistics as have been gathered the world over show that the industrial employment of married women does harm and only harm" and she specifies among the fruits of it "infanticide, a demoralizing tendency to husbands, and a lowering of men's wages."

Ellen Key, the great Swedish Feminist, holds the same opinion. She says that competition between the sexes produces overcrowding of the labor market, with low wages, uncertainty of employment, high infant mortality, and a debased domestic life with its consequences of drunkenness and crime. It also produces ill feeling between the sexes.

The truth of this last statement is unconsciously confirmed by Miss Anthony, who tells us how men, several centuries ago, solved the problem of competition between the sexes. She says:

In the middle ages, especially, women were prominent in the economic scheme. The records show that they were not excluded from any occupation. They were active as silk-weavers and silk-spinners, yarn-spinners, gold-spinners, hat-makers and embroiderers; in short they were quite generally engaged in the highly skilled production of apparel and tapestries of all kinds.

In the fourteenth century the guilds began to exclude women and to limit their work. They discovered that there was an old rule which declared that only those persons could be members who were able to bear arms. The terms in which the resolutions were drafted show that no attempt was made to conceal the purely competitive and egoistic spirit of the male workers by which the women were banished from the guilds and deprived of their means of livelihood.

The attitude of the guilds toward the women at this critical period was a compound of economic jealousy and sex-contempt. By the end of the seventeenth century, women had been wholly crowded out of the handicraft guilds and everywhere the male sex made the condition of admission.

This proves the truth of the anti-feminist contention that when competition between the sexes becomes keen, the woman, being the weaker, will go to the wall; and justifies the belief that *co-operation* between the sexes, not *competition* is the object to be striven for.

Miss Anthony dwells on the bitter antagonism of the German Feminists toward Ellen Key, long considered the leader of the Feminist movement in Europe. Because Miss Key declared that women were making a mistake in rushing indiscriminatingly into men's occupations, instead of freeing and enhancing the work which was peculiarly their own, she was bitterly attacked by the Feminists, who declare that she has retarded the progress of women's enfranchisement and of the entire woman's movement. Miss Anthony dubs her the "wise fool" of the woman movement!

Miss Key, after passing through various phases of feminist "thinking," at last worked out to the sane position which anti-suffragists have always maintained, that woman's great contribution to the world is as wife, mother and homemaker. Looking at the matter solely from the economic point of view, she declares that the wages of the married woman when expended for ready made clothing, generally of poor materials, and for ready made food, which is expensive and frequently adulterated, is less of a contribution to the family's well-being than her time and strength expended in the household, and used in purchasing wisely, cooking wholesome food, and making durable clothing. The mother in the home instead of in the factory would also lessen enormously the high rate of infant mortality, and decrease the number of neglected children.

It has been thoroughly demonstrated by many investigators that babies whose mothers "work out" do not thrive as well as those whose mothers can watch them.

Dr. John Lovett Morse, the child specialist of Boston, says that statistics show that one in every five bottle-fed babies dies before it is a year old, while only one in every thirty of breast-fed babies dies, thus giving the breast-fed baby six times as many chances to live as the bottle-fed baby. Evidently then, if the welfare of children and of the race is to be considered, the Feminist doctrine that mothers should return to their jobs in shops or factories six weeks after childbirth, is about as bad a program as could be devised.

But this doctrine, although it has all the weight of the world's experience against it, is hotly defended by the Feminist, who is obsessed by the idea that family life must be destroyed, and that woman must go out "into the world" to compete with man on equal terms.

The destructive character of the Feminist movement is clearly brought out in the following lines quoted by Miss Anthony:

Women have to demand a great many things which may not necessarily be good in themselves, simply because these things are forbidden. They have also to reject many things which may not be necessarily evil in themselves, simply because they are prescribed. The idea of obedience can have no moral validity for women for a long time to come. . . The only ethical course for her is to meet the requirements of her age, even if she is thereby condemned to enter a state of exaggeration and anarchy.

No better characterization could be chosen of the conditions for which the Feminists are striving than this "a state of exaggeration and anarchy." Miss Anthony has performed a real service to the reading public in setting forth so clearly the goal toward which the suffrage movement is tending, and in making it clear that what the Feminists call "Progress" is a backward movement toward conditions many of which have been long outgrown and discredited by civilized nations.

SOME CONSIDERATIONS AFFECTING THE REPLACEMENT OF MEN BY WOMEN WORKERS.

JOSEPHINE GOLDMARK,

Publication Secretary, National Consumers' League, New York City.

Read before the Industrial Hygiene Section, American Public Health Association, October 19, 1917, at Washington, D. C.

AMONG the many new and urgent problems of industry in wartime, none challenges our best thought more sharply than the replacement of men by women workers. This movement which has gone far abroad, is still in its infancy in this country; yet it is not too soon, it is, indeed, high time to gauge the tendencies and consequences of so radical a change. The replacement of men by women, proceeding in many industries and occupations in every state of the union, must of necessity react for good or for ill not only upon the girls and women so employed, but upon far wider circles, upon their families, their children, and upon the whole standard of living of their communities.

In this country it is too soon as yet to hazard an estimate of the numbers of women who are entering upon new occupations and taking men's places. The number of the women so employed is not yet numerically great; their employment is in many cases still experimental, but we are undoubtedly on the threshold of great innovations. Girls and women as messengers and elevator operators, as section hands and towermen on railroads, running drills and presses, working in powder-mills and sawmills, cleaning the outsides of railroad coaches and wiping engines, in the machine shop, in the munitions plant, in the airplane factory—these are some of the new figures in industry.

BENEFITS OF THE CHANGE.

Among the benefits from the new widening of women's employment one of the most important is the breakdown of prejudices. Women have in the past been hampered in advancing industrially by the prejudices of both employers and their fellow workmen, organized and unorganized. Women's sex and inexperience has been made the excuse not only for all manner of exploitation but for the refusal of employers to advance them to positions of responsibility and trust. One of the triumphs of women's wartime employment in England has been their response to opportunity: the intelligence and the speed with which they have reacted to instruction in intricate new work such as the manufacture of aero-engines and guns as well as in the simpler operations of making shells, fuses, hand grenades, etc. This is the universal testimony: to the unbounded surprise of all, women have proved their ability to enter upon and succeed in work hitherto closed to them on the sole ground of their sex.

And this success has been a triumph not only for women workers, but for

360

the new methods of instruction in industry. Instead of the old rule of thumb and the mere copying of fellow workmen by apprentices and new workers, there has been intelligent direction of the working women newly introduced into the workshops of England. Mr. Granville Baillie of the British Ministry of Munitions, at a conference on Women in Industry in London last May, told how the new training had enabled working women to surprise the world by their achievements in industry, by the speed, the accuracy and the responsibility with which they have mastered their new trades. The training has been most successful when carried on in the plant where the women are to work. Under the British Ministry of Munitions, training schools were established with a view to giving untrained women some general technical instruction for the simpler processes in the engineering and chemical trades. This has been best carried out in the individual shop rather than in technical schools.

Throughout the world women are entering these new fields. Between July, 1914, and January, 1917, the number of women gainfully employed in Great Britain had increased by almost one-third. According to the London *Labour Gazette* of August, 1917, 1,256,000 women are directly replacing men.* In Germany the number of women employed in metal trades alone in July, 1916, is reported to have been over 3,000,000. In France the Minister of Munitions stated just a year

ago that 300,000 women had gone into munition works; from Italy it is officially reported that the number of women employed in munition works in Lombardy has risen from over 4 to about 10 per cent of the total number of employes.†

Undoubtedly in this country many promising fields are opening for women from which they have been debarred and for which they are well fitted. Such are the new positions in many branches of the railroad service; for instance, as freight checkers, as ticket agents, and as information clerks, weeding and clearing the tracks; in banks and financial houses; in cost and production departments; as floor walkers in stores; as clerks in shoe stores, etc. In machine shops women are found to excel men at inspecting and testing and other operations requiring dexterity. In many instances, too, women are now receiving far higher wages than ever before for work no harder than women's traditional exhausting labor of scrubbing floors during long hours in dampness and wet. Yet, granting all that promises from such gains, no one can view without alarm the indiscriminate employment of women which is in process or impending in such heavy work as glass making, in some of the processes of steel mills exposed to extreme heat, as ballast tampers or freight handlers on railroads, as pilers of lumber and loaders of scrap iron, or in the bleachery pits of cotton mills,—to mention

† Child Labor in Warring Countries. A Brief Review of Foreign Reports. Industrial Series No. 4. The Children's Bureau. United States Department of Labor, pp. 12, 13, 14.

* Monthly Review of the United States Bureau of Labor Statistics, October, 1917, p. 41.

some of the occupations most needing scrutiny and care.

EVILS NEEDING SCRUTINY.

If the achievements of women workers challenge the world's admiration, we cannot neglect the obverse side of the picture. We have not yet learned the cost, the wastage of woman power.* There is no doubt that both abroad and in this country unmistakable dangers are inherent in many of the new occupations. Some indeed are totally unfit for women; some may be rendered fit by changes in method of management; in all of them the indispensable prerequisite is a new scrutiny of the workers and the effect of the work, a kind of intelligent supervision known hitherto in only a very small number of the most enlightened establishments but needed now wherever women are employed in new lines of activity if we are to preserve our national energies.

LIFTING EXCESSIVE WEIGHTS.

Of the specific dangers to be guarded against, one of the most obvious is the lifting of excessive weights. This has long been recognized as a source of injury for women. In no occupation hitherto engaged in have the chances of physical harm from lifting excessive weights been greater than, for instance, in the proposed employment of women in railroad freight yards. One road which has contemplated such a step, stated that the weight of goods to be lifted would run up to 100 pounds. No argument is needed to show that

such work, continued through the day, is unfit for women and should be totally prohibited. It is true that in laundries, another traditional employment of women, women are expected to lift bundles often weighing more than 100 pounds. This is undoubtedly a source of physical injury; in freight yards such burdens are not an occasional part of the work but constitute its main part. In one railroad yard girls themselves weighing not more than 115 pounds, were found wheeling metal castings in wheelbarrows up and down inclined planks and loading them into the cars.

A recent report from Germany shows that among women employed in the metal trades heavy lifting is a main cause of physical injury. The inquiry covered over 2,500 establishments employing more than 266,000 women and girls, an increase of 319 per cent over the number employed before the war. Projectiles weighing from 22 pounds to 82 pounds have to be raised breast high from the floor and clamped down, then unclamped and placed again on the floor. According to this report, given in *Soziale Praxis* of April 19, 1916, there is great complaint of abdominal trouble among the women who raise these weights. In one establishment which required very hard muscular work, it is reported that nearly a third of the 42 women employed "have been disabled by illness."†

Clearly, in any occupation which requires heavy lifting, as for instance in corerooms, a maximum weight

---

* See Women's Industrial News, London, July, 1917.

† Monthly Review of the United States Bureau of Labor Statistics, September, 1917, p. B4.

Replacement of Men by Women Workers 273

should be set. In New York State a maximum of 25 pounds has been fixed by law regulating women's work in foundries. A maximum of 25 pounds in lifting weights was adopted also in the valuable standards formulated by the Executives' Club of Detroit last spring representing 40 of the largest industrial plants in that city.*

The establishment of a maximum weight in lifting is obviously a rough measure of protection. In all occupations safety lies only in the physical examination of all prospective workers, or better in the medical supervision of workers, as Doctor Schereschewsky has well phrased it in a recent address.† For some women doubtless even 25 pounds is excessive, when lifting constitutes a large part of the day's work. The relation of the lifted weight to the chest and abdomen circumference, the total physical condition of the worker, should be determining and can be settled only by a medical examination before employment.

INDUSTRIAL POISONING.

Another obvious danger calling for close observation in some of the new occupations is that of industrial poisoning. Thanks to Bulletin No. 219 of the Federal Bureau of Labor Statistics by Dr. Alice Hamilton, we have knowledge of the extent and nature of industrial poisoning in the manufacture of high explosives, so far as it could be ascertained by investigation of the first order. In this country women have not yet been employed

* Industrial Management, August, 1917.
† Public Health Reports. Reprint No. 234, November 20, 1914.

in large numbers in the manufacture of TNT, in filling shells, or in those nitration processes whose victims show the same symptoms, suffer and die exactly as do the victims of gases in trench warfare. Yet it is known to the writer that in precisely one of the worst conducted TNT factories, where the sanitary precautions are nil and the TNT is allowed to cover the ground, the workroom and the workers themselves, women are among the operatives. As the manufacture of explosives grows by leaps and bounds in this country, and new gases are developed and manufactured, as other poisons are increasingly used such as the various dopes for airplane wings, women will increasingly be employed in these dangerous processes. As a sex they are known to experience more serious injury than men from such an industrial poison as lead. This may be true of other industrial poisons not yet studied. Safety here lies only in the enforcement of sanitary precautions, in periodic medical supervision, in the shortening of hours of labor and in the prohibition of night work for women.

OVERFATIGUE AND NIGHTWORK.

In all of the new occupations as in the old, too much emphasis cannot be laid upon the factor of fatigue in predisposing to illness and exhaustion. It did not need the well recorded wartime experience of England to teach us that output together with health and vigor fails when hours of work are excessive, when Sunday work is permitted and rest at night broken. Yet within the last year even the enlightened State of Massachusetts, the pioneer in labor legislation and for twenty years the leader in prohibiting night work for women employed in factories, has under the plea of war emergencies reëstablished night work and overtime by special permit to specified establishments.

It is well known that the greatest efforts have been needed to prevent the breakdown of labor laws in many states and the reëstablishment of excessive hours of labor for women.

The labor standards for European countries, especially for women and children, were in many respects lower than our own before the war. In the first, rush of industry, following the outbreak of the war, these standards abroad were still further lowered. Yet it soon proved that the relaxing of standards failed to achieve its purpose; in England and France and more recently in Italy definite steps were taken by the governments to restore the provisions of the labor law in order to maintain output and conserve the workers. In Italy indeed, the present standards are in some respects higher than before the war.*

Besides the recent reëstablishment of night work in factories, another new form of work at night for women in this country is in the elevator service. Here is an occupation newly open to women throughout the land. They are operating elevators in department stores, hotels and apartment houses, in large and small cities, from California and Utah to Texas and Maine.

---

* Child Labor in Warring Countries. Industrial Series No. 4. The Children's Bureau, United States Department of Labor, p. 61.

The work itself does not appear ill-adapted or injurious. The hours of duty, however, are often excessive and cannot fail to be harmful. In New York City for instance, girls are working in apartment houses 15 hours at a stretch; day and night work alternates each week and when the shifts change, the girls are on duty without relief from 6 p. m. to 12 o'clock noon, a continuous stretch of 18 hours. The girls are required to attend to the switchboard telephone as well as to run the elevator. Sunday work is required. One of the most serious abuses of this employment is the exposure of young girls to insult or danger on the all-night shift. In some instances no provision whatever is made for getting rest at night. In other cases an army cot is provided in a hall alcove. In another instance the young elevator attendant sought safety by running the elevator between the first and second landing to obtain sleep between summons.

Nightwork for women has been newly introduced also in the work of automobile cleaning. Women are being employed in New York City garages more than twelve hours each night—from 7 p. m. to 7.30 a. m. They clean from thirty to thirty-five cars during the night.

Another new occupation which exposes girls to moral dangers is the messenger service. In many cities girls are being increasingly employed to replace boys at this work, which should be closely watched. For the dangers involved in sending young boys to questionable houses or resorts has been so great that within the past few years legislation has been enacted in most of the states, raising the age limit of boys in the messenger service and prohibiting their employment after stated hours of the evening. It would indeed be a mockery if young girls were now employed at work which has been found unsafe for boys up to 21 years. To safeguard these young workers, legislation is needed so as to include the new occupations in the existing laws limiting hours of labor, etc. Other states might well follow the enlightened action of the State of Washington where the employment of female minors in the messenger service has recently been prohibited by ruling of the Industrial Welfare Commission. In some states, too, efforts are on foot to regulate by law the new employment of girls as bootblacks.

THE NEED OF EQUAL WAGES.

In regard to the general replacement of men by women workers, no single consideration is more important than the matter of wages. This is, moreover, not a social or economic question alone. It is primarily a question of health and must be of the first importance to all those concerned with public health issues. It was General Gorgas himself who put in a few trenchant words the close connection between wages and health. He ascribes to the results of increased wages of the common laborers the world-famous improvement in health at Panama. "I am satisfied," he said to a conference of health officers, "that to this improvement in social conditions, caused by our high wages, we principally owe our extraordinary improvement in general health conditions."*

2

Another medical opinion on the relation between wages and health has recently been well put in a study of Occupation and Mortality:† "We believe," say Doctors Wynne and Guilfoy, "that wages have a most important bearing upon the morbidity and mortality of any occupation, because, where real wages are high, the standard of living is correspondingly high, housing is better, food is more plentiful and more nourishing; and, in short, conditions are more favorable to physical and mental well-being, which results in greater resistance to disease, more recuperative power, and a healthier enjoyment of life, all of which stimulates the worker to preserve his health and makes him more alert to guard against accidents; whereas when wages are low, home conditions are of necessity unfavorable, and if in addition shop conditions are also bad, as they frequently are, the hazards of any occupation are increased manifold."

The great danger from the standpoint of health is that the employment of women should be resorted to merely in order to obtain cheap labor. As a matter of public health we must see to it that women are paid equal wages for equal work. Otherwise their employment can be and is daily being made the excuse for undercutting the standard wage of men and so reducing the whole standards of living in the community. The reports of the Children's Bureau and the Public

* New York State Department of Health Monthly Bulletin, December, 1915, pp. 369–70.
† Occupation and Mortality. Their Relation as Indicated by the Mortality Returns in the City of New York for 1914. Reprint No. 400, Public Health Reports, June 8, 1917.

Health Service have shown how infant mortality rises *pari passu* with a fall in wage.

It is true that in many of the new occupations women are unskilled and need training. Yet even while they are being trained they should as a matter of health be paid an adequate wage. The standards adopted by the Executives' Club of Detroit to which reference has been made, recommend that while learning, women shall be paid the flat day rate paid to men for the same work or operation.

There are many other pressing health problems in women's new employment needing wise consideration, which cannot even be enumerated here. Instances are beginning to multiply of the lack of decencies and sanitary provisions for women employed in railroad yards and round houses; the housing of women who must leave home is a pressing problem; the matter of clothing is highly important; women obviously cannot do men's work in ill adapted clothes such as skirts which are usually too full or too tight for safety and which are dust gathering in the dangerous trades, or in high-heeled shoes, more quickly inducing fatigue. Separate entrances should be provided for men and women especially in occupations involving heat and grime; the nutrition of the workers, and the provision of restaurants or lunch counters, is a chapter of immense importance.

SUMMARY: THREE ESSENTIAL SAFE-
GUARDS.

In summing up this brief survey of a large topic, emphasis should be laid upon three essential safeguards for girls and women entering upon men's occupations: equal wages, additional legislation and adequate medical supervision. I am aware that in making a plea for this last requisite, I am treading upon very difficult ground. The pressure for physicians for military and civilian needs is so great that a plea for new industrial supervision may appear ill-timed. Yet if any one truth has emerged from three years of warfare it is the indispensable nature of our industrial contribution. To preserve that is a part of the nation's self preservation.

The methods to be used in obtaining adequate medical supervision are of primary importance, and in this connection the National Consumers' League has engaged in a campaign for the establishment of industrial clinics.

Local conditions must determine whether these clinics should be under private, state or federal auspices. But the early diagnosis and treatment of workers suffering from industrial diseases by physicians who know industrial processes and conditions is the only means of more fully learning and controlling these diseases, hitherto little studied. The growing employment of women should be an added incentive to establishing industrial clinics, especially wherever large numbers of workers are engaged in dangerous processes. Where private means or enterprise are lacking and where work on government contracts is being done, it would seem peculiarly fitting for the Public Health Service to establish such clinics and so lead the way in measures of enlightened prevention as well as cure.

THE ANOMALY OF COEDUCATION

"EDUCATION will be entirely revolutionized by the war," says Dr. Nicholas Murray Butler. This is such welcome news that one should not question too precisely the inspiration of the prophet. After the tedious years of chronic reform with which education has been distressed, there is a gladdening hope in the crisis of revolution. Educational foundations are certainly quaking, traditions and prejudices are being jounced out of their ruts, and space cleared for new methods born of contemporary and demonstrated needs. Of the many things that are likely to happen in this revolution, one will surely be the recognition of the new status of women, and the necessity of providing as complete and specific an education for woman's life as for man's life.

In 1820 the mayor of Boston peremptorily closed the first school opened for girls, after a brief experience with its overflowing numbers, for the reason that it would "bankrupt the city to educate girls." From that significant event to the present hour, girls have been an embarrassment to the educational system, an aggressive responsibility that could not be easily shirked nor adequately assumed. Under the chastisement of public opinion by Horace Mann, early in the last century, girls were admitted to the New England academies. When the city high schools were opened, the girls crowded the boys uncomfortably for room, and aroused the hostility of the Philistines. In the seventies under the impulse given to higher education for women by the founding of the first women's colleges, young women forced their way into many of the old colleges for men, where they met with only a frigid and constrained welcome. All along the line of development, our educational system has shown a systematic discrimination against women and a shameless disregard for their specific educational needs. The record is a humiliating one.

The main instrument of this discrimination has been coeducation, a compromise that had its origin in economy and expediency, the red-letter virtues of the thrifty American pioneer. The chief and only substantial reason for its existence is, and always has been, that it is cheap. What was at first an economic necessity has become an economic habit; and with flagrant insensitiveness educationists still regard it as perfectly legitimate to economize on the education of women in order to be able to spend the more liberally on the education of men. Until quite recently no attempt has ever been made to justify coeducation on pedagogic or scientific principles, and every such attempt is an apology rather than an argument. It is called the American system, but there is nothing in this national habit to be proud of any more than in the survival of any other habit of poverty in a period of mature affluence. Coeducation is not a product, but an accident of democracy, and intrinsically is no more concerned with the democratic principle than is the institution of marriage.

The example of the great middle west is often used as an argument for coeducation, illustrating a characteristic American tendency to argue perfection from mere bigness. Western coeducation is impressive only for its vastness, as a prairie is impressive for its size but not for its beauty. The educational system of the west was developed under a régime of farm mortgages and pioneer economies, and in the state universities coeducation was automatically enforced by the Federal Land Grant of 1862. Western civilization is still young and transitional, not ripe enough in culture to furnish standards for the older sections of the country. Meredith Nicholson, a loyal westerner, in his recent book of praise, frankly says: "I do not share the opinion of some of my compatriots of the western provinces that culture and manners have attained any noteworthy dignity that entitles us to strut before the rest of the world." Moreover, in the "Valley of Democracy" there is already a wide reaction against prevailing educational methods. The courses provided for women in the colleges are far more liberal than those in eastern colleges. Chicago University has adopted a segregation plan, and other colleges are working toward it. Even the high schools in several large cities are experimenting with segregation. And here and there separate colleges are springing up, equipped for educating women as women.

The most vital and fundamental objection to coeducation, especially as administered in the colleges, is that it does not give to women what they want and most need—an education that will prepare them for employments in which by nature and the customs of civilized society they are destined to be engaged. The college education given to women is simply a man's education, the modifications to adapt it to the life of women being so slight as to be negligible in a general estimate. It is a singular circumstance that we are only just arriving at the point of discovering sex as a differentiating force in education. Many years ago the English scientist, Professor Romanes, sounded a warning against the habit of ignoring the natural differences between the educational needs of women and men. "If we attempt to disregard these differences,"

he says, "or try artificially to make of woman an unnatural copy of man, we are certain to fail, and to turn out as our result a sorry and disappointed creature who is neither the one thing nor the other."

If education is something more than abstract, cultural, mind-training effort, it should be functioned for a woman's actual career as it is now so strenuously functioned for a man's career. The reformers are crying at the top of their voices for an education that "correlates with life," an education that is "realistic," that "serves a purpose." But by an unfortunate oversight they fail to include woman's life in the tract of unfruitful life they propose to enrich with educational utilities. In the long evolution of the curriculum of men's colleges, the goal of effort, however ill defined or blunderingly pursued, has always been an ideal of well trained and efficient manhood. No such goal of ideal womanhood has ever been set up as a guiding principle by the administrators of women's education. The college girl is still an anomaly, without definition or destination. Inthe separate woman's college, she studies a curriculum copied from the catalogue of the nearest man's college. In the coeducational college she is tossed into the hopper with men, on the assumption that by some psycho-chemical process she will extract from the incongruous mixture the essence of ideal femininity. At graduation she finds herself surrounded by a rigid wall of professional opportunity, in which every gateway bears the sign, "No thoroughfare except for men." She has never been assisted by her instructors, not even permitted, to discover the professions belonging to her own sex. When young men are shuffled aside in this manner they rebel and get what they want—electrical engineering, commercial chemistry, sociology, what not that seems "practical"; but the young women must stand by in an attitude, as Mrs. Julia Ward Howe called it, of "passive and patient receptivity," like Milton's "hungry sheep that look up and are not fed." The result of this process of educating women as if they were men has been to graduate them into disillusionment and discontent, into a deplorable state of unpreparedness for the definite vocations which they must finally enter.

It is claimed that a liberal program of electives in the coeducational colleges will furnish all the specialized training needed by women. This claim is delusive. Electives primarily designed for women will be avoided by men, and thus segregation will already be in operation. Still more, electives suitable for both sexes are shunned by men when selected predominantly by women. This fact was emphasized by the late President Van Hise, in his effort to introduce segregation in Wisconsin University. "When in a given course," he says, "women for one reason or another become predominant, this acts as a deterrent to the free election of the course by considerable numbers of young men, and *vice versa*."

A still stronger disruptive force is working in the coeducational colleges. The women in these colleges are increasing more rapidly than the men. In the six years from 1910 to 1916 the increase of women was 70 per cent. and that of men 43 per cent. This means that coeducation is destined to be swamped in femininity, a result that has already been reached in some colleges. The attempt to stem the tide by arbitrarily limiting the number of women, as at Leland Stanford, Northwestern and elsewhere, is bound to prove a futile expedient. Public sentiment will not long tolerate such discrimination, but will demand that the colleges share their funds and equipment with women on a basis of real equality, by means, for example, of the

affiliated women's college, or finally turn over their business to the women.

There are certain natural incongruities and repugnancies connected with coeducation in college that can not be denied nor remedied. The system is essentially distasteful to boys and girls alike. Every girl to whom free choice is permitted will choose a separate or affiliated college for women. Similarly the boy with free opportunity will always choose a separate men's college. Students of limited means accept the compromise of coeducation as a necessity, and the instinctive aversion wears away into a habit of tolerance. Yet a restless discontent remains, especially where a woman's department has been grafted into an old institution with settled traditions and associations. There is resentment among alumni and students, becoming at times an active hostility amounting almost to rebellion. Students justly complain that coeducation breaks up the unity of college life and makes against college spirit and enthusiasm. The *esprit de corps* of the men's and of the women's section can not possibly be the same. There must be irreconcilable diversities of interests. Athletics, clubs, oratorical contests, etc., can not be representative of the whole college, and can not command loyal support when one half of the student body does not participate in these activities and exhibits for them only a gallery interest. Ideal college life as generally understood is impossible under conditions of coeducation, and some of the most valuable results of the college experience are sacrificed. Unless the diversities of men and women in mind and natural functions can be resolved into identities by some subtle form of hocus-pocus, there can be no perfect organization of college life for boys and girls bunched together. It is an attempt to balance two scales on a single pivot.

The spectacle of a college body of young women instructed for four years exclusively by men is manifestly too incongruous to need discussion. But the grievances are not all with the women. Coeducation forces young men into a competition that is unnatural and unfair. A college senior being asked why he objected to the women replied: "They drag all the prizes." This is a cogent epitome of some of the most serious difficulties inherent in coeducation. Girls are better students than boys, surpassing them in the power of application and the will to learn. They read more, write more, have a wider range of ideas and are proportionally more intellectual. The result is inevitable; academic honors fall disproportionately to the girls. Boys are content with a low standard of scholarship, and so long as the dominant interest of college is athletic rather than intellectual, this low standard of scholarship must prevail. Thus a young man who would win honors in a detached men's college is deprived of them in a coeducational college. Naturally he feels that he has been robbed of his rights, and in view of the acquiescent attitude of faculties toward the substitution of sport for scholarship, he is perfectly correct in his feeling of injustice. There is even a deeper feeling than this, a feeling of inherent impropriety in this unnatural race with women—an Atalantan race, more suitable for mythology than for real life. A young man's instinctive chivalry and generosity toward young women are assailed, but he can hardly be expected to possess the Platonic detachment in his regard for the sex that will enable him to forgive a young woman for humiliating him. The devices resorted to by faculties for the "adjustment" of these difficulties are more ingenious than just. The custom of distributing honors in such a way as to give the men and appearance of equality with the women in scholarship, is open to censure on the ground of both justice and morality. Such also is the inclination to favor the boy at the expense of the girl in the granting of scholarships. These and other devices of evasion are simply frauds perpetrated on the women to protect the men. Such practises are discreditable from every point of view, and should be made matters of conscience rather than expedients of custom. If coeducation can not be moral and just toward its women students, on that ground alone it stands condemned.

Coeducation is a house divided against itself. It is a case of two halves that do not make a whole, of two lines of human energy that can not be made to coincide or focus in a single point. At its very best, for higher education, the system is a lopsided compromise, temporary and expediential; above the age of adolescence it is psychologically indefensible. It was never the product of deliberate educational thought, and its wide persistence beyond the period of its economic necessity is due largely to lack of critical thought bestowed upon it as a serious educational problem. With characteristic American complacency we have accepted it as a matter of course, because it is American, ignorant or forgetful of its aboriginal origin, and stolidly indifferent to the injustice of its effects. It is time for revolution, a revolution that will give to woman a man's chance in education.

JULIAN W. ABERNETHY

A PLEA FOR FIRST-CLASS WOMEN

BY MARY SARGENT POTTER

IT is a truism, but one to which it is well constantly to
return, that the most important thing in the world is the
next generation. The limitations of the present one are
defined, its advance already discounted, its future, economically, of little importance. It has only to finish out its
task according to its already static abilities. The stage is
set for the oncoming young.

Thus the hope of the world very literally rests in these
young hands, and the supreme effort should be made to
equip them for the problems which they must inevitably
confront. No one can foresee what these problems will
be nor what turn history will take. But for the race as
for the individual the only adequate preparation, which
can be used in any emergency and for the solution
of any difficulty, whether personal or social, is best
expressed by that old-fashioned term, *Character*. It is the
only weapon with which this or any generation can successfully solve the difficulties and confusions which are
overwhelming the world, and which will again, in some
form or other, seek to overwhelm it.

Now character has come to be regarded as a dull and
negative force, something to be coupled with the worn-out
inanition of the Church, rather than to be allied with her
glorious and ideal potentialities. It was a factor in the
lives of our grandmothers, but it receives scant emphasis
in an age when " constructive work ", " intellectual progress ", " efficiency of organization ", " emancipation of the
individual " are the watchwords of the day. In its
proper analysis character presupposes and includes these
attributes. It would be a flabby personality which failed
to cultivate every endowment, physical, mental, and spiritual, to form that fine instrument of civilization—the well-
equipped man or woman. Without character, brilliancy

of intellect often runs amuck. Without character, efficiency becomes mechanical and falls short of its rightful fruition. Without character, the instincts of loyalty and service are crowded out by self-interest and greed. Without character, responsibilities which have become burdensome are laid aside with no sense of the high beauty of sacrifice, nor even of ordinary obligation. Character is the great engine which must put in action the complete efficiency of human beings.

Thus the supreme task of this generation becomes the development of the character of the one that is to follow it. The lives of the children have been and will always remain largely in the hands of the mothers. The function of motherhood is an elementary fact. What women therefore gain today in the way of emancipation, of intellectual advance, of practical knowledge, is not for any individual right or self-gratification, but that they may be better equipped for their eternal vocation. Unless this is the underlying purpose of every feminist movement, it will become devitalized and sterile.

What is the aim of the American woman? And I say " American woman ", because she is the leader of the world movement for the political and social emancipation of all women. Without doubt when this movement shall have attained its object and women shall have become economically and politically free, it will enormously strengthen the right relationship of all human beings. Yet the aim, I am frank to say, seems strangely confused. There is immense activity, but little coördination. Every segregated cause is represented by able women, but co-relation is an intellectual feat which they have yet to achieve.

What should be their ultimate aim? It is true that one cannot with advantage look too far into the future. Only one step at a time can be taken. Until that has been done, it is not clear in what direction the next step must be. Yet in periods of readjustment, of fluctuating values, of confused mental outlook, it is sometimes helpful to pause and endeavor to interpret present tendencies in order to clarify future hopes.

It would appear that women in their efforts to free themselves from old limitations, both intellectual and economic, are striving too much in the direction which has been marked out by men, and too little along original and personal lines. We are rapidly acquiring what seems to be a neutral sex, a body of women who will never rise higher than the grade of second-rate men. They scorn feminine qualities without the possibility of acquiring true masculine ones.

There can be but one logical aim for the feminist movement—the development of the first-class woman, just as the ideal of the man should be the masculine prototype. The abnormal and wholly artificial spirit of sex antagonism which has been roused in many quarters will have no lasting influence. Men and women are going to stick together, and they are going to remain as different as they have been from the beginning of the world. This does not mean that there is a superior and an inferior sex. Women should get it out of their heads that they are inferior, and must prove their equality. They are not inferior, but they are different, a difference which it is of the utmost importance to maintain and to emphasize. Biologically, they are eternally different. Their bodies are different, their minds are different, their functions are different, their work should be of a different character. There can be but one ideal for the inevitable relationship. It should be a partnership —a first-class man and a first-class woman, working together but along different lines, for the common good. Few women can ever be made into semblances of first-class men, just as few men, thank God, have the capacity to simulate first-class women, or if they have, they become undesirable and of no importance. The need is for first-class women and the standard for them has scarcely yet been set. Now in so far as the suffrage and other forms of advancement develop in them qualities of complete womanhood, they are good and desirable. But in so far as they are ends in themselves, they have neither value nor importance.

The most vital task of the world, then, the training of the Spirit of the oncoming generation, is largely in the hands of women. Every inch of progress gained, in whatever direction, should be not for themselves, but in order that, through inheritance and environment, each generation shall become, by a wide margin, the finest which has yet appeared. Though permanent progress must necessarily be gradual, there is no reason why it should not be speeded up, or why each generation should be content with so small an advance—so small that it is sometimes mistaken for retrogression—over the one which has preceded it. This can be accomplished, not by an even more feverish activity, but by a more widely-spread attention to child-life.

There is the old argument that a small proportion of women only become mothers and homebuilders, that the responsibility rests on the few, and that even for them it is a vocation which occupies a comparatively short period of their lives. This is a narrow view. The advance of the sex with its resulting influence must very largely alter the entire race. In addition, numberless women can have a share in motherhood, its opportunities and responsibilities, though they themselves do not bear children. When Roosevelt said that a woman's love of country could best be shown by the bearing and the rearing of a large family, trained to the service of the community, he uttered a sound principle. It is not an easy task, nor always a safe one, and it entails inevitable suffering, endless sacrifice. So do all forms of patriotism. But in the world as it is today, it is no longer possible, however great the desire, for much of the finest stock of the country, the intellectuals and the professionals, to have families of even moderate size, or any at all. However great the personal and social desire, economic conditions have rendered it impossible. Who is to enable this fine, potential motherhood, these women of refinement and character, to feel they have a right to bear children, because the children's opportunities are safe-guarded? If it is not done, the future will be controlled and destroyed by the products of haphazard and disastrous breeding in the slums. Inevitably it must lead to deterioration. This is a subject for advanced legislation in the form of grants, and one with which women should concern themselves. Then who is to see that the men and women to whom the education of the children is delegated are not so poorly paid that hope is very nearly precluded from their lives? Can men and women, themselves struggling against overwhelming odds, with no margin for physical needs, no channel through which nervous energy can be conserved, give to the training of mind and spirit those high qualities which such a task demands? Women should lead in the campaign to remedy the evil to a point far beyond the advance already won.

And the sick children of the world! With their pitiful lives unlived, what more glorious form of motherhood was ever given than that placed in the hands of the trained nurse? Who but herself, understanding the misery of physical distress, can teach little spirits that physical handicaps may become spiritual opportunities, that if they have been given sharp and difficult tools to work with, they can build with them more beautiful structures than ordinary lives, and that some of the finest of the world's work has been done by the world's invalids?

Today a woman's responsibility toward her individual children is often ended while she is still a young woman, yet she feels her social obligations as never before. She should realize that though one form of work is finished, her opportunities have increased, because she now has experience, judgment, knowledge. She recognizes her mistakes, she understands what principle led to her successes, she can speak with the authority of achievement. This great fund of trained, experienced motherhood should be released for the service of the oncoming generation throughout the world.

There is no end to the great work and destiny of woman, but her aim should be unmistakable and clear. Her vocation, her feminine qualities—not her feminine mid-Victorian weaknesses—should be guarded with jealousy and pride, and no advance deemed impossible in the interest of her cause, the development of that rare and beautiful thing—the First-Class Woman.

MARY SARGENT POTTER.

Acknowledgments

McIntosh, Maria J. "Social Evils—Woman Their Reformer." In *Woman in America: Her Work and Her Reward* (New York: D. Appleton and Company, 1850): 62–81.

"Correspondence Between Elisha Boudinot and George Washington." *Godey's Lady's Book* 43 (1851): 237–38.

"Editors' Table." *Godey's Lady's Book* 44 (1852): 293–95.

Chericot. "Men's Rights Convention at—. Extraordinary Proceedings, Exciting Scenes, and Curious Speeches." *Godey's Lady's Book* 44 (1852): 268–73.

Chericot. "Authentic Particulars of Alarming Disturbances Consequent on the Late Men's Rights Convention at—." *Godey's Lady's Book* 45 (1852): 535–42.

"Editor's Table: Women's Rights." *Harper's New Monthly Magazine* 7 (1853): 838–41. Copyright (1853) by Harper's New Monthly Magazine. All rights reserved. Reprinted from the November issue by special permission.

"Marriage." *Godey's Lady's Book* 49 (1854): 36.

"Married and Single Life." *Godey's Lady's Book* 49 (1854): 232.

"Editors' Table." *Godey's Lady's Book* 50 (1855): 172–75.

"Human Nature in Chunks. Chunk No. 1—Woman's Rights." *United States Review* (Nov. 1854): 434–40.

"Editors' Table." *Godey's Lady's Book* 52 (1856): 79–83.

"College Temple, Newnan, Georgia." *Godey's Lady's Book* 53 (1856): 154–55.

"Editors' Table." *Godey's Lady's Book* 53 (1856): 79–80.

Sands, Alexander H. "Intellectual Culture of Woman." *Southern Literary Messenger* 28 (1859): 321–32.

"Education of the Female Sex." *American Journal of Education* 31 (1863): 232–42.

Beecher, Catharine. "How to Redeem Woman's Profession From Dishonor." *Harper's New Monthly Magazine* 31 (1865): 710–16.

Brockett, L.P. Chapter 16 in *Woman: Her Rights, Wrongs, Privileges, and Responsibilities* (L. Stebbins: Hartford, Conn. 1869): 265–78.

"Woman's Rights Viewed Physiologically and Historically." *National Quarterly Review* 20 (1869): 79–101.

Allen, A.F. "The Sexes in Colleges." *Nation* 10 (1870): 134–35. Reprinted from "The Nation" magazine. Copyright the Nation Company, L.P.

Godkin, E.L. "Another Delicate Subject." *Nation* 11 (1870): 21–23. Reprinted from "The Nation" magazine. Copyright the Nation Company, L.P.

Meehan, Thomas. "Sexual Science." *Old and New* 5 (1872): 170–75.

Straker, David Augustus. "Citizenship, its Rights and Duties: Woman Suffrage." *New National Era* (1874): 3–19.

Johnston, George H. "Woman, Wrong and Right." *Mercersburg Review* (Oct. 1878): 524–45.

Dike, Samuel W. "Some Aspects of the Divorce Question." *Princeton Review* 13 (1884): 169–90.

Cooke, Rose Terry. "The Real Rights of Women." *North American Review* (Sept. 1889): 347–54.

Cooper, Samuel Williams. "The Present Legal Rights of Women." *American* 21 (Oct. 25, 1890): 27–28.

Eliot, Elton. "Women and Women." *Southern Magazine* 5 (1894): 199–203.

Winston, Ella W. "Foibles of the New Woman." *Forum* 21 (1896): 186–92.

Johnston, Helen Kendrick. "Introduction" and "Conclusion" in *Woman and the Republic* (New York: D. Appleton and Company, 1897): 5–9, 320–27.

Moody, Helen Watterson. "The Unquiet Sex: Third Paper—Women and Reforms." *Scribner's Magazine* 23 (1898): 116–20.

Wright, Theodore F. "The Collegiate Education of Women." *New-Church Review* 7 (1900): 112–16.

Mitchell, S. Weir. "When the College is Hurtful to a Girl." *Ladies Home Journal* (June 1900): 14.

Thompson, Flora McDonald. "Retrogression of the American Woman." *North American Review* (Nov. 1900): 748–53.

Gibbons, J. Cardinal. "The Restless Woman." *Ladies Home Journal* (Jan. 1902): 6.

Curtis, W.A. "Co-Education in Colleges: I.—A Man's View." *Outlook* (Dec. 13, 1902): 887–90.

Ramée, Louise de la. "The Woman Problem: Shall Women Vote? A Study of Feminine Unrest—Its Causes and Its Remedies." *Lippincott's* 83 (1909): 586–92.

Illinois Association Opposed to Woman Suffrage. "Modern Thought." Bulletin No. 15. (Chicago: Illinois Association Opposed to Woman Suffrage, 1912): 1–4.

Schlapp, Max G. Transcription of "Our Perilous Waste of Vitality." *Literary Digest* 44 (1912): 878–79.

Tarbell, Ida M. "The Irresponsible Woman and the Friendless Child." *American Monthly Magazine* 74 (1912): 49–53.

Stringer, Arthur. "The Renaissance of Woman." *Collier's* (July 27, 1912): 20–21.

Heape, Walter. "The Problems." In *Sex Antagonism* (New York: G.P. Putnam's Sons, 1913): 20–35.

Tarbell, Ida M. Excerpts from *The Business of Being a Woman. Ladies Home Journal* (Jan. 1913): 24.

"The 'Brute in Man' as an Argument Against Feminism." *Current Opinion* 56 (May 1914): 370–71.

Powers, Fred Perry. "Feminism and Socialism." *Unpopular Review* 3, no.5 (1915): 118–33.

Robinson, Margaret C. "The Feminist Program." *Unpopular Review* 5, no.10 (1916): 318–31.

Goldmark, Josephine. "Some Considerations Affecting the Replacement of Men by Women Workers." *American Journal of Public Health* 8 (1918): 270–76. Reprinted with the permission of the American Public Health Association.

Abernethy, Julian W. "The Anomaly of Coeducation." *School and Society* 9 (1919): 259–62.

Potter, Margaret Sargent. "A Plea for First-Class Women." *North American Review* (March 1920): 66.